D1555259

India in the Global Software Industry

India in the Global Software Industry

Innovation, Firm Strategies and Development

Edited by

Anthony P. D'Costa

and

E. Sridharan

First published 2004 by
PALGRAVE MACMILLAN
Houndmills, Basingstoke, Hampshire RG21 6XS and
175 Fifth Avenue, New York, N.Y. 10010
Companies and representatives throughout the world

PALGRAVE MACMILLAN is the global academic imprint of the Palgrave Macmillan division of St. Martin's Press, LLC and of Palgrave Macmillan Ltd. Macmillan® is a registered trademark in the United States, United Kingdom and other countries. Palgrave is a registered trademark in the European Union and other countries.

ISBN 1–4039–1252–1

This book is printed on paper suitable for recycling and made from fully managed and sustained forest sources.

A catalogue record for this book is available from the British Library.

Library of Congress Cataloging-in-Publication Data
India in the global software industry: innovation, firm strategies and development/edited by Anthony P. D'Costa and E. Sridharan.
    p. cm.
Includes bibliographical references and index.
ISBN 1–4039–1252–1
    1. Computer software industry – India. I. D'Costa, Anthony P., 1957–
II. Sridharan, Eswaran.

HD9696.63.I42I53 2003
338.4'7005'0954—dc21   2003053642

10 9 8 7 6 5 4 3 2 1
12 11 10 09 08 07 06 05 04 03

Printed and bound in Great Britain by
Antony Rowe Ltd, Chippenham and Eastbourne

To R. Narasimhan
A pioneer of computer science in India

Contents

Contributors

Gil Avnimelech is currently a PhD candidate of the School of Business Administration at Hebrew University of Jerusalem, and is also involved with the creation of a research centre there for 'High-Tech, Biotechnology and Globalization Studies'.

Rakesh Basant is Professor of Economics at the Indian Institute of Management, Ahmedabad. He has held Visiting Fellowships at the Economic Growth Center, Yale University, East–West Center, Honolulu and Daito Bunka University. He has published extensively in international and Indian journals and served as a consultant to the Intermediate Technology Development Group, London, United Nations University Institute of New Technologies, UNCTAD, the World Bank, and the International Development Research Center.

Deepti Bhatnagar is Professor of Organizational Behaviour at the Indian Institute of Management, Ahmedabad, where she has taught since 1984. She has been Visiting Professor of Management at the University of Maryland at College Park and at Fairleigh Dickinson University, and has taught at the Indian Institute of Technology, Kanpur, and Lucknow University, and worked in industry for five years.

Pankaj Chandra is Professor of Operations Management and Chair, Centre for Innovation and Entrepreneurship, at the Indian Institute of Management, Ahmedabad. He taught earlier at McGill University in Canada as Associate Professor, and has also been Professor and Associate Dean at the Indian School of Business, Hyderabad, and Visiting Professor at the University of Geneva. He has published extensively in international and Indian journals. He has also consulted for numerous companies in India and Canada, for the World Bank. He has been Associate Editor, *International Journal of Agile Manufacturing*, and a member of the editorial board of the *Asian Journal of Operations Management*. He has also been President, Society for Operations Management.

Anthony P. D'Costa is an Associate Professor of Comparative International Development, University of Washington in Tacoma and is affiliated with the university's International and South Asian Studies Programs in Seattle. He has published widely on the steel, auto and software industries, including *The Global Restructuring of the Steel Industry: Innovations, Institutions and Industrial Change* (Routledge, 1999), and is on the editorial board of *Asian*

Business and Management and a member of the Board of Trustees of the American Institute of Indian Studies, Chicago and Delhi.

Mukund R. Dixit is Professor of Business Policy at the Indian Institute of Management, Ahmedabad. He has been EEC Visiting Professor at ESSEC, France, and at the Rotterdam School of Management, Erasmus University, Netherlands. He has consulted widely for industry, served as a member of the Board of Public and Private Enterprises in India, and has been the editor of the management journal *Vikalpa*.

K. J. Joseph is Professor of Economics at the Centre for Development Studies, Trivandrum on secondment to the Centre for Studies in Science Policy, Jawaharlal Nehru University. He is the author of *Industry under Economic Liberalization: the Case of Indian Electronics* (Sage, 1998) and has contributed to numerous journals and edited volumes. He has been a Ford Post-doctoral Fellow at the Economic Growth Center, Yale University, and has held several advisory appointments in economic planning with the state of Kerala.

S. Krishna is Professor of Quantitative Methods and Information Systems, and Chairperson of the Software Enterprise Management Program at the Indian Institute of Management, Bangalore. He has also taught at the Indian Institute of Science, Bangalore, Indian Institute of Technology, Kanpur, and the Asian Institute of Technology, Bangkok. His research has been widely published in leading journals in India and abroad.

Rishikesha T. Krishnan is Associate Professor of Corporate Strategy, Indian Institute of Management, Bangalore, and a software entrepreneur. Apart from consulting for Indian industry, he has been a co-founder of two software start-ups, as Chief Executive Officer and Director, Knowledge Enabled Networks, and Partner and General Manager, Helios Antennas and Electronics, Madras.

Abhoy K. Ojha is an Associate Professor of Organizational Behaviour, Indian Institute of Management, Bangalore. Earlier he was an Assistant Professor at Laurentian University, Sudbury, Canada. He has published in several journals in India and abroad and is on the editorial board of *Human Resource Development International*.

Ashok Parthasarathi is Professor at the Centre for Studies in Science Policy, Jawaharlal Nehru University. A physicist and electronics engineer by training, he spent over three decades at the heart of science and technology policy in India, including as a Special Assistant for Science and Technology in the Secretariat of former Prime Minister Indira Gandhi. He was involved in the setting up of the Department of Electronics, Department of Space and Department of Science and Technology and several major projects in electronics, atomic energy, space and defence. He has published over 100 papers on various aspects of science and technology policy, planning and management and edited two books: *Pugwash on Self Reliance* and *Scientific Cooperation for Development: Search for New Directions*. He has been a consultant to leading United Nations agencies and has been elected as a member of the Board of Governors of the South Centre, Geneva.

Ganesh N. Prabhu is Associate Professor of Corporate Strategy, Indian Institute of Management, Bangalore. He has published widely in Indian and international journals and edited volumes, and has consulted for industry, including the software industry.

AnnaLee Saxenian is a Professor at the University of California at Berkeley with a joint appointment in the School of Information Management and Systems (SIMS) and the Department of City and Regional Planning. Her major recent publications include *Regional Advantage: Culture and Competition in Silicon Valley and Route 128* (Harvard University Press, 1994), *Silicon Valley's New Immigrant Entrepreneurs* (Public Policy Institute of California, 1999) and *Local and Global Networks of Immigrant Professionals in Silicon Valley* (Public Policy Institute of California, 2002). She is currently a member of the California Council on Science and Technology, Chair of the Board of the Center for the Future of China (CFC), and Adviser to the *Bay Area Economic Pulse* and to Joint Venture: Silicon Valley's *Index of Silicon Valley*.

E. Sridharan has been Academic Director of the University of Pennsylvania Institute for the Advanced Study of India (in New Delhi), the India affiliate of the Center for the Advanced Study of India, University of Pennsylvania, from its inception in 1997. He has held Visiting Fellowships at the London School of Economics, the Institute for Developing Economies, Tokyo, and the Center for the Advanced Study of India, University of Pennsylvania. He is the author of *The Political Economy of Industrial Promotion: Indian, Brazilian and Korean Electronics in Comparative Perspective 1969–1994* (Praeger, 1996), has co-edited two other books, and published numerous scholarly articles and book chapters.

Morris Teubal is Professor of Economics at the Hebrew University of Jerusalem. His research currently focuses on national systems of innovation, innovation and technology policy (both for advanced and developing economies), patterns of growth in high-tech companies, venture capital and policies for the promotion of venture capital, emergence and development of high-tech clusters and high-tech sectors. He has held visiting professorships at the University of Pennsylvania, Stanford University, University of Sussex and University of Buenos Aires. He served on the board of the International Schumpeter Society in 2000–2. He initiated the Israeli programme supporting generic, cooperative R&D (the Magnet Program) and is currently involved in the creation of a Hebrew University Centre devoted to research on 'High Tech, Biotechnology and Globalization Studies'.

Firms Researched or Cited

Acer America Inc
Aditi Technologies
Adobe Systems
Advantage
Alcatel
American Express
AmSoft
Analog Devices
AOL: America Online
Ashay Software Technologies
AT&T
Aztec Software and Technology Services
BA-HAL
Banyan Networks
Birla Soft
BUPT: Beijing University of Post and Telecommunications (China)
Cabletron Systems
Cadence
Canara Bank
C-DOT: Centre for the Development of Telematics (India)
China Telecom
Cisco Systems
Citicorp
CMC: Computer Maintenance Corp
CMIE: Centre for Monitoring Indian Economy
Concept Software
Cybercash
Cypress Semiconductor Corp
Daimler-Benz
Data General Corp
Data Software Research Company
Datamatics
Datanet Corportation
DBC
Dell
Dharma Systems
DoE: Department of Electronics
DSIR: Department of Scientific and Industrial Research
Eastern Software Systems

eCapital Solutions
ECIL: Electronics Corp of India
EID-Parry
Encore (formerly N-Core)
Encore Software
Ericsson
Far Mart
Founder
Fujitsu
GE: General Electric
Geodesic
Geometric
Great Wall Computers
HCL: Hindustan Computers
HCL Technologies
Hewlett Packard China
Hitachi
HP: Hewlett Packard
HSBC: Hong Kong and Shanghai Banking Corp
Hughes Software Systems
IBM
iCODE Software
IDC
IIM: Indian Institute of Management
IIS Infotech
IISc: Indian Institute of Science
IIT: Indian Institute of Technology
IL & FS: Infrastructure Leasing and Financial Services
IMF: International Monetary Fund
Infosys
Intel Corporation
ISRO: Indian Space Research Organization
ITI: Indian Telephone Industries
JL Informatrix
Karnataka State Financial Corporation
Karnataka State Industrial Development Corporation
Kshema Technologies
Kurt Salmon & Associates
L&T: Larson and Toubro
Legend Group
LG Software
Lucent, China
Macmet India
Macronix Co

Mastek
McKinsey
MICO Industries
Microland
Microsoft
Midas Communications Technologies
Mindtree
Mindware
MIT: Massachusetts Institute of Technology
Motorola
Mphasis (formerly BFL)
MPT: Ministry of Post and Telecommunications (China)
NASSCOM: National Association of Software and Service Companies
National Centre for Software Technology
National Semiconductor Corporation
NCR: National Cash Register
NetFront
Network Solutions
NIIT (formerly National Institute of Information Technology)
Nilgiri Networks
nlogue.com
Nokia
Nortel Networks
Nortel-Maitra
Oracle
Patni
Philips
Polaris Software Labs
R. S. Software
Ramco Systems
Reebok
RiteChoice Technologies
RITES: Rail India Technical and Economic Services
Robert Bosch
SAP
Saraswat Cooperative Bank
SAS (now Sasken)
Sasken (formerly Silicon Automation Systems)
Satyam Computer Services
Sharp
Siemens
Silicon Automation Systems (Sasken)
Siliconix
Silverline

Sonata
ST Microelectronics
Stone Group
STPI: Software Technology Parks India
Strand Genomics
Sun Microsystems India
Svam
Syntel
System Antics
System Logic
Tata Infotech
TCIL: Tata Consultancy India
TCS: Tata Consultancy Services
TeNet: Telecommunication Network
Texas Instruments
TISL
Toshiba
UACT: Usha Martin Academy of Communication Technology
UNDP: United Nations Development Program
UT Starcom
Vedika
Verifone
Virage Logic Corp
VLSI Technology
Wipro
XLRI: Xavier Labour Relations Institute
Yokogawa/Blue Star

Acronyms and Technical Terms

1S95	a code division multiple access (CDMA) digital cellular standard
Access Network	part of network that connects houses and offices to the local exchange
ASIC	application-specific integrated circuits
BCA	Bachelor of Computer Applications
BE	Bachelor of Engineering
BPO	business process outsourcing
BTech	Bachelor of Technology
CBS	Central Bureau of Statistics – Israel
CorDECT	a WLL solution for access networks
DIAS	digital instrument access system
DPS Chip	a general purpose chip
DSP	digital switch processing
ERSO	Electronics Research and Service Organization
ESOP	employee's stock option plan
FDI	foreign direct investment
GIS	geographic information systems
GSM	global system for mobile communications
HR	human resource
HTP	horizontal technology policy
ICs	integrated circuit(s)
ICT	information and communications technology
IPO	initial public offering
IS	information systems
IT	information technology
ITES	IT enabled services
ITI	industrial training institutes
ITP	Innovation & Technology Policy
ITRI	Industrial Technology and Research Organization
IVA	Israel Venture Association
M$	million dollars
M&A	mergers & acquisitions
MCA	Master of Computer Applications
ME	Master of Engineering
MNE	multinational enterprise
MS	Master of Science
MTech	Master of Technology
NASDAQ	National Stock Dealers Association Quotations

NASE	North American Stock Exchange
NASSCOM	National Association of Software and Service Companies
NRI	non-resident Indian
NSF	National Science Foundation
OCS	Office of the Chief Scientist, Ministry of Industry and Trade (Israel)
OEM	original equipment manufacturer
PC	personal computer
PGP	Postgraduate Programme (equivalent to a Masters in Business Administration)
PGSM	Postgraduate Program in Software Enterprise Management (equivalent to PGP)
PhD	Doctor of Philosophy
PHS	personal handiphone system, a standard used in Japan
R&D	research and development
SEI CMM Level X	a software company's quality certification level X
SIPA	Silicon Valley Indian Professionals Association
STP	software technology park
SU	start up or start-up company
TDM	time division multiplex
TDMA	time division multiple access, a telecom standard
TiE	The Indus Entrepreneurs
TNC	transnational corporation
VC	venture capital or venture capital company
WLL	wireless in local loop

Preface and Acknowledgements

This research volume is the first book-length study of the Indian software industry in the last seven years. The project originated with a suggestion made by R. Narasimhan, one of the pioneers of computer science in India. He was a senior member of the team which designed and built TIFRAC, the first electronic digital computer that was designed, built and operated in India (at the Tata Institute of Fundamental Research, Bombay, in the 1950s). E. Sridharan, director of the University of Pennsylvania Institute for the Advanced Study of India (UPIASI), expanded the idea and developed it into a fully-fledged proposal. The Institute, set up in New Delhi in 1997, is an affiliate of the Center for the Advanced Study of India (CASI), University of Pennsylvania in Philadelphia. The Center, established in 1992, was created to undertake studies of contemporary India. Sridharan raised funds from seven sources and identified participant scholars from several institutions in India, the United States, Canada and Israel. Anthony P. D'Costa, one of the invited participants, later came on board as a co-editor of the volume and played an active editorial role from the end of 2000 onwards.

The project was driven by the need to understand the factors that contributed to or hindered innovation in the Indian IT industry, especially the software sector. The Indian software industry was then one of the few internationally competitive and large export-oriented industries in India, and also classified as a high-technology industry. It was observed that the globally competitive Indian software industry, though expanding throughout the decade at an annual compound rate of 40–50 per cent, was overwhelmingly based on the export of personnel for low value-added, on-site work. It was evident that this business model of 'bodyshopping' would not be sustainable in the long run or would consign the Indian industry to low value-added activities. Indian IT would have to diversify its markets by reducing its dependence on the US market and go beyond 'bodyshopping' to innovate new products and services. Strategies would have to include exploiting new IT areas such as the Internet, creating niche products for both the domestic and world markets, integrating software and hardware in embedded IT products, and spinning off technologies developed for the defence/space complex into commercially successful products. A comprehensive research project on innovation in the Indian IT industry, it was believed, would be a useful first step towards this.

The project viewed innovation holistically, taking the view that developing new products at the R&D function level was not enough because successful innovation in a world of rapidly changing technologies had to be continuing and institutionalized. Technology had to be managed

xix

holistically so as to generate the virtuous cycle of revenues and investment in innovative activities. Only commercially successful IT products and services could generate the necessary revenues. Hence, innovation had to be located within the framework of corporate strategy, which in turn had to be contextualized in the larger domestic and world market structures and policy environments.

To capture the complexities of innovation, the study had to incorporate the following features:

- multi-level analysis with various units of analysis: firm, industry, inter-firm clusters, global outsourcing arrangements, domestic and global market structures, and policy environments;
- multi-methodological approaches, relying on the varied disciplinary backgrounds of the contributors;
- internationally comparative perspectives, taking into account relevant comparative locations of IT innovation activity, including India's actual and potential competitors as well as actual and potential markets;
- multifaceted and interdisciplinary frameworks, taking into account not only technological innovations but also the institutional, organizational and managerial (including financial) innovations and their cultural support systems.

Twelve studies, originally commissioned, investigated the various dimensions of innovation in the Indian IT industry. The researchers adopted a variety of mutually complementary perspectives, bringing out the heterogeneity of contexts, units or levels of analysis, and interactions between organizations, management, technology, firm strategies, domestic and international market structures, and policy environments. Thus, the project included product-level studies which examined the process of product development by teams within firms (Rishikesha Krishnan and Ganesh Prabhu, S. Krishna and Abhoy Ojha, and Subhash Bhatnagar), and firm-level studies which look at firm strategies for innovation for both products and services (S. Krishna and Abhoy Ojha, Anthony D'Costa, AnnaLee Saxenian, Gil Avnimelech and Morris Teubal, Subhash Bhatnagar and P. P. Gupta). Other dimensions included the organizational culture of firms and their impact on innovation (Deepti Bhatnagar and Mukund Dixit); inter-firm cluster studies examining collaborative efforts to innovate (Rakesh Basant and Pankaj Chandra); and global outsourcing arrangements which look at the potential for innovation for Indian IT firms in such arrangements (Rakesh Basant and Pankaj Chandra, Anthony D'Costa, AnnaLee Saxenian, S. Krishna and Sundeep Sahay). Three areas covering the domestic market included the indigenous high-tech software development for remote sensing satellites for advanced domestic needs, which led to IT-enabled high-tech exports of satellite imagery (A. R. Dasgupta and S. Chandrashekar), innovations aimed at the domestic market (S. Krishna and Abhoy Ojha, P. P. Gupta), and the small sector (P. P. Gupta). Most of the studies entailed comparisons and investigations of the effects of linkages with key global sites of IT innovation and export competitiveness. Such sites included not only Silicon Valley, Israel, Taiwan, China, Korea and Japan but also the visible expatriate Indian professional community. Taken together, the twelve studies, anchored around the issue of innovation in a global context, constituted an integrated whole. They yielded a wealth of firm and industry-specific data that were relevant for both corporate strategies and government policy.

UPIASI organized an initial and a final conference around the project, on 23–24 July 1998, and 18–19 August 2001, respectively. Individual fieldwork by participant scholars, carried out between 1999 and 2001, was funded by UPIASI. In 2002, some follow-up work was conducted. Acknowledgement of additional sources of funding, in the case of those scholars whose fieldwork coincided with fieldwork for another project, is made individually at the end of their respective chapters. This volume consists of revised and updated versions of the papers written for the project. For a variety of reasons only eight of the twelve original studies could be accommodated in this volume.

UPIASI thanks the Indian co-sponsors of this project: the Ministry of Small-Scale Industry and Agro & Rural Industries, the Ministry of Information Technology, Mahindra & Mahindra, Infosys, Tata Consultancy Services, the National Centre for Software Technology, and the Center for the Advanced Study of India, University of Pennsylvania. The editors would like to thank R. Narasimhan for his advice throughout the execution of the project. They would also like to thank G. Anandalingam of the University of Maryland, College Park (formerly of the School of Engineering and Applied Sciences and the Wharton School of the University of Pennsylvania), for his written comments on earlier drafts of the chapters. Invaluable support was provided by Ashok Parthasarathi, former Secretary of the Ministry of Small-Scale Industries and Agro & Rural Industries; N. R. Narayana Murthy, Chairman, Infosys; F. C. Kohli, Deputy Chairman, Tata Consultancy Services; Keshub Mahindra, Chairman, Mahindra & Mahindra; S. Ramani, former Director of the National Centre for Software Technology; and several officers of the Ministry of Communication and Information Technology (formerly Department of Electronics of the Government of India), particularly A. K. Chakravarti, S. Ramakrishnan, S. P. Nawathe, G. V. Ramaraju, and S. K. Vyas.

We would also like to thank Sage Publications India Pvt Ltd for permission to reproduce Chapters 3, 4, 5, 6 and 7, which are revised and updated versions of papers that were originally published in *Science, Technology and Society*, Vol. 7, No. 1 (January–June 2002).

The editors also thank Francine Frankel, Director, Center for the Advanced Study of India, University of Pennsylvania, for supporting UPIASI's involvement with the project and S. K. Singh, Secretary-General, UPIASI, for his enthusiastic overall support. Amanda Watkins of Palgrave Macmillan efficiently walked us through the entire publication process. We are grateful to

Adil Tyabji for copy editing the manuscript, Reuben Israel for technical support, and the UPIASI staff, S. D. Gosain, Ruchika Ahuja and Supan Manjhi, for their unstinting logistical support. We are of course indebted to the participants of the workshops and to the authors of this volume. We especially appreciate their patience during the editing process and thank them for bringing this project to a successful closure.

1
The Indian Software Industry in the Global Division of Labour

Anthony P. D'Costa[1]

1. Introduction

At the dawn of the twenty-first century India's traditional image as an impoverished nation is undergoing considerable change. While India continues to suffer from rampant poverty, persistent inequalities and internal political uncertainties, there has been a quiet revolution underway in India's high-technology industry. India, known for its tea, jewellery and garment exports, has now become a significant exporter of software. Consequently, the industry, the government and scholars are banking on the continued expansion of the sector. Considerable hope has been pinned on the sector's ability to address India's chronic developmental problems of low growth, unemployment, balance of payments deficits and technological backwardness.

In this volume we attempt to take a deeper look at India's software industry. Rather than assume that the rapid growth of software exports is a sure sign of the sector's strength or that exports will necessarily solve India's development problems, we critically examine the Indian software industry. This was prompted by three observable features of the Indian software industry: first, for all the hype of rapid sectoral expansion, the Indian industry has occupied a marginal position in the world market; second, notwithstanding high growth rates, India's exports have been largely low value output; and third, the size of the domestic market is less than a third of India's export market. These characteristics demand a closer examination of the industry to identify the sources of growth, the particular barriers facing it, and the possible strategic and policy responses that could raise the Indian industry to a higher trajectory. To accomplish this the industry must sustain its high growth rate for the foreseeable future and, relatedly, must move up the value chain to obtain such high growth. Consequently, much of the optimism regarding the sector's transformative capability on the Indian economy hinges on the industry's ability to innovate and cope with new competitors in a rapidly changing global information and communications technology environment.

This chapter lays out some of the basic features of the Indian industry in the context of the global sector. I argue that the Indian industry faces considerable

1

structural barriers to innovation because of its overt dependence on exports of software services to the US. Relatedly, the industry's growth is constrained by India's very small domestic market, limiting the diffusion of information and communications technologies (ICT) and information technology (IT) services. If this interpretation is correct, then the Indian industry must pursue a coherent set of strategies to break out of low value software and diversify export markets. There are also public policy issues which the Indian state must execute to facilitate the industry's transition from a low end trajectory to a high end one.

This collaborative project assesses the preparedness of Indian industry to meet the global challenges. It discusses how India fits into the international division of labour, the industry's trajectory, and how the industry and the government might harness the potential economic benefits of a dynamic Indian software industry. The project as a whole draws on the experiences of a number of firms and explicitly addresses the state of the Indian industry, its strengths and weaknesses, firm strategies, and the opportunities offered by the world economy. Each contributor identifies some of the challenges facing the industry, the strategic responses of firms to overcome barriers to innovation, and offers policy options for the government to make sustained growth a reality.

In the discussion that follows, I begin by briefly delineating some of the global structural barriers that prevent most developing countries from actively participating in the world economy. Second, I extend this exclusionary tendency to the Indian software industry by bringing out three forms of decoupling of the industry, which I argue place it on a low end trajectory. These are: (a) decoupling the software industry from the larger hardware sector; (b) disconnecting the industry from the domestic market; and (c) the specialized division of software into services and products.

Consequently, I show that Indian industry is neither large by global standards nor innovative. India's specialization thus far in a few niche markets, while consistent with contemporary economic globalization, is not consonant with the tremendous opportunities which the global information and communications technology (ICT) goods and services markets offer. The third section briefly explores how the principal challenges facing the Indian sector, namely the three kinds of decoupling, could be addressed. Anticipating competition from China and other countries, I refer to comparative data whenever possible throughout the discussion. The chapter ends with strategic implications for the industry as a whole, which the individual chapters in this volume take up in greater detail.

2. Structural dependence of developing countries

Historically, colonies suffered from a narrow specialization in primary exports. Export dependence locked in the local economy to a low accumulation path. Declining terms of trade and low income elasticities for primary commodities generated the 'export pessimism' and subsequent import substitution industrialization (ISI) strategy of early post-Second World War development thinking. However, by the 1970s even ISI was exhausted, due to narrow domestic markets, high costs and technological backwardness. For necessary economic transformation, as witnessed in East Asia, economic strategy for international competitiveness was switched in favour of export substitution. Exports facilitated learning through economies of scale and increasing returns, while foreign markets became a source for knowledge acquisition. The rise of East Asia demonstrated the importance of a market-augmenting role for the state and the significance of local learning anchored in export competition.

Today, the global economy is characterized by hyper-competition among mostly multinational corporations (MNCs) from the triad nations of the US, European 'Union and Japan. A handful of countries, such as South Korea, Taiwan, Singapore, India, China and Brazil, are attempting to upgrade their industrial activities. The rest of the developing world compete either vigorously in labour-intensive exports or are considered 'structurally irrelevant' (Hoogvelt, 2001: 189). Of the $12.4 trillion of global trade, the advanced capitalist countries had a share of 65 per cent, while the least developed countries, most of which are from Africa, had a mere 0.64 per cent (UNCTAD, 2002).[2] During 1999–2000, the triad economies accounted for 75 per cent of global foreign direct investment (FDI) inflows and 85 per cent of FDI outflows (UNCTAD, 2001: 9–11).

Home to nearly 50 000 MNCs and host to nearly 100 000 foreign affiliates, the triad's dominance of the world economy is virtually absolute. For example, US MNC affiliates in five IT industries had global sales of $202 billion, while total US exports of IT goods and services was only $113 billion in 1998 (US Department of Commerce, 2002: 54). The structural inequality is also evident from the size of firms (Table 1.1), suggesting the enormous difficulties in breaking into the world market. There are a few examples of East Asian countries capturing global market shares in manufacturing. The question is, can India do it in the software industry? Not only are the largest

Table 1.1. Size of firms and the structure of the world economy (averages of top 10)

Top 10 manufacturing MNCs (global) (1999)	$134 billion
Top 10 manufacturing MNCs (developing countries) (1999)	$24 billion
Top 10 ICT firms (global) (2000)	$63.4 billion
Top 10 software firms (global) (2000)	$5.9 billion
Top 10 Indian IT firms (2000)*	$278 million

Note: *Four were MNC subsidiaries.

Source: UNCTAD (2001:) for top manufacturing firms; OECD (2002: 63, 67) for top ICT and software firms; *Dataquest* (www.dqindia.com/top/20/) for top Indian IT firms.

MNCs from the industrialized countries but even the top developing country firms are about a sixth the size of such MNCs' gross sales. Similarly, on average, the top global ICT and software firms had sales revenues of $63.4 and $5.9 billion respectively, whereas the average for the top ten Indian IT firms was only $278 million.

Global competition suggests that not all firms can pursue all activities. Rather, outsourcing, joint-ventures, subcontracting, technical collaborations and alliances are institutional arrangements by which firms will try to specialize (Okhi, 2001: 85). Lacking core competence of a high technological order, most small firms are adjuncts to larger enterprises. For example, in Internet software development, smaller firms adjust to the standards set by giant telecommunications companies, while applications software developers are further down the industry hierarchy (Casper and Glimstedt, 2001). Large MNCs can be flexible if they outsource or subcontract some of their production and service needs. In practice, this means farming out non-critical, labour-intensive, low value activities to other suppliers as these activities are out of synchronization with MNC core competence (see US Department of Commerce, 2002: 54–7). This is both an opportunity and a constraint to growth for developing country firms. It permits breaking into markets hitherto closed to most but also condemns new suppliers to only those market niches the buyer is willing to forgo.

The Indian software industry is just such a case, facing both opportunities to move into new markets but at the same time locked into providing low wage services to rich clients abroad. The fact that many Indian firms provide software services to Fortune 500 companies is a cause for both celebration and sombre introspection as Indian exporters are very small in comparison to their renowned clients. However, just as many East Asian economies with considerable accumulation of technology have successfully upgraded their industrial capability, Indian firms are also at the juncture of strategically moving up the software value chain. To accomplish this, two concerted efforts will be critical: an emphasis on technological and commercial learning and a supportive institutional environment to encourage dynamic expansion. The constraints, in the form of industrial decoupling, which limit dynamic learning, are presented below. From this discussion some strategic responses are identified to make the Indian industry a global force as well as a contributor to India's developmental needs.

3. The decoupling of the Indian software industry

From hardware manufacturing

In the era of mainframe computers, most software was produced or subcontracted by computer manufacturers. With the diffusion of micro- and personal computers, the structure of the software industry changed dramatically. In addition to the in-house development of software by firms and by mainframe producers, there emerged independent software developers for external buyers as a distinct category, with many catering to the lucrative consumer-oriented applications market (Mowery, 1996: 4–6). As the installed base of PCs and other hardware such as telecommunications equipment increased, the production of software became delinked from hardware production. Increasingly, the independent developers of software are becoming more prominent as technological and organizational innovations permit greater flexibility in outsourcing customized software services to distant producers. In the area of software applications, whose production is less dependent on hardware production, there has been a proliferation of independent packaged software developers. Microsoft is the leading player in packaged software, separate from hardware manufacturing. However, its Windows operating system, acting as a dominant design, compels other hardware-independent application software producers to develop Windows-based applications.

Software, however, is complementary to hardware. Given the technological trajectory based on microelectronics, there is clear evidence of convergence of digital technologies (Dicken, 1998: 150). Consequently, the production and use of software are integrally linked to hardware, broadly classified as ICT goods. These include electronic data processing equipment (computers), office equipment, controls and instruments, communications equipment (radio, mobile systems, radar), telecommunications, consumer electronics, and components that go into these hardware.

India's position in the global ICT market is low, suggesting a disconnection between software development and a domestic hardware base. Recent data on global production of ICT goods (Table 1.2) reflect several characteristics of the international division of labour, the considerable asymmetry in this division, and India's poor standing. The OECD clearly dominates global production of ICT goods, with 77.5 per cent of the world total. Two OECD members – the US and Japan – together have 50 per cent of the global output and they dominate the production of various ICT goods. However, there is a distinct global division of labour in consumer ICT goods and components production, in which other economies actively participate.

Countries from East and South East Asia (including Japan) dominate these two segments, with Japan and China producing 44 per cent of consumer electronics, while Japan, Korea, China, Malaysia, Singapore and Taiwan control 55 per cent of components. As Japan consolidates its grip over high end consumer goods and components, China is making inroads into the low end. Korea, Taiwan and Singapore have specialized in memory chips, hard disks and other related segments (Okhi, 2001: 71). In this global division, India ranked 26th among 33 countries. Indian software producers in the early 1990s were confident that by the end of the decade India's hardware industry would be comparable to Taiwan's (Lakha, 1999: 148). In 1999, Taiwan's ICT goods production was ten times that of India's. Smaller countries

Table 1.2 World production of ICT goods (selected countries and OECD)

	1999 total ICT ($ m)	Share of world total (%)	1990–99 (CAGR %)	1995–99 (CAGR %)	1997–99 (% change)
US	320 840	29.5	5.8	4.4	20.3
Japan	220 728	20.3	2.3	4.0	1.3
Korea	57 597	5.3	10.8	4.2	19.2
Germany	47 545	4.4	0.5	4.4	37.9
Ireland	16 481	1.5	12.8	17.0	54.9
UK	47 734	4.4	6.2	6.9	28.4
OECD-21	843 121	77.5	4.2	1.4	16.5
China	59 738	5.5	19.8	20.1	NA
Malaysia	38 956	3.5	20.1	9.0	32.8
Singapore	40 755	3.7	11.9	0.7	−4.7
Taiwan	40 979	3.8	12.7	9.0	30.6
India	4 841	0.4	0.4	−0.3	5.5
Brazil	13 484	1.2	1.3	−5.0	−30.4
Israel	6311	0.6	14.6	11.2	35.5
Total	1 088 539	100.0	5.6	1.4	22.3

Note: CAGR = compounded annual growth rate.
Source: Adapted from OECD, 2002, 2000.

such as Ireland, the Philippines and Israel had greater production in these segments than India.

On the growth front, the ICT industry exhibits some consistent trends. During 1990–9, the decade of considerable technology-led expansion of the world economy, some smaller countries like Ireland and Israel have grown quite rapidly: 12.8 per cent and 14.6 per cent annually, respectively. It was also the Asian group (excluding Japan) that had some of the best rates of growth, varying from 10.8 per cent for Korea to 20.1 per cent for Malaysia. These were also economies that leveraged the global market during its expansionary phase, while India withdrew from it with its autarkic policies. India's growth rate in ICT goods in the 1990s lagged behind considerably with a paltry 0.4 per cent. In the second half of the 1990s, Ireland and East and South East Asia, excluding Japan and Singapore, grew the fastest. While Japan was reeling under the recession set in motion in 1990, Singapore was still recovering from the 1997 Asian financial crisis. India's growth rate fell before rising modestly in the 1995–9 period to 5.5 per cent in 1997–9.

The disconnection with the domestic market

The specialization of ICT goods production by Asia has been integral to upgrading manufacturing capabilities. Relatively early entry with multinational investments in combination with state promotion and aggressive learning strategies by business have contributed to this global specialization. India

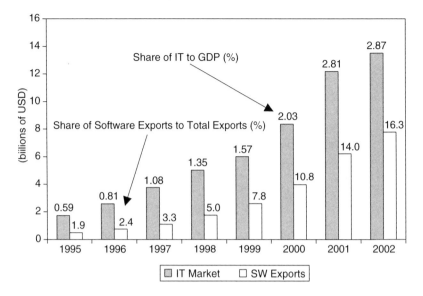

Figure 1.1 The recent growth of the Indian IT industry (1995–2003)

Notes: IT = hardware, peripherals, networking, domestic and export market for software and services.

Source: NASSCOM, 2002: 21, 28.

has essentially missed this manufacturing bus. Only now is the Indian IT seg-ment showing some signs of growth, being led by overall economic growth (Figure 1.1). This growth rate of IT has, however, been spearheaded by the rapid expansion of the software segment, especially for the export market.

The Indian IT market has clearly expanded in nominal terms. In 1995 the industry had under $2 billion in output. In 2002–3 it had reached $16.5 billion, representing 3.15 per cent of India's GDP. This share was over five times that of 1994–5. China's IT industry reported $27.4 billion value added in 2001, representing 4.2 per cent of GDP (US & Foreign Commercial Service, 2002a). During 1994–2002, India's exports of software and software services increased from less than half a billion dollars to $9.9 billion. This was a twentyfold increase, representing over 20 per cent of India's total exports in 2002–3. What is remarkable is the steady decoupling of India's hardware output from software production, evident from a rising ratio of software exports in relation to hardware output (Figure 1.2). Economic lib-eralization in the 1980s effectively forced Indian hardware firms to move into software specialization, thus reversing the earlier strategy of creating a national hardware industry (Sridharan, 1996).

Not coincidentally, this decoupling was not witnessed in the heavily guarded, nationally oriented supercomputer development. Past US restric-tions on the export of American-made supercomputers compelled Indian

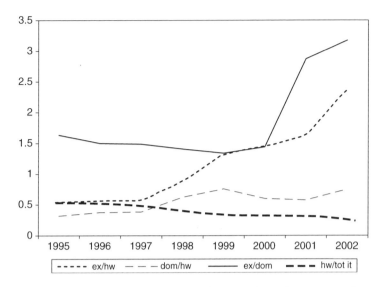

Figure 1.2 Decoupling of the Indian software industry (various ratios)

Notes: ex = exports of software; hw = hardware; dom = domestic software market; tot it = total

Source: Adapted from NASSCOM 2002: 21, 28.

organizations to develop their own. Though less powerful than American and Japanese machines (13–36 teraflops compared to India's one teraflop), these are considered by the industry to be the state-of-the-art. Built inexpensively by the Centre for Development of Advanced Computing (C-DAC) and the Indian Institute of Science (IISc), they have already sold seven units to Russia, Canada, Germany and Singapore (India Abroad News Service, 2002). This is illustrative of India's hardware capability and its wherewithal to overcome global structural dependence.

Decoupling is also reflected in the declining share of hardware in relation to total information technology output. However, there appears to be a stable relationship between domestic output of hardware and software. This can be interpreted as a slow-growing domestic market for IT in general, which is not inconsistent with a demand-constrained economy. Finally, there is a decoupling of software export markets from the domestic market (Kattuman and Iyer, 2001: 216). Domestic projects are assumed to be more complex, such as Mumbai's stock exchange and Indian railways' reservation systems, both designed and implemented by the Computer Maintenance Corporation (OECD, 2000: 135). This suggests limited spillovers from the wide range of project experience obtained from the domestic software market. The exogenously driven Indian software industry is captured by an increasing ratio of software exports relative to the domestic software market

(Figure 1.2). India also has an unusually high share of software production in relation to the total IT market in India, ranging from nearly 50 per cent in 1995 to over 75 per cent in 2003. This contrasts very sharply with the 1997 OECD norm of 13.4 per cent (OECD, 2000: 62). The corresponding ratio for China in 2001 was 18.5 per cent (US & Foreign Commercial Service, 2002a).[3]

The software services and products divide

The third form of decoupling is India's specialization in software services, an activity quite distinct from developing software packages. The spectacular growth of Indian exports, averaging over 50 per cent in most years, has been through software services. Exports accounted for 60 per cent of the total Indian IT market in 2002–3. Of the total software market, $9.88 billion or nearly 80 per cent was exported (NASSCOM, 2003: 21, 45). What is missing from the basket of software exports is software products or packages. This is in sharp contrast to Ireland's software export profile. In 2000, Ireland's packaged software exports amounted to $3.82 billion. However, as foreign companies for tax purposes book their revenues in Ireland, Irish software production has been artificially inflated (Arora et al., 2001: 1270). There is no comparable figure for India, suggesting negligible presence in this market niche. The closest India comes to software products is installing and integrating 'packaged software' created by multinational firms. The value of such exports from India was estimated to be only about $300 million (NASSCOM, 2003: 36).

In and of itself, exports of software services are a market strength. They are also a source of employment. The ability to mobilize large numbers of technical professionals has made Indian firms adept at quickly providing low cost software and IT services to foreign clients, many of them MNCs. However, specialization is also a result of India's inability to penetrate other market niches, such as software packages. There are several reasons for this. First, product development requires a dynamic domestic market in general. Second, without a large installed base of hardware the benefits of network externalities cannot be captured, thus limiting the market size. Third, packaged software development demands intensive interfacing between users and producers, which neither small markets nor geographically distant producers can support. Fourth, software products demand heavy marketing outlays, exacerbated by first-comer advantages. The latter places most small firms at a disadvantage; developing country firms are further disadvantaged.

According to NASSCOM's 2002 *Strategic Review*, the bulk of India's service exports fell under two categories: first, legacy application management, maintenance services and migration, comprising 27 per cent of exports; and second, customized services comprising 30 per cent of total exports. Both these categories of services (though not necessarily all their sub-categories) are generally considered to be low value additions (NASSCOM, 2002: 29). In the 2003 *Review*, the first category was not listed, while the second category was estimated to account for 35 per cent of exports. A third category, IT-Enabled Services (ITES), comprising 20 per cent of exports, also consists of low value services such as customer interaction centres and business process outsourcing (BPO). In 2001–2 their combined contribution was 65 per cent of ITES exports, which is likely to increase as ITES as a whole expand. There was a 60 per cent growth in ITES exports over the 2001–2 and 2002–3 periods (NASSCOM, 2003: 58). It might be pointed out that the growth in ITES exports is good for employment. Capturing a sizeable share of this market, with global spending estimated at $1.2 trillion in 2006 (NASSCOM, 2003: 57), would reduce India's chronic unemployment of non-technical graduates. However, the larger issue has to do with the general problem of low value service exports. According to NASSCOM's earlier report (2002: 24), the global demand for IT services, which includes customized services and ITES, will be $700.4 billion in 2005. India's current strength is in customized services, which is expected to be sustained in the future. However, this segment of the global IT services market has been estimated to be only 4.4 per cent of the global market in 2001 and is expected to fall to a mere 3.6 per cent by 2005 (see Table 1.3).

If the market segment in which India excels is small to begin with, and it is likely to witness a relative decline in a few years, then it is clear that India needs to diversify its markets away from this segment. This may mean moving into high value software services for which there are considerable opportunities, such as systems integration, packaged software support and installation, and processing services. This does not, however, mean that India should give up all low end services. For example, low wage ITES is a growth sector with significant absorptive capacity for India's large pool of educated, non-technical personnel. Much would depend on the supply of skills in India and their global demand (Desai, 2001). What is incontrovertible, however, is that India must develop not only higher order skills in general but also widen experience in complex project design and execution so as to cope with the rapidly changing global ICT market. This demands an innovative strategy that takes into account India's current endowments but also foresees future competitive strengths in creative ways.

4. Strategic responses to exploit global opportunities

The characteristics of the Indian ICT sector as a whole suggest that Indian producers will have an uphill battle protecting their current position in software exports, let alone becoming a global IT powerhouse, unless there is some radical rethinking on competitive strategies. As it is neither practical nor intellectually productive to present an exhaustive list of 'to do' items (many are elaborated in the individual chapters), I present a discussion centred around the three forms of decoupling and relate them to innovation strategies for the software sector.

Table 1.3   Forecast of global IT services and India's opportunities

	Global market (2001)		Global market (2005)		India's exports (2001, US $ b)	India's global share (%, 2001)	Potential for exports
	US $ b	% share	US $ b	% share			
Professional services	142.9	32.5	238.7	34.1	5.3	3.7	
IT consulting	21.3	4.8	31.5	4.5	0.1	0.3	Low–Medium
Systems integration	81.1	18.4	142.1	20.3	0.1	0.1	Low–Medium
Custom applications	19.3	4.4	25.3	3.6	4.5	23.1	High
Network consulting & integration	21.2	4.8	39.8	5.7	0.7	3.3	Low
Product services	117.9	26.8	176.9	25.3	0.4	0.3	
IT training & education	25.5	5.8	40.9	5.8			High
H/W support & installation	44.4	10.1	49.4	7.1			Low
Packaged software support services	48.0	10.9	86.6	12.4	0.4	0.7	Medium–High
Outsourcing services	179.2	40.7	284.8	40.7	0.1	0.0	
Processing services	78.4	17.8	103.8	14.8			High
IS outsourcing	64.0	14.5	100.2	14.3			High
Application outsourcing	13.4	3.0	39.0	5.6			Low–Medium
Network infrastructure management	23.4	5.3	41.8	6.0	0.1	0.3	Medium–High
Total	440.0	100.0	700.4	100.0	5.7	1.3	

Notes: IT = information technology; IS = information services; H/W = hardware.

Source: Calculated from NASSCOM, 2002: 24, 46.

First, a strong link between production of ICT goods or hardware and the Indian software industry is necessary to foster learning and thus inter-industry synergy in ways that are currently not possible. Second, a strong home market engendered by a dynamic ICT sector can also foster software opportunities, which could provide an alternative to the customized software services India currently exports. As this niche is limited by the extent of the global market, and as India's current strengths lie in this particular segment, it is of the utmost importance consciously to reduce this excessive dependence. It is here that development of software packages with business and government promotion becomes critical. Entrepreneurship and its explicit institutional support through venture capital are likely to be key ingredients in this market-diversifying strategy.

Third, India's innovative capability can be enhanced by intensifying the interfaces between users and producers of software, a possibility made difficult with distant export markets. Subsequently, a greater domestic orientation could induce strong linkages among firms (foreign and domestic), universities and governments. Fourth, the deepening of the domestic market can be leveraged to attract overseas Indians (non-resident Indians or NRIs). Much has been reported about the successes of Indian engineers in Silicon Valley and much is expected from such talent if they were to return to India with their technical knowledge, market contacts, entrepreneurial energy and business savvy. An integral understanding of these cumulative causal mechanisms helps us understand the ways by which the decoupling of the industry might be resolved. If followed through by appropriate strategic responses by firms, the industry and the government, the Indian industry could be well positioned in the global economy for sustained growth.

Hardware production to build technological capability

East and South East Asian economies are not strong in software but they have large domestic ICT markets. For example, Japan, South Korea, Taiwan, Singapore and Malaysia have successfully created a viable high-technology manufacturing base. The basic mechanism has been to establish dynamic linkages with the world economy that rest on strong domestic capabilities for manufacturing hardware (Dedrik and Kraemer, 1998: 23). Even Brazil, plagued with macroeconomic instability, external indebtedness and high costs of protectionism, has been able to foster a viable hardware sector (Evans, 1995; Sridharan, 1996). Even more remarkable is Ireland's global presence in both the hardware and software industries. In 2000, Ireland, with less than four million people, exported and imported nearly $25 and $16 billion respectively of ICT equipment (OECD, 2002: 273). In 2001, Ireland had nearly a $4 billion market in packaged and IT services software, suggesting a link between the hardware and software sectors (OECD, 2002: 320).

Many would argue against the establishment right now of an investment-intensive fully-fledged hardware sector in the small Indian market. Others will point to the severe competition afflicting the sectors in Asian economies (Dedrik and Kraemer, 1998: 312). Yet others are likely to point to the economic robustness of 'specialization' and India's premier position in global software outsourcing. These are all reasonable arguments, but only from a static point of view. In a dynamic context, factor prices, costs, markets and industry structures do not remain fixed. Instead, increasing returns from increasing economies of scale and industrial agglomeration could have substantial spillover effects. The synergy between expanding hardware and software sectors can be a significant source for learning in the overall ICT industry.

Consider the case of Singapore, where software development capability lags behind India's. However, Singapore provides a window not only to what can be done to promote hardware manufacturing but also how hardware manufacturing capability could be leveraged to induce learning in the ICT sector in general. The convergence of American business interests and the strategic intervention by the Singaporean government to create a high technology industry demonstrates the possibility of creating world class manufacturing capability even in a tiny city state (McKendrick, Doner and Haggard, 2000). From low-wage based assembly operations, Singapore now specializes in design and manufacturing of hard disk drives. While this suggests the advantages of (manufacturing) specialization rather than diversification, it is evident that ultimately it is the diffused learning process that matters most in industrial competitiveness. Wong's (1995) 'dynamic interaction' model demonstrates why this is so. His model (see Figure 1.3) shows this interaction among three factors: entrepreneurial innovation, state intervention and agglomeration of competitive advantage (Dedrik and Kraemer, 1998: 249). The learning process entailed a virtuous cycle of sector-specific targeting, spillover effects into related industries, skill building in the electromechanical and electronics industries, a deepening supplier base, and the clustering of industries that contributed to competitive advantage.

Singapore's broad manufacturing capability can now be leveraged to move into other ICT development activities. We see some evidence that this is occurring. For example, while Singapore has not specialized in software development, it has been able to attract numerous software professionals as well as entrepreneurs from India. One important case has been the relocation of Vedika Software from Kolkata (formerly Calcutta) to Singapore. The company started in Kolkata in 1987 and produced a successful accounting package called FACT (personal interview with Vedika staff, Kolkata, April 1998). The software is now used by over 9000 companies in nearly twenty-five countries. The IT-friendly Singaporean environment, in which ICT goods production is a critical ingredient, facilitated Vedika's international presence, suggesting that hardware manufacturing can be a centrepiece of national competitiveness and can act as a catalyst for software development.

China provides another example where strength in hardware manufacturing could be a springboard for software growth. In 2000, China's software

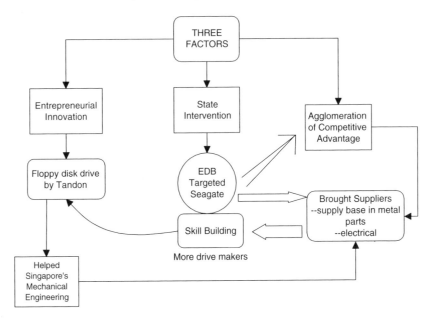

Figure 1.3   Learning through dynamic interaction in hardware manufacturing

Note: EDB = Economic Development Board of Singapore.

Source: Adapted from Pom-Kam Wong (1995) in Dedrik and Kraemer (1998: 249).

exports totalled a mere $220 million (Wong and Wong, 2002: 6).[4] This represented 8 per cent of China's total software market, which translates roughly to a domestic market of $2.5 billion. This is virtually identical in size to India's $2.45 billion domestic software and services market (NASSCOM, 2002: 46). Where China excels is in the manufacture of ICT goods. In 2001 it ranked as the world's sixth largest ICT market (OECD, 2002: 58). Between 1992 and 2001, China had the highest annual growth rate (over 50 per cent), increasing from under $10 billion to nearly $70 billion. India's ICT market grew at a respectable rate of 40 per cent per year during the same period, expanding from less than $5 billion to about $20 billion. However, China's lead in hardware production, rising cross-border foreign direct investment from Taiwan, steady increases in skilled personnel, and the continued promotion of China's science and technology establishment places it in a very advantageous position (Saxenian, Chapter 7, and Sridharan, Chapter 2). Recently, *Current Science* highlighted India's decline in scientific publications from the eighth position in 1973 to now fifteenth in the world (in Jayaraman, 2002a: 100). Between 1980 and 2000, India's science-related publications fell from 14 983 to 12 127, while China's rose from 924 to 22 061. Over the long haul, the absence of strategic business and government policy could render temporary India's current lead over China's software competitiveness.

There are other competitors in the fray. The former Eastern bloc and the former Soviet Union are well-endowed with high technical skills to exploit emerging IT opportunities. Between October 1999 and February 2000, Russia received 1.7 per cent of H1B visas (OECD 2002: 168).[5] While this is a very small share in relation to India's, Russia's ratio of 55 engineers for every 10 000 people places its skill profile far ahead of India's (Kozlov, 2001). Russia's IT market has been estimated at $3.9 billion in 2002 (Lakaeva, 2002). It is entering both low value and high end development work. For example, just like India it is getting into business process operations and IT-enabled services but also complex projects such as application-specific integrated circuit (ASIC) chips for Nortel (Kozlov, 2002). With its own overseas technical diaspora, Russia is being advised to lure back its emigrant engineers (see Goyal, 2001). The Eastern European countries (the Czech Republic, Hungary, Poland and Slovakia) are still behind India's software output, but their IT markets (both packaged software and IT services) are on the upswing (OECD, 2002: 320). In 2000, Hungary exported $5.24 billion of ICT goods, with nearly an equal volume of imports, suggesting considerable activity in the IT industry (OECD, 2002: 273). These are also markets with significant technical talent and low disposable incomes, suggesting future competitive pressures on the Indian industry.

Diversifying software development

As we have seen, India specializes in the export of customized software. Nearly 60 per cent of India's export revenues comprise legacy applications and customized services (NASSCOM, 2002: 29). Software export revenues for India, while on the rise, have not been particularly high when compared to other software exporting economies such as Ireland and Israel. For example, India's revenue per employee has been between $20–30 000 compared to Ireland's $60–80 000 (Arora et al., 2001: 1269–70; Heeks, 1996). The very nature of customized software for specific clients restricts wide applicability to other sectors and thus constrains economy-wide learning (Kumar, 2001). Relatedly, the focus on ITES as a driver of software exports, while perfectly logical from a resource allocation view, reinforces the low wage segment of the value chain. This sentiment is echoed by industry representatives when they say that Indian software firms 'take up projects after people conceptualize something' or that the Indian industry must get into products (Sircar, 2002).

Higher skills add higher value. Skill development is a product of formal training as well as accumulated learning experience. As this chapter has suggested, a strong hardware sector and a large installed computer base can facilitate learning, neither of which is prominent in India. It is therefore not surprising to find that in the area of *high* value customized software services requiring high skills, India has not been able to capture much of the global market. These services include systems integration, packaged software integration, network infrastructure management, consulting, turnkey projects, product development and design, embedded software, and R&D services. India's combined exports in these areas in 2001–2 totalled $2.67 billion or 35 per cent of total software exports (NASSCOM, 2003: 36). Curiously, the 2002 *Report* for the same information for the same year showed an export of $1.5 billion or less than 20 per cent of total software exports (NASSCOM, 2002: 29). The most visible change in the new export data was for R&D services of $1.21 billion or a 110 per cent increase in the new estimate. Two other categories that did not exist in the previous report are product development and design ($300 million) and embedded software ($910 million). These are encouraging signs as they all entail higher order services (Sridharan, this volume). However, India's global shares in other high value service areas such as systems integration, packaged software integration, network infrastructure management, and consulting were a mere 0.1, 0.7, 0.3 and 0.3 per cent respectively, while India's total exports amounted to only 1.3 per cent of the global market (NASSCOM, 2002: 24, 29). If Indian firms had the necessary skills and project experience, India's exports in these areas and as a whole would have been much higher.

The principal drawback to developing products is a weak domestic market. However, there are other non-technical factors that influence product development (Krishnan and Prabhu, Chapter 6). Most products and applications are off-the-shelf software programmes, such as word-processing, financial programmes, statistical packages and the like. The question as to why India is not good at making products has to do with the size of the domestic market (Desai, 2001), which is influenced by the installed base of hardware in the economy and its associated network externalities. Product development is also stunted by the lucrative services export market, while geographical distance dissuades firms from taking up product development for export markets (D'Costa, Chapter 3). Others have emphasized the importance of effective copyright protection and an established intellectual property rights regime, which are still evolving in India. The huge costs in development, short marketing span, and follow-up support services, which are all integral to the product development chain, can deter firm entry. At the same time, applications software have a more stable environment with low entry barriers as they are based on standard hardware and operating system platforms (Casper and Glimstedt, 2001: 273). However, application software is also dependent on user community feedback. Hence, domestic market development is likely to have a favourable impact on software product development.

To successfully develop software products, firms must be able to accumulate domain expertise in areas such as banking and finance, retail trade, engineering and design, industry, education, entertainment, health and the like. Expertise is developed through high R&D investment and from firm-specific knowledge in the context of an expanding, dynamic market. Thus far the Indian software industry has not demonstrated much proclivity towards R&D (Parthasarathi and Joseph, Chapter 4). The small, albeit growing, domestic market continues to constrain deep interaction that is possible with a large user base and thus limits software product development. India's presence in the packaged software or products market is negligible. A few companies, large and small, have attempted software products but found the market difficult (Desai, 2002). A handful of firms have viable products. Of the large ones, for example, Infosys, Tata Infotech and Ramco have financial and enterprise resource planning products, while Vedika Software, a small firm, has an accounting package. The presence of this limited number of software products concentrated in the area of financial and banking-related services illustrates the importance for product development of the large Indian market for these services.

The question is whether other markets can be developed for various applications software. While it would be difficult to overcome the technical challenges associated with creating products for distant users (in export markets), firms can diversify their software portfolio to capture the huge benefits from product development by focusing on longer product cycles and intermediate product niches, such as middleware that bridge telecommunications architectures with applications software (Casper and Glimstedt, 2001: 268–72). Targeting the home market, as the installed base and Internet connectivity increase, would be a significant redirection of the Indian industry. Products will also spread the risks of limited export market growth in standard customized services. However, to translate ideas into new products, firms must be innovative in conceptualizing novel applications with complex functionalities. They must also be commercially savvy enough to bring new products to the market quickly and effectively. One promising avenue is open source software development, which permits distributed innovation (Kogut and Metiu, 2001). Here too, the user-driven feedback is critical for fitness of products and reducing the time to bring them to market. More importantly, because of the distributed nature of software development, large numbers of Indian engineers could be mobilized to develop software to serve the domestic market. A recent open source Linux operating system has been applied to the 'Simputer', a low cost machine developed by the Indian Institute of Science in Bangalore (Jayaraman 2002b: 359).

The high risks associated with products, resulting from high development and marketing costs, software piracy, and weak intellectual property rights, demand a multi-pronged institutional approach to reduce market risks. Open source development is one way of overcoming the rigidities of copyright laws and fostering new product development. The development of a venture capital (VC) market is another institutional arrangement which could underwrite some of the risks of product development.

An innovation of Silicon Valley (SV) that accompanied and led the high technology boom, VC market development has been quintessentially a US phenomenon. With particular forms of social networks at the core of the technology industry (Saxenian, 1994), transferring the SV model *in toto* to the Indian institutional context would be problematic (Dossani and Kenney, 2002: 227–8; Casper and Glimstedt, 2001). However, the evolutionary nature of VC formation in the US and the changing business and macro-economic environment in India suggest that VC development is possible in India, albeit adapted to India's particular conditions. The Taiwanese and Israeli experiences, approximating an SV model (Dossani and Kenney, 2002; also Saxenian, Chapter 7; Avnimelech and Teubal, Chapter 5) illustrate the significance of VC to new start-ups and product development. For example, given Israel's small market, it has been relatively successful in particular product niches. The development of a VC market in India will be critical to launching start-up companies and altering the institutional environment to support greater entrepreneurial activities such as product development (Kumar and Jain, 2002). Thus far the VC market is small and immature by US standards, but it has been growing consistently, except for the 2001–2 financial year. The Indian VC market expanded from $20 million in 1996–7 to $1.2 billion in 2002–3 (NASSCOM, 2003: 152). A nearly ninefold increase ($10 billion) in VC disbursements is predicted in 2007–8. As non-resident Indians (NRIs), especially from Silicon Valley, get more involved with the Indian IT industry, they are also likely to emerge as supporters of a fledgling VC market and a source for entrepreneurial initiatives (Saxenian, Chapter 7; Krishna and Ojha, Chapter 9).

Developing the domestic market

What is perhaps most disconcerting is the assumption that somehow India's current lead in the export services market will be maintained. Already India's low wage advantage is eroding, certainly in the higher-order skill levels. This is evident, though not conclusively, from the recent interest shown by a few Indian firms such as Satyam Computer Services to set up a development centre in China.[6] China offers tremendous market opportunities as its economy continues to grow at high rates. The internationalization of Indian software firms means that they will also behave like other MNCs seeking cost reductions and new markets elsewhere.

China is the only other country where both cost and market objectives could be met. There is a large supply of IT professionals, wage costs are low, and the Chinese economy is displaying robust growth. With a large hardware industry, a strong science and technology establishment, and a growing number of Internet users, China is well poised to challenge India in the software industry (Trivedi, 2002). China's heavy investment in Internet infrastructure despite a later start than India has placed it well ahead of

India (Press et al., 2002). According to the CIA estimate, in 2002 China had 47.8 million Internet users compared to India's 16.6 million (Press et al., 2002: 21).[7] China's international bandwidth is roughly twice that of India with 3297.8 megabytes per second and the gap in the installed base of PCs is widening in China's favour (Press et al., 2002: 6, 11). According to the *Computer Industry Almanac*, China has 34 million PCs compared to India's 5.2 million (compared to 3.7 million versus 1.1 million in 1996). China's ICT spending is also surging ahead of India's, with considerable investment in chip-making facilities to meet the demand of the domestic electronics industry (Einhorn, 2002a). It is estimated that by 2005 China's chip output will exceed $8 billion. With nearly $60 billion in 2001, China was well ahead of India's ICT spending of $20 billion. Comparable figures for 1997 were roughly $30 and $10 billion respectively. Even India's English language advantage could be eroded as China aggressively introduces English language training for their software engineers (Einhorn, 2002b).

The significance of leveraging the domestic market for export competitiveness is well illustrated by the Chinese ICT trajectory. One industry official squarely attributed India's great disadvantage to the 'soft demand from local customers' compared to China's booming domestic market (Gordon Brooks, in Einhorn, 2002b). India's surge in software exports, which is decoupled from an ICT base and a dynamic domestic market, means that the industry must innovate up the value chain. Otherwise, the Indian industry will face increasing competition due to the erosion of its labour cost arbitrage. Rising wage costs would automatically dampen the industry's propensity to serve the domestic market and reinforce the sector's penchant for exporting customized software services in a path-dependent fashion (D'Costa, Chapter 3). This would also mean excessive demand on the supply of Indian talent, exacerbated by the global shortages of IT workers. A redirection of emphasis towards the domestic market is expected to alleviate some of the shortcomings of an overly export-dependent, software services sector. While leapfrogging with ICT production is difficult, the enclave nature of software production in India must be reoriented to spread the benefits of the digital economy (Mansell, 2001: 285–8).

The global shortage of IT skills, especially in the US, Germany, the UK and Japan suggests widespread poaching of Indian talent for multinational operations. This puts further pressure on the wage level in India. An ageing society combined with shortages of researchers in science and engineering has created a massive demand for non-immigrant labour in the US (Larson and Brahmakulam, 2002: 41). This by itself is not an unfavourable outcome as Indian firms will be compelled to move up the innovation chain. Currently, about 500000 Indians are employed by the Indian technology sector. However, with global demand outpacing supply even India is likely to face shortages of critical skills. For 2004–5 these shortages are estimated to be 64000 'knowledge' professionals assuming 'minimum' industry growth, and 533 500 under an 'optimistic' scenario (NASSCOM, 2002: 65). Even if only 20 per cent of these are likely to be ITES workers, who are not part of the high skill group, there will be shortages of skills.[8]

In the absence of a dynamic domestic market, Indian skilled professionals will continue to be lured away to foreign firms and markets. The US has relied on H1B visas to secure a large number of Indian technical workers: nearly 50 per cent of the total number of visas in 1999, while China obtained less than 5 per cent (OECD 2002: 179). Even Indian firms in the US such as Syntel, Wipro and TCS relied on the H1B visa system to recruit Indians. Under this scenario, considerable effort must be expended to retain highly skilled IT professionals in India as well as persuade NRIs to conduct higher order IT activities. To guarantee that these professionals will 'circulate' back to India, as is currently being observed (Kripalani, 2002), the Indian domestic economy itself has to be raised to a higher level and the quality of life vastly improved.

To extricate the Indian industry from narrow specialization of customized software service exports a comprehensive and multi-pronged approach to domestic market development will be critical. This is not expected to be at the expense of the export market. Rather, it is aimed at generating the necessary intersectoral linkages in high technology manufacturing, fostering the accumulation of technological know-how, and providing a domestic foundation for high value added software exports. Admittedly, late entry in manufacturing is not easy. The global economy today is highly competitive, prices of commodity components are declining, and several ICT industries are saddled with excess capacity. However, with inter-firm arrangements, developing domestic capability becomes feasible (Basant and Chandra, Chapter 8). As alliances among firms with different competencies become routine, Indian firms need to actively seek out and team up with those that can offer relevant technologies, markets and exposure. Both less risky and more pragmatic, partnerships among firms and between firms, universities and research labs are viable ways of promoting local learning and engendering technological spillovers in the wider economy.

Recent efforts by Indian firms such as Encore Software and the Indian Institute of Science (IISc) have led to the development of an indigenous and inexpensive computer called Simputer. Similarly, HCL Infosystems has launched unicode compatible PCs to support seven Indian languages. Both are examples of serving the domestic market with hardware and software, and not at the expense of the export market. Already the affordable Simputer is being targeted to other developing countries in Asia and Africa. Nor should India's solid achievements in creating indigenous supercomputers be ignored. What is needed is a more institutionally driven, large-scale concerted thrust towards raising the technical and commercial profile of the Indian software industry, which would in the end meet India's developmental needs.

5. Conclusion

It is evident that the massive growth rate of the Indian software industry has caught the world's attention. One of the poorest countries in the world, better known internationally for its uncompetitive industries, India has come a long way with its high-growth software industry. However, by examining India's particular position in the larger global division of labour, this chapter demonstrates that there are still many hurdles to overcome. First, Indian firms are small by global standards, suggesting considerable fragmentation of the Indian industry. To be global players it is important for Indian firms to consolidate their operations and focus, where applicable, on particular core competencies (Kattuman and Iyer, 2001: 217). This will necessarily require strengthening technical, commercial and organizational innovative capabilities of firms (Bhatnagar and Dixit, Chapter 10). India already boasts a few 'world class' companies such as Wipro, NIIT, C-DOT and Infosys (Ghoshal, Piramal and Budhiraja, 2001). The challenge for the country and the industry is to diffuse them throughout the economy.

Second, the Indian industry faces several structural barriers, as revealed by the three kinds of decoupling displayed by the Indian software industry. These are the disconnections between ICT manufacturing and software development, between export markets for software and domestic markets, and between software products and services. The net result has been narrow specialization at the lower end of the value chain, erosion of the wage advantage, emerging new competition from other countries such as China, the growing scarcity of skills, and forgoing of huge opportunities by not leveraging the ICT and IT industries for domestic development. While India's share is globally quite high in the customized software services market, this segment is expected to have less than 4 per cent of the global software market. India's predicted presence is also expected to be low in high-growth niches such as systems integration and packaged services. This makes it all the more urgent to extricate the industry from its low end trajectory.

To counter these challenges both the industry and the government must respond strategically. Linkages for innovation must be promoted systemically (Freeman, 1997) among software-related institutions. The precise details of these broad strategies are discussed in the individual chapters. However, two areas for concerted action deserve mention here. The first is to deepen India's innovative capability so as to capture more lucrative software niches; and the second is to nurture the domestic market so as to generate spillovers through dynamic interaction. Some of the interrelated sector-specific initiatives, in no particular order, would include the following:

- large-scale investments in ICT manufacturing
- diffusion of IT-related applications throughout the economy

- emphasis on learning and accumulation of technological capability, including staying abreast of the technological frontier, such as embedded software (ubiquitous computing), Linux and wireless technologies
- superior quality of physical and ICT infrastructure
- expansion in the quality and quantity of education infrastructures for skill building
- greater engagement with science and engineering and associated R&D
- a risk-reducing environment for entrepreneurial initiatives, such as venture capital
- identification of strategic partners, between MNCs and domestic firms; between business, university and government; *and* among domestic firms.

Many of these areas, such as infrastructure provision, VC market development, skill enhancement, and some types of institutional partnerships are being addressed. Regarding the domestic market, a number of ad hoc developments have taken place. Recently there have been small investments from East Asian firms for the manufacture of some hardware and components. There are also state-owned enterprises manufacturing ICT goods, such as C-DOT and Indian Telephone Industries. Even as many Indian firms undertake chip design work (a high value activity), there does not appear to be any discussion on establishing chip manufacturing units such as those set up in China. IT diffusion has been sporadic, covering the modern corporate sector (Miller, 2001), citizen services in Andhra Pradesh, preventive health care programmes, and delivery of agricultural information (World Bank Group, 2002), to name a few. What is not self-evident is that these Internet-based services require ICT goods, many of which make use of advanced wireless technologies. Outside the prosperous parts of the urban economy, IT diffusion is not widespread. It cannot be, given India's large illiterate population and very low per capita incomes. This suggests the importance of strategic intervention with investment in software-related industries and infrastructure within the broader imperatives of raising the overall level of Indian economic development.

The external sector has played a very important role in the recent evolution of the software industry. The principal benefit has been sourcing foreign technologies and capturing markets. With dominant designs and industry standards set by MNCs, it is evident that Indian firms will have to be followers. However, this need not come in the way of learning and innovative capability so long as firms are willing to undertake more complex projects by investing in skill development and R&D, and exploiting new opportunities such as open source software. Many of the software development centres of MNCs in India have begun high level work for their in-house needs. Texas Instruments has successfully designed a chip, yielding considerable global revenues; while Oracle has developed a substantial part of its operating system in India. This certainly points to the salubrious effects of MNC activity, resulting from the availability of human capital (Patibandla and Peterson, 2002; Ghemawat and Patibandla, 1997). The question, however, is to what extent in-house projects for distant users result in the synergy often associated with local users or, to put it in another way, what kind of learning takes place when the entire industry interacts nominally with the domestic economy? While this remains an empirical question, it is suggestive of specialization in low value services and various forms of economy-wide distortions (D'Costa, 2003). What matters now is the resolution of the three disconnections by leveraging the domestic economy for export competitiveness and balanced home development. Only then will the industry begin to 'walk on two legs' (Schware, 1992).

Notes

1. I thank E. Sridharan and Janette Rawlings for their editorial comments. Errors and omissions are mine alone.
2. http://www.unctad.org/Templates, accessed 11/27/2002 3:30 p.m.
3. Cross-national data are not strictly comparable. China's ratio was obtained by dividing $2.9 billion of software (IT services and packages) by the sum of IT services and packages ($2.9 billion) and hardware ($15.7 billion) (US & FCS, 2002b).
4. I am grateful to Pete Suttmeier for bringing this source to my attention.
5. These are work visas given by the US government to foreign skilled, non-immigrant workers, which are valid for six years but must be renewed after three years.
6. Information obtained from http://custom.marketwatch.com, retrieved on 11 Nov. 2002.
7. I thank Pete Suttmeier for bringing this publication to my attention.
8. This 20 per cent was arrived at using the current norm of ITES workers in relation to total software professionals (NASSCOM, 2002: 63). This ratio could be higher as India continues to promote ITES and the industry is unable to penetrate the high value segments of the customized services area.

References

Arora, A. et al. (2001) 'The Indian Software Services Industry', *Research Policy*, 30 (8): 1267–87.

Casper, S. and H. Glimstedt (2001) 'Economic Organization, Innovation Systems, and the Internet', *Oxford Review of Economic Policy*, 17 (2): 265–81.

D'Costa, A. P. (2003) 'Uneven and Combined Development: Understanding India's Software Exports', *World Development*, 31 (1): 211–26.

Dedrik, J. and K. L. Kraemer (1998) *Asia's Computer Challenge: Threat or Opportunity for the United States and the World?* (New York: Oxford University Press).

Desai, A. V. (2001) 'The Peril and the Promise: Broader Implications of the Indian Presence in Information Technologies', Workshop on the Indian Software Industry in a Global Context, Indian Institute of Management, Ahmedabad, India.

—— (2002) 'The Dynamics of the Indian Information Technology Industry', Centre for New and Emerging Markets', London Business School, unpublished.

Dicken, P. (1998) *Global Shift: Transforming the World Economy* (New York: Guilford Press).

Dossani, R. and M. Kenney (2002) 'Creating an Environment for Venture Capital in India', *World Development*, 30 (2): 227–53.

Einhorn, B. (2002a) 'High Tech in China: Is it a Threat to Silicon Valley?', *BusinessWeek/online*, 2002.

——(2002b) 'Shenzhen: the New Bangalore?', *BusinessWeek/online*, http://www.businessweek.com/technology, accessed 12/17/2002 9:47 a.m.

Evans, P. B. (1995) *Embedded Autonomy: States and Industrial Transformation* (Princeton: Princeton University Press).

Freeman, C. (1997) 'The "National System of Innovation" in Historical Perspective', in D. Archibugi and J. Michie, *Technology, Globalisation and Economic Performance* (Cambridge: Cambridge University Press), pp. 24–49.

Ghemawat, P. and M. Patibandla (1997) 'India's Exports Since the Reforms', in J. Sachs, A. Varshney and N. Bajpai, *India in the Era of Economic Reforms* (Delhi: Oxford University Press).

Ghoshal, S., G. Piramal and S. Budhiraja (2002) *World Class in India: a Casebook of Companies in Transformation* (New Delhi: Penguin Books India (P) Ltd).

Goyal, A. (2001) 'Intellectual Capital: IT or Not to IT, That is Not a Question', *The Russia Journal*, http://www.outsourcing-russia.com, accessed on 12/19/2002 2:07 p.m.

Heeks, R. (1996) *India's Software Industry: State Policy, Liberalisation and Industrial Development* (New Delhi: Sage Publications).

Hoogvelt, A. (2001) *Globalization and the Postcolonial World: the New Political Economy of Development* (Baltimore, MD: Johns Hopkins University Press).

India Abroad News Service (2002) 'India Beats US Curbs to Produce Supercomputer', http://www.siliconindia.com, accessed 12/17/2002 9:50 a.m.

Jayaraman, K. S. (2002a) 'India's Scientists Agonize Over Fall in Publication Rate', *Nature*, 419: 100.

——(2002b) 'India Online', *Nature*, 415: 358–9.

Kattuman, P. and K. Iyer (2001) 'Human Capital in the Move Up the Value Chain: the Case of the Indian Software and Services Industry', in M. Kagami and M. Tsuji, *The 'IT' Revolution and Developing Countries: Latecomer Advantage?* (Tokyo: Institute of Developing Economies, Japan External Trade Organization), pp. 208–27.

Kogut, B. and A. Metiu (2001) 'Open-Source Software Development and Distributed Innovation', *Oxford Review of Economic Policy*, 17 (2): 248–64.

Kozlov, V. (2001) 'Report Wary on Future of Russia's IT Sector', http://www.outsourcing-russia.com, accessed on 12/19/2002 2:06 p.m.

——(2002): 'Russian Firms See ITES & BPO as Competitive Advantage', http://www.outsourcing-russia.com, accessed on 12/19/2002 2:00 p.m.

Kripalani, M. (2002) 'Calling Bangalore: Multinationals are Making IT a Hub for High-Tech Research', *Businesseek/online*.

Kumar, N. (2001) 'Developing Countries in International Division of Labour in Software and Service Industry: Lessons from Indian Experience', Workshop on the Indian Software Industry in a Global Context, Indian Institute of Management, Ahmedabad, India.

Kumar, V. and P. K. Jain (2002) 'Commercializing New Technologies in India: a Perspective on Policy Initiatives', *Technology in Society*, 24 (3): 285–98.

Lakaeva, I. (2002) 'Trends in the Russian IT Market', US & Foreign Commercial Service, US Embassy, Moscow.

Lakha, S. (1999) 'The New International Division of Labour and the Indian Computer Software Industry', in J. Bryson et al., *The Economic Geography Reader: Producing and Consuming Global Capitalism* (Chichester: John Wiley & Sons Ltd), pp. 148–55.

Larson, E. V. and I. T. Brahmakulam (2002) *Building a New Foundation for Innovation: Results of a Workshop for the National Science Foundation* (Santa Monica, CA: Science and Technology Policy Institute, RAND).

Mansell, R. (2001) 'Digital Opportunities and the Missing Link for Developing Countries', *Oxford Review of Economic Policy*, 17 (2): 282–95.

McKendrick, D. G., R. F. Doner and S. Haggard (2000) *From Silicon Valley to Singapore* (Stanford: Stanford University Press).

Miller, R. R. (2001) *Leapfrogging? India's Information Technology Industry and the Internet* (Washington, DC: International Finance Corporation).

Mowery, D. C. (1996) 'Introduction', in D. C. Mowery (ed.), *The International Computer Software Industry: a Comparative Study of Industry Evolution and Structure* (New York: Oxford University Press), pp. 3–14.

NASSCOM (2002) *The IT Industry in India: Strategic Review 2002* (New Delhi: National Association of Software and Service Companies).

——(2003) *The IT Industry in India: Strategic Review 2003* (New Delhi: National Association of Software and Service Companies).

OECD (2000) *OECD Information Technology Outlook: ICTs, E-Commerce and the Information Economy* (Paris: OECD).

——(2002) *OECD Information Technology Outlook: ICTs and the Information Economy* (Paris: OECD).

Okhi, H. (2001) 'International Division of Labor in East Asia's IT Industry', in M. Kagami, and M. Tsuji, *The 'IT' Revolution and Developing Countries: Late-Comer Advantage?* (Tokyo: Institute of Developing Economies, Japan External Trade Organization), pp. 63–91.

Patibandla, M. and B. Petersen (2002) 'Role of Transnational Corporations in the Evolution of a High-Tech Industry: the Case of India's Software Industry', *World Development*, 30 (9): 1561–77.

Press, L. et al. (2002) 'The Internet in India and China', *First Monday*, 2002.

Saxenian, A. L. (1994) *Regional Advantage: Culture and Competition in Silicon Valley and Route 128* (Cambridge, MA: Harvard University Press).

Schware, R. (1992) 'Software Industry Entry Strategies for Developing Countries: a "Walking on Two Legs" Proposition', *World Development*, 20 (2): 143–64.

Sircar, A. (2002) 'The Issue: What If We Don't Move Up the Value Chain?', *Dataquest*, 2002.

Sridharan, E. (1996) *The Political Economy of Industrial Promotion: Indian, Brazilian, and Korean Electronics in Comparative Perspective, 1969–1994* (Westport, CT: Praeger Publishers).

Trivedi, A. (2002) 'India's Software Supremacy and the Chinese Threat', siliconindia. com, 2002.

UNCTAD (2001) *World Investment Report 2001: Promoting Linkages* (New York: United Nations).

——(2002) 'Statistics: Value of Exports and Imports of Goods in 2001 (millions of dollars)', (UNCTAD Secretariat, New York).

US & Foreign Commercial Service (2002a) 'IT Product Distribution', US & Foreign Commercial Service.

——(2002b) 'Computers/Peripherals and Growth of Internet (Users, Computers, Handheld Devices)'.

US Department of Commerce (2002) *Digital Economy 2002*, US Department of Commerce, Economics and Statistics Administration (Feb.).

Wong, J., and C. K. Wong (2002) 'China's Software Industry (I): On the Fast-Track', East Asia Institute, Singapore.

Wong, P. K. (1995) 'Competing in the Global Electronics Industry: a Comparative Analysis of the Strategy of Taiwan and Singapore', International Conference on the Experience of Industrial Development in Taiwan, National Central University, Taiwan.

World Bank Group (2002) *Information and Communication Technologies: a World Bank Group Strategy* (Washington, DC: World Bank Group).

2
Evolving Towards Innovation? The Recent Evolution and Future Trajectory of the Indian Software Industry

E. Sridharan[1]

1. Can the Indian IT industry develop the capacity to innovate? Some central issues

This chapter reviews the evolution of the Indian software industry over the past decade, addressing the issue of whether it can graduate to technologically more complex and higher value-added projects, software products and integrated hardware – software products and systems. It has been argued that while the Indian software industry has been a success story of exports based on exploiting the labour cost differential between India and the US for fairly low value-added software services, it will need to innovate to move up the value chain if it is to sustain and enhance its competitive position in the coming years. Why the focus on innovation? What is critical to any overall effort to compete successfully and sustainably in world markets, which includes modernizing and making the best use of the installed capacities in industry and infrastructure, is the capacity for, and quality of, innovation. To get to grips with what is happening on innovation in the Indian software industry, the literature on innovation offers several approaches to the issue of the context of innovation in India in the IT industry. A useful starting point, theoretically, for a study of the context of innovation in such a case, would be a broad Schumpeterian definition of innovation as consisting not only of new products and processes, but also of new materials, new markets and new forms of organization. Thus, innovation would consist not only of patentable/copyrightable inventions to create new markets, but also appropriate intermediate processes, products/tools. New hardware and the emerging networked environment would then be the equivalent of new materials. Innovation is a multifaceted phenomenon covering not only technological innovation but also institutional, organizational and managerial (including financial) innovation, and their attitudinal and cultural support systems. Indeed, technological innovation, whether in firms or in research institutions, is nested in managerial–cultural, institutional, organizational and macro-policy settings.

The next step, following from the market structure and innovation literature (Kamien and Schwartz, 1982), would be a more focused approach that views Indian IT firms as small, specialized suppliers (Pavitt, 1990; Pavitt, Robson and Townsend, 1989) of services, and potentially products that have found or could find a niche in the world economy. Both India's software and hardware exports would, at first glance, by and large, fit this description. The key strength of such firms is the ability to match technology with specific customer requirements. The content of their technological strategies consists in finding this match, including the acquisition or development of technologies to do so, competing on the basis of innovation and not low costs alone. The key strategic management tasks, and hence technology strategy tasks, are to find and maintain a stable product and/or service niche, find or create new product and/or service niches, and absorb user experience to continue to match technology to user needs and maintain/create stable new product and/or service niches. The question that can then be posed is: how well do Indian software and other IT firms perform such strategic management and technological tasks?

The next step would be, following Pavitt (1990), to ask how company structure, company culture and company strategy play a role in the formation of technological strategy. Innovation studies have come to robust conclusions that, apart from technical work, strong horizontal linkages between functional departments, with customers, and with outside sources of information (including academia–industry, government–industry linkages) are the key to successful innovation. This would lead the study to focus on firm structures and strategies.

A very important approach, given the significant clustering of Indian IT firms in some major cities and software technology parks, is that of Saxenian (1994) who focuses on the broader context of firm strategies, specifically how the regional network-based industrial cluster of Silicon Valley 'promotes collective learning and flexible adjustments among specialist producers of a complex of related technologies'. Studies of inter-firm collaboration, including those in global outsourcing relationships involving technology/product development, would be very important.

Given the context of globalization of IT, the technological spillover literature could also throw light on the conditions under which such spillovers are maximized. The literature emphasizes that the productivity level of an economy depends not only on its own R&D but also on the R&D of the rest of the world (Grossman and Helpman, 1991). The increase in productivity from such draws on world R&D through various mechanisms, i.e. the indirect benefit or externality, is called the technological spillover effect. Spillovers can take place through imitation, reverse engineering, technology purchase, technological collaboration, foreign direct investment, and absorption of tacit knowledge. The most significant finding (Coe and Helpman, 1995) is that the impact of foreign R&D capital stock on domestic R&D is stronger the more open an economy is to foreign trade. This could be expected to apply strongly to the globalized Indian software industry. However, spillovers require investment in domestic R&D and the creation of appropriate skill pools, which in turn require firm-level incentives and supportive policies.

The central point in the literature is that innovation is situated in firm strategy, and the latter in the larger market and technological environment, and multilevel policy regime. Firm strategy need not necessarily include innovation as a priority, for example, if it is not faced with competitive pressure, or if competition is based on implementing existing routines, as has been argued is being done in some types of software service exports, or if import of technology is available as a short-term solution to modernization needs. The challenge is to design policies that create incentives for firms to incorporate and institutionalize innovation as a core component of their strategy for survival and growth.

This capsule survey of the possible approaches that can be followed from the literature indicates the need for multilevel studies – the product, project and firm levels, and a range of policy levels, micro-, meso- and macro- (Avnimelech and Teubal, Chapter 5) – of the factors affecting the environment of the firm, and the question of the emerging world technological and market environment and opportunity structure (D'Costa, Chapter 1). The studies in this volume, all based on field research, analyse this issue from a range of theoretical and methodological perspectives at a variety of levels and units of analysis: product, project and firm levels, inter-firm alliances and global outsourcing arrangements, with comparative perspectives on the Indian IT diaspora in Silicon Valley and a study of the Israeli case of graduating to high-tech IT entrepreneurship.

The volume breaks new ground in that it is the first multilevel, comprehensive scholarly effort that examines Indian innovation in the wider context of moving up the value chain. The existing book length studies of the Indian IT industry (computers, software, telecom) largely focus on the hardware industry (Grieco, 1984; Subramanian, 1992; Mani, 1992; Evans, 1995; Brunner, 1995; Sridharan, 1996; McDowell, 1997). Two recent studies that deal with software (Heeks, 1996; Bhatnagar and Schware, 2000) are either somewhat dated or concerned with rural IT applications. None of these takes a close look at Indian firms to explain the industry's recent technological trajectory nor addresses the significance of innovating up the value chain.

Since 1991, the macroeconomic, industrial and trade policy regime changes have eased rapid access to imported technologies. Several scholars have critiqued the earlier policy of indiscriminate technological import-substitution, arguing that technology import can be a net stimulant to the development and commercialization of indigenous technological efforts

(Desai, 1985, 1988, 1990; Fikkert, 1995; Sridharan, 1995; Kumar and Agarwal, 2000). Imported technologies represent both challenges and opportunities for indigenous technological and other innovative capabilities. Neither price-led markets nor open economies are a guarantee to innovative capability as increased dependence on technology imports can drive growth only in the short run. However, indigenous innovative capability can follow a phase of absorption and follow-up on imported technology, as has been emphasized in technology development studies, especially with regard to Korea and Taiwan (Bagchi, 1987; Amsden, 1989; Wade, 1990).

Can the Indian software industry follow a path to higher value-added products analogous to the semiconductor industry in Korea and Taiwan from the 1970s to the 1990s? As has been well-documented (Amsden, 1989; Wade, 1990; Mody, 1990; Evans, 1995), Korea and Taiwan began as assemblers of semiconductors, with indigenous firms undertaking contract work for multinationals outsourcing assembly work. These firms then moved up technologically by vertically integrating backwards into wafer fabrication and design. They thus overcame the decoupling between these activities (D'Costa, Chapter 1 for the decoupling of hardware and software, foreign and domestic markets, and services and products in the Indian IT industry). They imported technology and designs but built local capability through indigenous follow-up R&D investments and a gradual development of the home market in the semiconductor-using computer and electronics industry. All this was within the framework of export-led growth, with the world market generating the competitive pressures for innovation but the state orchestrating the development model (Wade, 1990). This model forced firms to continually upgrade so as to be able to remain competitive, and indeed, anticipate and create comparative advantage, to the surprise of much of the world, in a high-technology industry like semiconductor design and fabrication. A major role was played in this by exposure to the world market and its shaping of firms' incentives to invest in innovation, and also, no doubt, by technological spillovers in manufacturing and R&D, particularly by the influx of technology embodied in capital goods, the targeted import of codified technology, and the acquisition of tacit technological and market knowledge.

If the Indian software industry is to follow an analogous path to innovation, what might be the appropriate corporate strategy for technological creativity? What should be the national policy and global market conditions that might elevate the Indian industry on to a higher innovation trajectory? Does such a strategy require a reorientation towards the domestic market to avoid export-oriented path-dependency perpetuating a low value-added trajectory? Does export orientation on the outsourcing model prevent transfers of key technologies except piecemeal as these are centralized, and does it prevent the development of user-feedback linkages that are the key stimulants and drivers of incremental innovation in software development

(D'Costa, Chapter 3)? Or are these effects overpowered by the technological and market knowledge spillovers from export activity that are not captured by formal R&D and formal technology import figures? Can the Indian diaspora in Silicon Valley be leveraged to make this transition? What lessons does the Israeli case of successful transition to high-tech IT exports offer and will the export-oriented business model auto-generate incentives for companies to upgrade technologically so as to stay competitive over the long run? The chapters in the rest of the volume focus on these issues.

2. The evolution of the Indian IT industry up to 2002–3: the need for innovation

An overview of the principal features of the Indian software industry, the segment of the Indian IT industry that is internationally competitive, reveals the following picture (NASSCOM, 2003, 2002, 2000; Rastogi, 2001; Soni et al., 2001, for the figures in the following paragraphs). The Indian IT industry consisted mainly of, and Indian IT policy was overwhelmingly focused on, the hardware industry until the 1990s. The hardware industry was considered part of a wider electronics industry encompassing the entire microelectronics-based complex spanning electronic components, consumer electronics, computers, telecom equipment, and aerospace/defence electronics. Policy was historically focused on import-substitution both in production and in R&D so as to build up local manufacturing and technological capabilities in what was considered a strategic industry both from the point of view of long-term economic development and the needs of the national security complex of arms, nuclear and space programmes (Grieco, 1984; Subramanian, 1992; Mani, 1992; Evans, 1995; Sridharan, 1996). This was in sharp contrast to the growth of the computer industry and the wider microelectronics-based complex from semiconductors to consumer electronics in developing East Asia which were export-oriented from the outset. The software industry was a combined spin-off of the growth of the Indian computer industry in the 1980s, the emergence of independent software firms in the US following the emergence of the personal computer (PC), and the outsourcing of low end software work to low wage locations offshore where appropriate software skill pools existed.

The software industry grew in stages with the following telecom-infrastructural and policy developments. Software exports in the 1980s and through the 1990s took place through body-shopping or on-site services in which the Indian firm sent software personnel to the client's site in the US to undertake the labour-intensive aspects of software development such as data entry, coding and testing. The New Software Policy of 1986, following the New Computer Policy of 1984 that promoted domestic manufacture of PCs and the spread of computerization, was export-oriented from the outset, recognizing the potential for software exports and the futility of import-substitution. In 1986, the first satellite link became operational. Texas Instruments gifted the link to the government and began software export operations from Bangalore. Software technology parks for software export firms were set up, each with dedicated satellite links for the firms in the park; private links were still not permitted.

However, the shift to offshore software development, that is, from India as against on-site, gathered momentum only after computer import was freed from licensing, import duties on them reduced, and dedicated private satellite links permitted in 1992 following the new industrial and trade policy changes after the launch of the economic liberalization programme in 1991 (Desai, 2002). The relative weight of offshore development increased and that of body-shopping declined over the decade that followed until offshore exports overtook on-site exports in 2001–2 (Table 2.1). Offshore development also facilitated more complete and complex projects rather than piecework, a greater degree of retention of talent in India, and greater net exports, that is, greater retention of export earnings in India net of outgo on account of reduced expenditure on personnel abroad. All this contributes to the growth of firm capabilities, including specialization in particular domains and services such as custom application development for banking, insurance, airlines and the like, and hence brand-building.

The next major techno-infrastructural development was the spread of the Internet in the second half of the 1990s. This lowered entry barriers for firms that did not have a satellite link and increased interactions between companies and their clients. It also opened the door to IT-enabled services, particularly those involving customer interaction, that have taken off since the late 1990s. The arrival of broadband cable in the near future will hugely increase the tele/datacom transmission capacity available and will further boost the above trends.

This growth pattern has led to a software industry whose profile in terms of specialization and domain is roughly as follows. India's software exports are overwhelmingly concentrated in certain specializations, such as custom applications development (35 per cent in 2001–2) and application outsourcing (23 per cent in 2001–2). Application outsourcing was classified as legacy application management, maintenance and migrations, a broader category

Table 2.1   Mode of delivery of software exports from India

	Year					
	1994–95	*1998–99*	*1999–2000*	*2000–1*	*2001–2*	*2002–3 E*
Onsite	61.0	58.18	57.43	56.08	45.21	38.95
Offshore	29.5	33.92	34.70	38.62	50.68	57.89
Products and unclassified	9.5	7.90	7.87	5.29	4.11	3.16
Total	100%	100%	100%	100%	100%	100%

Note: E = Estimate.

in earlier years, and was 27 per cent in 2000–1. IT-enabled services (23 per cent), comprising customer interaction centres, business process outsourcing (BPO), GIS and engineering services and others, was the third largest component. Software products and 'unclassified' as a category has a share of only 4 per cent in 2001–2, and this has been shrinking over the past few years. Custom application development is where the software exporter designs the customer firm's IT software and IT system for specific functions, e.g. for a bank or an airline company. Legacy application management consists of integrating new software with existing older software and computer systems to ensure compatibility, the latter usually consisting of a large number of servers and workstations connected in networks in multiple locations. This type of work requires software skills and can result in the accumulation of knowledge that allows the exporting firm to move up the value chain in software services and perhaps product design, unlike most IT-enabled services, such as call centres and other customer interaction services, which are usually low tech and employ personnel who do not need advanced software skills.

However, most Indian software exports are concentrated in these two niche segments that occupy only 8 per cent of global IT services spending in 2001 and are not projected to grow substantially by 2006. There are only three other specializations in which India's export potential is considered high and in which the world market is expected to grow significantly by 2005: IT training and education, processing services (including BPO), and IS outsourcing. Medium-to-high prospects exist in packaged software support and installation, and in network infrastructure management, the world markets for both of which will also grow significantly by 2005–6. All these are, however, based not on advanced skills of Indian software firms but on significant cost advantages, the existing skill base due to custom application development and maintenance, and upgrading legacy systems. The one segment that differs from all the above is the export of R&D services, which has emerged as a separate category in the past two years, and recorded $1.21 billion in 2001–2.

The specialization pattern in terms of domain is roughly as follows. Indian software firms have significant penetration in only three domains (verticals) – finance (banking, insurance, financial markets), communications and media (basically telecom equipment), and manufacturing – in both the US and Western Europe, less so in the latter. Finance has been the mainstay domain of Indian software firms, particularly the largest firms, with a share of 35 per cent in Indian software and services exports by verticals, with telecom equipment and manufacturing 12 per cent each in 2001–2 (NASSCOM, 2003: 30).

In 2001–2, software exports were $7.66 billion, and domestic sales $2.10 billion, grossing $9.76 billion (Table 2.2). Compared to 1994–5 when IT hardware, peripherals and networking still represented 48 per cent of the

Table 2.2   Indian software sales, 1993–4 to 2002–3 (US $ million)

Year	Domestic sales					Exports							Total sales	Share of exports % in total sales
	Software	% of software	ITES	% of ITES	total	Software	% of software	ITES	% of ITES	R&D services	% of R&D services	Total		
1993–94	230				230							330	560	59
1994–95	242				242							485	727	67
1995–96	419				419							734	1153	64
1996–97	648				648							1085	1733	63
1997–98	1031				1031	1759						1759	2790	63
1998–99	1246	98	21	2	1267	2600						2600	3867	67
1999–00	1370	97	39	3	1409	3397	86	565	14			3962	5371	74
2000–01	1807	96	70	4	1877	4730	76	930	15	550	9	6210	8087	77
2001–02	2032	97	73	3	2105	4950	65	1495	19	1210	16	7655	9760	78
2002–03 E	2297	96	94	4	2391									
Annual rates of change (%)														
1994–95	5.2				5.2							47.0	29.8	
1995–96	73.1				73.1							51.3	58.6	
1996–97	54.7				54.7							47.8	50.3	
1997–98	59.1				59.1							62.1	61.0	
1998–99	20.9				22.9	47.8						47.8	38.6	
1999–00	10.0		85.7		11.2	30.7						52.4	38.9	
2000–01	31.9		79.5		33.2	39.2		64.6				56.7	50.6	
2001–02	12.5		4.3		12.1	4.7		60.8				23.3	20.7	
1994–5/ 2001–2	739.7				769.8							1478.4	1242.5	
2002–03	13.0		28.8		13.6									

Note: E = Estimate.

Source: NASSCOM (2000, 2002, 2003).

total IT industry revenues in India, in 2001–2 it is estimated that software will garner 71 per cent of IT industry revenues, of which software exports alone will constitute 56 per cent. If one disaggregates the software industry into software services and products and IT-enabled services, there was a significant slow-down in the exports of the former in 2001–2 and 2002–3 but the latter continued to rise.

India's software exports amounted to 19 per cent of the cross-border customized software market but only 1 per cent of the cross-border packaged software market in 1999–2000. In 2001–2, the market share of Indian software exports in global IT spending continued to rise to 1.9 per cent compared to 1.5 per cent the previous year due to the higher growth of the former compared to the latter. By destination, 68 per cent of software exports went to North America, overwhelmingly to the US, 21 per cent to Europe, 2 per cent to Japan, and 10 per cent to the rest of the world. The compound annual growth rate for software exports over 1995–2000 was 61 per cent, for the domestic software market 46 per cent. Software exports continued to grow at the impressive rate of 23 per cent in 2001–2 despite the global economic slow-down, considerably higher than the 12 per cent growth rate of domestic software sales (Table 2.3). The *McKinsey Report* (1999) on the Indian software industry projects $50 billion IT exports by 2008; possible at the recent 50 per cent compound annual growth rate in software exports. This is projected to comprise 50 per cent in software services, 10 per cent in hardware, and the rest in e-commerce of which $17 billion, or one-third, will be in IT-enabled services. The *Report* also forecasts a domestic market of $37 billion by 2008, and sees major potential in IT services, software products, IT-enabled services and e-commerce. IT-enabled services include human resource-related services such as customer interaction, e.g. call centres, financial processing, and accounting and data management.

In the shorter run, NASSCOM sees potential in IT-enabled services due to the wage cost advantage and low skill requirements, particularly in BPO in domains like finance, insurance and airlines. Potential also exists in the IT training and education sector, and in penetrating the government, health care and utilities domains in the US and Europe for existing professional services, in the specializations of packaged software support and installation, in systems integration, and in some R&D services.

The structure of the Indian software industry in 2001–2 was pyramidal, with the top five firms having sales of over Rs10 billion ($200 million) (Table 2.4), the largest being Tata Consultancy Services (TCS) with $813 million (Table 2.5). The Tier 1 (top 5, over $200 million sales in 2000–1), TCS, Wipro, Infosys, Satyam and HCL Technologies, account for nearly a third of India's software exports, are primarily US-oriented, offer a comprehensive professional services portfolio, and have a large number of Fortune 500 clients (D'Costa, Chapter 1, Table 1.1 for comparisons with international

Table 2.3　Composition of Indian software exports, 2000–1, 2001–2 to 2002–3 (US $ billion)

	Exports			Domestic sales			Total sales		
	2000–1	2001–2	2002–3E	2000–1	2001–2	2002–3E	2000–1	2001–2	2002–3E
Software and services	4 730	4 950	7 475	1 737	1 960	2 200	6 467	6 910	
Legacy applications/application outsourcing	1 700	1 750					1 700	1 750	
Custom application development	1 950	2 650		352	401	437	2 302	3 051	437
Packaged software integration	300	300		426	442		726	742	
E-business solutions	550						550	0	
Wireless integration	75						75	0	
System integration	75	150					75	150	
Network infrastructure management	50	50					50	50	
Consulting	50	50		159	204	229	209	254	229
Turnkey projects				362	378	437	362	378	437
Captive development				438	580	685	438	580	685
IT enabled services	930	1 495	2 400	70	73	94	1 000	1 568	2 494
Customer interaction centres	185	350					185	350	

Business process outsourcing	295	600					295	600
GIS and engineering services	350	450					350	450
Other	70	75					70	75
R&D services	550	1 210					550	1 210
Training				511	306	312	511	306	312
Total	6 210	7 655	9 875	2 318	2 339	2 606	8 528	9 994	2 806

Notes:

1. E = Estimate; all 2002–3 figures are estimates.

2. Legacy applications and application outsourcing are largely but not wholly overlapping categories. Legacy applications is the category that applies for the figures for 2000–1 while application outsourcing applies to the figures for 2001–2.

3. The amounts for individual service lines in software and services exports and in ITES exports, and likewise for domestic sales do not add up to the totals for these categories exactly due to definitional and data deficiencies. In the case of exports the new category, application outsourcing, the disappearance of E-business solutions and wireless integration in the service lines for 2001–2, and the doubling of the estimate for R&D services from NASSCOM 2002, are responsible for the discrepancy.

4. For domestic sales by service lines, figures are available only for selected service lines.

Source: NASSCOM (2002, 2003).

Table 2.4   Structure of Indian software exports industry (Indian rupees)

Annual turnover (Rs m)	No. of companies	
	2000–1	2001–2
Above 10 000	5	5
5 000–10 000	7	5
2 500–5 000	14	15
1 000–2 500	28	27
500–1 000	25	55
100–500	193	220
Below 100	544	2 483

Note: Rs 48 = $1 approx for the year concerned.

Source: NASSCOM, 2003.

Table 2.5   Top 20 IT software and services exporters from India

Rank	Company	US$ million
1	Tata Consultancy Services	813
2	Infosys Technologies Ltd	535
3	Wipro Technologies	481
4	Satyam Computer Services Ltd	357
5	HCL Technologies Ltd	277
6	IBM Global Services India Pvt Ltd	160
7	Patni Computer Systems	153
8	Silverline Technologies	126
9	Mahindra – British Telecom Ltd	113
10	Pentasoft Technologies Ltd	96
11	HCL Perot Systems Ltd	94
12	Pentamedia Graphics Ltd	90
13	NIIT	84
14	Mascot Systems Ltd	84
15	i-Flex Solutions Ltd	82
16	Digital Globalsoft Ltd	69
17	Mphasis BFL Group (Consolidated)	66
18	Mascon Global Ltd	64
19	Orbitech	55
20	Mastek Ltd	54

Source: NASSCOM, 2003.

firms). Tier 2 ($20–200 million sales) have just over a third of exports and a narrower range of service specializations. Multinational subsidiaries, most of which do in-house work for the parent company, being largely captive off-shore development centres for large system integrators, OEMs or professional services firms, have about 22 per cent of the software services export market and 45 per cent of the largely low-tech ITES exports. These include GE, American Express, Texas Instruments, HSBC, Hewlett-Packard, Intel, Dell, AOL, Microsoft, Cisco Systems and others. It needs to be noted that most Indian software firms and 73 per cent of the industry in terms of software services export revenues alone, consist of Indian-owned firms. These are largely firms started by India-based entrepreneurs, with very few started by 'return entrepreneurs' from Silicon Valley or elsewhere, although there may be a dense network of personal connections with software and IT hotspots, in the US in particular (Desai, 2002; Saxenian, Chapter 7).

The overall picture that emerges is that the Indian IT industry needs to move beyond software services, on-site services still constituting 39 per cent of exports (Table 2.1). In recent years there has been steady movement from on-site to offshore (from India) services, and upwards to more complex projects. However, there has been very little software product innovation, and still less in integrating hardware and software.

If the Indian software and associated IT industry is to have any realistic prospect of achieving these targets, particularly given the restructuring provoked by the slowdown in 2001–2, then the industry will have to step up its efforts both to diversify specializations and domains, and to make a quantum move towards higher value-added activities. Simultaneously, there will have to be supportive and facilitative policy shifts in four areas: (1) an enabling legislation and policy framework, particularly on convergence, independent regulatory bodies, intellectual property rights and cyberlaws, and an appropriate hardware policy; (2) infrastructure provision, particularly in telecom; teledensity is only 4.0 direct lines per 100, cellphones about 11.3 million at the end of 2002, PC penetration only about 8.68 million, and Internet connections only about 2.5 million indicating a user population of 12.85 million, three-quarters being businesses; (3) a quantum leap in computerization of the economy especially in the vast government and public sector, including the public financial sector; (4) finally, human resource development to supply the estimated 2.2 million IT professionals, including 1.1 million in software, necessary to achieve these targets in comparison to the Indian software industry's estimated 650 000 high-level professionals in March 2003, and total employment of 1.3 million in 2000. Since then it has been reported that India now graduates 167 000 engineering graduates, of whom 50 000 major in IT-related disciplines, and 455 000 science graduates every year (NASSCOM, 2003: 140).

3. R&D and innovation in the Indian software industry: trends and scenarios in the context of rapid change

To understand innovation in the Indian software industry it is useful to situate it in the context of trends in innovation in Indian industry following the liberalization of the economy since the 1991 reform initiative. Historically, post-Independence India has been an import-substituting economy with very high protection for industry and limited competitive pressures operating on industry from within. Neither product nor process innovation defined itself as a high priority for most of Indian industry. What R&D effort and innovation there was in most manufacturing sectors was largely adaptive and incremental innovation, with the principal thrust being adapting imported technologies to Indian conditions (Desai, 1988). Indian industry did not produce any major product innovations or become competitive in world markets on the basis of product or process innovations. Some industries, like pharmaceuticals, saw reverse engineering for manufacturing the same product through different processes, as Indian patent laws did not recognize product patents, enabling the industry to become a competitive exporter of many bulk drugs. However, this was more an exception than the rule.

Overall, R&D expenditure as a percentage of GNP increased from 0.27 per cent (1965–6) to 0.58 per cent (1980–1) to 0.79 per cent (1990–1) just prior to liberalization, to 0.81 per cent (1998–9), dipping to 0.71 per cent (1995–6) (DST, 2002a: 70). The peak years were 1987–8 (0.91 per cent) and 1988–9 (0.90 per cent). In 1998–9, the latest year for which figures are available (DST, 2002), 68 per cent of Indian R&D took place in the central government (62.5 per cent) and public sector companies (5 per cent), 8 per cent in state government agencies, 3 per cent in higher education, and 22 per cent in the private sector. Thus, industrial R&D, both public and private, constituted only 27 per cent of R&D expenditure. Twelve major scientific agencies accounted for 83 per cent of central government and public sector companies' R&D expenditure, or 56 per cent of national R&D expenditure, of which again as much as 65 per cent was R&D in atomic energy, defence and space. These three heads constituting the national security complex thus accounted for 36 per cent of national R&D expenditure compared to 27 per cent for public and private industry, including manufacturing, communications, transport and other industrial sectors including IT; most of the rest being accounted for by agricultural (21 per cent) and medical research (9 per cent).

This pattern of Indian R&D expenditure being overwhelmingly on the part of the central government, and dominated by the national security complex, has been consistent since the 1960s; the only significant change in the 1980s and 1990s has been the relative increase of R&D expenditure in the public and private industrial sector from 4 per cent in 1956–66 to 12 per cent in 1985–6 to 27 per cent in 1998–9 (Sridharan, 1995 for trends up to the 1991 industrial liberalization reforms). The relative increase in the 1990s was due to slow growth in central government R&D expenditure due to budgetary pressures, and faster growth in private R&D expenditure (DST, 2002a: 69), probably due to a combination of greater actual or anticipated competitive pressure following liberalization and the need to adapt increasing infusions of both disembodied and embodied technology (capital goods) to local conditions in a decade of liberalized imports of both capital goods and technology. If so, this would be more 'serious' R&D, unlike the earlier pattern in which firms often engaged in R&D to avail of tax rebates for such activity (DST, 2002b) and did not depend on it to modernize to face local (given protectionism) competition, taking recourse to repeated rounds of technology import without successful absorption and follow-up.

However, Kumar and Agarwal (2000: 2) note that the growth rate of industrial R&D in the 1990s was slower than in the 1980s, and that R&D expenditure in real terms had fallen in twelve out of twenty-eight broad industries in the 1990s, and even where it had increased the R&D intensity had stagnated or declined. However, they also note that outward orientation and disembodied technology imports both positively influence R&D behaviour by local firms, a point relevant for the software industry. It is too early to say whether the increase in both import of technology and industrial R&D will lead to a virtuous cycle of better technology absorption laying the foundation for local innovation and competitiveness on the historical Japanese and Korean pattern of building on originally imported technologies, which had been noticed in India even under the intensive import-substitution regime (Desai, 1988) of firms importing technology more also tending to engage in genuine R&D and incremental innovation.

Another important point to be noted is that the huge national security complex, while having considerable technological depth, as manifested in the Indian civilian and military nuclear programmes, and the space and missile programmes, remains a black box. It has not led to any civilian commercial spin-offs or technological spillovers to the civilian sector in sharp contrast to defence and space spending in the US which have spawned myriad civilian technologies and associated commercial spin-offs, particularly in the microelectronics-based complex of industries. Two exceptions exist as far as exports are concerned. One is the export of satellite imagery by the Indian Remote Sensing Satellite IRS 1C, which for a window of time in the mid-1990s offered amongst the highest resolution civilian satellite images, an achievement made possible by R&D in IT within the Indian Space Research Organization's Space Applications Centre. The second is the export of the Centre for the Development of Advanced Computing's (CDAC) parallel processing supercomputers to even advanced countries such as Canada and Germany (Sridharan, 1996: 139), and more recently its teraflops-capable machine, developed in 2002, to Russia. However, these are exceptions to the rule. Thus, the civilian–defence/space sector decoupling remains a fourth decoupling present in the Indian IT industry in addition to the three noted by D'Costa (D'Costa, Chapter 1).

In IT, the following R&D trends are apparent. Government expenditure in R&D in IT has been overwhelmingly concentrated on hardware and on the requirements of technological import-substitution for self-reliance in advanced equipment, largely for defence and space, but also for telecommunications (Sridharan, 1996: 138–40). In terms of formal R&D, we see that the IT industry as a whole, in the most recent three years for which figures are available, 1996–9 had a higher R&D intensity (3.4 per cent of sales) in the two public sector companies and in the eighteen private sector companies (1.4–1.8 per cent of sales) compared to the industry average of 0.28 per cent and 0.67 per cent respectively for the public and private sector companies in the database of 160 public sector and 968 private sector companies that had registered R&D facilities (DST, 2002a: 82–3). However, we may immediately note that this is only a tiny fraction of even software companies alone, NASSCOM having 520 member firms in 1998–9, rising to 854 by December 2001. These figures are corroborated by Parthasarathi and Joseph (Parthasarathi and Joseph, Table 4.9, Chapter 4) whose figures (for only listed companies) indicate that only 7–9 per cent of a database of 115 to 238 firms covered in the years 1997–8 to 2000–1 reported R&D. Although they averaged 2–7 per cent R&D intensity in the various years, the R&D intensity of the software industry as a whole, given that only such a small fraction of firms did R&D, ranged from 0.17 to 0.63 per cent (this would appear to indicate that the larger firms in the sample did R&D).

This paucity of formal R&D among software firms sits uncomfortably with recent data that shows that a new category of service exports, that of R&D services, has emerged in 2000–1 and 2001–2, worth $550 million and $575 million (estimated) respectively, or around 9 per cent and 7 per cent of software exports respectively. According to more recent information (Sunil Mehta, Vice-President, NASSCOM, interview 14 December 2002), R&D services revenues in 2001–2 were about $1 billion excluding such wholly MNC-owned R&D units such as Oracle, SAP, Microsoft, Adobe, Intel, etc. Of this $1 billion, Wipro and HCL Technologies earned $200 million each, Infosys $60 million, Hughes Software $40 million, and all others including TCS, $300 million. NASSCOM estimates that this will grow to $4 billion by 2004–5. A useful comparison would be Israel, which exported $3 billion worth of software and integrated hardware–software IT products in 2001, almost all high-tech in character but including MNCs like Intel, etc. (Mehta interview, referred to above.) Telecom MNCs are the major R&D outsourcers to India (Basant and Chandra, Chapter 8, for a case study of Nortel) and networking R&D is the huge area, both wireless and wireline. Desai (2002), however, lists pharmaceutical and biochemical firms that require large amounts of data-processing, often repetitive, and experiments to be carried out iteratively as the work begins to be outsourced. NASSCOM (2002: 55–62) lists ASIC development, broadband networking, biometrics, bio-informatics, and health as emerging opportunities, not necessarily for R&D services.

Recent reports (Kripalani, 2002; Singh, 2002; Dubey, 2003) indicate considerable R&D relocation to India. Over seventy multinational firms have invested in R&D facilities in India from 1997–2002 which, taken together with earlier investments, brings the number of multinational-owned R&D

facilities located in India to nearly 100 (Dubey, 2003). This list excludes purely software development activities but includes IT hardware, including investments in semiconductor design. There is a spurt in investments of the latter kind by MNCs, centred around Bangalore, as well as the emergence of local semiconductor design firms doing contract work for MNCs. This again does not sit well with the paucity of formal R&D. It is reported that recent investments by US MNCs in Bangalore are turning the city into a base for genuine R&D. For example, Texas Instruments has its biggest chip design centre outside the US in Bangalore where 900 engineers design chips; this accounts for 30 per cent of TI's global R&D work. Likewise, Intel too has its largest non-US chip design centre in Bangalore, and plans to spend $200 million over the next five years to triple its number of engineers to 2700. Texas Instruments' success has drawn companies such as ST Microelectronics, Europe's biggest chip-maker, National Semiconductor Corp, Analog Devices, Cypress Semiconductor Corp, Virage Logic Corp, Cadence, Cisco Systems and others to Bangalore. Some local firms like Wipro and Sasken have also entered chip design and other high end work. Among non-semiconductor IT firms, Germany's SAP has a 500-engineer facility, Oracle a 2400-engineer centre.

At the beginning of 2001, 230 MNCs had invested in Bangalore, with some 25000 engineers working in various Bangalore labs in R&D work, largely in telecom applications development and chip design (Kripalani, 2002). This number is predicted to grow to 65000 in just three years, taking it to the scale of many US research hubs. Much of this genuine R&D produces significant intellectual property for the investing firms. Thus, Intel's labs have produced sixty-two patents for semiconductors, telecom switching equipment and routers.

At the same time, over 1999–2002 an estimated 30–40 chip design start-ups have been set up in India by Indian entrepreneurs, many of them returnees from the US but some also spin-offs and initiatives from the national security complex like the Defence Research and Development Organization (DRDO) and the public sector defence and space needs chip-maker Semiconductor Complex Limited (SCL) (Hari and Anand, 2002). Exports of Indian-made chip designs now account for $200 million, but are expected to grow to $7 billion by 2007. Estimates by Frost and Sullivan (Hari and Anand, 2002) show that India accounts for 4 per cent of the $1.5 billion sales of system-on-a-chip designs with eighty companies involved and fifteen engaged in Silicon IP (intellectual property), that is, pure design.

What are the drivers behind this development? One is the vertical disintegration between chip design and fabrication since 1990, pioneered by the Taiwanese, leading to the emergence of pure fabrication facilities or fabless chip manufacturers who manufactured US-designed chips at lower cost. This led to huge increases in manufacturing efficiencies, leading in turn to increases in transistor densities of 5–10 million gates on a chip with 0.13 micron linewidths compared to 20000–100000 gates on chips with 0.8 micron linewidths a few years ago. As chip designers struggled with this increasing complexity, designer productivity began to lag behind transistor density leading to a 'design gap'.

This 'design gap' in turn led to three things: (1) a huge increase in the demand for chip designers as more designers are needed to design a single chip, and hence for low cost Indian designers; (2) more significantly, a further dis-integration in the chip design process itself with the emergence of modularity in which the modules are common 'blocks of logic' that can be used across different chips, these 'blocks of logic' being called Silicon IP, that lent themselves to outsourcing to fabless chip design firms and hence the emergence of start-ups of such firms; (3) most importantly for India, a shift in the content of chip design work from 90 per cent hardware to a projected 60 per cent software content in a few years which favours the Indian software industry skills.

To return now to the question: how does one explain this very recent emergence of R&D relocation and outsourcing to Indian IT and software firms given the largely low-tech services exports of the sector, concentrated in custom applications development and legacy work, and given the relatively few firms engaged in formal R&D? The answer, following from the above account of recent R&D relocation to India and the emergence of chip design start-ups (but which now can only be speculative as we seem to be at the beginning of a trend, if one indeed develops), seems to be, (a) that formal R&D does not capture innovation in the software industry given the extremely important role of tacit and embodied knowledge, and technological spill-overs from global technological advance; indeed, custom applications development, the mainstay of Indian software exports, can lead to product development (Krishnan and Prabhu, Chapter 6); (b) that the kinds of work that Indian firms have been doing lend themselves to incremental innovation for both process innovation in the delivery of services and as a base for outsourced product development of software products and software-intensive telecom and chip design products; (c) and most crucially, the availability of the right engineering and software skills for software R&D and chip design amongst sufficiently large numbers of people. The crucial attraction of India, and Bangalore in particular, is that it graduates 220000 computer science and engineering graduates a year, 25000 alone in Bangalore (this is probably a broad definition including diploma holders), with wages of one-fifth to one-sixth of those in the US. Additionally, 'Bangalore is awash with veterans with global experience' (Kripalani, 2002: 25), creating a cluster effect.

Does this then mean that the Indian software and larger IT industry is about to take off to climb up the value chain and compete on the basis of innovation? Three cautionary notes are relevant. First, these are extremely new developments that need to be watched for the next five years at least. Second, *unlike* Indian software exports, 73 per cent of which are by locally owned firms, the great bulk of the relocated R&D is being done in labs wholly owned by MNCs. Thus, it is *not* the Indian software majors who have moved up the value chain to more high-tech activities but a *new* set of players, except for some like Wipro, Sasken, HCL Technologies and MindTree. This relocated R&D thus resembles the early stages of outsourcing of software, driven by the need for cheap skills (analogous to MNCs being relatively dominant in low tech-, low skill-, low wage-oriented ITES exports, the low end of software exports in 2001–2). Third, the chip design firms emerging are also either a new set of entrepreneurs or MNCs, building on increasingly important cheap software and engineering skills rather than Indian software majors.

However, the trends outlined above in the emergence of the 'design gap' in chip design, the emergence of chip design start-ups, some by engineers from a hardware background and from the national security black box, and the increasing software-intensity of chip design make possible in the coming years (with many caveats and cautionary notes) the *recoupling* (see D'Costa, Chapter 1, on three types of decoupling) of software and hardware, software services and software products, and civilian industry and the national security complex, industry and academia collaboration, and if all this happens, the creation of true local networks on the Silicon Valley model spanning the gamut from software services exports to R&D and chip design, and eventually, with the growth of a more IT-intensive national economy, recoupling domestic and world markets. However, this does not mean that the existing Indian software majors will lead; it will most certainly mean they will have to continually reinvent themselves (Bhatnagar and Dixit, Chapter 10) to carve out a place among a host of new players.

4. The chapters in this volume

The chapters to follow are organized around focus areas such as structural constraints and opportunities, the significance of domestic markets and supportive institutions for innovative capabilities, the international sources of knowledge and technological capability such as technical networks, strategic alliances, entrepreneurial initiatives, and firm-level responses to challenges and forays into new areas such as software products.

In 'Export Growth and Path-Dependence: the Locking-in of Innovations in the Software Industry', Anthony D'Costa argues that the industry's growth path, dependent on exports and overwhelmingly on the US market, 'locks-in' the sector to a lower innovative trajectory. This is because, as advanced mission-critical tasks are not outsourced due to geographical and cultural distance, the industry misses out on user-feedback linkages critical to developing innovative capabilities. Relatedly, domain knowledge, vital for developing innovative capabilities in higher order activities such as embedded software, does not develop. What exporting Indian firms tend to do is to reproduce successful routines rather than innovate. He recommends, without turning away from export-orientation, the promotion of innovation to meet domestic IT needs, which will over time lead to a virtuous cumulative cycle feeding back into a higher level of international competitiveness in IT, and at the same time a diversification of export markets away from the US, specifically towards East Asia.

Ashok Parthasarathi and K. J. Joseph, in 'Innovation Under Export Orientation', argue that the Indian IT sector developed in the 1970s and 1980s under state initiatives, developing a broad and deep technological base in both hardware and software in designing and manufacturing complex equipment for the domestic market, led by public sector firms. Even the growth of the software export sector in the 1990s should be seen in the context of this background of capability creation, infrastructure provision, and other interventions by the state to specifically promote software exports. They argue, from a cross-sectional analysis of a database of 262 observations of software firms over the four years 1997–8 to 2000–1, varying from 50 firms to 89 firms in different years, created by merging the databases of the National Association of Software and Services Companies (NASSCOM) and the Centre for Monitoring Indian Economy (CMIE) that, counter to expectations from the standard neoclassical literature, export intensity and import intensity, though positive, are not statistically significant, and that the nature of export demand is not conducive to innovation. In general, export-orientation has led to competition in low value-added areas with low productivity, and on the basis of labour cost advantage, without promoting innovative capacities. They emphasize the complementary role of the domestic market and recommend for the coming years a reorientation to developing total systems solutions for complex, large-scale domestic infrastructural and industrial needs without turning away from exports.

Gil Avnimelech and Morris Teubal, in 'The Indian Software Industry from an Israeli Perspective: a Systems/Evolutionary and Policy View', view the potential for graduation of the Indian IT industry to higher value-added, product-oriented activities, and high-tech entrepreneurship from the perspective of the Israeli experience. They focus on high-tech entrepreneurial start-up companies in the context of the various kinds of domestic policy support, horizontal or targeted, that are possible in the context of the globalization of asset markets, foreign direct investment, and venture capital. They begin with an account of the three-phased Israeli experience culminating in the successful development of a high-tech IT industry in the 1990s with distinct types of policy interventions that promoted the Silicon Valley model of development, that is, the promotion of venture capital, high-tech start-up firms, and integration with global asset markets, in a broad, dynamic–evolutionary perspective. With fieldwork-based explorations of the experience of three Indian software firms, each of a different type, they draw tentative conclusions for the replicability of the Israeli model, which is itself once removed from the original Silicon Valley experience.

Rishikesha Krishnan and Ganesh Prabhu in 'Software Product Development in India: Lessons from Six Cases', analyse six cases of software product development in six different Indian firms (including two large services companies and four product software companies), among which are three financial sector (one banking, one financial accounting, one stockbroking), two enterprise resource planning, and one Arabic script-based desktop publishing software products. Graduating from software services exports to the development of branded software products, beginning in specific niches, is seen as a mark of an innovative trajectory and a desirable path for the Indian software industry, especially as India's labour cost advantage erodes over time, but is a direction that very few Indian firms take. It is interesting to note, among other things, that software products can be a spin-off from customized software development by services companies. The authors explore the incentives and disincentives, and all the various problems associated with the transition from relatively profitable and low-risk services activities to much riskier product development in different market, technological and firm-level capabilities contexts. They draw lessons for both companies and policy-makers.

AnnaLee Saxenian, in 'The Silicon Valley Connection: Transnational Networks and Regional Development in Taiwan, China and India', compares the role of the Indian-origin high-tech diaspora in Silicon Valley with that of their Chinese- and Taiwanese-origin counterparts in linkages with their home country IT industries. She argues that over the past decade the 'brain drain' has increasingly given way to a process of 'brain circulation' in which informal cross-national networks of engineers and entrepreneurs are transferring technology, know-how and skills to their home countries, and that such networks and home country clusters create 'return entrepreneurship' and promote high-tech development in home country regional clusters more effectively than conventional foreign direct investment. She shows that despite its great potential, Indian engineers in Silicon Valley have been slower to build a transnational network feeding into the development of IT clusters in India, focusing on the case of Bangalore, than their counterparts of Chinese and Taiwanese origin. The policy framework in the receiving country and other local-contextual factors are the key to exploiting the technology, skills and contacts of the diaspora. In the Indian case, both global and local networks are weakly institutionalized with less policy support.

Rakesh Basant and Pankaj Chandra, in 'Capability Building and Inter-Organizational Linkages in the Indian IT Industry', explore the role of inter-organizational linkages in capability building, including firms, academic institutions and research organizations. Given the strategic intent of using linkages to build capabilities for developing new products and services for commercialization, do organizations of different types follow different paths resulting in different outcomes in terms of capabilities and spillover benefits? They examine the nature and extent of inter-firm linkages in the telecommunication sector of the Indian IT industry, study two technology development networks created in the telecom sector by a Canadian multinational, Nortel, in India and China, and contrast the nature of these foreign firm networks with one initiated by a domestic Indian organization. The foreign firm networks are of two types, one established by the multinational with firms in India, and the other with a public sector technical university in China. The network established by the domestic Indian organization comprises linkages between a public sector technical university, the Indian Institute of Technology (IIT), Chennai, and domestic/foreign firms. These comparisons provide useful insights into capability building through network linkages. The methodology employed in this chapter involved analysis of primary survey data and case studies on Nortel's linkages with Indian and Chinese organizations and the network, the TeNet Group, developed by IIT, Chennai.

Abhoy K. Ojha and S. Krishna in 'Originative Innovation and Entrepreneurship in the Software Industry in India', survey sixteen entrepreneurs in the software industry in Bangalore, in a study of entrepreneurship and innovation covering eleven start-up firms that have chosen to venture into what they call an originative rather than a derivative activity strategy. This, unlike software services exports, is a high-risk strategy. The results suggest that successful IT entrepreneurs come from diverse family backgrounds, mainly middle-class homes, are educationally well qualified, have prior work experience, and have adequate management knowledge. They are driven by strong motivations, including a deep-seated desire to put India on the high technology global map, have strong personalities, and an ability to deal with risk and ambiguity, can maintain a large network of professionals, friends and family, and also seem to focus on simple ideas in the early days of the venture. The findings of the study, however, are that there is neither the local market nor the available financial resources for entrepreneurs who want to engage in originative work; the key to survival and growth is the identification of niche markets, primarily global.

Deepti Bhatnagar and Mukund Dixit in 'Stages in Multiple Innovations in Software Firms: a Model Derived from Infosys and NIIT Case Studies', focus on the important issue of organizational innovation for competitiveness, and present a model of stages in multiple innovations in the software sector. The chapter is based on an in-depth study of organizational innovations over two decades in two software majors, Infosys and NIIT. Both were founded in the early 1980s by professionals with comparable academic background and larger-than-life visions for their organization. They responded to the opportunities and challenges posed by the external environment and internal resource constraints through multiple innovations. The chapter develops a concept called 'strategic imbalance' that triggers the development of innovations and innovation-enabling contexts. Innovations occur when organizations recognize and initiate efforts to reduce their strategic imbalances. The response of the external environment to the first round of innovations of the organization decides the nature of subsequent imbalance and innovations. The conceptualization of stages in generating multiple rounds of innovation is the distinct contribution of this study. It has particular relevance for the study of ways in which software firms continually reinvent themselves or incrementally adapt to challenges, both of which are essential for them.

Note

1. I thank Anthony D'Costa for detailed comments.

References

Amsden, Alice (1989) *Asia's Next Giant: South Korea and Late Industrialization* (New York: Oxford University Press).

Bagchi, Amiya K. (1987) *Public Intervention and Industrial Restructuring in China, India and the Republic of Korea* (New Delhi: ILO-ARTEP).

Bhatnagar, Subhash and Rober Schware (2000) *Information and Communication Technology in Development Cases from India* (New Delhi: Sage).

Brunner, Hans-Peter (1995) *Closing the Technology Gap: Technological Change in India's Computer Industry* (New Delhi: Sage Publications).

Coe, D. and E. Helpman (1995) 'International R&D Spillovers', *European Economic Review*, 39.

Department of Science and Technology (DST) (2002a) *Research and Development Statistics 2000–1* (New Delhi: Government of India), May.

—— (2002b), *Research and Development in Industry: an Overview* (New Delhi: Government of India), Dec.

Desai, Ashok V. (1985) 'Foreign Technology Suppliers View of Indian Industry', collection of papers in *Economic and Political Weekly*, 20 (45–7) (Special Number), Nov.

—— (1988) 'Technology Acquisition and Application: Interpretations of the Indian Experience', in R. E. B. Lucas and G. F. Papanek (eds), *The Indian Economy: Recent Developments and Future Prospects* (New Delhi: Oxford University Press), pp. 163–84.

—— (1990) 'Recent Technology Imports into India: Results of a Survey', *Development and Change*, 21 (4).

—— (2002): 'The Dynamics of the Indian Information Technology Industry', Centre for New and Emerging Markets, London Business School, London, unpublished.

Dubey, Rajeev (2003) 'India as a Global R&D Hub', *Businessworld*, 17 Feb.: 28–37.

Evans, Peter B. (1995) *Embedded Autonomy: States, Firms and Industrial Transformation* (Princeton: Princeton University Press).

Fikkert, Brian (1995) 'Reforming India's Technology Policies: Impacts of Liberalization on Self-Reliance and Welfare', IRIS Center, University of Maryland at College Park, IRIS India Working Paper no. 2, Sept.

Grieco, Joseph M. (1984) *Between Dependency and Autonomy: India's Experience with the International Computer Industry* (Berkeley: University of California Press).

Grossman, Gene M. and Elhanan Helpman (1991) *Innovation and Growth in the Global Economy* (Cambridge, MA: MIT Press).

Hari, P. and M. Anand (2002) 'Chip's Off the Block', in Annual Session and National Conference on Innovating to Excel, 14 June, Manufacturer's Association for Information Technology (MAIT), New Delhi.

Heeks, Richard (1996) *India's Software Industry: State Policy, Liberalisation and Industrial Development* (New Delhi: Sage Publications).

Kamien, Morton I. and Nancy M. Schwartz (1982) *Market Structure and Innovation* (Cambridge: Cambridge University Press).

Kripalani, Manjeet (2002) 'Calling Bangalore: Multinational are Making it a Hub for High-Tech Research', *Business Week*, 11 Nov., 24–5, http://www.businessweek.com/magazine/content/02_45/b3807151.htm.

Kumar, Nagesh and Aradhna Agarwal (2000) 'Liberalization, Outward Orientation and In-house R&D Activity of Multinational and Local Firms: a Quantitative Exploration for Indian Manufacturing', RIS-Discussion Paper #07/2000, Research and Information System (RIS) for the Nonaligned and Other Developing Countries, New Delhi.

Mani, Sunil (1992) *Foreign Technology in Public Enterprises* (New Delhi: Oxford & IBH Publishing Co).

McDowell, Stephen D. (1997) *Globalization, Liberalization and Policy Change: a Political Economy of India's Communications Sector* (New York: St. Martin's Press and Basingstoke: Palgrave Macmillan).

McKinsey & Co (1999) *The Indian IT Strategy* (New York: McKinsey & Co; New Delhi: NASSCOM).

Mody, Ashoka (1990) 'Institutions and Dynamic Comparative Advantage', *Cambridge Journal of Economics*, 14: 291–314.

NASSCOM (2000) *The IT Software and Services Industry in India: Strategic Review 2000* (New Delhi: NASSCOM).

—— (2002) *The IT Industry in India: Strategic Review 2002* (New Delhi: NASSCOM).

—— (2003) *The IT Industry in India: Strategic Review 2003* (New Delhi: NASSCOM).

Pavitt, Keith (1990) 'What We Know about the Strategic Management of Technology', *California Management Review*, Summer.

Pavitt, K., M. Robson and J. Townsend (1989) 'Technological Accumulation, Diversification and Accumulation in UK Companies, 1945–1983', *Management Science*, 35 (1), Jan.

Rastogi, Rajiv (2001) 'Indian Electronics and IT Industry Production Profile: 2000', *Electronics: Information and Planning*, 28 (6–7): 169–98.

Saxenian, AnnaLee (1994) *Regional Advantage: Culture and Competition in Silicon Valley and Route 128* (Cambridge, MA: Harvard University Press).

Singh, Abhay, (2002) 'India Beats China as Designer of Intel, Texas Instruments Chips', Bloomberg.com, http://quote.bloomberg.com/fgcgi.cgi?ptitle=Technology%20News&T=markets_box.ht&middle=ad_frame2_all&s=Ape.X.haBSW5kaWEg.

Soni, G., S. C. Mehta, P. N. Gupta and C. Muralikrishna Kumar (2001) 'Role of DOE/MIT in the Development of IT Education', *Electronics: Information and Planning*, 28 (6–7): 199–213.

Sridharan, E. (1995): 'Liberalization and Technology Policy: Redefining Self-Reliance', in T. V. Sathyamurthy (ed.), *Industry and Agriculture in India Since Independence* (New Delhi: Oxford University Press), pp. 150–88.

—— (1996) *The Political Economy of Industrial Promotion: Indian, Brazilian and Korean Electronics in Comparative Perspective 1969–1994* (Westport, CT: Praeger).

Subramanian, C. R. (1992) *India and the Computer* (New Delhi: Oxford University Press).

Wade, Robert (1990) *Economic Theory and the Role of Government in East Asian Industrialization* (Princeton: Princeton University Press).

3
Export Growth and Path-Dependence: the Locking-in of Innovations in the Software Industry

Anthony P. D'Costa[1]

1. Introduction

The Indian software industry is growing rapidly. Whether firms can actually sustain this high rate of growth remains an empirical question. The ability to maintain the momentum of software export growth will ostensibly be determined by innovative capability. Notwithstanding the immense benefits accruing from the external orientation of the Indian software industry, there are good theoretical reasons why innovation may not be a pervasive feature of Indian software firms. I use a structural argument to suggest that the sector's overt export-dependence on one single (US) market contributes to a lower innovative trajectory (also Parthasarathi and Joseph, Chapter 4). The lock-in effects associated with serving a spatially distant market, albeit vibrant and profitable, detracts the Indian sector from undertaking a more long-term innovative strategy (D'Costa, Chapter 1). Interrelatedly, the sector's weak domestic orientation truncates the immense technological spin-offs possible with finding software (IT) solutions to local problems (D'Costa, 2002a). An inescapable outcome is uneven development in its most pronounced form: a highly dynamic software sector in the midst of various lagging sectors and a few innovative software firms coexisting with numerous low end software service providers (D'Costa, 2003a, 2003b).

The implications of such lock-ins for long-term policy are in two areas: one, a macro policy that specifically reduces the excessive dependence on the external market so as to generate a more balanced (complementary) relationship between foreign and domestic markets, and second, a global strategy that diversifies India's export markets, both geographically as well as in functional areas. For example, a shift in favour of the Japanese market and towards greater involvement with embedded software would meet both diversification requirements. The lack of domain expertise and user knowledge erects barriers to building knowledge systems and IPRs. Pricing projects is also difficult and therefore the potential to underprice Indian services is rampant. What is needed is a wider and deeper exposure to global markets and state promotion. Such interventions raise questions on the utility of national innovation systems, most of which are not directly addressed here (Nelson, 1997). However, given the neoliberal environment in which multinational corporations (MNCs) are leading players, it is imperative that we examine the innovative capability that might arise with MNC interaction. At the same time, to strengthen local networks so as to maximize learning from external sources a supportive role by the state is necessary, and therefore the relevance of a national innovation system cannot be assumed to be trivial (Porter, 1990).

The objective of this chapter is to identify how the export dynamic might be denying the full realization of India's innovative capability. This hypothesis is theoretically informed by synthesizing three sets of interrelated literatures. They are: (a) path-dependence and technology lock-in, (b) international technology management, and (c) political economy of development.

The study is divided into five main parts. First, the literature to bring out the 'logic' of path-dependence and lock-in is reviewed. It suggests the possible mechanisms by which the Indian software industry could be following a lower innovative trajectory. This section also reviews the literature that addresses the ways by which learning and innovation can be fostered under globalization. The next section outlines the basic methodology and data sources. Then an empirical assessment of the Indian software sector is provided to bring out the evidence of lock-in effects, such as low productivity and low value output. Using firm surveys, this part demonstrates India's specialization in low value services such as legacy systems solutions (D'Costa, Chapter 1). Additionally, the favourable time zone which India enjoys with the US is alternatively interpreted as a form of lock-in. The fourth section presents the findings of the survey and outlines some of the challenges facing the industry. This section also illustrates how some firms are trying to break the path-dependent nature of sectoral evolution. Based on my survey, different types of firms are discussed to indicate some of their learning strategies. The final part briefly recaps the low end trajectory being followed by Indian firms and outlines some of the broader strategies for a high road to accumulation. It re-emphasizes the complementary role of the domestic market to exports. It also suggests diversifying export markets in favour of East Asia, increasing the possibility of substantially adding chip design and manufacturing and embedded software to its export basket. Market diversification, generation of IPRs, and institutional arrangements, such as university–business partnerships will be critical to sustain a dynamic sector.

2. Exports, globalization and innovation

What's the 'path' in export dependence?

Path-dependency refers to an evolutionary trajectory of technological change, implying that past institutions and historical events leave their imprint on the future development of technology (Rosenberg, 1994: 9–10). Both systemic and idiosyncratic factors are involved, making the process essentially historical and cumulative, thus bringing out the interplay between a host of factors, both local and global. This lock-in is seen in terms of relatively easy entry in a high-growth sector. This, I argue, reproduces and consolidates successful routines, making alternative strategies less attractive. Relatedly, the limits to carrying out skill-intensive activities in geographically dispersed locations locks in Indian firms to a lower trajectory. Multinational strategy, the importance of face-to-face interaction in generating tacit knowledge, and market proximity are seen as influencing India's software capability. In the absence of local technological synergy, the benefits of spatial dispersion of high skill activities are truncated. From an economic development perspective, exports are seen as an engine of growth. However, export dependence can induce narrow specialization and lock in firms to a low local accumulation path.

Historically, declining terms of trade and low income elasticities for primary commodities generated the 'export pessimism' and subsequent import substitution industrialization strategy of the early post-Second World War developmental thinking. Breaking out of ISI exhaustion implied a changed strategy in favour of export substitution by which export competitiveness of manufactures, as evidenced by East Asia, was seen as necessary to economic transformation (Cypher and Dietz, 1997). The economies of scale associated with exports induced increasing returns and knowledge acquisition, thus contributing to higher growth rates. The rise of East Asia demonstrated the importance of a market-augmenting role of the state and export-driven model without downplaying local learning or the domestic market (Amsden, 1989; Kim, 2000; Lall, 2000).

Specifying some of the mechanisms by which India's software industry is articulating with the global one would be one way of understanding its innovative capability. Balasubramanyam and Balasubramanyam (1997) suggest one kind of lock-in effect resulting from export dependence. Notwithstanding the gains from exports, the Indian software industry is said to 'misallocate' valuable talent by luring away human capital from other sectors (D'Costa, 2003a, 2002b). In the early 1990s the Indian industry was reportedly trapped at the low-return end of software exports (Evans, 1995: 194–6). To put it in another way, India's software capability allows MNCs to reallocate their talent for higher order activities. Thus, it is not surprising to find that the bulk of R&D is done in the MNCs' home countries (Mariani, 1999; Narula, 1999) despite some evidence to the contrary (Cantwell and Santangelo, 1999; Reddy, 1997; Patibandla and Peterson, 2002). The strategies of the actors in this international division of labour and the significance of exports in these strategies are likely to reveal the specific nature of lock-in effects. Specific learning strategies, as well as public policies, could counteract some of the tendencies of a powerful export driven market.

Evolving international division of labour: firm strategy, tacit knowledge and market proximity

The software sector is a relatively new one and the ensuing division of labour even more recent (D'Costa, Chapter 1). The bulk of software production and consumption is in the US, followed by Western Europe and Japan. A handful of newly industrializing countries, including India, have made a dent in this typical triadic structure of the global economy. India's exports are driven by favourable supply conditions, such as the availability of a large pool of English-speaking, technically trained workers, excellent location, particularly relative to the US, and low labour costs. Exports are all the more attractive because of the structural weakness of and chronic balance of payments problems faced by the Indian economy. Exports are based on both on-site services and offshore development. The former involves Indian engineers working at the client's site on a temporary basis. The latter entails work in India itself, either on a subcontracting basis by local firms or through an intra-firm arrangement, whereby an MNC outsources its requirements from its own subsidiary in India. Offshore development captures larger economic benefits for the local economy. While this is a welcome development, it is still unclear whether local firms are merely providing low end services for their clients or increasingly adding value to their services by upgrading their innovative capability.

Evidence about MNC behaviour indicates that parent firms generally do not transfer critical work, i.e. those that have a significant bearing on immediate revenue earnings. Some of the reasons are weakness of local competence and a greater desire to control technology leakages from foreign subsidiaries. From MNCs' point of view, costs tend to be high with geographical dispersion, hence the tendency to centralize proprietary information. This is especially the case when substantial science-based production and industry-specific core technologies are involved. Both of these entail unpackaging tacit knowledge and therefore requires 'face to face interaction' (Cantwell and Santangelo, 1999: 104). Distance shrinking technologies, such as ICT, are unlikely to reduce the importance of proximity because knowledge is diffused by close interaction between clients and suppliers (Amin and Wilkinson, 1999: 122–3; Maskell and Malmberg, 1999: 180). Even in the EU, enjoying geographical proximity and with similar legal and social conditions, organizational coordination is still problematic (Narula, 1999). Socialization becomes the basis for transferring tacit knowledge, which obviously calls for geographical and cultural proximity (Schmitz, 1999: 232). When this condition is unmet, MNCs prefer to farm out tasks that are not part of their core competence, subsidiaries having to remain content to serve as adjuncts to central functions.

In the absence of countervailing developments, exports and MNC strategy suggest a low-innovation trajectory for the local industry. This lock-in effect is exacerbated by the absence of a dynamic local network, which mimics

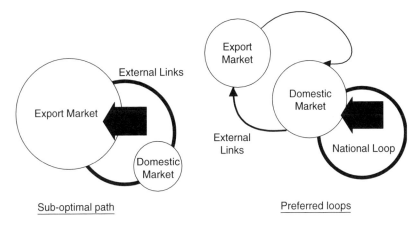

Figure 3.1   Sub-optimal path versus preferred loops

attributes of a Silicon Valley model (Saxenian, Chapter 7; Avnimelech and Teubal, Chapter 5). While exports may reveal international competitiveness, it is likely to be sub-optimal as local spillovers are not strong enough to complement the externally driven innovations. Cross-border learning proves to be residual, which is tapped from an external dynamic that is structurally designed to serve the external market (Figure 3.1).

Learning to innovate under globalization

If geographical and cultural distance gets in the way of close interaction, how does learning for innovation take place? There is evidence that external links can act as sources of innovation through learning in its myriad forms (Teece, 2000; Archibugi and Michie, 1997; Bell and Albu, 1999; Bell and Pavitt, 1993). However, significant public support for local knowledge creation and firm-level innovative strategies are necessary to break the lock-in effects. The recent focus on industrial agglomerations provides some clues. By co-locating in (geographic/sectoral) clusters, firms find themselves in synchrony with one another in a virtuous loop. As globalization is both a dispersive and an integrative process, in theory and practice, firms in different clusters can be tightly interlinked. Each cluster provides a localized dynamic which the different branches of the firm exploit by internalizing the relevant knowledge. However, such tight links are most possible under an MNC multi-subsidiary model, with the assumption that the production–development process can be broken down into relatively self-contained subsystems, each with its own core competence. In manufacturing this has been achieved through subsidiaries as well as by independent but dedicated subcontractors.

The question is what sort of learning is propagated when the service-oriented Indian software sector is geographically dispersed and consists of small independent firms? Furthermore, what does the innovative trajectory look like when the dynamism of local firms is fuelled by distant markets? It should be noted that despite geographical clustering of software firms, as in Bangalore or in the Santa Cruz Export Processing Zone in Mumbai, the local agglomeration effects are still weak because, unlike manufacturing, software does not have the same intensity of backward and forward linkages. Furthermore, high export dependence suggests strong links with foreign firms and not among domestic firms themselves (Basant and Chandra, Chapter 8). It has some links with local firms due to high labour turnover, which could result in knowledge spillovers (Patibandla and Peterson, 2002). However, IPR protection and proprietary concerns limit this type of flow of knowledge.

Knowledge, based on learning, is of two types: codified and tacit. The former is generic and easy to transfer, while the latter, as we have suggested before, is more specific and difficult to replicate. Tacit knowledge is typically generated within the firm subject to the particularities of the local context. The context includes the industry as a whole, the (internationalized) cluster of which the firm is a part, and the national–institutional arrangements. Tacit knowledge is experiential, heavily influenced by user needs, and hence less amenable to easy capture and transmittal. Tacit knowledge is converted to core competencies through 'problem-solving activities' and deep 'socialization' based on both geographical and cultural proximity (Cohendet et al., 1999: 227, 231–2). Competencies arise from fine tuning routines for solving problems, setting off increasing returns (Arthur, 1994). However, by stabilizing successful routines through repetition (Coombs and Hull, 1998: 242) firms could lock themselves into technological inertia. The established routines themselves might be suboptimal to begin with, as implied by the geographical dispersion of innovation. While the benefits from established knowledge keep on expanding, switching to new routines (or technologies) becomes prohibitively costly (David and Greenstein, 1990; Rosenberg and Frischtak, 1985: 147). With the establishment of a successful routine (akin to the effects of a dominant design), the lock-in effects become even more severe.

If building up tacit knowledge is critical to software development, then diversity of project experience is essential. However, if successful experience leads to technological lock-in, there must be systematic initiatives to 'unlearn' existing, successful routines.[2] While software exports from India, whether in the form of on-site services or offshore development, can provide experiential learning, a heavy reliance on foreign clients can limit the range of activities possible for Indian firms. The expanding export revenues based on several successful systems maintenance projects, for example, reinforce the firm's desire to specialize in such projects. This specialization, while lucrative, and subject to increasing returns, imposes a high switching cost when diversifying to other software services. Whatever diversification might take place is likely to be ad hoc and piecemeal at best. For example, rather than hiring people with skills in developing and implementing new operating systems, a firm could continue to expand linearly in systems maintenance rather than seizing alternative opportunities. Consequently, firms continue to reproduce their commercial successes with the 'same frame of mind' (Hamel and Prahalad, 1994), locking themselves tightly to client-driven, externally generated demand. With learning by doing, successful routines will be consolidated, leading to path-dependent 'learning trajectories' (Maskell and Malmberg, 1999: 180) in which increasing returns seem to take on a 'more-of-the-same-loop' configuration.

Furthermore, as tacit knowledge is dependent on socialization, distance becomes a liability. The socialization is not only among the suppliers themselves but also between users and developers (von Hippel, 1988). Silicon Valley is a quintessential example of clustering, where most learning is based on the interaction between different technologies, products, suppliers and users (Rosenberg, 1982; Saxenian 1994). With a weak user base in India, the complementary effects of the local market are missing, thus locking in the Indian software industry to the dictates of foreign demand. The contradiction is apparent: the strategy of multinationals is to centralize core activities while socialization is heavily influenced by shared ideas. To get around this, partitioning of projects, and thus reducing importance of close interaction, is resorted to. Hence, under this arrangement, far-flung clients can only approximate 'local relational fabric' (Cohendet et al., 1999: 232) and not substitute for it. The decoupling of production and consumption in India effectively limits the extent of local 'collective learning' (Maskell and Malmberg, 1999: 168; D'Costa, Chapter 1). Even with space-shrinking technologies, it is difficult to capture tacit knowledge for local innovation.[3]

No firm wants to co-locate critical projects overseas due to coordination and communication problems (D'Costa, 2002b). These problems arise because of the 'modular' approach to software development. Each project/ product is decomposed into self-contained modules, each with varying demands on tacit knowledge, making it possible to co-locate certain modules in certain places. However, the tension between increasing coordination costs and the criticality of certain modules limits what can be done offshore in India. Total learning with modular projects is constrained since exposure of Indian engineers to innovative projects is only partial. This hinders domain and systems integration expertise, spheres of considerable import for building competence. It also limits 'transferability' of tacit knowledge as user-based interaction is constrained. Also, rising costs in the more user-driven iterative process make geographically dispersed modular software outsourcing risky, thereby limiting suppliers' market exposure (Kogut and Turcanu, 1999).[4]

Building tacit knowledge will require intense interaction with users and co-designing of complete projects at home. Alternatively, Indian firms can go to the (foreign) market directly and produce there. The former is challenging given the geographical and cultural distance and the centralization of high end R&D functions. The latter means Indian firms must move overseas, in which case innovations resulting on foreign soil will not fall under 'Indian' innovations unless linkages with the home base remain strong. When Indian firms open offices abroad, as many are currently doing, they are attempting to override the shortcomings of long-distance outsourcing.[5] Relatedly, as non-resident Indian entrepreneurs initiate start-ups in India, client-based knowledge might spill over into the India-based segment of the software industry. However, to be effective the Indian economy must be sufficiently prepared to absorb this 'brain circulation' (Saxenian, Chapter 7).

Therefore the issue is not whether exports enhance tacit knowledge but rather to what extent. While there is 'creeping migration of knowledge' with internationalization (Ernst, 1999), the chances of lock-in are also quite high. This is not readily apparent as the industry as a whole is expanding rapidly. To unlock the various forms of lock-in, India's innovation *context* itself must be transformed, from one of heavy export reliance to *complementary* domestic development. Within this macro shift, greater export market diversification, geographic as well as product/service niches must necessarily follow, suggesting the reduction of India's overt dependence on the US market and on routine, low-level, cost-based outsourcing arrangements for software services. Both will require significant initiatives at the national, sectoral and firm levels. The current form of lock-in can be weakened with increased tacit knowledge, enhanced by the undertaking of challenging turnkey projects in a variety of markets at home and abroad, and, ironically, by tapping into the huge network of talent of US-based Indian software developers.

As innovation is linked to the ability of firms to differentiate themselves from others, there will be a question of 'fitness' of firms in the evolution of the sector. Firms can distinguish (select) themselves by deepening their skill profiles, which can be enhanced with total solutions, including architectural and detailed design. As modular production, the principal form of exports, is not congruent with turnkey solutions, developing local markets and diversifying foreign markets are likely to offset this lopsided development. Under the umbrella of heterogeneous users at home and abroad, the generation of tacit knowledge is expected to be enhanced, radically altering the innovation context. Software exports to diverse markets will be complemented by a strong domestic loop where local users will be also informed developers.

3. Methodology and data sources

Given the strategies of MNCs to outsource from India and the commercial attractiveness of export markets, Indian firms prefer to pursue less risky, more predictable projects. It is the *structural* position of the Indian industry in the larger global context that constrains its innovativeness. The weak user–producer links in the home economy limit the increasing returns that are possible with international exposure. This is not to suggest that all Indian firms are structurally positioned at the low end of the competency spectrum. There will certainly be a few firms that will actively seek to break out of the path-dependence engendered by export dependence. It is therefore the task of this study to first present an empirical assessment of the sector to bring out the evidence of lock-in effects (the suboptimal path), such as low productivity and low value output. Second, I also examine those firms that are attempting to break the cycle of path-dependence. By taking on more complex projects and building up their skill base, these firms are consciously moving up the value chain.

Two kinds of data were sought. The first was aggregate sectoral data, which could capture the broad trends of the industry. Such published data was obtained from NASSCOM and other organizations. The second kind, which forms the bulk of the analysis, was obtained first-hand through a semi-structured survey of firms in India (see Appendix). The firms were selected from the NASSCOM 1998 Directory, both on the basis of size, types of software projects handled, and geographical distribution of firms. In all, thirty firms were contacted, three of which declined to participate in the survey. Not all firms responded equally to all the queries. However, coverage was considered sufficient to capture the range of activities carried out by the industry and to identify the challenges faced by it.

The survey investigated five broad interrelated areas:

- general firm/corporate data, such as employment, skill availability, size of projects undertaken and exports;
- information on the three most challenging projects, in terms of clients, value, time taken, the complexity of these projects and the learning experience;
- information on innovations, in terms of products, process, the hurdles faced, novelty and the replicability of the experience gained for project diversification;
- the use of tools, such as object-oriented language, design, methodologies and work group techniques;
- links to the domestic market, such as clients, the hardware sector and manufacturing industry.

4. The evidence of lock-in

Low value output

In 2001–2 India exported $7.78 billion worth of software and services. The domestic market for software and services was $2.45 billion. Over 60 per cent of exports were for the US market. In 2002, the triad nations of North America, Western Europe and Japan absorbed 90 per cent of total exports (NASSCOM, 2002a: 26).

Nearly half of the exports in 2001–2 were low value, on-site development services. While this is a significant improvement from the 90 per cent share in 1988, the other half, which falls under offshore development (in India), is also subject to low value addition (D'Costa, Chapter 1). On-site services include a range of activities such as programming, conversions, testing, debugging, porting, installing and maintaining systems (Heeks, 1996: 81–3). Most of this work is tedious, less skill-based and uncreative as the bulk of the instructions and specifications come from the client. Turnkey projects, which entail design activity and systems integration, are more skill demanding. About 20 per cent of exports in 2001–2 comprised integration of packaged software, wireless, and systems, GIS/Engineering and R&D services (NASSCOM, 2002a: 29). However, even these activities have their low value tasks, such as coding, conversions, debugging and testing, most of which are carried out offshore (in India) for cost reasons.

The gradual shift from on-site to offshore development is indicative of greater skill-based activity providing the Indian developers with increased autonomy. However, this is not perceptibly visible when we look at export revenues per employee. Okazaki (1999: 142), using NASSCOM's *Indian Software Directory, 1998*, shows that eighteen firms (about 8 per cent of 235 firms included in the analysis) which were only moderately export-oriented earned on average under $30 000 per employee, compared to $13 400 for 100 per cent export-oriented firms (representing 62 per cent of total firms studied).[6] The figure rises somewhat to $14 500 for firms exporting 80–100 per cent of output. Fragmentary data show annual revenues of $18–25 000 per employee at TCS, the largest exporter in the mid-1990s (Heeks, 1996: 98–9).[7]

The persistently lower US dollar-base is a result of both the depreciating rupee and lower wage costs. Indian salaries represented anywhere from 7 to about 40 per cent of US figures, depending on the job classification (INFAC Information Products and Research Services 1998: 23) (see Table 3.1). Low revenues reflect low end, routine work, much sought after by both large and small firms. It could also be the result of Indian firms' inability to command higher prices due to a credibility gap, resulting either from mistrust, lack of tacit knowledge arising from geographical and cultural distance, or a race to the lowest bid for fear of losing the contract. Okazaki (1999) shows that in 1998, revenues per employee were the lowest for firms with ten or less employees ($11 528) and highest for those with 500 or more ($36 372). It is evident that large firms have higher revenues/employee due to increasing returns resulting from a larger number of employees and more capital equipment. There was considerable difference in revenues per employee between companies with 10–100 employees ($14 670) and those

Table 3.1 Comparative costs and revenues

Size of firm	Revenue/employee (1998)		Type of worker	Indian salaries as a % of US salaries (1997)*
	INR	USD		
0–10	484 166	11 528	Programmer	6.8–7.4
10–50	686 704	16 350	System analyst	17.8–18.6
50–100	617 832	14 700	Programmer analyst	13.8–14.0
100–200	681 197	16 219	Network administrator	43.6–34.9
200–500	689 418	16 415	Database administrator	29.1–28.4
500+	1 527 652	36 373	Help-desk support technician	21.6–19.7
			Software developer	32.0–28.4

Note: INR = Indian rupees, USD = US dollars, exchange rate used is 1USD = 42INR. *The 'Indian salaries' column was derived from Arora et al. (2001) and % share based on lower and upper values of Indian salaries corresponding to US salaries.

Source: INFAC 1998 and Okazaki 1999, Arora et al. 2001: Table 12, p. 1278.

with over 100 employees ($37 950). The average revenue per employee for the top ten Indian firms with more than 3000 employees in 2000–1 was $45 965 (computed from NASSCOM, 2002b). Revenues per employee in Ireland in the late 1990s ranged from $60 000 to $80 000 (Arora et al., 2001: 1269–70). Among exporters, those who exported less had higher productivity, indicating that the export market, despite arguments to the contrary, is not inevitably lucrative.

These figures suggest a heterogeneous software sector, with most comparatively smaller companies generating low revenues. In 2001, there were 576 companies with less than 250 employees (NASSCOM, 2002b). It also suggests that over-dependence on export markets truncates the salutary complementary effects of a vibrant domestic market. The implication of this is that lower entry barriers encourage firms to export, while subsequent growth reinforces the export routine cumulatively.

Locked in to what?

To understand why, despite rapid growth of exports, productivity is low it is necessary to examine the type of services being exported. A rigorous categorization of firms capturing their range of software services is beyond the scope of this chapter. However, given that large firms tended to have higher productivity, relatively large, mostly export-oriented firms were surveyed (see Appendix). Many of these firms were set up to be 100 per cent export-oriented units to avail themselves of numerous government incentives. Software services and products ranged from the low-technology Y2K, various Enterprise Resource Planning (ERP) packages for an array of businesses to complex CAD/CAM, telecom, chip and IC design, and real-time embedded systems. In the absence of longitudinal data for each firm, information on individual projects and firm specialization will allow us to comment on the innovation trajectory for the sector as a whole.

The notion of 'complexity' of a project can be used to examine the strengths of the Indian software sector.[8] The complexity of a project arises because of technical requirements and the challenges that are thrown up by the environment in which such technical specifications are applied. Thus banking, telecom and embedded software represent different domains, each offering different degrees of technical and environmental complexity. Technological complexities arise from the different platforms used, such as hardware, software and language. The number of functions offered and the quality of performance expectations will also dictate the difficulties of the project. Also, products, unlike most projects, are not expected to have an end. They call for continuing improvements and hence remain open-ended. If projects are real-time systems then there is greater interdependency among different components and hence they are expected to be robust, adding to the complexity.

The environmental complexity results from several factors. For example, project size is a major contributor to complexity. If there are several trans-formations of inputs to outputs, each emerging from and leading to other transformations, the software is rendered complex. Thousands of simulta-neous users of software as opposed to a few hundred pose a scalability chal-lenge. The cycle time during which the project must be completed and ready to be used significantly increases complexity. Thus, given certain resources, a project could be designed and executed within, say, six months. However, if the client, for marketing or competitive reasons, demands that it be done in three months, the complexity of the project would increase substantially, particularly in figuring out and coordinating the tasks that can be done in parallel and those that cannot. Deploying more people can speed up the process, but there is a risk of communication complexity. The interdepen-dency of the different components of the project also demands tight sequencing of tasks, making the project more challenging.

It is inevitable that firms with little experience will not begin with com-plex projects. Thus, early on, Indian software firms provided on-site services to cater to legacy problems. These included providing Y2K compliance, con-version projects (moving from one system to another, retrofitting the old with new, whether hardware or software), basic consultancy, Euro conver-sion, and a variety of data conversions (see Table 3.2). The legacy systems were a ready-made market for Indian firms. Literally hundreds of companies could quickly mobilize low cost talent to provide labour-intensive, low value-added software services, such as programming and coding, testing and maintenance. During 1998–9, exports of Y2K software solutions comprised about $560 million or 21 per cent of total exports. The largest of Indian firms and even multinationals cashed in on this bonanza in the early phase. For example, Birlasoft, Data Software Research, HCL, Rolta, TCS and Wipro

Table 3.2 Areas of specialization and application

Specialization	(% of firms)	Applications	(% of firms)
Legacy systems		Engineering industries	29
On-site projects	57	Telecommunications	39
Year 2000 solutions	39	Banking/insurance/financial/ stock exchange	64*
Consultancy	62	Manufacturing/retail/trading	54
Euro-currency solutions	15	Public administration/ office automation	22
Data-processing/conversion	27	Electronic commerce	23
Enterprise solutions		Electronicss/robotics	20
RDMS/datawarehousing/ datamining	43		
Systems integration	57**		
ERP/MRP	35		
Imaging/scientific programming	19		
GIS/imaging			
CAD/CAM/CAE	15		
Systems/real-time programming			
Telecom/networking/ communications	39		
Multimedia/graphics	27		
Others			
Web Tech/Internet	52		
Client-server computing	58		
Total no. of firms in survey	406		

Notes: I have collapsed individual areas of specialization to broad categories with the assistance of Sanjoy Chatterjee of Entomo Inc, US.

* high legacy content, ** legacy and ERP content

Source: Adapted from NASSCOM (1998).

were active in the Y2K market in the US. In 1998–9, Birlasoft had 20 per cent of its revenues from Y2K projects (*Dataquest*, 31 July 1999: 181). Some MNCs, such as Syntel, relied on cheap Indian labour for Y2K services. In the absence of tools, most on-site work is tedious and labour-intensive. Today, the use of a variety of Y2K tools has automated the process, making such projects even more routine. It is evident that most firms entered the market through legacy systems, inferred partly from the high proportion of firms surveyed in 1997–8 still claiming to conduct such work.

The slowing down of Y2K demand as the millennium approached compelled many Indian firms to transfer their international exposure to other areas, many of which included low end conversion projects. Conversion projects included the mixing and matching of different hardware platforms, different operating systems, applications software, moving over to new databases, and the Euro conversion. The latter entailed reconfiguring information systems impacted by the move to a common currency and common regulations among EC members. However, Indian firms have been less active in this market due to some of the complexities arising from a highly heterogeneous market, the presence of Ireland and other relatively low cost European suppliers, and the ample alternative opportunities offered by the US market. Conversion projects could be challenging, especially if the knowledge gap between the old and new systems was particularly large and there was a scalability problem. For example, if the gap between raw hardware and the operating system was large enough it would warrant a creative application solution. However, conversion projects often entail simple 'plug and play' operations, whereby the different interfaces have already been worked out leaving little room for creativity. On the surface, none of these types of projects is particularly challenging in a technical sense. Legacy problems, such as the Y2K and some conversion work, entailed good programming skills and coding capability. They did not generally demand deep conceptual activities. An offshoot of on-site work was systems maintenance. As Indian labour was cheap relative to the US, it made sense for American firms to outsource the maintenance services from Indian companies, many of which acted as talent brokers. In 2001–2, nearly 27 per cent of exports consisted of legacy application, management and migrations (NASSCOM, 2002a: 29).

The diversification of projects began with offshore development, itself an outcome of a gradual decline of on-site services, albeit still high, rising costs of doing business on-site, government investment in ICT infrastructure, such as satellite-based data communication links with foreign clients, and increasing hostility from US programmers, reflected in the fluctuating H1B visas granted to foreigners for work in the US. Satyam Computers diverted 75 per cent of its people to ERP after the Y2K slowdown. Opportunities for diversified exports arose as the credibility of Indian firms with their clients also increased by delivering services on time and cost-competitively. The perceptible shift towards offshore development began with rising trust leading to the transfer of more projects to India.

With offshore development centres, a variety of work has been transferred to India. Nearly 70 per cent of the firms surveyed reported undertaking offshore work (NASSCOM, 1998). However, a substantial share of it has remained at the low end, even if offshore work relative to on-site is collectively at the higher value end. For example, ERP and telecommunications software (discussed below) are certainly more revenue-generating and technically more complex than Y2K and conversion projects. The new areas included ERP for supply chain management, human resource management, manufacturing, finance, inventory control and the like. ERP is designed to increase enterprise efficiency, reduce response time, make transactions transparent, lower costs, and better integrate enterprise-wide systems.

A substantial number of firms, about 35 per cent, are engaged with ERP projects (see Table 3.2). Strictly speaking, ERP is not low value-added, especially when projects tend to be large-scale. This is because of massive back end operations required for ERP implementation. However, barring some specific enterprise application, most ERP projects are not subject to increasing complexity from an innovation point of view. An investment in 'face-to-face interaction' for building domain expertise is critical to ERP projects. The fact that most Indian firms engaged in ERP projects customize multinational products, such as SAP, Baan and Oracle, reflects the skilled labour cost advantage and not necessarily innovative capability. There are of course a few exceptions, such as Ramco, an Indian company, having implemented SAP projects for Swiss watch companies, among others, which now has its own ERP package (Prabhu and Krishnan, Chapter 6). In this line of work there is limited scope for repeatability as each client's requirements and the business (domain) in which it is applied are quite specific. If the opportunity to provide similar services exists, firms are likely to capture some generic logic of that particular business. Unfortunately, the *foreign* ERP market is itself on the downswing, undermining the full utilization of skills already built up by Indian firms.

The low end lock-in is still found under new guises. For example, under 'enterprise solutions' (Table 3.2) we also have systems integration, an area of considerable technical complexities. However, the category is broadly understood to mean integrating various components, which not coincidentally includes not only various turnkey projects and ERP but also various legacy systems. For example, old hardware could be phased out or new software applications added on. Again, this is not particularly challenging. Similarly, applications in banking, etc. (Table 3.2), in which nearly 64 per cent of the firms reported to have expertise, incorporates a sizeable proportion of legacy systems. There is either replacement of hardware, upgrading, or installing new software. Application software for stock exchanges is generally not part of legacy systems.

In addition to solid systems' integration skills, imaging and scientific programming, such as GIS and CAD/CAM, real-time programming, such as telecom and multimedia, e-commerce, and electronics and robotics clearly demand excellent technical knowledge and commercial acumen. A sizeable number of firms have already entered these areas, especially telecom (39 per cent of firms), the market for which is growing rapidly at home and abroad. Scientific programming is commercially weak in India, even though the technical talent exists. Multimedia (27 per cent of firms) is also a growing area and is technically challenging. However, multimedia has its low end 'content' and high end 'infrastructure' components. The former is more in the area of graphics, while the latter is in complex encoding/decoding, encryption, 'fat data through thin pipes' type of tasks. Though it is difficult to ascertain exactly how much of multimedia work falls under the infrastructure type of projects, the number of firms engaged in such work cannot be high. Lastly, e-commerce and web-based development are still immature and thus the most promising areas of growth. Both demand considerable skills in understanding the logic of interconnections between multiple players. However, they too have their broad definitions and may include low end work. For example, software developed to accept credit card numbers online is relatively simple and could be claimed to be e-commerce work. Similarly, web page designs could be claimed as high end web technologies.

An unrelated low end offshore development has been IT enabled services. This entails the digitization of various financial, retail and other service-oriented transactions, such as online information and help and support through call centres, telemarketing, data entry and conversion, back-office dataprocessing, airline reservations, medical transcription, insurance claims, web content development and the like. Thanks to new telecommunication and data communication links in India, today's Indian companies can provide a variety of services, such as processing of parking data for New York and Washington, DC, processing of airline tickets and insurance claims. Cheap labour and English proficiency remain the driving force in securing labour-intensive activities. This development is not altogether unwelcome. It absorbs labour in a labour-abundant nation and brings in scarce foreign exchange. In 1998, 28 000 people were employed with revenues totalling $231 million. In 2001–2, the corresponding employment was estimated at 106 200 and revenues at $1.53 billion (NASSCOM, 2002a: 41). This is expected to increase to 1.1 million persons and nearly $18 billion of revenues in 2008 (NASSCOM, 2002a: 41). The development of this segment conforms to the geographical dispersion of low wage activities and employment expansion in a relatively low skill segment. There are non-pecuniary spillovers such as employees' exposure to technologically modern and professional environments.

5. The immediate challenges: export dependence and innovative capability

At the general level, the challenge for the Indian software sector is to move from low end services to becoming a high end solutions provider, from simple outsourcing projects to value-adding, management of (turnkey) projects. As outsourcing from a client's point of view is coordination-intensive, those projects that present the least interfacing problems tend to get outsourced. While demand for software in general and outsourcing in particular continues to grow, the deepening of skills cannot be taken for granted. There are a number of structural problems that afflict the Indian software segment, precisely because of its heavy reliance on an externally driven dynamic. This external constraint imposes a cost that is not immediately visible nor easily eliminated. As shown by others (Parthasarathy and Joseph, Chapter 4), net software exports are quite low. Considerable effort by firms and the government in the larger institutional context will be necessary to move the sector to a higher innovation and accumulation trajectory.

Low revenues per employee also result from the weak domain experience of Indian firms. Most export projects are priced on time and material used, and thus tend to be the low value type. Clients pay for software services provided. Earnings are based on either hourly or weekly revenues, determined by the number of people deployed and the length of time. For complex assignments, T&M is not feasible as it entails design and analysis, in addition to programming, based on user requirements. This would require a fixed or contract price which in turn demands significant domain expertise or at least being able to conceptualize and translate the user's needs. In the absence of substantial experiential learning, the Indian subcontractor, for fear of losing the project, is compelled to under-quote the price. While offshore development reduces costs, fixing a price beforehand still poses difficulties as considerable effort must go into the iterative process of determining the user's needs before the final delivery of the project. The challenge here is to develop domain knowledge, endowed largely with the user. Indian software developers could be earning far more revenues than they do now because of their inability to fully capture the benefits of fixed price projects.

In the absence of a vibrant domestic market, the Indian software industry is dependent on external clients, and therefore is rarely in a position to dictate the concepts behind new products and services. Software products provide the largest margins as they entail concept building and marketing. India-based developers have been unable to penetrate the global product market. Outsourcing also means most Indian firms find it difficult to develop core competency. They will attempt to capture whatever projects come by as the strategy is to maximize absolute revenues rather than revenues per unit of labour. While the issue of core competency cannot be settled here, and for all practical purposes it does not make sense for Indian firms to specialize too narrowly at this stage of sectoral evolution, it is evident that without some specific domain expertise, such businesses run the risk of spreading expertise thinly over a wide variety of projects. For large firms this is a feasible strategy, but for small firms it could lead to a rudderless trajectory.

Firms can pre-empt lock-in effects associated with outsourcing by investing resources in learning strategies. By systematizing the experiential knowledge gained from projects, firms are able to build certain strengths. Such formalization takes on a number of avenues. A number of Indian firms have begun using object-oriented tools, but many others have not shown any inclination to utilize them. Mastek was the first user of object-oriented tools and developed a tool (Merit) for defect recording. TCS also developed a tool (Mastercraft) for custodial solutions for managing records of stocks and foreign exchange transactions. However, the use of automation, CASE tools, development of tools and libraries, various methodologies, such as rapid applications and prototyping, reusability of code, and auto code generation are still limited in India. Both tools and libraries are critical for developing products quickly, a requirement imposed by the highly competitive environment. Reusability is low because of the newness of Indian firms but also because projects are not within the same domain. AmSoft, a small firm, has a code reuse of only 10–15 per cent compared to Hitachi's nearly 50 per cent.

Also, considerable effort is necessary to document and record various in-house processes and track a wide range of metrics. The systematization of knowledge and quantification of productivity have been achieved by a number of firms, beginning with the ISO9001 and the Software Engineering Institute's Capability Maturity Model, among others. In 1998, of the top 250 companies, 36 per cent already had some form of certification, largely ISO9000, and 54 per cent were in the process of acquiring it. By 2002, of the 300 top firms, 274 of them will have some international quality certification (NASSCOM, 2002a: 108). Individual firms have also added their own forms of knowledge development. In some cases, such as AmSoft, the detailed documentation of processes and source codes are kept on a server. This information is shared as part of a knowledge bank, which both users and clients can access. Similarly, L&T in 1999 initiated a Centre of Excellence to provide documentation of learning. In these cases there is a build-up of specific knowledge all around. However, it should also be noted that with international clients, the user knowledge is not fully captured in the producer's economy.

The structural position of Indian firms contributes to the inability of either generating or retaining intellectual property rights (IPR). First, the dominance of the export market and the outsourcing arrangement makes Indian firms surrender virtually all IPR to the client. Second, whatever IPR is developed by multinational subsidiaries in India is captured by the multinational firm. As a cost centre, the stream of income associated with an IPR is missing. There are other arrangements by which IPR generated locally is not locally retained. One of Wipro's IPR was not licensed to users. Instead, the company accepted a one-time fee under the 'fee bearing application-specific worldwide usage right', an act not unlike a 'distress sale'. Indian firms prefer to cash in on the IPR developed as marketing it globally is beyond their capability. Another variant was TCS paying royalty to SEGA but securing licence fees from its clients. With more brand equity and deep financial pockets, multinationals are able to lure away locally generated IPR. MNCs are also able to provide higher compensation to local talent, driving up wages for local firms, and secure large projects even in the Indian market. For example, recently, Alcatel of France bagged a very large Tata project, while Tata-Infotech (one of the larger Indian firms and exporters) failed to beat IBM for a Reserve Bank of India project. Both cases exemplify the importance of market clout.

Trying to learn, learning to unlock path-dependence

Going by an evolutionary understanding of learning, the shift from low to high end software development over time seems inevitable. No matter what the project or service content, there will always be some (scope for) learning. The question is how to translate such experience into tacit and codified knowledge. Switching away from the same routines does not appear to be a sectoral strategy. As we have seen, there are a number of factors working against such an outcome, and two strong assumptions will have to be made in order for it to be realized. They are: (1) external demand growth will continue to accommodate Indian output and, (2) the structure and participants of the international division of labour will remain unchanged. For the long haul neither of these assumptions is reasonable. Witness the impact of the recent 'dotcom' downturn in the US. Lay-offs in the US and the excess IT professionals in India, cynically dubbed B–B (Back to Bangalore!), have been reported (*Business Standard*, 2002). China is aggressively upgrading its capability, while Indian firms are eyeing China as a low cost outsourcing possibility.

If a conscious shift must be made, turnkey solutions must be sought to understand user requirements and substantial investments must be made to capture domain knowledge. Added to the fact that users are abroad, there could be proprietary information that could limit the access to domain knowledge. For example, a small company, AmSoft, could not replicate the bus architecture for a phone project for several years due to an unwritten, voluntary clause. In e-commerce, the most recent software development area, the issue has more to do with capturing 'user experience' in a cognitive systems sense. How will Indian companies gain such experience when e-commerce is really in its infancy and largely found in the US? NIIT, a rapidly expanding education-oriented firm, which is undertaking such innovative research, is an exception rather than the rule.

The deep interaction necessary for turnkey projects is difficult to foster under arm's-length relationships with the client. Even so-called virtual software organizations, in which Indian firms dedicate entire floors to servicing foreign clients' requirements, cannot capture the user–producer dynamic synergy very well. However, firms could strategically initiate certain learning-based measures which would in the long haul extricate them from the clutches of a low end trajectory. There are many examples of this in India that reflect a general strategy of moving out of outsourcing (simple, modular) to project management (complex, total), from low end services (Y2K conversions) to providing 'solutions' (ERP-like with business intelligence, e-commerce, and embedded systems). Table 3.3 presents some of the

Table 3.3   Selected evidence on local learning strategies

	Research	Design	Manufac. domain/ hardware	University partnership	Code reuse tools	Economies of repetition	Local projects for Japanese clients	Foreign partnership
HCL	x	x	x					x
NIIT	x							
TCS				x		x		x
Mastek					x			
AmSoft					x			
L&T			x		x			
Geometric	x		x					x
Wipro	x		x				x	x
BFL							x	
SCT	x	x						x
CMC		x					x	
C-DOT	x						x	

Source: Field survey, Aug.–Sept. 1999.

reported learning strategies pursued by a variety of Indian firms selected for the survey.

The learning strategies of firms have varied. A few are engaged directly in research, often in conjunction with university affiliation. NIIT is one such example. Several other firms have exploited their existing domain experience in manufacturing, engineering knowledge, and computer hardware manufacturing. They include L&T, Geometric, Wipro, SCT and C-DOT. Both L&T and Geometric are spin-offs from their traditional engineering and manufacturing activities. While L&T has pursued business solutions for manufacturing firms, Geometric has focused on CAD/CAM applications (see Figure 3.2). It conducts relatively high end development research in Pune.[9] Despite the cutting-edge nature of Geometric's development, it has decidedly opted out from devising its own 'geometry' and instead supports the foreign products with its own technology in specific software kernels.

Computer hardware manufacturers like HCL and Wipro have also been able to apply their manufacturing expertise to software development. Also, Wipro and BFL (a non-manufacturing firm) have captured some of the learning for complex products from Japanese clients. On the other hand, DSQ's reliance on Japan-based Oki and NEC for telecom and various device drivers has been superseded by standardization of operating systems and 'smart' hardware with significant built-in diagnostics, debugging capabilities and functionalities. Besides, many external devices have now become part of main systems, and complex devices, such as medical or phone switches, are rarely outsourced.[10] Several firms, like Wipro and BFL, have developed systems integration capability because of the need to interface Indian-made software with Japanese

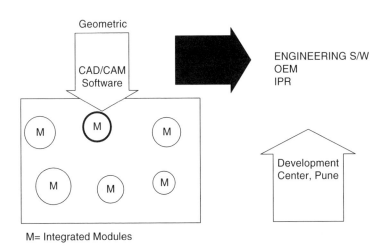

M= Integrated Modules

Figure 3.2 Unlocking low end trajectory by Geometric

hardware. Tata-Infotech, through its many alliances with well-known US firms, has also developed considerable systems integration competency.[11]

Large public sector firms, such as CMC and C-DOT, the latter with manufacturing capability, have developed solid project experience with design and implementation of large-scale projects for the domestic market. CMC is responsible for developing the Indian railway reservation system, while C-DOT has made its mark in telecommunications hardware for the rural sector.[12] Not all state firms have had fortuitous starts. A joint venture between state-owned Hindustan Aeronautics and British Aerospace (BA–HAL) began with financial and business management software rather than aerospace-related. The attractiveness of using cheap labour, for outsourcing by British Aerospace and generating revenues for HAL, was apparent. However, with a low error rate (a third of commercial software) and cheap manpower costs, it was in the interest of British Aerospace to move into more demanding projects. This was an ad hoc response rather than a systematic strategy for developing products and systems.

Other learning strategies include code reuse, use of tools, and greater reliance on research. AmSoft, a small Delhi-based firm, exploited code reuse, albeit on a small scale. Mastek and TCS developed and used tools: Merit and Mastercraft respectively. TCS also explicitly captured some of the benefits from economies of repetition by undertaking similar projects. Smaller, more entrepreneurially driven firms, such as Sasken Communication Technologies (SCT), have pursued high end, research-driven activities from the very outset.

Learning through multinational subsidiaries

Virtually all major IT-related multinationals are represented in India. Most of their work is routine, aimed primarily to assist the parent firm abroad through outsourcing. They are cost centres rather than profit centres. This means that the full market value created in these MNC subsidiaries is not captured by the Indian economy. Instead, revenues earned by the unit are based on costs plus some reinvestment funds. Philips, Motorola, Hewlett Packard, Citibank Texas Instruments, Verifone, LG Electronics, Lucent and others fall into these categories. Very few of these companies do critical work in India, and the value of work done relative to the firm's total is likely to be a small fraction. Citicorp, a 100 per cent subsidiary of Citibank, produces low value IT solutions pertaining to the financial and banking needs of Citibank. However, other firms, such as TI, have moved from an initial foray in CAD tools to chip design, in what has become its largest R&D centre outside the US (D'Costa, 2002b). TI's first major breakthrough came in 1998, thirteen years after its inception in India, when it developed the 'Ankur' digital signal processing (DSP) chip. 'Ankur' is a complex product, requiring significant technical skills in architecture, logic and layout design, and deployment of high level language (verilog). While a considerable stream of technological learning has been captured by TI's Indian employees, the commercial benefits are largely retained by its corporate headquarters in the US. As of now, there are no plans for TI, India to be profit-oriented. It will continue to serve TI, USA's needs through intra-firm transfers.

Other MNCs have launched small projects in embedded software systems. Both Daimler-Benz and Philips have taken a long-term outlook towards their India operations. Such software is demanding, requiring tacit knowledge, domain expertise and significant formal training. As hardware, such as consumer electronics and automobiles, begins to absorb more software for their operations and control, the architecture of these products is becoming increasingly software driven. Daimler-Benz in India is developing encryption software for remote diagnosis via satellites for its Mercedes Benz vehicles. Philips is devoting its initial efforts to testing software for consumer electronics. With experience and investment in hardware, it hopes to carry out non-routine software development, such as IC design, speech processing, and medical equipment manufacturing in India. Indian engineers are thus expected to be exposed to new technologies and learning possibilities.

6. Conclusion: forging ahead with multi-pronged strategies

In this chapter, given India's significant export growth in software services, with considerable dependence on the US market, I have raised questions about the sector's innovative capability. I hypothesized that the Indian sector was actually locked into a low level innovation trajectory. The reasons were: (1) that only those segments of software development that did not entail significant 'face-to-face' interaction would be farmed out, (2) multinationals tend to centralize high end, mission-critical segments, in the user-markets, which India is not, and (3) the Indian sector, given particular endowments, quickly seized the lucrative export markets, thereby shying away from alternative opportunities. These are largely determined by the structure of the global IT industry and India's place in it. The empirical materials suggested the lock-in effect, with the Indian sector exhibiting neither high productivity nor any untoward penchant for innovations.

However, the data did suggest that some firms were indeed diversifying their software activities. Indian firms are aware of the need to innovate and move up the value chain. They have introduced various quality-enhancing systems in their workplace, but these are few and far between with little depth. Only a handful of firms of the nearly 500 surveyed could really boast any sort of core competence. Clearly ERP, telecom, and e-commerce are growing markets, while scientific-based programming along with telecommunications software are demanding fields. Indian firms are present in these areas, but the content of their activities reveals that only a few are engaged in highly innovative activities, confirming the lock-in effects associated with offshore development centres.[13]

To break the path-dependent nature of India's innovation trajectory, two macro strategies are necessary. The first is to systematically reduce external dependence, especially on the US. The second is to diversify external markets, with the understanding that both strategies are compatible with a vibrant domestic market. A number of avenues exist, none of which excludes the others. However, ultimately the capability of the Indian software sector will depend on the tight linkages and deep relationships that develop between domestic users and producers. This domestic backbone can be best assured through a diffusion of IT in general, an area in which the state cannot abdicate its responsibility. The recent target set by the IT Task Force to make India an IT superpower is laudable. Broad economic reforms are compelling Indian business to respond to increased competition (D'Costa, 2000). Indian banks are thus adopting IT for competitive advantages. The adoption of such competitive practices in all other sectors, including public administration, is expected to contribute to the diffusion of IT. The conversion of cable TV network to a bi-directional system for Internet communication coupled with the dispersion of IT kiosks to rural areas for information access and dissemination will also be significant ways of enhancing this backbone. Finally, the introduction of C++ in the high school curriculum might contribute to a deeper dissemination of software writing skills and a wider awareness of IT in general.

For late developers, government policy has been important to the evolution of innovative capability. In manufacturing, the East Asian governments have successfully fostered high-tech competitive industries through a wide range of fiscal and non-fiscal policy instruments (Dedrik and Kraemer, 1998). On the other hand, protectionist regimes in Brazil and India have had greater difficulty in fostering competitive manufacturing. In the Indian context, especially in the computer hardware sector, restrictive policies did encourage certain local capabilities through what Evans terms a 'greenhouse' approach (Evans, 1995: 168). Several Indian firms were compelled to use limited imported know-how and build their own computer hardware. However, with economic reforms and market liberalization, whatever hardware capability was generated dissipated under international competition.[14] Most Indian hardware manufacturers had to abandon this line of business and focus solely on software. The retreat of the government from regulatory intervention had its favourable outcomes in the software industry. Unlike other established sectors which are still dependent on captive markets and residual state protection, the software industry is internationally competitive. However, it must be noted that the state still plays an important role, albeit market-augmenting, on behalf of the software industry. Duty free imports for exports, tax free export income, infrastructural support, such as data communication links, and a taken-for-granted supply of technical talent from government educational institutions are all products of state-sponsorship.

Beyond the US, there are tremendous opportunities in East Asia. Virtually all hardware is now software-intensive, hence the growth of this market is virtually limitless. Second, the talent for writing embedded software algorithms is available in India. Renowned MNCs such as Texas Instruments, Philips, LG Software, and Motorola, among others, are developing such embedded software. As one Philips official confided, East Asia's high-tech manufacturing based on 'fast-copy' will be matched by India's cutting edge software analytical capability and, ultimately, design skills. This indicates that embedded software is possible, especially if embedded software development can be more fully transferred because of greater scientific (codified) content. This development is likely significantly to alter the path of software evolution in India from its software service orientation.

It is evident that a vibrant domestic manufacturing sector will be needed that will also demand semiconductors. A few firms have begun such development. Some firms like TCS and Am Soft have begun developing embedded software. Hardware manufacturers, such as CDOT, on the other hand, have been able to support upstream industries through their demand for switching equipment parts. The understanding of hardware is crucial in any kind of embedded systems development and the Indian economy is well placed to provide formally trained computer scientists and other specialists. Unfortunately, such specialists are taking opportunities in the commercially lucrative business sector, which is generally decoupled from such specialized training.[15] The argument that there is no local demand for high end embedded systems is at best specious and at worst shortsighted.

Another promising avenue for cultivating domestic linkages is with academia, either local or foreign. For example, TCS, Tata Infotech and NIIT have long-term arrangements to work with academics in the US and India. Even multinational subsidiaries are beginning to work with Indian universities. Daimler-Benz and a few others in Bangalore are working with Indian Institute of Science faculty in areas such as cryptology. What this means is that innovation must take on a knowledge-footing. Tacit knowledge is the key to innovative capability and understanding the business (or users) is critical to the success of projects. Hence, being close to the market redeems the shortcomings of geographically dispersed development sites. What better way is there to diversify to high end export markets than establishing a solid national market? The involvement of the academic community will not only be served well through such endeavours but, more importantly, they could be an important source for IPR generation.

The issue then is not to promote the domestic market at the expense of the export one. Rather, it is to allow the former to play a more significant, complementary role to the latter. Considerable rethinking will be necessary to extricate the Indian industry from its low end trajectory. The institutional support of the industry by the government is one of the principal steps towards this strategy. As Sridhar Mitta, Chief Technology Officer of Wipro, bluntly put it: 'Most Indian companies are at the second level' (*Computers Today*, April 1998: 36), the first level being acquisition of programming, design and systems skills; the second, learning domains, processes and interfaces. The third level is a thorough knowledge of domains and understanding market needs and the last is commercial exploitation of ideas. It is evident that to move up the rungs of adding value, a vibrant domestic market is essential, for in the same article, Mike Shah, a software consultant, suggests that 'the geographic distance from the place of end use makes it difficult for the development team to understand the requirements' (ibid.). The challenges to a path-dependent, locked-in trajectory could be redirected by several initiatives on both the demand and supply side. These include IT diffusion, emphasis on science and technology, long-term research, the infusion of ideas from universities to industry, greater reliance upon open-source development, VC development for start-ups, adequate compensation and emphasis on IPRs, and the general commitment to optimally use local talent for local development. Recognizing some of the hidden problems behind the Indian success of software exports could be the beginning of our appreciation for some of the more serious national development concerns in a structurally lopsided world.

Notes

Originally published in *Science, Technology and Society*, 7(1) (January–June 2002). Copyright © Society for the Promotion of S & T Studies, New Delhi, 2002. All rights reserved. Reproduced with the permission of the copyright holders and the publishers, Sage Publications India Pvt Ltd, New Delhi.

1. The fieldwork was supported by the University of Pennsylvania Institute for Advanced Study of India, New Delhi (1999) and by a Senior Fellowship from the American Institute of Indian Studies (1998). E. Sridharan and his staff at UPIASI attended to the elaborate logistics of carrying out this project during the last four years. Salvatore Torrisi provided some crucial ideas on the questionnaire used. Gary Hamilton, through the Taylor Institute of my university, provided writing support in the early stages. I would also like to thank an anonymous reviewer and the numerous firms, government institutions and individuals in India and the US who willingly shared their views on the software industry. Janette Rawlings, as always, provided substantive editorial comments. I am grateful to all these institutions and individuals.

2. See D'Costa (1999) for the path-dependent trajectory of the US steel industry as a response to high switching costs for new technologies.

3. Anecdotal evidence from new small start-ups in the US indicate that even in the US it is difficult to coordinate activities between Portland and Seattle on the west coast (personal communication with V. B. Suresh, Entomo Systems, Seattle, March 2000).

4. Several iterations are necessary as clients modify their requirements frequently during the course of development and implementation. In one business to business e-commerce product, it took the developers about nine months to understand the client's needs, which were still subject to future modifications.

5. Kogut and Turcanu (1999) suggest that innovation is possible in India because 'the market itself comes to Bangalore'. Even if Indian engineers were able to define user requirements, as in this example, it is unclear how it might be generalized for other software requirements when the users are abroad. The community model of e-innovation, made possible by open-source codes and modular development, cannot be a substitute for locally based users.

6. Rupee values converted to USD at Rs 42/USD.

7. The replication of Okazaki's analysis with more recent data is left for another study.

8. For example, there are four types of complexity: inherent (dependent on basic property of a problem), unnecessary (complexity built into a solution not inherently required), psychological (neither inherent nor unnecessary), and communication (dependent on number of individuals and method of communication required for the project).

9. Its particular strength is in 'Feature Recognition' which is part of the larger Solid Works, a programme that allows parametric feature recognition of static 3-D data. Geometric has created modules around a proprietary 'core geometry' of firms to create a wide range of functionalities. It has also developed several off-the-shelf libraries and toolkits, particularly nesting technology that optimizes metal cuttings.

10. Personal communication with Sanjoy Chatterjee, Vice President, Entomo, Seattle, 16 December 1999.

11. The earlier assessment of systems integration being part of legacy problems still holds in the case of Tata-Infotech. For example, software implementation, consultancy, outsourcing, training, education, and software products, all part of systems integration, could entail legacy systems. Of the ten largest firms with over than 3000 software employees, Tata-Infotech had the lowest revenues per employee ($23 991 compared to $45 965, which was the average for the group) (computed from NASSCOM, 2002b).

12. CDOT offered challenging projects but could not compete with MNCs in the area of salary. However, as CDOT had a high turnover, it was clearly supplying highly trained personnel to other (private) firms.

13. A cursory examination of the firms listed in Appendix 1 in NASSCOM (2002b) suggests that most firms since 1998 had expanded into telecom, e-commerce, general business solutions, and ITES but were still conducting conversion and maintenance projects. Those few firms that had moved into embedded software, ASIC, VLSI design and CAE were already present in closely related activities.

14. In contrast, IBM's supercomputer 'Blue Gene', designed to understand molecular biology underscores the importance of hardware to software. With this hardware it is hoped that computer science students will take up graduate studies and advanced research rather than simply opt for the lucrative Internet start-ups and stock options (Lohr, 1999).

15. Anecdotal evidence suggested that a number of engineering students working on projects at the Indian Space Research Organization in Bangalore eventually joined commercial software companies (personal interview, Indian Space Research Organization, Bangalore, July 1998).

Appendix
List of firms surveyed

Company	Location	Year established	Type	Capital (Rs m)	S/W revenues (Rs m)	S/W exports (Rs m)	Specialization	No. of S/W employees
Alcatel*	Gurgaon, ND	1992	MNC	833.0	69.2	69.2	Digital switching equipment	63
AmSoft (X)	New Delhi	1991	Indian	66.0	145.6	145.6	Graphics/multimedia/embedded systems/AI	70
BA-HAL	Bangalore	1993	JV (MNC-GOI)	60.0	122.0	109.0	Application s/w (transportation related), systems maintenance	150
Mphasis (formerly BFL)	Bangalore	1992	Indian	171.4	1 728.7	1 728.7	Database, object-oriented applications, networking, telecom, embedded s/w	776
Birla Soft #	NOIDA, ND	1995	Indian	45.0	2 755.1	2 755.1	Y2K, on-site maintenance	482
CDOT@	New Delhi	1984	GOI	360.0	–	–	Telecom, real time OS, s/w engineering tools	903
Citicorp **@	Mumbai	1985	MNC	20.0	326.0	326.0	IT solutions for banking applications	465
DSQ	Chennai	1992	Indian	202.5	639.0	639.1	Mainframe, telecom, CAD/CAM	1 530
Data S/W Res.**@	Chennai	1973	Indian	150.0	600.0	600.0	Mainframe, hotel mgmt appl, Y2K, professional education services	700
Datamatics (A)@	Mumbai	1975	Indian	–	106.0	–	Migration, tools dev, banking, telecom	123
Daimler-Benz (X)@	Bangalore	1998	MNC	–	–	–	Encryption, communications, embedded software CAD/CAM	–
Geometric	Mumbai	1994	JV	52.4	448.7	448.7	software CAD/CAM	350
HCL +	NOIDA, ND	1991	Indian	569.8	14 051.0	12 502.0	Client-server, object-oriented, Y2K, telecom	3 975
L&T	Mumbai	1997	Indian	150.0	2 390.0	2 218.4	Mainframe, SAP, client-server, CAD/CAM, embedded ERP/banking, manufacturing	1 811
Mastek	Mumbai	1982	Indian	166.0	2 611.0	2 550.0	telecom	868
Robert Bosch (A)	Bangalore	1998	MNC	43.8	722.0	647.5	Auto. related real time embedded systems	629
NIIT	New Delhi	1981	Indian	386.0	6 828.0	5 700.0	Systems integration, education s/w, multimedia	2 143
Patni **	Mumbai	1978	Indian	closely held	5 180.0	5 150.0	Migration, porting, IBM mainframe, Y2K, client-server, ERP	3 104

Philips	Bangalore	1996	MNC	60.0	1 314.9	1 314.9	Consumer electronics, IC design, medical equipment	686
Ramco	Chennai	1989	Indian	80.8	2 131.9	1 259.6	ERP, simulation, real time control systems	700 (1998)
Rolta	Mumbai	1982	Indian	636.9	1 908.0	586.6	CAD/CAM/GIS, conversion, Y2K, banking solution	1 300
Sasken (formerly SAS)	Bangalore	1989	Indian	private limited	1 413.0	1 362.3	Telecom, design, signal processing	837
Silverline	Mumbai	1992	Indian	856.5	7 070.0	7 010.5	Banking, education, telecom, hospitality, maintenance, migration	1 950
Sonata	Bangalore	1986	Indian	100.0	1 289.2	1 070.2	ERP, manufacturing, telecom billing, business, financial service	623
Syntel (A)@	Mumbai	1992	MNC	5.0	180.2	180.2	Outsourcing, on-site, Y2K	1 473
TCS	Mumbai	1968	Indian	–	31 420.0	28 700.0	Management, re-engineering, migration, telecom, CAD/CAM/CAE	16 880
Tata-Infotech	Mumbai	1978	Indian	183.8	3 341.3	2 880.3	Offshore, systems integration, education	3 054
Texas Instrum.	Bangalore	1985	MNC	3.0	1 281.0	1 281.0	IC Design, s/w design	565
WIPRO	Bangalore	1981	Indian	464.9	26 429.2	17 670.4	Telecom, health care, Y2K, e-commerce	8 573
Yokogawa/Blue Star@	Bangalore	1987	JV	87.5	104.0	104.0	computer control systems, re-engineering services, manufac. control systems	230 (1998)

Notes: @data is for 1998, no data available in 2002 Directory; * previous joint-venture with Modi is now defunct; (X) not part of the original survey list; # renamed from Birla Horizon International Ltd.

** declined to be interviewed, (A) contacted but could not schedule meeting (previously MICO-Bosch), + met with head of another HCL division. Interviewed Mindtree in 1999 during its formation. Other firms interviewed in 1998: Advantage, TISL, Microland, SAS, WIPRO, Aditi, STPI, Bangalore, STPI, Delhi, STPI, Calcutta (1999), Mindware, Infosys, Hewlett Packard, Motorola, Verifone, LG Software, Svam, Oracle, CMC, NIIT, IDC, IIS Infotech, Cadence, R.S. Software, Vedika, ISRO, Encore (formerly N-Core).

Source: NASSCOM (1998, 2002 Directories) and author's field research, 1998 and 1999.

References

Amin, A. and F. Wilkerson, (1999) 'Learning, Proximity and Industrial Performance: an Introduction', *Cambridge Journal of Economics*, 23(2): 121–5.

Amsden, A. H. (1989) *Asia's Next Giant: South Korea and Late Industrialization* (New York: Oxford University Press).

Archibugi, D. and J. Michie (1997) 'Technological Globalization and National Systems of Innovation: an Introduction', in D. Archibugi and J. Michie, *Globalisation and Economic Performance* (Cambridge: Cambridge University Press), pp. 1–23.

Arora, A. et al. (2001) 'The Indian Software Services Industry', *Research Policy*, 30(8): 1267–87.

Arthur, W. B. (1994) *Increasing Returns and Path Dependence in the Economy* (Ann Arbor: University of Michigan Press).

Balasubramanyam, A. and V. N. Balasubramanyam, (1997) 'Singer, Services and Software', *World Development*, 25(11): 1857–61.

Bell, M. and M. Albu (1999) 'Knowledge Systems and Technological Dynamism in Industrial Clusters in Developing Countries', *World Development*, 27(9): 1715–34.

Bell, M. and K. Pavitt (1993) 'Technological Accumulation and Industrial Growth: Contrasts between Developed and Developing Countries', *Industrial and Corporate Change*, 2(2): 157–210.

Business Standard (2002) '55,000 IT Engineers Jobless', *Business Standard*, 22 Aug: iv.

Cantwell, J. and G. D. Santangelo (1999) 'The Frontier of International Technology Networks: Sourcing Abroad the Most Highly Tacit Capabilities', *Information Economics and Policy*, 11(1): 101–203.

Cohendet, P. et al. (1999) 'Knowledge Coordination, Competence Creation and Integrated Networks in Globalized Firms', *Cambridge Journal of Economics*, 23(2): 225–41.

Computers Today (1998) 'Where is India's Windows or Java', April.

Coombs, R. and R. Hull (1998) ' "Knowledge Management Practices" and Path-Dependency in Innovation', *Research Policy*, 27(3): 237–53.

Cypher, J. M. and J. L. Dietz (1997) *The Process of Economic Development* (London: Routledge).

D'Costa, A. P. (1999) *The Global Restructuring of the Steel Industry: Innovations, Institutions and Industrial Change* (London: Routledge).

—— (2000) 'Capitalist Maturity and Corporate Responses to Economic Liberalization in India: the Steel, Auto, and Software Sectors', *Contemporary South Asia*, 9(2): 141–63.

—— (2002a) 'Technological Leapfrogging: the Software Challenge in India', in P. Conceição et al., *Knowledge for Inclusive Development* (New York: Quorum Books), pp. 183–99.

—— (2002b) 'Software Outsourcing and Policy Implications: an Indian Perspective', *International Journal of Technology Management*, 24(7/8): 705–23.

—— (2003a) 'Uneven and Combined Development: Understanding India's Software Exports', *World Development*, 31(1): 211–26.

—— (2003b) 'Catching Up and Falling Behind: Inequality, IT and the Asian Diaspora', in K. C. Ho, R. Kluver and C. C. Yang, *Asia Encounters the Internet* (Routledge: London), forthcoming.

Dataquest (1999) 31 July.

David, P. and S. Greenstein (1990) 'The Economics of Compatibility Standards: an Introduction to Recent Research', *Economics of Innovation and New Technology*, 1, Fall: 3–41.

Dedrik, J. and K. L. Kraemer (1998) *Asia's Computer Challenge: Threat or Opportunity for the United States and the World?* (New York: Oxford University Press).

Ernst, D. (1999) 'How Globalization Reshapes the Geography of Innovation Systems: Reflections on Global Production Networks in Information Industries' (unpublished paper, 1st draft), Copenhagen Business School, Denmark.

Evans, P. (1995) *Embedded Autonomy: States and Industrial Transformation* (Princeton: Princeton University Press).

Hamel, G. and C. K. Prahalad (1994) *Competing for the Future* (Boston: Harvard Business School Press).

Heeks, R. (1996) *India's Software Industry: State Policy, Liberalisation and Industrial Development* (New Delhi: Sage Publications).

INFAC (Information Products and Research Services (I) Pvt. Ltd) (1998) 'Software Industry: Market Status', Consultancy Report, INFAC, Mumbai.

Kim, L. (2000) 'Korea's National Innovation System in Transition', in L. Kim and R. R. Nelson (eds), *Technology, Learning, and Innovation: Experiences of Newly Industrializing Economies* (Cambridge: Cambridge University Press), pp. 335–60.

Kogut, B. and A. Turcanu (1999) 'Global Software Development and the Emergence of E-Innovation', unpublished paper, Carnegie Bosch Institute, Pittsburgh.

Lall, S. (2000) 'Technological Change and Industrialization in the Asian Newly Industrializing Economies: Achievements and Challenges', in L. Kim and R. R. Nelson (eds), *Technology, Learning, and Innovation: Experiences of Newly Industrializing Economies* (Cambridge: Cambridge University Press), pp. 13–68.

Lohr, S. (1999) 'IBM Plans a Supercomputer that Works at the Speed of Life', *New York Times*, 6 Dec.

Mariani, M. (1999) 'Next to Production or to Technological Clusters? The Economics and Management of R&D Location', unpublished paper, University of Maastricht, the Netherlands.

Maskell, P. and A. Malmberg (1999) 'Localised Learning and Industrial Competitiveness', *Cambridge Journal of Economics*, 23 (2): 167–85.

Narula, R. (1999) 'In-House R&D, Outsourcing or Alliances? Some Strategic and Economic Considerations', unpublished paper, University of Oslo, Norway.

NASSCOM (1998) *Indian IT and Software Services Directory, 1998* (New Delhi: NASSCOM).

—— (1999) *The Software Industry in India: a Strategic Review* (New Delhi: NASSCOM).

—— (2002a) *The IT Industry in India: Strategic Review 2002* (New Delhi: NASSCOM).

—— (2002b) *Indian IT and Software Services Directory, 2002* (New Delhi: NASSCOM) (CD ROM).

Nelson, R. R. (1997) 'Foreword', in D. Archibugi and J. Michie, *Globalisation and Economic Performance* (Cambridge: Cambridge University Press).

Nooteboom, B. (1999) 'Innovation, Learning and Industrial Organisation', *Cambridge Journal of Economics*, 23 (2): 127–50.

Okazaki, T. (1999) 'The Productivity of the Indian Software Industry', in 'New Dimensions of Indian Industrial Development', *Konodai Bulletin of Economic Studies*, 11 (1), (Special Volume): 135–48.

Patibandla, M. and B. Petersen (2002) 'Role of Transnational Corporations in the Evolution of a High-Tech Industry: the Case of India's Software Industry', *World Development*, 30 (9): 1561–77.

Porter, M. E. (1990) *The Competitive Advantage of Nations* (New York: Free Press).

Reddy, P. (1997) 'New Trends in Globalization of Corporate R&D and Implications for Innovation Capability in Host Countries: a Survey from India', *World Development*, 25 (11): 1821–37.

Rosenberg, N. (1982) *Inside the Black Box: Technology and Economics* (Cambridge: Cambridge University Press).

——(1994) 'Path-Dependent Aspects of Technological Change', in Rosenberg, *Exploring the Black Box: Technology, Economics and History* (Cambridge: Cambridge University Press), pp. 9–23.

Rosenberg, N. and C. Frischtak (eds) (1985) *International Technology Transfer: Concepts, Measures and Comparisons* (New York: Praeger).

Saxenian, A. (1994) *Regional Advantage: Culture and Competition in Silicon Valley and Route 128* (Cambridge, MA: Harvard University Press).

Schmitz, H. (1999) 'Collective Efficiency and Increasing Returns', *Cambridge Journal of Economics*, 23 (4): 465–83.

Teece, D. J. (2000) 'Firm Capabilities and Economic Development: Implications for the Newly Industrializing Economies', in L. Kim, and R. R. Nelson (eds), *Technology, Learning and Innovation: Experiences of Newly Industrializing Economies* (Cambridge: Cambridge University Press), pp. 335–60.

von Hippel, E. (1988) *The Sources of Innovation* (New York: Oxford University Press).

4

Innovation Under Export Orientation

Ashok Parthasarathi and K. J. Joseph

1. Introduction

By enhancing access to information and augmenting the process of information exchange, information and communication technologies (ICTs) offer enormous opportunities for growth, enhanced productivity and improvement in efficiency in all spheres of human activity. Unfortunately, however, the fruits of this ubiquitous technology are very unevenly distributed across different countries. On the one hand, we have a few countries like the US with a high level of IT diffusion (about 400 computers per 1000 people), where IT contributes significantly to GDP.[1] At the other extreme are a number of developing countries, where the extent of IT diffusion remains very low.[2] The observed 'digital divide' is best summarized by the fact that 'more than half of humanity has never made a phone call'.[3]

It may, therefore, appear paradoxical that in an era of 'digital divide' India enjoys enormous comparative advantage in the export of software. Going by the available statistics, during the last decade software export from India recorded annual compound growth rates of over 60 per cent in rupee terms (at current prices) and around 45 per cent in dollar terms. In consequence, the share of software export in the total export earning of the country increased from 1.9 per cent in 1994–5 to about 20 per cent in 2002–3. Studies indicate, however, that the comparative advantage of Indian ICT firms has been in on-site export of services and related customized software development (Arora and Asundi, 1999). Very few well-known software products or proprietary packages have been developed by Indian firms and put on the international market. Moreover, the focus of Indian firms has mostly been at the lowest end of the value chain (see D'Costa, Chapter 1), carrying out low-level design, coding and maintenance (Kattuman and Iyer, 2001) and often mere computerization of analog data, for example, medical records. Consequently, the revenue per employee in the conventional private sector software firms ($16000 in 1999) was found to be only about one-tenth that of Israel and one-fourth even of Ireland (Arora et al., 2000).

Moreover, and particularly crucially, the net export earning has been only around 50 per cent of the gross export (Joseph and Harilal, 2001). As ICT is one of the most dynamic technologies with, perhaps, the shortest product lifecycle, in order to sustain the observed rate of growth in exports it is imperative that the industry moves up the value chain and progressively increases domestic development with a focus not only on software products but also on systems. The available evidence indicates that the prime factor behind the current comparative advantage is the relatively low labour cost in India (Mahajan, 2000; Kumar, 2001). Given the flexible international division of labour, the potential threat of this industry migrating to other countries, in the event of a rise in wage cost, cannot be ruled out. There is therefore a need for a change in the current strategy of competing on the basis of pure 'labour cost advantage' to one based on efficiency and induced by productivity based on innovative capacity.

Against this background, this chapter seeks answers to the following issues: Have the policy measures and the institutional interventions under-taken in the 1990s been instrumental in fostering an innovation-based com-parative advantage? What has been the innovative strategy, if any, of firms that have adopted export orientation? What are the factors that govern the innovative performance of firms? What new or additional policies need to be adopted to foster India's innovation-based comparative advantage and to enable software firms to move up the value chain and have the competence to address software demand in the huge *domestic* ICT market?

The organization of this chapter is as follows. In the next section we deline-ate the background for the analysis that follows by presenting a brief analy-sis of the structure and growth of software service exports during the last decade. In the third section we analyse the policy measures and institutional interventions made by the government towards the development of ICT in general and the software sector in particular. The fourth section analyses the innovative behaviour of firms followed by an analysis of the determinants of innovative performance under the strong export-oriented regime (section five). In the last section we highlight the major findings of the study and present perspectives for the future.

2. Structure and growth of software exports

Conceptually, software export is amenable to analysis within the framework of trade in services. Unlike trade in goods, trade in services could be carried out in different ways. In the literature on trade in services (Nayyar, 1988; Sampson and Snape, 1985), we largely find four different modes of service export:

- trade taking place with the movement of provider to receiver;
- trade in which the receiver is mobile not the provider;
- no movement of either the provider or the receiver is involved;
- transactions in which both the provider and the receiver move.

Trade in software, which is akin to service trade, is carried out principally through (a) on-site services; (b) offshore services; and (c) offshore products and packages. The underlying distinction between them is the movement of the provider and the receiver. Let us now briefly deal with each of them in some detail, for it is important in understanding innovative behaviour and export performance.

On-site services, popularly known in industry circles as 'body-shopping', occur when the factors move to the site of the receiver. Here, very often the software firms provide the client with software programmers and analysts on a temporary basis. In its extreme form, this occurs when software manpower is exported to help resolve the users' software-related problems. In a sense, here the exported item is not software but manpower, and the exporting firms need not necessarily have a complete understanding of user requirements. Therefore, there is little need for the exporting firm to be innovative because the requirement analysis, high level designs, and other stages involving high value addition will be undertaken by the importing firms. On-site services could also involve undertaking the task of total software development to resolve specific problems. In such contexts, given the restrictions on export of manpower, on-site services might result in uneconomic utilization of manpower (Sen, 1995). This is because there can be situations in which highly skilled manpower engage themselves not only in the design of the software but also in coding and testing which could be undertaken by less trained manpower (D'Costa, 2002). Under this mode of export, it has been argued that the net export earning will be substantially lower than the total export earning because a part of the foreign exchange earned will have to be spent in the importing country itself (Heeks, 1996).

The second mode of software export is in terms of offshore services. This involves limited movement of both the factor and the receivers. The software is developed offshore in accordance with specified requirements and exported to the users. This entails greater investment in hardware and the communication network. This method could lead to more effective use of software manpower and be cost effective because the software development process is carried out in the domestic country. In comparison to on-site services, the net export earning could also be higher. Firms engaged in offshore services are likely to be more innovative than those engaged in on-site services because in this mode of export, firms are more likely to undertake all the stages involved in software development: from conceptualization and design to installation and testing. This argument, however, should not be stretched too far because it is not necessary that all offshore service projects entail undertaking all the stages in software development. If the offshore services entail only carrying out the last stages in software development, such as coding, testing and post-production support, there will be scarcely any motivation for the exporting firm to be innovative.

The third mode of export is offshore packages or software product development. Here, neither the factor nor the receiver of the service moves. The firms will necessarily be undertaking all stages in software development such as requirements analysis, design, coding, testing and post-production support. To be competent in effectively undertaking all these stages, the firms need to be innovative and invest substantially in research and development. In addition, there is also a need to incur substantial marketing cost. The net export earning will be higher in this mode of export in comparison to the others. On the whole, it appears that the structure of export has a bearing on the innovativeness of the firms and the extent of net export earning and domestic value addition and, of course, vice versa, over time as capabilities get built. Hence, one of the major objectives of India's policies towards software exports has been to increase the offshore component and to induce firms to move up the value chain. It may be seen from Table 2.1 (Sridharan, Chapter 2) that, over time, there has been a considerable increase in the share of offshore projects whereas the share of software products has shown a declining trend.

Export performance

We shall begin with an analysis of export trends based on NASSCOM data. The issue of net export earning is then taken up using firm level data. Table 4.1 presents data on export earning as reported by NASSCOM, an often quoted data source on exports. We have presented export earning in both dollars and rupees for the data are at current prices.[4] By comparing export in rupee and dollar terms, one gets an idea of the possible effect of devaluation.

From the data presented in Table 4.1 the following observations may be made.[5] To begin with, the recorded rate of growth in exports (around

Table 4.1   Trend in software export from India

Year	Rs million	Growth rate	$ million	Growth rate
1990–91	2 500		128	
1991–92	4 300	72.00	164	28.13
1992–93	6 750	56.98	225	37.20
1993–94	10 200	51.11	330	46.67
1994–95	15 350	50.49	485	46.97
1995–96	25 200	64.17	734	51.34
1996–97	39 000	54.76	1 085	47.82
1997–98	65 300	67.44	1 750	61.29
1998–99	109 400	67.53	2 650	51.43
1999–00	172 000	57.22	3 900	47.17
2000–01	283 500	64.80	6 217	59.40
Annual compound growth rates (percentage)				
1990–91 to 1995–96		78.18		54.74
1995–96 to 2000–1		62.26		53.31
1990–91 to 2000–1		60.49		47.44

Source: NASSCOM, *Indian Software and Services Directory*, various years.

50 per cent in the sub-periods as well as for the whole period), both in rupees and dollars, is almost unprecedented in any other sectors of the Indian economy. Secondly, there is a wide margin between the recorded rate of growth in terms of rupees and dollars which reflects the possible effect of devaluation of the Indian rupee *vis-à-vis* the US dollar. Third, the observed difference between the rate of growth in terms of the Indian rupee and the US dollar (exchange rate effect) comes down from 24 per cent during 1991–5 to 9 per cent during 1995–2001. This probably reflects the reduced role of devaluation in sustaining export growth.

The phenomenal increase in export growth has to be viewed, inter alia, in terms of the growing world demand, the comparative advantage that India has on account of its highly skilled, low cost, English-speaking manpower, and the time difference between India and the US. At the same time, it is important to enquire into the role of state and industry associations such as NASSCOM[6] in facilitating the observed growth performance. While the cost of ICT and software manpower in India is much lower than in developed economies, it is much higher than the prevailing wage rate in other sectors in India. More importantly, the salaries of software personnel have been growing at a rate of 25–30 per cent per annum (Kumar, 2001). This has to be viewed against the backdrop of growing world demand, on the one hand, and excess demand for software personnel, on the other.

Import intensity

So far we have been dealing with gross exports. However, in economies with balance of payment problems, policy-makers are concerned more with net exports. Hence, let us examine the trend in net export earning as revealed from the firm level data provided by the Centre for Monitoring the Indian Economy (hereafter CMIE), the only source from which reliable import data are available.[7] At the outset, it needs to be noted that the argument of net export earning should not be stretched too far because our analysis is based only on a sample of firms. Second, from a macroeconomic perspective, it is not necessary that each sector in an economy is a net export earner. Table 4.2 presents the details of the number of firms as well as their mean export and import. From the table it is also evident that the total export from the sample of firms increased from Rs1240 million in 1992–3 to over Rs145 303 million in 2000–1. At the same time, imports also recorded a commensurate increase. The result has been that the import per rupee of exports remained around 60 paise till 1996–7. There has been a decline in the import intensity after 1996–7 to reach a level of 44 paise per rupee in 1998–9. In 1999–2000 there has been a marginal increase in import intensity and it has stabilized at that level of 48 for the last two years. If the data presented in Table 4.2 are any indication, one could safely conclude that the recent decline in import intensity notwithstanding, the net export earning from India's software export is not more than 52 per cent of the gross exports.

Table 4.2   Trend in export, import and import export ratio for a sample of software firms

Year	Total exports	Total imports	Import export ratio
1992–93 (20)	1 243.4	751.8	0.60
1993–94 (34)	2 532.8	1 463.1	0.58
1994–95 (59)	4 297.0	2 383.5	0.55
1995–96 (74)	6 672.7	4 122.5	0.62
1996–97 (87)	8 943.2	5 395.7	0.60
1997–98 (115)	18 404.5	9 607.0	0.52
1998–99 (155)	34 265.2	15 085.3	0.44
1999–00 (238)	84 371.3	41 102.6	0.48
2000–01 (217)	145 303.4	69 027.7	0.48

Note: Total exports and imports are given in Rs million, figures in the brackets show the number of firms in the sample.

Source: Estimates based on PROWESS, Centre for Monitoring Indian Economy.

3. State initiatives

In the light of the discussion so far, we shall now proceed to explore the role of the state in facilitating the recorded growth performance and the innovative behaviour of firms. There is a point of view, prevalent at least in some quarters, that the dynamism in the software export sector is an outcome of 'benign neglect' rather than active, strategic support by the state (Kattuman and Iyer, 2001). To test the veracity of this argument and, more importantly, to place the forthcoming discussion in a proper perspective, we begin with an overview of the various state initiatives towards the development of the software industry in India. These initiatives ranged from a series of policy measures to active institutional interventions.

Policy measures

Contrary to popular and scholarly perceptions and analysis, the importance of promoting software development, particularly for export, had been recognized by the erstwhile Department of Electronics (hereafter DoE), and suitable policies and programmes were put in place as far back as 1972. An important element of the policy was permitting import of computer systems on a custom-duty-free basis provided the computer importing companies signed a bond that they would export twice the CIF value of the imported computers within a specified period. Another element of that policy was encouraging 100 per cent foreign-owned companies to set up software export operations provided they were located in the Santa Cruz Electronics Export Processing Zone (Government of India, 1972). Later, in January 1982, a software export promotion policy was initiated by the DoE (Government of India, 1982). However, the direct attention of policy-makers to the importance of software as a major export earner came about only with the PC revolution in the early 1980s.

The Computer Policy of 1984 gave a further thrust to software development. For example, the policy called for the setting up of a separate Software Development Promotion Agency (SDPA) under the DoE. Imports of inputs needed for software development were liberalized. Computer production rose phenomenally after 1984 leading to a rationalization of the policy for import and manufacture of software, and using this base for promoting software exports. At the same time, world trade in computers was expected to be of the magnitude of US$100 billion by 1990, of which over half was estimated to be in terms of software (Government of India, 1986). The seventh plan had a software export target of US$300 million, accounting for about 0.6 per cent of the world trade in software. Accordingly, in 1986 an explicit software policy was announced and software was identified as one of the key sectors in India's agenda for export promotion.

With the initiation of economic reforms in the early 1990s, an assessment was made by the finance ministry that, apart from the general orientation of all industries towards export markets, India's comparative advantage in the IT sector was in software and not hardware. Accordingly, new policy measures were initiated, which included inter alia: abolition of entry barriers for foreign companies, measures to make available faster and cheaper data communication facilities, and reduction and rationalization of taxes, duties and tariffs[8] (Narayana Murthy, 2000).

Along with the policy measures initiated by the central government, most state governments also enacted IT policies with a view to promoting software. These policies generally focus on the key issues of infrastructure, electronic governance, IT education and provision of a facilitating environment.

Institutional interventions

In addition, the government also undertook certain institutional interventions. No less than four major national task forces have studied all aspects of IT over 1998–2001, and most of their recommendations, particularly those relating to software exports, have been acted upon by the government.[9] More significantly, the chief executives of leading private sector software companies have been fully involved with these task forces. A number of government agencies involved in different aspects of ICT were brought together in an integrated Ministry of Information Technology. This was followed by an IT Act to deal with the wide variety of issues relating to the IT industry (Parthasarathi, 2001).

A notable institutional intervention has been the establishment of software technology parks[10] (STP) to provide the necessary infrastructure for software export. The first ones to come into being were those at Pune, Bangalore and Bhubaneshwar in 1990. In 1991, four more STPs were set up by the DoE at Noida, Gandhinagar, Trivandrum and Hyderabad.[11] As of now, there are eighteen STPs in different parts of the country, and the companies registered with them account for about 68 per cent of the export of software from India. The infrastructure facilities available at these STPs include, among other things, modern computers and communication networks that are beyond the reach of individual firms. The STPs also have a transparent policy environment, and a package of financial and regulatory concessions.

Measures to address skill bottleneck

While the policy measures and the setting up of the STPs have led to a substantial increase in the investment for software exports (Ventakesh, 1995), the supply of technical personnel appeared to be a major constraint (Schware, 1987; Sen, 1995). Software development is a skill-intensive activity, although the intensity of the skill requirement varies across different activities in software production. The development of software involves broadly the following stages: requirement specification, prototyping, designing, coding, testing and maintenance. While the first few stages require highly skilled manpower (person power to use a gender-neutral term), the skill requirement is relatively low in the later stages (Schware, 1987).

Traditionally, the principal sources of ICT and software professionals have been the public sector education institutes such as the IITs (Indian institutes of technology), engineering colleges and ITIs (industrial training institutes). To facilitate the entry of the private sector in training software personnel, the DoE initiated the accreditation scheme based on certain objective criteria.[12] In consequence, a large number of private organizations were set up to provide training for durations ranging from three weeks to a year or even more. Available estimates show that in 1999 there were over 1832 private educational institutions that trained over 68 000 computer software professionals that year (NASSCOM, 1999). The structure of the current out-turn of technical manpower from these institutes indicates that three categories – BTechs, diploma holders and ITI certificate holders – account for nearly 70 per cent of the total (Table 4.3), BTechs accounting for as much as 24 per cent. The share of MTechs and PhD holders is only 3.14 and 0.14 per cent respectively.

From the above discussion, it is evident that any international competitiveness and credibility software firms have been able to establish over the years has not entirely been the handiwork of prophets of the market. Rather, a series of state initiatives taken on a systematic and sustained basis have played a significant role. The form and content of state intervention has, however, changed since 1991–2. The role of the state during this phase has been that of a facilitator of private sector initiatives with a concomitant reduction in the role of the state as a direct participant. Moreover, the focus of the state initiatives has been primarily on promoting the software sector as a foreign exchange earner rather than as in the 1980s as a foreign

Table 4.3 Structure of the outturn of software manpower (1999)

Course	Number	Per cent
PhD	95	0.14
MTech	2 130	3.14
BTech	16 160	23.84
MSc	2 800	4.13
BSc	3 200	4.72
BCA/MCA	7 700	11.36
PG. Diploma	6 000	7.38
Diploma	16 700	24.64
ITI	14 000	20.65
Total	68 785	100

Source: NASSCOM (1999).

exchange saver. However, what seems to have been missed out in the obsessively export-oriented strategy pursued in the 1990s is a concerted effort to diffuse and apply what one might call the 'New IT' (that is, PC server and portal-based IT) into core sectors of the domestic economy. Thus, it appears that under the influence of strong export demand for low end software services generated by the OECD countries, and particularly the US, the role of the huge domestic market, both to meet domestic needs and as a springboard for export seems to have been discounted by policy-makers, industry, industry associations like NASSCOM and the media.

4. Innovative behaviour under export orientation

The role of innovation in sustaining long-run competitiveness and growth in the context of a dynamic sector like software cannot be over-emphasized. The process of innovation in turn, inter alia involves the ability to develop new products/processes/systems, new markets and new organizations. Generally, innovation is specific to each country, and hence the process that governs the dynamics of innovation in a developing economy is inherently different from that of developed countries. In a general sense, innovation in a developing economy is viewed as an outcome of the combined effect of both the transfer and generation of technologies. The technology transfer could be either from external or domestic sources. It may take either an embodied (in capital goods) or disembodied form (technical drawings, source codes and the like). It has been argued that the technology transferred from an industrialized country is often not suited to local conditions in a developing country and has to be adapted to the local environment. Moreover, it is generally understood that the strategic technologies (those that, scientifically or technically, have large spread effects and are complex and sophisticated, or have backward and forward linkages) are R&D- and IPR-intensive. What is more, such state of the art technologies are very often also not available from the international technology market. All these considerations necessitate domestic R&D effort, both in order to adapt imported technology to local conditions and to develop altogether new technologies. The development of technologies may be carried out either by the firms through their own in-house R&D effort and/or through an interface with or contract between the companies concerned and the academia or the R&D system in the country, or through global links such as partnerships, collaboration, OEM subcontracts and the like (Basant and Chandra, Chapter 8; Saxenian, Chapter 7; and Sridharan, Chapter 2). Given the large number of non-resident Indians (hereafter NRIs) abroad, it is also likely that the industry draws on such NRIs to enhance their innovative capacity.[13] In the discussion that follows we examine some of the components of innovative effort in the context of software.

Technology import

Our analysis of technology import is based on the Department of Scientific and Industrial Research (hereafter DSIR) dataset on foreign collaborations in India. At the outset, it may be noted that the DSIR database provides information on foreign collaboration approvals and not actuals. Therefore, the conclusions drawn may be treated as indicative only.

It is found that the number of foreign collaborations in the software sector increased from eight in 1991 to 262 in 1999. The share in the total number of collaborations increased from 0.8 per cent to about 12 per cent during the last decade. While there was hardly any financial collaboration in 1991, their number increased to 197 in 1999. In line with the economy-wide trend, almost 75 per cent of the collaborations have involved foreign equity (Table 4.4).

In terms of the country-wise distribution, the US accounted for over 40 per cent of the collaborations in 1999, and it was found that over 43 per cent of those for the period as a whole (1991–9) stemmed from there. This is in contrast to 20 per cent of collaborations from the US for the economy as a whole in the 1990s. Table 4.5 also reveals that the share of all the other countries put together accounts for only about 35 per cent. The regional concentration of foreign collaborations may be viewed in the context of the domination of the US in ICT technologies. It might also be seen as a strategy of Indian firms to gain access to the US market which is the largest in the world.

It has been found that about 58 per cent of graduates in computer science from the Indian Institute of Technology (IIT), Chennai, migrated abroad during 1964–86 (IAMR, 2000). It has also been argued that IT and software export has benefited immensely from the presence of a substantial number of Indians working in US companies (Lateef, 1997). In this connection, it

Table 4.4   Trend in the number of foreign collaborations
in IT software and services

Year	Technical	Financial	Total
1991	Nil	8	8
1992	7 (19.4)	29	36
1993	12 (29.3)	29	41
1995	16 (21.3)	59	75
1996	14 (13.2)	92	106
1997	20 (15.3)	111	131
1998	34 (25.4)	100	134
1999	65 (24.8)	197	262
Total	168 (21.2)	625	793

Note: Figures in the parentheses show share in total. Data for 1994
were not available to us.

Source: Department of Scientific and Industrial Research (DSIR),
Foreign Collaboration: a Compilation (various years) (New Delhi:
Ministry of Science and Technology).

Table 4.5   Country-wise distribution in the number
of foreign collaborations

Year	NRI	USA	Others	Total
1991	0	2	6	8
1992	4	18	14	36
1993	6	23	12	41
1995	10	39	26	75
1996	10	48	48	106
1997	11	51	69	131
1998	27	57	50	134
1999	45	106	121	262
Total	113	344	336	793

Source: Department of Scientific and Industrial Research
(DSIR), *Foreign Collaboration: a Compilation*, various years.

may be of some relevance to look at the extent of collaborations involving
NRIs. The number of such collaborations increased from a mere four in 1992
to forty-five in 1999, accounting for 17 per cent of the total number of collaborations approved by the government (Table 4.5).

However, such an analysis purely in terms of the number of foreign collaborations has severe limitations. Hence, let us look at the extent of equity
participation by the NRIs. While NRIs accounted for a substantial number
of collaborations, their share in the total foreign direct investment still
remains negligible. Thus, it appears that while the NRIs have an immense

potential to help boost the Indian software sector, this source is yet to be fully tapped. If the experience of China, which has been successful in attracting substantial investment from the overseas Chinese (see Saxenian, Chapter 7), is any indication, an enquiry into the ways and means of promoting investment and technology flows from NRIs is bound to provide rich dividends. As in the case of the number of foreign collaborations, the US accounts for over 47 per cent of the total FDI in the software sector in 1999.

As we have already stated, given the obsessively export-oriented growth strategy adopted in the 1990s, restrictions on the inflow of FDI as well as the extent of foreign equity participation have almost been done away with. It may therefore be of relevance to examine the extent of foreign control over the decade. Table 4.6 presents data on the distribution of foreign equity participation. It is evident that there has been a substantial increase in the number of 100 per cent export-oriented units. Their share increased from about 25 per cent in the early years of this decade to over 50 per cent in 1999. Also, the share of collaborations involving more than 50 per cent equity participation increased from 50 per cent in 1991 to reach a level of about 80 per cent in 1999.

An interesting aspect of foreign technology transfer (collaborations) agreements concluded over the 1990s in the software sector relates to the terms under which the collaborations were entered into. Unlike other industries, the incidence of royalty and lump sum payments has been found to be minimal, and over time the share of cases involving neither royalty nor lump sum has increased (Table 4.7). This may be viewed against the widely prevalent practice of costing adopted in the offshore projects which is the dominant form of ICT exports. A common practice of pricing in the offshore projects is the 'cost plus pricing' in which the client provides to the exporting firm a margin over the cost involved in 'time and materials' (Arora and Asundi, 1999). Hence, for the foreign firm it is important that the local firm

Table 4.6   Distribution of foreign equity participation

Year	<10	10–25	25–50	>50	100	Total
1991	0	1	3	4	2	8
1992	1	1	8	19	6	29
1993	1	1	2	25	14	29
1995	4	3	11	41	22	59
1996	2	4	11	75	34	92
1997	3	5	13	90	45	111
1998	0	3	2	97	71	102
1999	7	11	23	158	106	199

Source: Department of Scientific and Industrial Research (DSIR), *Foreign Collaboration: a Compilation*, various years.

Table 4.7   Terms of foreign collaborations

Year	*Percentage of cases involving*			
	Only royalty	Only lump sum	Both	Neither
1991	12.5	12.5	0	75
1992	11.1	2.8	0	86.1
1993	0	7.3	4.9	87.8
1995	2.7	6.7	1.3	89.3
1996	2.8	2.8	1.8	92.6
1997	2.3	0.8	0.8	96.1
1998	0	2.2	0	97.8
1999	7.3	0.8	0	91.9

Source: Department of Scientific and Industrial Research (DSIR), *Foreign Collaboration: a Compilation*, various years.

does not overstate the 'time and material cost'. In order to obviate the possibility of overcharging, the foreign firms might find it advantageous to have an equity stake so that issues of overcharging and shirking do not arise. Therefore, many of those cases involving neither royalty nor lump sum may not entail any significant transfer of technology.

What is intriguing is that unlike the common practice in which the royalty rate is higher for exports than domestic sales, in the case of software we find that the royalty rate in most cases is higher for domestic sales. (Details of such foreign collaboration agreements approved in 1999 are given in Table 4.8.) We have not been able to find a satisfactory explanation for this phenomenon. However, as this is the first case in which we have come across such 'inverted' royalty rates, we propose to investigate this matter further in our future research. In the meantime, we are inclined to infer that as of now the foreign firms, in their attempt to enter India's large domestic market, are using licensing agreements as means of erecting entry barriers to prevent Indian firms entering the domestic market. This is indeed a cause of considerable concern, particularly in the current context in which there is an imperative to develop and exploit the domestic market.

In-house R&D effort

Now let us turn to the other side of the coin: in-house research and development. In a skill-intensive sector like IT software and services, it is likely that many firms may be carrying out R&D as an important normal activity even if there is no division designated exclusively for it. However, given the fact that some of the firms engaged in value added services and development of software products, like Infosys, Tata Infotech and Satyam, have reported R&D expenditure, it may be instructive to examine the extent of R&D activity so that some inferences, though tentative, may be drawn.

Table 4.8   Details of foreign collaborations approved in 1999 involving higher royalty rate for domestic sales than for exports

Local firm	Foreign firm	Royalty on domestic sales (%)	Royalty on exports (%)
ASB Infotech Pvt Ltd, Mumbai	Patrick Clinton, USA	2	1.5
Altar Consultancy Pvt Ltd, Chennai	Martin Vomstein, Germany	5	2
Baroc Technologies Pvt Ltd, Pune	Joost Derlamans, Switzerland	7.5	5
Cybernet Sustems Inc, New Delhi	Cybernet Sustems Inc, USA	5	2
Magic Software Enterprises, Pune	Magic Software Enterprises, Israel	7	5
Maxion Systems Pvt Ltd, Cochin	Maxion Systems Inc, USA	7	5
Microwave Systems & Components Pvt Ltd, Bangalore	Conserv Inc, USA	2	1
Natural Bleach Earths Pvt Ltd, Hyderabad	Natural Bleach SDNBHD, Malaysia	5	2
Network Solutions Pvt Ltd, Bangalore	Intel Pacific Inc, USA	5	2
Premium Power Software Ltd, Mumbai	Draper India International Inc, Mauritius	5	2
Rediff Communication Pvt Ltd, Mumbai	Queenswood Investment Ltd, Mauritius	2	1.5
ST-CMS Electric Company Pvt Ltd, Chennai	CMS generation Neyveli Ltd, Mauritius	2	1.5
Satyam Ge Software Service Pvt Ltd, Hyderabad	Ge Pacific (Mauririus) Ltd	7	5
Srishti Communications Pvt Ltd, New Delhi	Ritu Mehta, Spain	7	5
Staffing Solution India Pvt Ltd, New Delhi	John Kevin Kopra, USA	5	2
Sunram Systems India Pvt Ltd	Sunram Systems Inc, Canada	7	5

Source: Department of Scientific and Industrial Research (DSIR), *Foreign Collaboration: a Compilation,* various years.

To examine the R&D activity of firms we have made use of the CMIE database. At this point a few remarks about this database may be relevant. The CMIE data are drawn from the annual reports of the companies incorporated in India, and most of these are listed in the Indian stock exchanges. The disclosure norms under the Indian Companies Act, as periodically amended, require companies to report all heads of expenditure that account for over 1 per cent of their turnover. If the R&D expenditure is less than 1 per cent of the turnover, it is up to the management to decide whether or not to report it separately. Hence, when a company does not report R&D expenditure, the only inference that one can draw is that its R&D expenditure is less than 1 per cent of the turnover. It is likely that at least some of the firms not reporting R&D might be undertaking R&D, but as the expenditure is less than 1 per cent of their turnover they have decided not to report it.

Table 4.9 presents information on the number of firms reporting R&D, their R&D expenditure and R&D intensity (R&D expenditure as a proportion of sales) in the private corporate sector firms. It may be noted that, notwithstanding the substantial growth in the number of firms, there has not been any corresponding increase in their innovative effort in terms of the number of firms reporting R&D or their R&D intensity. R&D intensity for the industry as a whole remained at less than 1 per cent for all the years under consideration. It may, however, be noted that in the case of those firms performing R&D, their R&D intensity increased from a little over 2 per cent in 1997–8 to nearly 7 per cent in 1999–2000. However, the number of such firms undertaking R&D was found to be only seventeen out of a sample of 217. Such firms have been increasingly engaged in developing new software products with higher value addition (see Krishnan and Prabhu,Chapter 6). Hence, on the basis of the available evidence, we are inclined to infer that the export-oriented strategy has not induced the firms to substantially increase their investment in research and development. This perhaps points towards the nature and composition of export demand, in which the task assigned to the Indian firms by the foreign counterparts did not require any R&D effort.

It may be noted here that a range of complex (often state-of-the-art) software packages has been developed and successfully used in the domestic market, largely at the instance of public sector units. These encompass both stand-alone application packages and packages forming parts of complete

Table 4.9 Profile R&D effort in IT and software service sector

Year	Sample size	Firms reporting R&D (number)	R&D (Rs million)	R&D intensity
1997–98	115	9	213.44	2.03 (0.17)
1998–99	155	14	244.28	2.82 (0.63)
1999–00	238	16	703.29	6.82 (0.49)
2000–01	217	17	763.19	4.91 (0.39)

Note: R&D intensity is for the firms reporting R&D and figures in the brackets show R&D intensity for the industry as a whole.

Source: CMIE, PROWESS database.

systems. Many of these systems, incorporating such packages, have also been exported. What is significant about such exports is that they have originated largely from public sector companies or R&D institutions. They have been in frontier areas of IT applications, for example, major port automation, airport automation, automation and management of international sporting events, and telecommunications, both switching and transmission. The exporting firms involved in these areas are quite different from the 'standard pack' of Infosys, Wipro or Satyam. They are public sector companies like CMC, RITES, TCIL, Bharat Electronics and Electronics Corporation of India Ltd (ECIL) and private sector firms like Shyam Telecom, Larsen & Toubro, and Cromption Greaves. CMC is the company which undertook the IT-based automation system of Felixstowe port in the UK (having cut its teeth on a similar job on Nhava-Sheva port near Mumbai), Bremerhaven port in Germany, and part of Rotterdam port in Holland. It has also been responsible for the airport runway lighting control system at Changi airport, Singapore, and the air traffic control systems at the same world-class airport. To this, one may add the complete automation of the Mediterranean Games in Damascus and a project on the ticketing of the London Underground. These projects were won against stiff international competition and were multi-million dollar systems. What is more, each involved substantial value addition, hardware content, and deep software development, installation, commissioning, training, and considerable revenue from after sales support and maintenance (CMC, Annual Reports, various years).[14]

While these were under way, another group of some fifteen firms in both the public and private sectors, specializing in telecom, licensed the highly software intensive manufacturing know-how for the Centre for Development of Telematics (C-DoT) digital electronic switching systems and set up large manufacturing systems plants based on them. For a four-year period from April 1996 to March 2000, these fifteen firms supplied the equivalent of around $2 billion of goods and services to the Department of Telecommunication (now Bharat Telecom Nigam Ltd). This was done against stiff global competition from several telecom TNCs including Alcatel, Fujitsu, Ericsson and Nortel. The Indian firms secured around 65 per cent of the total number of lines tendered because their bids were 30 per cent cheaper than those of the TNCs. In consequence, of the approximately 32 million telecom lines in the national network by the end of March 2000, some 50 per cent were those supplied by C-DoT licensee companies. What is more, the fifteen C-DoT licensees had over the same period also exported millions of such wireless lines to around twelve countries, including the established markets of TNCs such as Saudi Arabia[15] (C-DoT, Annual Reports, various years in the 1990s).

While this development was taking place in the switching area, the joint R&D programme of IIT, Chennai with M/s Analogue Devices, USA, on the one hand (for the microchips needed), and with four national telecom manufacturers, on the other – ECIL and BEL in the public sector and Shyam

Electronics and Cromption Greaves Ltd in the private sector – has led to the large-scale licensing of the jointly developed Wireless in Local Loop (WILL) based telecom technology (trade marked Cordect) to companies in seven countries, including China, South Korea and Taiwan, at a licence fee of $2 million plus substantial royalty payments for 15–18 years (C-DoT Annual Reports, various years in the 1990s). What is more, in a tender for the manufacture and supply of one million such wireless lines floated by the Malaysian Telecom Authority two years ago, the designated Indian licensee company, ECIL, emerged as the lowest price, technically compliant bidder for a $400 million tender. The second lowest bidder was Alcatel of France, 7.8 per cent higher in price than ECIL![16]

Academia–ICT industry partnerships

Traditionally, industry in general has had low levels of interaction with academia in India. However, the new economic policy of 1991, which emphasized competition and globalization, forced the firms to be technologically dynamic. At the same time, the progressive devaluation of the rupee has made securing foreign technical and knowledge inputs (particularly technology in disembodied form and technical services) progressively more and more expensive for the industry. Concurrently, government policy has placed increasing emphasis on academic institutions earning higher shares of their financial requirements from industry through contract research, training, etc. These two factors have led to growing academia–industry collaboration and partnerships, particularly during the second half of the 1990s (Basant and Chandra, Chapter 8).

The software sector has taken a lead in this. It is using academic faculty as consultants, placing R&D contracts with institutions and using them for specialized training. The respective roles of the two types of actors have been broadly along the following lines:

Educational institutions

- increase industrial awareness among students through faculty and the nature and content of the curriculum;
- allocate appropriate resources, especially faculty and students, to make the partnership effective;
- provide a platform in the academic environment for industry as spokesperson; and
- realize the results of projects and investigate research problems perceived by industry.

Industry

- recognize and allocate resources for providing inputs to academic institutions, especially subject matter experts in technologies and domains, hardware/software infrastructure, books and periodicals;

- identify senior corporate mangers and subject matter experts to teach on sabbatical in academic institutions;
- develop programmes for faculty, especially in new and emerging technologies;
- invite faculty members for relevant knowledge sharing sessions/training programmes conducted in-house; and
- provide all possible assistance during curriculum and syllabus development, mainly relating to advanced technologies.

While no formal study on the precise number of such partnerships is available, there is considerable circumstantial evidence that it is occurring across a broad front. For example, the major telecom and computer group Bharati Telecom has become the first Indian corporate to fully fund a school for Telecom and Management Studies at IIT, Delhi. The Kanwal Rekhi School of Information Technology at IIT, Mumbai, has also recently become operational. (Rekhi is a non-resident Indian in Silicon Valley.) The Usha Martin Academy of Communication Technology (UACT) has been set up as a joint venture between Usha Martin Infotech and IIT, Chennai. Table 4.10 indicates the profile of sponsored research projects and consultancy in information technology at IIT, Delhi, undertaken over the last five years. Such project assignments apart, several major ICT companies, both domestic and foreign, have set up complete laboratories and R&D centres at the IITs.

5. Determinants of innovative performance: an empirical analysis

In this section we deal with one of the basic issues addressed in this chapter: has the export-oriented growth strategy been instrumental in enhancing the innovative performance of the software sector? It has been argued that liberal economic policies associated with export orientation facilitate technological advancement and hence faster growth of output. Studies on the dynamic effects of technological change, learning and growth have

Table 4.10 Sponsored research projects and consultancy undertaken by IIT Delhi

Year	Sponsored research ($ mill)	Consultancy ($ mill)
1994–95	1.10	0.3
1995–96	1.60	0.5
1996–97	1.70	0.9
1997–98	4.10	1.0
1998–99	3.50	1.0

Source: IIT, Delhi, *Annual Reports*, various years. Also see Ishani Datta Gupta, 'Back to School', *Economic Times*, New Delhi, 23 July 2000.

generally taken three different approaches: (a) firm level case studies (for example, Lall, 1987 for India and Katz, 1987 for Latin America); (b) cross-industry studies (Subrahmanian, 1988; Katrak, 1989; Deolalikar and Evenson, 1989; Siddharthan, 1988); and (c) cross-country studies.[17] While the literature in this area is enormous and still growing, Rodrik (1995) states that the analytical foundations of most studies have been too ambiguous and the preferred method of proof ranges from casual appeal to common sense. Yet, we are living in a world in which export-oriented policies have been religiously pursued as a panacea to most problems being faced by the developing world even in the case of big emerging markets (BEMs) such as India and China. In this context, the relevance of empirical verification of the issue raised above cannot be over-emphasized.

As a primary step towards the empirical analysis, we have to address the issue of defining innovative performance. It has been generally acknowledged in the literature that the primary manifestation of innovative performance is the improvement in productivity. Productivity could be defined either in terms of partial productivity (output per unit of any of the inputs like labour or capital) or total factor productivity. In this chapter, given the human capital-intensive nature of the process involved, we measure innovative performance in terms of labour productivity (output per unit of labour employed).

The influence of an export-oriented strategy is measured in terms of the following variables:

- export intensity, measured in terms of the proportion of output that is exported;
- import intensity, measured in terms of the ratio of total imports to sales;
- foreign collaboration dummy which takes the value one for those firms having foreign collaboration and zero for those having no foreign collaboration; and
- MNC dummy, which takes the value one if the foreign equity share is more than 10 per cent and zero otherwise. (This is in line with IMF classification.)

Going by the theoretical premises of an export-oriented growth strategy, all these variables are hypothesized to have a positive effect on innovative performance. In terms of the theoretical premises of the Structure–Conduct–Performance paradigm,[18] innovative performance (here labour productivity) is, however, affected by a number of other firm-specific, industry-specific and economy-wide factors. Given the fact that we are dealing with a cross-section of firms operating in one specific industry, the industry-specific and economy-wide factors are assumed to be the same for all the firms and, therefore, are not taken into account in our analysis. What follows is a brief description of other firm-specific factors incorporated in the analysis.

In the innovation literature in the neo-Schumpeterian tradition, firm size is generally considered as having positive influence on the innovative performance of firms. Nelson and Winter (1982) have justified the positive effect of firm size on the ground that larger firms are better able to appropriate the returns from their innovative activity. However, in the empirical literature we find hardly any consensus on this issue. Detailed review of empirical studies (Cohen, 1995; Kumar and Siddharthan, 1997) on the innovative activity and innovative performance of firms have reported mixed results. In the Indian context, earlier studies have reported a positive effect of firm size on the innovative activity of firms (e.g. Lall, 1983; Katrak, 1985). A few studies also reported an inverted U-shaped relationship between firm size and innovation (Siddharthan, 1988). Literature also provides empirical evidence of a cubic relationship with two thresholds acting on the firm size and innovation (Kumar and Aggarwal, 2000). In our dataset also, which covers a wide range of firm size, the relationship might be characterized by two thresholds. Hence, while postulating a positive relationship between firm size and innovative performance, quadratic and cubic terms are included to capture possible non-linearities. In this study, firm size is measured in terms of the sales turnover of the firms.

The role of R&D in promoting innovative performance is very obvious. Therefore, we have also incorporated R&D intensity (R&D as a proportion of sales) in the model. In a skill-intensive industry like software, one could postulate a positive relationship between innovative performance and the skill profile of the firms. However, the available dataset does not permit us to define skill profile with precision in terms of the academic qualifications and experience of the employees. Given the available dataset, we measure the ratio of software employees to total employees as a proxy for skill intensity. We hypothesize a positive relationship between innovative performance and skill intensity. As in the case of size, one could also expect a non-linear relationship between innovative performance and skill. To test for the existence of any non-linear relationship we have included a square term in the estimated model. We have also included the age of the firms to discern the possible effect of accumulated experience. Finally, following Siddharthan (1988), we have incorporated the ratio of selling cost to sales to highlight the influence of sales effort.

The influence of the different variables identified above has been empirically verified using the following regression equation:

$$\text{Productivity} = a_0 + a_1 \text{export Intensity} + a_2 \text{import Intensity} + a_3 \text{colldum}$$
$$+ a_4 \text{mncdum} + a_5 \text{size} + a_6 \text{size}^2 + a_7 \text{size}^3 + a_8 \text{skill}$$
$$+ a_9 \text{skill}^2 + a_{10} \text{sellingcost} + a_{11} \text{age} + \text{error term.}$$

The regression equation above has been estimated by using the new dataset that we have developed by merging the NASSCOM and CMIE data set for four years (from 1997–8 to 2000–1). The unbalanced panel that we have obtained consists of 262 observations. The distribution of firms across different years is as follows: 50 firms for the year 1997–8, 59 for 1998–9, 84 for 1999–2000, and 69 firms for 2000–1.

Results of the model

Table 4.11 presents the results of the estimated model. The relatively high R^2 and the statistically significant F value reflect the robustness of the model.

To begin with, the estimated model reveals that none of the coefficients of its variables representing export orientation is statistically significant. Export intensity, the most important variable in the model, has a positive sign but is not statistically significant. This tends to suggest that export orientation has no significant bearing on the innovative performance of the firms.[19] Thus the nature of export demand does not seem to be conducive to inducing the firms to be more innovative. This goes well with our finding on the emerging structure of software exports reported in the first section and the observation made by earlier studies. It has been observed that the comparative advantage of Indian firms has been in the export of services such as customized software development, with very few well-known products of proprietary packages in the international market (Arora and Asundi, 1999). Here again, the focus of the Indian firms is at the lower end of the value chain, on low design, coding and maintenance (Kattuman and Iyer, 2001). Thus, the Indian ICT and software services sector competes primarily

Table 4.11 Results of the regression model on the determinants of innovative performance

Variables	Estimated coefficients	
Export intensity	0.00474	(0.308)
Import Intensity	0.01397	(0.609)
Collaboration dummy	0.00543	(0.460)
MNC dummy	−0.01695	(−1.015)
Size	0.00099	(8.760)*
Size^2	−5.45e−07	(−4.963)*
Size^3	9.77e−11	(3.753)*
Selling cost	−0.26001	(−2.671)*
R&D intensity	−0.12976	(−0.696)
Age	−0.00002	(−1.145)
Skill	−0.00011	(−6.169)*
Skill^2	6.97e−09	(2.717)*
Constant	0.92644	(8.509)*
Number of observations	262	
Adjusted R^2	0.3423	
F	10.80	

Note: Figures in the brackets show t values.
* Indicates statistical significance at 1 per cent level.

on cost advantage with very limited innovation capacity (Mahajan, 2000). The empirical evidence, therefore, points to the need for a greater focus on the domestic market to promote innovative performance on the part of the software industry where opportunities for much higher revenue per employee exist.

Among the other variables incorporated to reflect on the influence of an export-oriented growth strategy, import intensity is found to have a positive sign but is not statistically significant. The coefficient of a MNC dummy has a negative sign but is again not statistically significant. Similarly, the coefficient of a collaboration dummy, though positive, is not statistically significant. The result thus indicates that greater outward orientation or increased import of both embodied and disembodied technology and foreign participation is not likely to have any significant bearing on the innovation performance of software firms.

Among the firm-specific variables, size, selling cost and skill intensity have proved to be statistically significant. In the case of size, it appears that there is a non-linear relationship. A cubic relationship (horizontal S-shape) is found to be a good fit for the sample. While the coefficient of size is positive, that of $size^2$ is negative and $size^3$ positive. This tends to suggest that very small firms have very low innovative performance, but that the innovative performance increases with firm size up to a threshold beyond which it declines up to another threshold before rising again with size. To illustrate, some of the largest firms like Infosys and Wipro are found to record much higher labour productivity levels than very small firms (sales $<$ \$200 000) in the sample. The relationship between skill and productivity is also found to be a non-linear, U-shaped relationship. Given the fact that skill is defined in terms of the proportion of software employees, the decline in productivity might point towards the presence of the number of medium-sized firms mostly engaged in data entry type of activities where the labour productivity is lower but employment is higher. Here again, firms with large software employment are found to have higher productivity. The negative influence of selling cost may be viewed against the current structure of exports in which software services, especially on-site services, still have a significant and declining share of software products and packages. Selling cost is relevant largely in the case of software products. It has been noted that in the case of high value added software products, large multinational companies dominate the market and spend up to 60–65 per cent of the price component of packages on marketing and distribution (Kumar, 2001).

The estimated model also shows that age does not have any significant influence on innovative performance. Perhaps, in a highly dynamic area like ICT and software, in which the product lifecycle is very short, older firms may not have any comparative advantage as against the new ones. The coefficient of R&D intensity also proved to be statistically not significant. This, as we have already noted, has to be viewed against the fact that there are

only a very few firms that are engaged in R&D, and even their R&D intensity is not very high.

6. Conclusion: towards a perspective

Given the manifold ways in which information technology can contribute
to human welfare, developing countries have invested in information and
communication technologies as a short cut to prosperity (UNDP, 1997;
World Bank, 1999). India is, in fact, one of the pioneering developing countries to undertake a series of initiatives to promote the software sector. These
efforts seem to have paid rich dividends in terms of the sector emerging as
one of the vibrant components in India's export basket and accounting for
as much as 20 per cent of total exports. Moreover, India has been able to
establish credibility in international ICT markets, which appears unique
when compared to most of the other items in India's export basket. Higher
growth rates in total exports notwithstanding, there have been substantial
imports associated with software exports. Our study observed that the net
export earning has been substantially lower and not more than 52 per cent
of gross exports. It has also been observed that the present structure of
exports is one in which the software service sub-sector dominates and the
share of software products, with higher net export earnings and value addition, is almost negligible, and even that has shown a decline in recent years.
Given the fact that innovative capacity is a key factor in enabling the firms
to move up the value chain and taking our current comparative advantage
to new heights, an attempt has been made in this chapter to analyse the
innovation behaviour of our firms and their performance.

We have argued that the international competitiveness and credibility, if
any, that the ICT and software service sector has been able to establish over
the years, have not fallen like manna from heaven. As A. K. Sen (1983: 752)
puts it in the context of the South Korean performance in the 1970s: 'if this
is a free market, then Walras's auctioneer can be surely be seen as going
round with a government white paper in the one had and a whip in the
other'. The point we make is that the series of state initiatives have played
an important role in the Indian software sector. The policy measures and the
other initiatives of the 1990s have been overtly export-oriented and the role
of the domestic market as a springboard for export seems not to have
received adequate attention. Moreover, there appears to have been hardly
any attempt towards enhancing the innovative capability of the firms to
enable them to move up the software value chain.

The innovative behaviour of firms under export orientation has been one
in which they have depended heavily on collaboration with foreign firms.
Here, again, similar to the case with exports, there has been very high
regional concentration, with the US accounting for over 40 per cent of the
total number of foreign collaborations and FDI. NRIs have accounted for

over 17 per cent of the number of collaborations, and their share in total FDI is negligible. Hence, while NRIs have immense potential to help boost the software sector, this source to yet to be fully tapped. It was also found that the recent trend in the terms of collaboration is one in which the royalty rates are higher for sales in the domestic market as compared to export markets. Thus, there appears to be a tendency for foreign collaboration to erect entry barriers to the domestic market! At the same time, going by the available information, there is a growing interface between the software sector and academia, which is expected to earn rich dividends in the near future.

The results of our analysis of the determinants of innovative performance using cross-section data have been highly revealing. None of the variables, specified in the model to represent export orientation, is found to have any statistically significant influence on the innovative performance of firms. Perhaps the nature of export demand, mainly from the OECD countries, especially the US, and the structure of exports that emerged under the export-oriented strategy has been one that did not provide sufficient inducement for the firms to be innovative. This finding tends to underscore the need to recognize the complementary role of the domestic market in export promotion and greater integration of domestic and export production and sales (see also D'Costa, Chapter 3). Indeed, it is encouraging to note that in the recent past, particularly as a result of the downturn of the US economy, both the ICT firms and the government are 'returning' to realize the enormous potential of India's domestic market. This was the market that was the basis of the building up and growth of the ICT industry in the 1980s. Then in the 1990s came the credo, fuelled by globalization, that our domestic market was 'too small' to create and sustain a high growth ICT industry. Now a long overdue and very welcome correction of this serious distortion and imbalance in policies and macro- and microeconomic orientation is coming in. There have been many straws in the wind in both governmental and business circles to this effect. Representative of them is the recent address of Azim Premji, chairman of the Bangalore-based IT company WIPRO, India's second largest company in the field. Premji's entire address focused on the domestic market. He stated: 'If ICT and software services have put India squarely on the global map, they have *a lot more to contribute to industries in India*'[20] (emphasis added).

In the recently finalized tenth five-year plan (2002–3 to 2007–8) the government targets a GDP growth rate of 8 per cent. In government circles there has been a deep concern about the steep reduction in the growth of industrial output: from the eighth plan (1990–1 to 1995–6) average of 10 per cent to an expected ninth plan (1997–8 to 2001–2) average of only 6.5 to 7.0 per cent. The target set for the tenth plan is to raise the rate of growth in the industrial sector to at least the level achieved during the eighth plan. Consequently, heavy investments to expand several core sectors of the industrial economy are projected for the tenth plan.

All these sectors are highly ICT-intensive. For example, ICT-based process control and enterprise resource planning are involved in all the subsectors of the energy sector: coal, oil and gas, and electric power. Telecom, process control, management of pipelines and tank farms, petroleum products distribution, and accounting of billing of product pipelines are all involved in the huge 60 000 km network of pipelines to be set up for which the government has established a massive state-owned company called PETRONET with an initial equity base of $5 billion. The number of telephone lines is to be doubled and another 60 000 km of optical fibre links laid. There are plans to enable tracking of the 12 000 trains and 300 000 wagons on the Indian railways (the largest railway system in the world), including maintenance and repair of wagons so as to minimize delays, turnaround times and wagon 'sickness'. A huge nationwide project called the Freight Operations Information System (FOIS) involving an investment of Rs 350 million ($70 million) is to be completed during the tenth plan on a turnkey basis by the public sector ICT software, services and systems company CMC (formerly Computer Maintenance Corporation). If such a project were to be implemented by a company from North America or Western Europe, it would have cost eight to ten times as much, and that too in hard currency.

The 1990s have seen the ICT inputs into these core sectors of the economy provided overwhelmingly by direct import from the OECD countries or transnational corporations which have set up subsidiaries/joint ventures in India. They have therefore made little, if any, contribution to the demand for ICT software, services and systems, and hence to the employment of ICT personnel oriented to production for the domestic market. A considerable change is now in the offing in the tenth plan, thereby enabling absorption of Indian ICT professionals returning home because they have been laid off in the USA. This should also help in stemming further outflows of such professionals. What is more, these projects will lead to huge savings of foreign exchange. In addition, ICT exports will be enabled to move rapidly towards high value products and systems.

Notes

Originally published in *Science, Technology and Society*, Vol. 7, No. 1 (January–June 2002). Copyright © Society for the Promotion of S & T Studies, New Delhi, 2002. All rights reserved. Reproduced with the permission of the copyright holders and the publishers, Sage Publications India Pvt Ltd, New Delhi.

We have benefited from the helpful comments on an earlier draft by P. K. M. Tharakan and an anonymous referee. Helpful comments and encouragement from Anthony D'Costa and E. Sridharan are also gratefully acknowledged.

1. For a quantitative analysis of the impact of the investments in IT on economic growth in a cross-section of thirty-nine countries, see Pohjola (2002).
2. In the African countries, for example, it is estimated that the number of computers per 1000 population is 0.3. Even in India, the number of computers per 1000 people is only about 1.5, Internet connections only one in ten.

3. This is a statement made by Thabo Mbeki, Vice President of the Republic of South Africa, as quoted in Pohjola (1998).
4. It would have been ideal to convert the export earning into constant prices. In the absence of an appropriate deflator, we are obliged to carry out the analysis at current prices.
5. For a detailed analysis of the trend in software exports during the period prior to 1990, interested readers may refer to Schware (1992), Pronab Sen (1995), Venkatesh (1995), Heeks (1996) and Joseph (1997).
6. For a discussion on the role of NASSCOM in promoting software exports, see Joseph (2002).
7. For detailed discussion on different datasets relating to the Indian software and service sector, see Parthasarathi and Joseph (2002).
8. Mention needs to be made of the substantial reduction in the duties and tariffs across the board for components and sub-assemblies, zero duty on software import, and zero income tax on profits from software exports.
9. The task forces include the national task force on IT, task force on human resource development for IT, task force on knowledge society, and the National Advisory Committee on IT comprising the chief executives of leading IT companies.
10. A Software Technology Park (STP) is in all respects similar to a free trade zone exclusively for software. The specific objectives of the STPs are:

   - to establish and manage the infrastructural resources such as data communication facilities, core computer facilities, built up space, common amenities, etc.;
   - to provide services (import certification, software valuation, project approvals, etc.) to the users who undertake software development for export purposes;
   - to promote development and export of software and software services through technology assessments, market analysis, marketing support, etc.; and
   - to train professionals and to encourage design and development in the field of software technology and software engineering (Government of India, 1995).

11. In 1991 there was a policy change as regards the management of the STPs. The earlier autonomous societies for managing each park were dissolved and a new society, called the Software Technology Park of India, registered in June 1991. This was given the charge of managing all the STPs in India through an individual executive in each of the parks. Under the new scheme, the participating companies have the advantage of being fully involved in all decision-making, including fixing of rent, selection of hardware, etc. The companies are represented on the executive board, which manages the park under the overall supervision of the governing council.
12. The IT task force also made a series of recommendations to tackle the manpower bottleneck, including greater participation by the private sector and a transparent policy environment. See, for details, IT task force, IT human resource development, http:///www.IT-Taskforce.nic.in.
13. The case of the Government of India attracting home the leading telecom engineer Satyen G. Pitroda, from his telecom company in Chicago, USA, to act as adviser to the newly created Centre for Development of Telematics (C-DoT) wholly funded by the government to design, develop, field test and evaluate, and then transfer to some fifteen telecom companies, the complete technology for a whole range of state-of-the-art digital electronic switches exchanges with capacities ranging from 128-line Rural Automatic Exchanges (RAX) to 40000-line internationally competitive MAX exchanges for metropolitan areas is a classic case of major success involving an NRI in the high-tech area of telecom. See for details Meemamsi (1993).

14. Rites and TCIL have undertaken similar major IT-based export projects but space does not permit us to discuss them here.
15. See for details, *C-DoT Annual Reports*, various years in the 1990s.
16. Based on Ashok Jhunjhunwala, IIT, Chennai, various documents and information obtained from ECIL.
17. Here the reference is to the growing number of studies carried out in the framework of endogenous growth models.
18. Early contributions in this area have been made by Bain (1944, 1951) and Scherer (1970).
19. Parthasarathi and Joseph (2002) reported a negative and statistically significant relationship between labour productivity and export intensity while analysing the data for two years (1997–8 and 1998–9). On careful examination of the data it was found that the correlation between export intensity and size (measured as log of sales) is 0.38 which was statistically significant. To overcome multicollinearity, in this chapter we have measured size in terms of the sales turnover of the firms. The possibility of multicollinearity was pointed out to us by Prof. P. K. M. Tharakan, and we are greateful to him.
20. See 'Premji Sees Export Potential in Europe', *Business Age*, New Delhi, 27 April 2001.

References

Arora A. and Jai Asundi (1999) 'Quality Certification and Economics of Contract Software Development: a Study of Indian Software Industry', NBER working paper no. 7260, National Bureau of Economic Research, Cambridge MA.

Arora, A., V. S. Arunachalam, J. Asundi and F. Ronald (2000) 'The Indian Software Services Industry', *Research Policy*, 30 (3): 1267–87.

Bain, J. S. (1944) *The Economics of Pacific Coast Petroleum Industry* (Berkeley, CA: University of California).

—— (1951) *Barriers to New Competition* (Cambridge, MA: Harvard University Press).

Centre for Development of Telematics (various years) *Annual Reports* (New Delhi: C-DoT).

Centre for Monitoring Indian Economy (2000) 'PROWESS' (computerized database on India's Corporate Sector), CMIE.

Cohen, W. (1995) 'Empirical Studies of Innovative Activity', in P. Stoneman (ed.), *Handbook of the Economics of Technological Change* (Cambridge, MA: Blackwell Publishers), pp. 182–264.

Computer Maintenance Corporation (various years) *Annual Reports* (New Delhi: CMC).

D'Costa, A. P. (2002) 'Software Outsourcing and Policy Implications: an Indian Perspective', *International Journal of Technology Management*, 24 (7/8): 705–23.

Deolalikar, A. and R. Evenson (1989) 'Technology Production and Technology Purchase in Indian Industry', *Review of Economics and Statistics*, 71: 689–92.

Department of Scientific and Industrial Research (DSIR) (various years) *Foreign Collaboration: a Compilation* (New Delhi: Ministry of Science and Technology).

Government of India (1972) *Annual Report* (New Delhi: Department of Electronics).

—— (1982) *Annual Report* (New Delhi: Department of Electronics).

—— (1986) 'Policy on Computer Software Exports, Software Development and Training' (Department of Electronics, New Delhi).

—— (1995) *STP Info Data Base* (New Delhi: Department of Electronics).

—— (1998) Report of the IT Task Force, http://www. IT-Taskforce. Nic.in.

Gupta, P. (2000) 'The Indian Software Industry', in R. Ravichandran (ed.), *Competition in Indian Industries: a Strategic Perspective* (New Delhi: Vikas Publishing House).

Heeks, R. (1996) *India's Software Industry: State Policy, Liberalization and Industrial Development* (New Delhi: Thousand Oaks; London: Sage Publications).

Indian Institute of Technology (IIT), Chennai (various years) *Annual Report* (Chennai: IIT).

Indian Institute of Technology (IIT), Delhi (various years) *Annual Report* (Delhi: IIT).

Institute of Applied Manpower Research (IAMR) (2000) *Manpower Profile: India Year Book 2000* (New Delhi: IAMR).

Joseph, K. J. (1997) *Industry Under Economic Liberalization: the Case of Indian Electronics* (New Delhi: Thousand Oaks, London: Sage Publications).

—— (2002) 'Growth of ICT and ICT for Development: Realities of the Myths of the Indian Experience', Discussion paper no. 2002/78, UNU/ WIDER, Helsinki.

Joseph, K. J. and K. N. Harilal (2001) 'Structure and Growth of India's IT Exports: Implications of an Export-Oriented Growth Strategy', *Economic and Political Weekly*, 36 (34): 3263–70.

Katrak, H. (1985) 'Imported Technology, Enterprise Size and R&D in a Newly Industrializing Country: the Indian Experience', *Oxford Bulletin of Economics and Statistics*, 47 (3): 213–30.

—— (1989) 'Imported Technologies and R&D in a Newly- Industrialising Country: the Experience of Indian Enterprises', *Journal of Development Economics*, 31 (1): 123–39.

Kattuman, P. and K. Iyer (2001) 'Human Capital in the Move up the Value Chain: the Case of Software and Services Industry' (mimeo.), Department of Applied Economics, University of Cambridge.

Katz, J. M. (ed.) (1987) *Technology Generation in Latin American Manufacturing Industries* (London: Macmillan).

Kumar, N. (2001) 'Indian Software Industry Development: International and National Perspective', *Economic and Political Weekly*, 36 (44): 4278–90.

Kumar, N. and A. Agarwal (2000) 'Liberalization, Outward Orientation and In-house R&D Activity of Multinational and Local Firms: a Quantitative Exploration for Indian Manufacturing', discussion paper no. 07/2000, Research and Information System for the Non-Aligned and Other Developing Countries, New Delhi.

Kumar, N. and N. S. Siddharthan (1997) *Technology Market Structure and Internationalization: Issues and Policies for Developing Countries* (London and New York: Routledge).

Lall, S. (1983) 'Determinants of R&D in a LDC: the Indian Engineering Industry', *Economic Letters*, 13 (3): 379–83.

—— (1987): *Learning to Industrialize: the Acquisition of Technological Capability in India* (London: Macmillan).

Lateef, A. (1997) 'Linking with Global Economy', International Institute of Labour Studies, Geneva.

Mahajan, R. (2000) 'Moving India's Software Industry up the International Value Chain: the Role of the State in Creating the Institutional Capacity for Innovation', paper presented in the Third Triple Helix International Conference, Rio de Janeiro, 26–29 April.

Meemamsi, G. B. (1993) *The C-DoT Story* (New Delhi: Kedar Publications).

Narayana Murthy, N. R. (2000) 'Making India a Significant IT Player in this Millennium', in Romila Thapar (ed.), *India: Another Millennium* (New Delhi: Viking, Penguin, India).

National Association of Software and Service Companies (NASSCOM) (1999a) *Directory of Indian Software and Service Companies* (New Delhi: NASSCOM).

—— (1999b) *The Software Industry in India: a Strategic Review* (New Delhi: NASSCOM).

—— (2002) *The Software Industry in India: a Strategic Review* (New Delhi: NASSCOM).

Nayyar, D. (1988) 'The Political Economy of International Trade in Services', *Cambridge Journal of Economics*, 12 (2): 79–98.

Nelson, R. R., and S. G. Winter (1982) *An Evolutionary Theory of Economic Change* (Cambridge and London: Harvard University Press).

Oberoi, S. S. (1991) 'Software Technology Park: Concepts, Procedures and Status', *Electronics Information and Planning*, 19 (3): 42–6.

Parthasarathi, A. (2001) 'Tackling the Brain Drain from India's Information and Communication Technology Sector: Need for a New Industrial and S&T Strategy', paper presented in the ACU Conference of Executive Heads on Configurations in Globalization, Cyprus, 22–26 April.

Parthasarathi, A. and K. J. Joseph (2002) 'Limits to Innovation with String Export Orientation: the Case of India's Information Communication Technologies Sector', *Science, Technology and Society*, 7 (1): 13–49.

Pohjola M. (1998) 'Information Technology and Economic Development: an Introduction to the Research Issues', working paper no. 153, UNU/WIDER.

—— (2002) 'Information Technology and Economic Growth: a Cross Country Analysis', in M. Pohjola (ed.), *Information Technology, Productivity and Economic Growth* (Oxford: Oxford University Press), pp. 242–57.

Rodrik, D. (1995) 'Trade and Industrial Policy Reform', in J. Behrman and T. N. Srinivasan (eds), *Handbook of Development Economics*, vol. IIIB (New York: Elsevier), pp. 2923–81.

Sampson, G. and L. Snape (1985) 'Identifying Issues in Trade in Services', *World Economy*, 8 (2): 171–82.

Scherer, F. M. (1970) *Industrial Market Structure and Economic Performance* (Chicago, Ill: Rand McNally).

Schware, R. (1987) 'Software Industry in the Third World: Policy Guidelines, Institutional Options and Constraints', *World Development*, 15 (10/11): 1249–67.

—— (1992) 'Software Entry Strategies for Developing Countries', *World Development*, 20 (2): 143–64.

Sen, A. K. (1983) 'Development Which Way Now?', *The Economic Journal*, 93 (372): 745–62.

Sen, P. (1995) 'Indian Software Exports: an Assessment', *Economic and Political Weekly*, 30 (7&8): 2053–58.

Siddharthan, N. S. (1988) 'In House R&D, Imported Technology and Firm Size: Lessons from Indian Experience', *Developing Economies*, 26 (3): 212–21.

Subrahmanian, K. K. (1988) 'Technological Transformation: an Assessment of India's Experience', in Surendra Patel (ed.), *Technological Transformation of the Third World* vol.1, *Asia* (Ahmedabad: Gujarat Vidyapith), pp. 61–143.

UNDP (1997), UNDP and the Communications Revolution, http://www.undp.org/undp/index.html.

Venkatesh, P. (1995) 'India's Software Exports: a Study with Special Reference to Technology Parks', MPhil dissertation, Centre for Development Studies, JNU, Thiruvananthapuram.

World Bank (1999) 'Knowledge for Development', *World Development Report* 1998–99 (New York: Oxford University Press).

5

The Indian Software Industry from an Israeli Perspective: a Systems/Evolutionary and Policy View

Gil Avnimelech and Morris Teubal

1. Introduction

This chapter has two objectives: first an analysis of the evolution of Israel's high-tech sector and cluster over the past thirty years to identify aspects of Israel's IT high-tech experience of the 1990s which may be useful in assessing the prospects of India's IT high-tech sector during this decade; the second to suggest policy directions or policy issues that, if put into effect, might contribute to accelerating the evolution, alongside India's existing software/IT industry, of a more R&D-intensive, 'Silicon Valley'-type segment of high-tech.

The objectives are strongly linked to three strands of the literature: the high-tech cluster literature (Saxenian, 1998, 2002; Bresnahan, Gambardella and Saxenian, 2002; and Avnimelech and Teubal, 2002b, among others); the venture capital (VC) literature (Gompers and Lerner, 1999, 2001; Dossani and Kenney, 2001; Kenney, 2001; and Avnimelech and Teubal, 2002a,b, among others); and various strands of the policy literature, particularly evolutionary/systemic innovation and technology policy (ITP) (see Metcalfe, 1996; Teubal, 2002b; Avnimelech and Teubal, 2002c).

For our first objective we start by describing the two principal phases of evolution of Israel's high-tech industry: an initial R&D penetration phase in the 1970s and 1980s, and a Silicon Valley phase that emerged during the 1990s. Throughout we focus on two principal co-evolutionary processes: a policy–business sector co-evolution process which spans both phases; and VC–SU co-evolution which is a central vector in the emergence of the second phase. Section two succinctly describes the two phases of Israel's high-tech industry within such a systems/evolutionary perspective. We show that the first electronics-dominated R&D penetration phase (1970–89) was a *critical background condition* for the 'emergence' of a VC industry in the Silicon Valley phase (decade of the 1990s); and for the associated reconfiguration of Israel's high-tech cluster to the Silicon Valley model (characterized by large numbers of SU companies, of VCs, and strong links with global capital markets). In section three we underscore the critical role that ITP played in both phases, including the *targeted VC-directed policy* implemented in 1993–7. Whenever our analysis focuses on VC, and in contrast to most of the VC literature, it is concerned less with the *operation of an existing VC industry* and more with the process of *VC emergence* (Avnimelech and Teubal, 2002a, 2002b). Throughout, an explicit evolutioary/systemic approach to policy is adopted. Thus, we strongly emphasize the importance of 'learning processes', including learning by policy-makers; the importance of considering not only R&D as an objective of policy but also non-R&D factors such as issues of VC organization, the need for both incentives programmes and institutional changes (including aspects of liberalization and deregulation), and the like. Moreover, we refer also to a number of co-evolutionary processes, particularly VC–SU co-evolution (Avnimelech and Teubal, 2002b) and ITP–business sector co-evolution (Avnimelech and Teubal, 2002c).

The most important implication for India is the possibility that the current software services phase of India's IT industry may be the basis upon which a Silicon Valley segment of IT high-tech might emerge during this decade. Our basic thesis is that India is extremely well poised to enter into a 'Silicon Valley phase' of its IT industry, and that this will entail both further expansion of the existing software industry and entry into new higher value added areas, part of the latter involving large numbers of SUs and VCs.[1] This view follows from our analysis of the Israeli case and the conditions for its, sometimes remarkable, high-tech development during the past three decades. It also coincides with the predictions, the implications of which can be surmised from the analyses of Dossani and Kenney (2002), Bowonder and Mani (2002), *Business Week* (2002) and Gates (2002).

A second implication for India of the Israeli experience is that putting into effect the above potential may require specific policy actions over and beyond the policies that have successfully been implemented in the past. In view of the need to rapidly achieve critical mass for collective learning and the rapid enhancement of the emerging segment's reputation, and as part of the effort to engage foreign venture capital on a much larger scale than hitherto, a *targeted VC-directed policy may be necessary*. Israel's Yozma programme could be a model worth considering in this endeavour.

After considering the evolution of Israel's high-tech sector and of Israel's ITP (sections two and three), the chapter summarizes the findings from the fieldwork conducted in Mumbai (Bombay) and Bangalore during September 1999 in which nineteen software companies and two 'supporting institutions' were interviewed. In section four we focus on three companies that represent three different company types that could play an important role in the future evolution of the IT industry in India. One was an independently created start-up company; another, a large successful domestic software services company; and the third, a multinational company operating in India. A number of issues, including policy issues, emerge from these discussions.

The chapter utilizes a framework of analysis that we recently developed to analyse Israel's high-tech transformation of the 1990s (Avnimelech and Teubal, 2002c) to identify policy implications of potential relevance for India (due to the enormous complexity of the task we naturally hesitate to propose *specific* policy recommendations). As with the Israeli case, this chapter utilizes both industry (or meso-level) information *and* microeconomic information and insights pertaining to high-tech companies.

The importance of microeconomic analysis

Sectoral research oriented to policy, and involving very dynamic sectors such as the Indian software industry, require analysis at three different levels: (a) firm (micro)-level, (b) cluster/sector (meso)-level, (c) policy level. Both the micro and the meso levels should, to some extent, be integrated into policy analysis for the latter to be relevant to reality. One implication is a multi-methodological perspective to policy-relevant research.[2]

Also, from a 'positive' analysis perspective (in contrast to a 'normative' or policy perspective) sectoral/cluster analysis alone is frequently not enough; it must be complemented with a study of individual companies, particularly very successful companies whose direct and indirect (through spillovers) contribution to the cluster/sector and to the economy is high. Frequently, the growth and transformation of a very dynamic sector are triggered by initiatives or pioneering efforts of firms (or individuals) who 'show the way'. The path subsequently followed by the sector as a whole cannot, therefore, be understood without reference to those key firms or key agents.[3] This has been the approach followed by Saxenian in her analysis of Silicon Valley dynamics – in that analysis a special role was played by firms such as Hewlett Packard (creating and diffusing the so-called 'HP-Way', the culture of openness and informality both within the firm and beyond) during the period of 'cluster emergence'; and by companies such as Sun Microsystems and specialized chip producers during the 'cluster reconfiguration' that occurred during the 1980s (Saxenian, 1998). Such key firms were not only very successful in themselves but played 'key' roles for the cluster as a whole. They created a set of norms and values (the 'culture of openness'); strategies, organization and business models (open systems, decentralization, outsourcing, etc.); and promoted the creation of sector-specific institutions and organizations (e.g. business associations, link organizations with local governments, and the like) with wide repercussions for the sector as a whole. A similar conclusion is arrived at in a very dynamic segment of Israel's software industry: the data security sector.[4] Four very successful companies out of a total of nineteen comprising the sector in 1998 contributed a dominant share of total sector sales, profits and market capitalization (85–95 per cent); and they also made very significant contributions to high technology and to the economy. The Israeli study draws a clear distinction between very successful companies that remained indigenous (two out of four), and those that were acquired by multinational software companies (e.g. Computer Associates). Both the direct and the indirect contribution of the indigenous ones seemed to be higher than of those acquired (Avnimelech and Teubal, 2002b) This aspect of successful company growth might be of relevance to the Indian case, and might have policy implications.

2. Israel's high-tech sector and cluster: characteristics and evolution

Central features of the high-tech cluster of the 1990s

During the 1990s the Israeli economy continued the process of structural change initiated in the 1970s (Teubal, 1993) but in an accelerated mode (Justman, 2001). Within manufacturing (and probably within services) we observe a sharp increase in the weight of high tech. The share of these industries in manufacturing employment increased from 14 per cent in 1980 to 19.5 per cent in 1998, an apparently higher share than in any OECD country (Avnimelech et al., 2000: Table 1.1). IT high-tech sales and exports quadrupled or increased over that level from 1991 to 1999: from $3.6 billion and $2.2 billion respectively to $12.5 billion and $11 billion; and the share of high-tech exports in total manufacturing exports, which has grown steadily throughout the last three decades, grew by approximately 60 per cent. Moreover, we see a sharp rise in the relative importance of the

Table 5.1   Israel's high-tech cluster of the 1990s

	99/00	90	80
Number of SU	~3,000	~300	~150
Number of VC companies	~100	2	0
Funds raised by VCs: M$	3,400	~49	0
Capital invested by VCs: M$	1,270	~45	0
Accumulated no of IPOs (high tech)	~150	9	1
Accumulated VC-backed IPOs	~80	3	1
Share of foreign sources in total SU funding	67%	NA	NA
Share of IT exports in total manufacturing exports	45.7%	~33%	~20%
Capital raised in US capital markets during preceding decade B$	~10	NA	NA
Mergers and acquisition (M&A): B$	~10	NA	NA

Note: Frequently the figures in the box are approximations due to gaps in data, multiple sources of information, and fragmentary information from non-official sources.

Source: Avnimelech and Teubal (2002c). SU numbers come from three sources: CBS, OCS and IVA.

software and communications equipment segments (and lately, of Internet-related areas) and a relative decline in the more traditional electronics and instruments-based segments which characterized high tech during the 1980s. Finally, the processes of globalization have generated a new type of export good: the sale of high-tech start-up companies to foreign multinationals (this would be part of the process of mergers and acquisitions, M&A). This is a *sale of technological assets* rather than the traditional merchandise/services exports. It has become one of Israel's most important category of exports.

No less important than the quantitative high-tech changes are the qualitative ones. Thus, the high-tech cluster that emerged during the 1990s was very different from the cluster dominated by military industries in the 1980s (see Table 5.1). The changes include: (1) large numbers of SU companies; (2) significant venture capital investments; and (3) strong links with the US both in terms of product market links (e.g with Silicon Valley) and capital market links (e.g. NASDAQ). These are elements of what can be termed the 'Silicon Valley model' of high tech (Saxenian, 1998).

Background conditions[5]

The success of Israel's high-tech ICT sector during the 1990s would not have been possible without the continued deepening of the globalization process during the 1990s and the continued ICT technological revolution. Globalization of technology and knowledge, organizational forms, capital markets and skills created new opportunities which some countries more than others (or earlier than others) happened to exploit due to their flexibility and capacity to adapt. Israel was one of the first countries outside the US which was fortunate enough to have exploited such opportunities, at least during the 1990s. In the early 1990s some US investment banks and private equity investment corporations came to Israel in search of high-tech investment opportunities. The subsequent government-owned venture capital company, Yozma, was a result of an attempt at harnessing such behaviour for the benefit of Israeli high tech.

Israel's success with high tech and its 'reconfigured cluster' seems to have been linked to a number of processes operating more or less in parallel. These include:

- the 'Silicon Valley' model of ICT high tech *diffusing* to other countries;
- strong links to US (and to some extent other countries') asset and capital markets were forged;
- significant foreign investments into Israeli high tech, particularly in ICT areas, and including M&A activity occurred;
- strong *personal professional* and *business links* and networks have been forged between Israeli engineers, managers, investors and their counterparts in the US (and also to some extent elsewhere).

The first is a central feature of today's globalization process. The latter three are proximate causes of Israel's successful adaptation in the 1990s, i.e. of being one of the first Silicon Valley 'model' offshoots beyond North America. They are explained by other fundamental variables, such as the availability of large numbers of high-level technical personnel (the numbers of engineers as a percentage of population is one of the highest worldwide); a pre-existing high-tech sector in the 1980s with at least moderate success; the existence of a set of country-specific institutions such as the army research units; and strongly revealed entrepreneurial capabilities (particularly at the SU phase of company growth, and much weaker in the subsequent phases). Other countries and regions in Europe and in the Far East are bound to follow suit and reconfigure their existing high-tech clusters (or incorporate 'Silicon Valley' elements), e.g. India and Korea. There are a number of mechanisms explaining this diffusion process: 'imitation' and learning from others; enhanced cross-border links; and enhanced selection pressures derived from the successful Silicon Valley model.

Capital market links

The proximate causes mentioned above co-evolved with the evolution of the high-tech cluster during the 1990s.

A central distinguishing feature of Israeli high tech is the extent of its integration with US asset and capital markets (this is not the case with other

Table 5.2   Number of IPOs of Israeli companies in the US and EU capital markets

Year	All public offerings			VC-backed public offerings		
	*Number of Offerings**	*Capital Raised (M$)***	*Number of IPOs*	*Number of Offerings*	*Capital Raised (M$)***	*Number of IPOs*
1979–92	~30	~1,000	~25	4	~60	3
1993	18	529	16	7	103	6
1994	10	336	8	5	35	4
1995	16	608	12	7	210	5
1996	31	1,037	24	13	535	12
1997	24	1,074	16	8	175	5
1998	14	907	14	5	144	5
1999	20	3,172	20	16	1,073	14
2000	36	2,842	31	29	1,530	24
2001	3	143	2	2	83	2
Total 1990s	~202	~1,1200	~168	96	3,950	80

* Including IPOs, secondary and debt offering of all Israeli and Israel-related companies (high-tech and non high-tech) that are traded or were traded on the NASDAQ.
** US capital markets only.

Sources: Avnimelech and Teubal, 2002c and website of NASDAQ, NASE, EU capital markets, Yahoo Finance, and *Globes Newspaper*.

high-tech clusters of the 1990s, e.g. those of Europe). Links with the US in many ICT areas and capital market links are critical both because of the size of the US market and because the US market sets the trend and pace of technological and market developments. Apart from the US, Israel is next only to Canada in terms of having the highest number of IPOs (initial public offerings) on the NASDAQ and, till 1997 at least, its total number exceeded the cumulated IPOs on the NASDAQ of all other countries combined (again, excluding Canada).[6] Another instance of asset market links are M&A with US and other foreign companies, particularly acquisitions of small and young Israeli SUs by US companies.[7] Large chunks of Israeli ICT high tech seem to have been internationalized through this mechanism. M&As also comprise an important share of the growing flows of total direct foreign investment into Israeli high tech. Table 5.2 provides information on public offerings in the US by Israeli companies between 1993 and 1997.

Importance of SU companies and venture capital

As mentioned, the high-tech cluster of the 1990s becomes much more 'intensive' in SU and VC companies. Table 5.3 shows, year by year, trends in capital raised by VCs, gross additions to SU companies, and gross additions to VC-backed SU companies. We would like to emphasize a number of important points:

(1) VC emergence, i.e. the appearance of a distinctive VC industry, c. 1993–8;[8]
(2) VC–SU co-evolution, starting in 1990–3 when we observe an excess supply of SUs (i.e. unsatisfied demand for VC), followed later by a sharp increase in VC capital raised and invested (the latter a policy-induced 'supply response' (see below);
(3) A targeted VC-directed programme (Yozma) triggered VC emergence and VC–SU co-evolution.

A significant increase in SU numbers occurred during VC emergence: about 750 start-up companies were founded during 1993–7, and many more during the late 1990s. Yozma funds are widely believed to have triggered a dynamic/cumulative process, inducing industry entry financed by other private funds (both limited partnerships and other private equity

Table 5.3   Capital raised by VCs and new SUs backed by Israeli VC firms ($ million)

	1991	1992	1993	1994	1995	1996	1997	1998	1999	2000	2001	Total
Capital raised by VCs	58	160	372	374	156	397	727	675	1752	3288	1600	8559
New VC-backed SUs	10	20	80	90	80	200	219	252	338	513	221	1802
New SUs	40	40	50	50	100	200	350	350	550	850	NA	2605

Source: IVA (statistics and estimates).

companies); collective learning and other 'positive feedback' effects. The one time $100 million programme had direct and indirect effects. The direct impact of Yozma is reflected in the growth of (gross) accumulated numbers of new VC-backed SU companies from 110 in 1993 to 730 in 1998. After 1995, the annual flow of new SUs has been such that it exceeds the annual flow of new VC-backed SUs (thus reversing the situation of 1994 and 1995). This suggests an indirect impact of VC expansion, namely an acceleration of SU formation. All in all we observe a sharp rise during the 1990s in the proportions of VC-backed SU companies. Our thesis of strong VC–SU co-evolution (Avnimelech and Teubal, 2002b, d) is consistent with this data.[9]

3. Innovation and technology policy and its impact (1969–2000)

There are two distinct phases in Israel's R&D strategy, and possibly a third (induced by the high-tech crisis of the last couple of years) is now emerging. The first phase corresponds to the process of introduction and diffusion of R&D throughout the business sector; the second corresponds to the emergence and development of a distinct high-tech cluster largely modelled on Silicon Valley lines (1990–2000).

R&D penetration phase (1969–90)

The Israeli government's innovation/technology policy towards the business sector began in 1969 with the creation of the R&D Industrial Fund at the recently created Office of the Chief Scientist (OCS) at the Ministry of Industry and Trade. This programme was, and to some extent continues to be, the backbone of the country's R&D/innovation/technology strategy so far as the business sector is concerned. It supports the R&D of individual companies with the aim of creating new or improved products (or processes) directed to the export market. This type of R&D could be termed 'regular' or 'classical' R&D to differentiate it from generic, cooperative R&D, a more infrastructural type of R&D.[10]

The Industrial R&D Fund is an example of a *horizontal technology policy (HTP) programme*, that is, a programme directed towards the business sector as a whole and open in principle to all firms in that sector rather than to a specific industry or technology (programmes supporting the latter would be targeted programmes). These programmes embody an important component of 'neutrality in incentives'. In Israel this expressed itself as a 50 per cent subsidy to every R&D project submitted to the OCS, regardless of the industrial branch the submitting firm belonged to, whatever the product class towards which the proposed R&D was oriented, and whatever the technology underlying such a product class (Teubal, 1982, 1993). From $2.5 million in the late 1960s, the programme involved disbursements which almost reached $300 million in 1996/7.[11]

Due to the central role played by the Industrial R&D Fund, Israel's explicit R&D strategy or innovation/technology policy (directed to the business sector) over the past thirty years can be termed an *HTP-led strategy*. That programme was the first of the set of others comprising Israel's programme portfolio, and it was and still remains the dominant one in terms of government disbursements and probably (at least till the 1990s) in terms of impact. Moreover, the dynamic processes unleashed by its successful implementation led to the other programmes that made up Israel's innovation and technology policy of the last ten years.

To appreciate the impact of the Industrial R&D Fund, let us recall that the objective was penetration and diffusion of 'regular R&D' throughout the business sector.[12] While a neoclassical perspective would focus on the need to provide incentives due to market failure (caused by knowledge spillovers by firms undertaking R&D), an evolutionary perspective would focus first and foremost on the absence of R&D/innovation capabilities as a major obstacle to diffusion of R&D. Initially, when first implemented, such capabilities were either non-existent or existed only in 'islands' within the business sector. Therefore the major objective during the infant phase of implementation was the promotion of learning about R&D/innovation.[13] Much of this is 'collective learning', that is, R&D performing firms mutually learn from each other, and much of this relates not directly to technology or R&D proper but to organizational and managerial matters. Box 5.1 illustrates some specific aspects of 'collective learning' during 1969–90 in Israel.[14]

Experience with Israel's implementation of the Industrial R&D Fund showed that programmes following a 'learning/evolutionary' perspective would be facilitated by, or would require, the following:

- assuring a critical mass of projects as early as possible (this is a condition for 'collective learning');
- creating a policy implementation network to ensure learning by experience on the part of policy-makers;

Box 5.1 Collective learning during the implementation of the 'Industrial R&D Fund' (first 20 years)

Firms learned about the importance of marketing (thereby overcoming the previously held view that 'my invention is so good that it will sell automatically').

Officials and experts of the OCS learned, partly through exchange of information within an informal 'policy network' (a) to better assess the quality and potential of the projects submitted; (b) how to help firms configure good projects.

Firms acquired capabilities for identifying new projects, including 'complex' projects which built upon prior 'simple' projects.

- generating policy-relevant typologies of R&D in favour of innovation;
- special attention might have to be given to promote a wide diffusion of R&D;
- explicit attention to enhancement policy capabilities;
- other: flexible budgets, use of grants rather than loans (and rather than tax concessions, at least in the initial, infant phase of implementation); and bottom-up determination of projects.

The backbone regular R&D support programme was widely regarded as having been a success in terms of stimulating R&D in the business sector, in stimulating exports resulting from R&D, and in contributing to the creation of a civilian high-tech sector during the 1980s (see Teubal, 1993; Toren 1990 and 1999; Justman and Zuscovitch, 1999).

Expansion and diversification

Successful implementation of the core or backbone programme *through an evolutionary/dynamic process* led to the emergence and implementation of a set of other programmes in the early 1990s (see Box 5.2).

Throughout this period (the 1990s) the regular R&D grants of the OCS continued to grow; together they amounted to $440 million during 2000 (see Table 5.4).

Box 5.2 Programme sequencing: Israel

The successful implementation of Israel's backbone 'Industrial R&D Fund' programme since 1969 led, together with other changes in the external environment, to a spate of new programmes in the early 1990s:

1. **Yozma** (1992–7) – a $100 million government-owned venture capital company which invested in ten funds that operated in Israel. Each fund had at least one major US investment bank/private equity investment company, is backed by at least one major local financial institution, and corporations/individuals (both domestic and foreign). Yozma, which triggered the emergence of a domestic VC industry, was privatized in 1997.
2. **Magnet Programme** (1992–) – a $60/70 million a year horizontal programme supporting cooperative, generic R&D involving two or more firms and at least one university. Widely regarded as a successful venture.
3. **Technological Incubators' Programme** (1992–) – a $20/30 million a year programme supporting entrepreneurs during the seed phase of their project for a period of three years. The incubators are privately owned and managed. Both they and the projects approved receive financial support from the government. The programme complements the Industrial R&D Fund (projects could be submitted to either programme). It contributed to the transformation of Israel's high-tech cluster during the 1990s, particularly during the early years.

Table 5.4   Summary of activities of the Office of the Chief Scientist (OCS) in 1997

	1987	*1990*	*1993*	*1997*	*1999*	*2000*
Number of firms requesting support	~350	451	656	623	600	504
Number of first time start-ups requesting support	32	34	179	170	138	126
Number of project support requests submitted	690	920	1,513	1,342	1,316	1,370
Number of firms' support requests approved	~300	352	474	479	486	488
Number of project support requests approved	580	670	1 09	974	1 007	908
Grants approved	$87m	$137m	$200m	$397m	$428m	$440m
Royalties paid by companies	$4.2m	$14m	$42m	$103m	$139m	$134m
No. of projects in 26 technological incubators	0	0		212		

Source: Slide presentation of Chief Scientist, Orna Berry, 1999 and other OCS information.

Israel's targeted VC directed programme: Yozma (1993–7)[15]

Yozma is reputed to have triggered the emergence of Israel's VC industry. The spurt in VC activity that accompanied implementation of the programme in 1993 gives credence to this view. It was based on a $100 million fund (of the same name) oriented to two functions: (a) investment in ten private Israeli owned and managed VC funds, mostly limited partnerships ('Yozma Funds' $80 million); and (b) direct investments in high-tech companies: $20 million. The basic idea was to promote the establishment of a domestic, professional VC industry. Each fund would have to involve a reputable foreign institution and a well-established Israeli financial institution. The objective of the funds was early phase investments in young Israeli high-tech start-ups. Once a fund fulfilled these conditions, the government would invest (through Yozma) up to $8 million, approximately 40 per cent of the capital. Each fund also had a call option on government shares, at cost (plus interest), for a period of five years. All this was supposed to create a solid base for the industry, to learn the business from foreign partners, and to access a network of international contacts. The government was willing to grant a bonus or premium to foreign institutions willing to invest in Israeli VCs despite the latter's lack of experience.

In all, ten 'Yozma funds' were created: five in 1993, two in 1994, two in 1995 and one in 1996. They managed $310 million and invested in over 200 SU companies. They started a dynamic, cumulative process involving: learning by doing and imitation/learning from foreigners (this was a collective learning process); exploitation of economies of scale and specialization; and advantages brought about by consolidation of the overall new high-tech cluster in Israel (we could say the VC co-evolved with SU and, more generally speaking, with high tech).

An indication of their success in triggering the growth of the industry is their expansion which took the form of 'follow up' funds. Each of the Yozma funds (and some other funds as well, which indirectly learned from the Yozma experience) was followed by one or more additional funds managed by an expanding but related core of managers. The total sums managed by this group in 2000 approximated $5 billion,[16] constituting a large share of the total VC industry funds.[17]

We conclude with the view that Israel's restructured 'programme portfolio' of the 1990s, and particularly the Yozma programme, had a strong impact on the growth of high tech and on the emergence of the new 'Silicon Valley'/VC-and SU-intensive cluster. Over and beyond Yozma's *direct* effect (as measured by, e.g., the share of VCs with Yozma funds in accumulated VC capital raised), this assertion is based on the fact that the data are consistent with Yozma having triggered VC–SU co-evolution, on the 'microeconomic insights' of entrepreneurs and policy-makers, and on it being correlated with the strong growth of high tech during the 1990s. As many other countries did not seem to have benefited to the same degree from the high-tech product and technology capital market bonanza of the 1990s, it is very likely that Israel's success owes a great deal to ITP, particularly to the *targeted VC-directed policy* which was implemented.

4. Issues emerging from an analysis of three Indian IT companies[18]

Several papers have been written on India's software industry (Arora et al., 2001; NASSCOM, 2002) and a summary of some of the important trends can be found in Chapters 1 and 2. We will only mention some important facts. The Indian IT sector grew from $1.73 billion in 1994–5 (0.59 per cent of GDP) to an estimated $13.5 billion (2.87 per cent of GDP) in 2001–2. Sixty per cent of the estimated level for 2001–2 involves *software and services* (around $8 billion), and of these exports are $6.217 billion. Software and services exports have consistently recorded a growth rate of over 50 per cent between 1994–5 and 2001–2.

This section does not make use of industry level data nor purports to be a study of that nature. Its distinctive feature is a microeconomic analysis based on interviews of the representatives of several companies, in particular a detailed study of three. Our presumption was (and remains) that numerous issues relevant to our analysis of the prospects of India's IT and software industry could emerge.

The representatives of nineteen companies were interviewed in Bangalore and Mumbai (Bombay). They included large software services companies such as Wipro, Infosys, Satyam and Tata Infotech; a small number of 'entrepreneurial' companies engaged in developing 'product software' such as SAS (now Sasken); and subsidiaries of multinational companies (IBM, Hughes Software and the like). As with the Israeli study mentioned above, and given the limitations of time and resources, it was important after the interviews to focus on a small number of companies only.

The companies chosen were

- Wipro, from the group of large software services companies;[19]
- Sasken, an entrepreneurial, product software company;
- Hughes Software, a foreign subsidiary.[20]

When reading the following accounts it must be realized that the objective is *not* to identify and measure a given set of variables or aspects across the three companies. Rather, by focusing on companies of different type, our objective is to further our understanding of how different segments of the existing IT industry might contribute to the new Silicon Valley type segment of the future. This, and the constraints of interviewing time, explain why *different* sets of variables were emphasized in each of the cases.

Sasken

Sasken Communications Technology Limited is a leading provider of telecommunications software services and solutions to network equipment manufacturerers, mobile terminal vendors, and semiconductor companies. Since its inception in 1989, Sasken has grown to be over 1000 strong with headquarters in Bangalore and offices in Canada, Japan, the UK, USA and Sweden. It clocked revenues of $ 31.3 million for the financial year ending March 2001 (NASSCOM, 2000: 629).

It is representative of an important category of software companies: an entrepreneurial, product-software company which was 'independently' born. Its apparent 'high quality' probably situates it within a small class of potentially large, global companies. The founders had extensive experience in Silicon Valley and decided (a team of four) to leave their jobs in 1989 and come to India to set up a company to design and build a front end tool for VLSI design. At some stage in the development of the company it got involved in DSL (Digital Subscriber Lines) products, developing a PC-based solution. The development process involved explicit participation in the relevant international standards' committee where the company acquired market/need knowledge, reputation, and links with potential partners, all contributing to what appeared to be a successful product. The company had in September 1999 around 500 employees of whom 440 were technically qualified (50 per cent had Masters degrees in computer science and in electronic engineering, and there are twenty PhDs).

We group the issues that emerged from the interview into four categories.

1 *Strengths of the Indian software/IT sector (which favoured the firm)*

Sasken's successful development was facilitated by a number of features of the Indian context and by the globalization process. These include: (1) the Silicon Valley experience of the founders (this is indicative of at least a measure of personal and professional links between the Indian system and Silicon Valley); (2) high quality research universities (Indian Institutes of Technology), from which both professors, students and graduates were drawn to the firm; (3) the attractiveness of India to multinationals such as Nortel who was looking to outsource its R&D towards the mid-1990s.[21]

2 *Benefits from globalization (favourable to Indian companies like Sasken)*

These include the possibility of participation in the standards committee relevant for the ASDL technology it was developing (this possibly reflects the openness of the international system in the sense that Indians can participate in some 'global' institutions. It also reflects a measure of the maturity in the Indian software cluster in the sense of being able to exploit such features of the world system.).The above not only enabled adaptation of local efforts to ongoing developments, including those of 'complementary' technologies and products, but also generated important links with key players in the area. It set the base for subsequent agreements with Intel (and, directly or indirectly, probably with other companies too).

3 *Weaknesses of the software/IT cluster or system*

In parallel with the undoubted academic excellence in science and engineering, there was a felt need for a stronger practical orientation of at least some aspect of academic institutions. Moreover, there seemed to have been insufficient interaction between government labs (including defence labs) and business (this is a reflection no less of future potential as it is of current weakness). The globalization of asset/capital markets in the 1990s had not yet affected the company by 1999: no foreign venture capitalist seems to have invested in the company, nor was any IPO issued.[22] At the time, only large companies seemed to have had an opportunity of issuing an IPO in global markets. One possible cause was insufficient venture capital funding and the relatively underdeveloped VC industry in India at the time. A final point is that the firm was only weakly linked to knowledge networks at the time, and this was considered by it to be an important obstacle to innovation success (a possible *system failure* in India).[23]

4 *Policy issues addressed by the interviewee*

The central point here was the significant felt change in the attitude of the Indian government towards the software industry after 1996: the government was now (1999) speaking the language of enterprises like SAS. However, there were still many areas of 'need' where policies did not provide answers or were non-existent, e.g. *seed finance* (an area in which the interviewee was looking forward to some action, e.g. incubators); *the support structure*, e.g. educating more practically oriented graduates; changing the governance of institutes/universities to enable and induce researchers to create/manage/ own companies, etc; and *promotion of business–university links*.

5   *Other policy issues*

The interview with Sasken suggested a number of potentially relevant policy issues or policy directions. The most important of these is the *desirability of continuing with a targeted policy favouring the software and IT industries* in which India has a clear competitive advantage in world markets. However, other elements in the overall policy portfolio or package may be required. Up to now the package involves 'framework conditions' and infrastructure (e.g. Electronic City in Bangalore); liberalization;[24] and means to reduce bureaucracy. Two other policy objectives suggested by the Israeli experience are the *support of R&D/innovation* (e.g. through a grants or conditional loans scheme); and the *support of venture capital*. The Israeli experience also suggests that at the current stage of the Indian IT high-tech cluster the support of R&D/innovation should be considered to be complementary rather than a substitute to targeted support of venture capital. Both would be *strategic priorities* as both promote entry of SU into the branded software and IT 'product' segment of high tech.[25]

Conclusion

The Sasken experience suggests that, given the existence or the potential for generating large numbers of very good SUs, certain components of the Silicon Valley 'model' might be relevant for India (e.g. a well-developed VC industry involving domestic and/or foreign funds). On the other hand, it suggests that the existing national/regional setting is such that explicit policies, including innovation/technology policies and targeted VC promotion policies, could accelerate the above-mentioned evolutionary process.

Hughes Software Systems

Hughes Software Systems (HSS) specializes in convergent network software and is the foremost communications software company in India. Assessed at SEI-CMM level 4 for all its development centres and all projects, HSS has been an ISO 9001 company since 1996. It has a team of 1500 world class professionals at its development centres in India (NASSCOM, 2002: 362).

The company was created in 1992 as a subsidiary of Hughes Network Systems which is a joint venture of Hughes Electronics and General Motors. The reason for the establishment of the subsidiary was similar to those underlying the decisions of other multinationals, particularly the availability of very low cost skilled labour in comparison to its cost abroad. At that time Hughes held 76 per cent of the shares while a group of venture capitalists held the remaining 24 per cent. The focus of this company was software services and a large proportion of sales were directed to the parent company.

In 1996 a group of employees suggested to Hughes' management a change in strategy that would contribute to their motivation to stay with the company by responding to their desire to become 'businesspersons'. This included the development of 'product' software (or at least software modules) for the market rather than services to a single customer. The company's management responded positively and instituted a change in strategy. In this context, it undertook an aggressive marketing strategy during 1998–9 while struggling to extricate itself from a purely 'engineering' perspective – and US customers were beginning to buy. By September 1999 over 50 per cent of sales still went to a single customer, but the goal was to reduce it to 25 per cent. Subsequently, the company became the first multinational in IT to go public in India (Mumbai Stock Exchange during October 1999), and Hughes' holding was diluted to 56 per cent.

Possible lessons or implications of the case

The above points to a situation in which an MNE can directly and indirectly contribute to the eventual emergence of an Indian (or largely Indian) company involved both in developing 'product software' and in downstream 'marketing' activities. An important condition suggested by the Hughes case is the existence of a strong, domestic stock market (for the Indian case, see Dossani and Kenney, 2002) where the MNE subsidiary could float shares. It suggests the existence of an important mechanism in India for further developing and 'reconfiguring' the existing software and IT cluster. The mechanism usually mentioned in the literature on high-tech clusters focuses on the market/management/technological spillovers and spin-offs from MNEs (Bresnahan, Gambardella and Saxenian, 2002). These are very strong in Israel and presumably in Ireland, and will become even stronger in India given the frenetic efforts of MNEs to create R&D facilities in India (*Business Week*, 2002). What a strong domestic capital market can give in addition to spillovers is a mechanism for the restructuring of the MNE subsidiary itself, a process leading to a mixed pattern of ownership (both foreign and domestic); and to a new set of activities and an increase in the scope and variety of spillovers (over and beyond those emerging from an MNE's lab).

More specifically, the restructuring of Hughes enhanced the accumulation of market/marketing/client-related assets, which is a richer set of spillovers than the hitherto apparent dominance of engineering-related spillovers in the original phase after establishment of the subsidiary (frequently MNE subsidiaries that undertake R&D generate a lot of technological spillovers and many lower market and client-related spillovers). It follows that if future priorities of the Indian software and IT industry involve (a) a vigorous development of software and IT products and venture capital, and (b) the emergence of a segment of indigenous companies with high growth rates and eventual global status, then the above-mentioned partial shift to product software *and* accumulation of client/marketing/market-related and reputation assets that follow the change in ownership could be helpful for the next phase in the development of the industry.[26, 27]

Conclusion

The Hughes case, together with the framework of analysis that emerged from our Israeli study suggests two possible mechanisms for generating global indigenous companies in IT 'product' areas: (1) the *Israeli pattern*, which is based on the existence of large numbers of high-tech SU companies and on a system which, during the 1990s, facilitated a small subset of very good companies to issue IPOs on the NASDAQ rather than to be acquired very early by a foreign multinational (see Teubal and Avnimelech, 2002a,b); and (2) the *Hughes example* which suggests that the pre-existent MNE which populated the first phase in the development of the Indian software industry, by floating the local subsidiary in the domestic capital market, may eventually become or increasingly behave like an Indian company while simultaneously diversifying into 'product software' areas. We suggest that both mechanisms should be explored and their policy implications unravelled. Note that while the latter mechanism might be a real possibility in India without major changes in its system of innovation, the former Israeli-type mechanism for generating 'indigenous companies' in India would require a 'system' driven by venture capital and large numbers of SU companies (see the Sasken case above and the inferred policy implications).

Wipro Infotech

The company is part of a large conglomerate, one of the largest in India, and is one of India's largest software companies. The conglomerate made a decision to enter the IT area in 1980 in response to restrictions on the import of minicomputers. At that time only larger categories of machines, such as mainframes, were allowed entry, giving rise to the prospect of producing minicomputers. Wipro developed, in its first phase, strong skills in hardware design, and had a clear growth objective that entailed both proprietary products, distribution partnerships, and an explicit building-up of in-house expertise. It became the foremost vendor in the country offering a wide range of products.

The company entered the software business in 1989, initially with a strategy for developing 'product software' which failed for marketing reasons. It then reoriented to software services, including the creation of an offshore development centre where development was undertaken for companies like Nortel and General Electric. Later, it started offering integrated software/ hardware design services. Some product development activity has also been undertaken, but this represented (in 1999) a minor share of the company's activity.

Total sales in 1998 were $350 million, of which $100 million were accounted for by hardware and the rest divided among two software groups: the software and software services group; and the systems and services group (both independent groups within Wipro).

Subsequent (post-1999) activity

The next phase would involve going up the value chain, e.g. fixed price transactions for the development of application software; specialization in vertical segments such as finance, retail and the like; and the development of some reusable software components that might represent building blocks for large software projects of clients abroad. They represent system integration, solutions development, and operations support activities of a higher level of sophistication than in the past. Until September 1999 there seemed to be no plans to enter even more sophisticated consulting business such as IT or business processes consultancy.

Possible implications

The Wipro case suggests that large opportunities do exist in India for the continued growth of software services and customized software up the value chain, and that for a long time to come this will continue to be the basis for the growth of the Indian software industry.[28] Moreover, given Wipro's ownership of a Silicon Valley company and a one-shot transfer of technology to another company there, the case suggests how large Indian software companies could, indirectly or directly, promote the development of SU in the IT and software areas , and even of venture capital. The latter would have a strong effect if spurred by a change in strategy, e.g. in response to changes exogenous to the company.

The mechanisms by which large domestic incumbent companies may contribute to the new segment of IT high tech include: (1) undertaking product software development activity with or without spinning it off as an independently managed subsidiary (probably in conjunction with other companies and/or investors) or joint venture; (2) personnel spin-offs, including managers, founding or joining SU or VC companies;[29] (3) investment in Indian SU companies; (4) agreements or partnerships with SU companies.

Implementing the above involves important strategic and organizational issues for the large, services-oriented software company. These, in turn, could be more or less stimulated by government policy, both in terms of incentives and 'institutional changes' (stimulation of VC in terms of corporate VC funds as well as limited partnerships, direct support to R&D, taxation issues, bankruptcy laws, corporate governance, regulation of financial markets, regulation and taxation issues related to M&A, and the like).

5. The prospects for Indian IT and possible policy implications[30]

The prospects for Indian IT industries

Our analysis (here and in Avnimelech and Teubal, 2002b) of the emergence and development of a venture capital industry in Israel and its role in the recent successful growth of Israel's high-tech cluster suggest the important role played by five groups of factors, events, or subprocesses: (1) *favourable background conditions*; (2) events or features of the *immediate pre-emergence period (1989–92)*; (3) *targeted policies* that directly triggered VC emergence (1993–96/7); (4) the onset of a *complex, cumulative dynamic process* including multifaceted 'collective learning' and strong VC–SU co-evolution; and (5) *global capital market links* (IPOs and M&A).[31] Israel's evolution towards a (or pattern of emergence of the) Silicon Valley model of high tech was based on spurring VC–SU co-evolution through a targeted, VC directed programme implemented during 1993–7 (Yozma).

Favourable background conditions included the prior existence of an electronics industry that had developed during the 1970s and 1980s both R&D/innovation capabilities and links with the US; a large pool of skills; a process of liberalization and improvement in the business environment; and other favourable external and internal conditions. Moreover, during a pre-emergence period (1989–92), VC (partly non-formal) or proto-VC activities already existed as well as significant numbers of SUs that represented *an unsatisfied demand or need* for VC services. Finally, the design and timing of Yozma was such that it led to the early and rapid accumulation of reputation and capabilities.

Our central point is that, despite the obvious differences between Israel then and India now, there are similarities between these two countries in terms of *favourable background* conditions for the emergence of a software/IT segment of high tech with Silicon Valley characteristics. Partly as a result of a *targeted* policy implemented during the 90s, India presently enjoys a comparative advantage in the software and IT services industry which will enable it, with the aid of other internal and external factors, to create 'advantages' in other segments of IT, including branded software products and high-tech SU companies. This possibility is real. Some of these factors parallel those operating in Israel during the late 1980s to early 1990s: large numbers of high quality and low cost IT graduates (over 220 000 software and computer science engineers graduates every year: see *Business Week*, 2002); the success and reputation of the existing software and services industry ($13.5 billion estimated output for 2001–2); the existence of large, highly reputable software companies which, notwithstanding their being overwhelmingly involved today in high quality and highly reliable customized software applications/software services, could contribute directly and indirectly to the new IT segments; and a web of personal linkages with Indians working in Silicon Valley and elsewhere (see Dossani and Kenney, 2002; and

Saxenian, 2002). Moreover, as the case of Sasken, and other successful high-tech R&D-intensive SUs demonstrates, there already exists a measure of innovation and high-tech entrepreneurship capabilities on the Indian scene (Saxenian, 2002: 142–3).

In addition, to some degree favourable *pre-emergence conditions* seem to have appeared in India towards the late 1990s. These include a significant increase in venture capital and of VC organizations that are owned by Indian or foreign companies;[32] the apparent disposition of increasing numbers of NRI to come to India in search of (and invest in) projects, and the like. We are less certain about other factors we considered important in our analysis of the Israeli case: the creation, prior to emergence, of large numbers of SUs that represent *demand* for the services of a VC industry expected to emerge in a few years (in Israel this was induced by specific policies); policy experimentation and learning that can set the base for further refinement and complement the existing package or portfolio of policies directed to the software/IT industries; and further improvements in the institutional and business environment. Moreover, it is not clear to us the degree to which a mechanism has been put in place to systematically support SUs and business sector R&D and, indirectly, the accretion of R&D/innovation capabilities (at least till venture capital can take over most of this function). It is our belief, however, that both public and private agents in India are (or will) find solutions to the above and other problems.

Still, the transition requires a strong, cumulative process of growth of 'product' software and IT hardware, with a potential vector SU–VC co-evolution. True, the existing IT/software industry (particularly large software incumbents and R&D lab subsidiaries of MNEs) could serve as a springboard for the emergence of such a segment, e.g. through spin-off companies, technological, market/marketing, and managerial 'spillovers'; networking and reputation effects; investments in new ventures or in VCs, etc. Despite this possibility, *the certainty of a cumulative, self-reinforcing process may require a more focused policy than that undertaken till at least 2000–1* (this is also consistent with the view held by Dossani and Kenney, 2002). The Israeli experience would suggest that such a complement of targeted policies could trigger the above cumulative process and assure its continuation by assuring a critical mass in a short period of time. Moreover, policy may also be required to further reinforce the pre-emergence conditions mentioned in the previous paragraph.

Policies supporting software/IT transformation

Under a systems/evolutionary perspective to ITP (Teubal, 2002a), a fundamental distinction should be drawn between, (a) *strategic priorities*, on the one hand (the outcome of the 'strategic dimension' to innovation and technology policy that starts with a *vision and a strategy* to achieve it); and (b) their *translation into a new or restructured set of incentives programmes and set of institutional changes*. The *vision* for India's future software/IT industry could include, first, continued growth in existing services/customized software areas and accelerated entry into higher value added activities; and, second, the emergence and development of a thriving, competitive, R&D-based product software and IT hardware segment of high tech.

The strategy or strategic priorities to achieve the above vision could include: (1) creation of large numbers of SU companies in product software areas (hundreds every year); (2) reinforcement of the domestic, *early phase-oriented* venture capital industry with characteristics similar to those of the US and Israel; (3) assurance of a mutually supporting process of VC–SU co-evolution; (4) assurance of the effective transition of SUs from the R&D to post-R&D phase, and the emergence of a subset of high-growth SU companies ('gazelles') and of a set of large domestic companies in the software products area which have acquired world status; and (5) facilitating enhanced links with global capital markets, particularly the NASDAQ.

We propose two axes to the new elements or components of the package of policies that could be applied. The first, a set of incentives programmes whose objective would be to trigger and sustain VC–SU co-evolution; the second, liberalization, deregulation and institutional changes. The raison d'être of the former is our presumption that the best way for VCs and SU companies to be created is for them to *co-evolve*. This means transforming their creation into a strongly *endogenous* process. The role of policy in this context would be to trigger this process of co-evolution and to sustain it for some time (till full endogeneity is achieved, i.e. without government inducements). Note that achieving this strategic priority may require the implementation of more than one incentives programme, e.g. a *targeted* VC-directed programme and another programme directly stimulating SU creation and growth (in Israel this function was performed by 'horizontal' R&D grants to the business sector that did not discriminate against small companies; and by the Technological Incubators programme).

The second axis is a group of policies aimed at creating a favourable business environment for the new software/IT industry segment. Following Dossani and Kenney (2002) and others, this should include both 'general' liberalization (including the gradual assurance of currency convertibility) and further deregulation of the VC industry. Our experience suggests also that attention may need to be given to other aspects of the institutional framework, e.g. corporate law/governance, and the like.

Notes

Originally published in *Science, Technology and Society*, 7 (1) (January–June 2002). Copyright © Society for the Promotion of S & T Studies, New Delhi, 2002. All rights reserved. Reproduced with the permission of the copyright holders and the publishers, Sage Publications India Pvt. Ltd, New Delhi.

Many thanks to E. Sridharan and Anthony D'Costa for their extensive comments on an earlier version of this chapter.

This chapter was made possible by the generosity and assistance of P. Sudarshan (Chairman and Managing Director, Intel Southtech Ltd), H. N. Keshav (Business Development Executive, Pentasoft, Bangalore), and Rakesh Basant (Professor, Indian Institute of Management, Ahmedabad), and representatives and officials of nineteen Indian software companies and two Indian institutes associated with high tech who Teubal interviewed in 1999. The institutes were: National Centre for Software Technology (S. P. Mudur, Associate Director and head of Division, Graphics and Computer Aided Design) and Software Technology Parks India (B.V. Naidu, Director; B. Mahesh, Joint Director; and R. Padmini, R-NITS). Special thanks to all the other individuals who helped with the research.

1. The tremendous strides taken in the past by the Indian IT software and services industry are very well described in NASSCOM (2002). This report also discusses India's prospects in these areas; and while it does analyse trends in venture capital it does not explicitly address the prospects of 'diversification' into the Silicon Valley model of high tech.

2. See Teubal (1999), Bartzokas and Teubal (2002), and Avnimelech, Gayego, Teubal and Toren (2000). The methodological implications of the last two items followed from an analysis of two segments of the Israeli software and IT industries.

3. From a systems innovation and evolutionary perspective we could say that such Schumpeterian firms/individuals introduce new 'variety' into the system being analysed, which is then selected out by other agents, thereby initiating a cumulative development process. See Nelson (1995) for an analysis of evolutionary theory as applied to the study of economic and social change.

4. See Teubal and Avnimelech (2002) and Teubal, Avnimelech and Gayego (2002). All the companies in the study were engaged in developing 'product software' although some (including two out of the four very successful ones) were involved in 'security services' during the early phase of their growth.

5. For a detailed analysis of Israel's R&D Penetration Phase and of the background conditions setting the stage for the 'cluster reconfiguration' of the 1990s, see Avnimelech and Teubal (2000a, b).

6. See Blass and Yafeh (2001).

7. In January and June 2000 the highest company values to date were obtained from acquisitions of Israeli start-up companies by foreign multinationals: $1.6 billion (Intel's purchase of IDPC); and $4.7 billion (Lucent's purchase of Chromatis).

8. For a definition of VC emergence, see Avnimelech and Teubal (2000c).

9. Note that the vast increase in capital raised by VCs in Israel during 1999–2000 coincides with a tremendous spiral worldwide: the sums raised in the US, for example, increased phenomenally from around $15 billion per year to over $60 billion.

10. The latter's objective is to generate knowledge, capabilities and components rather than directly marketable outputs. Its output would facilitate (or become inputs to) subsequent 'regular' R&D activity directed to new products or processes.

11. It is well known that horizontal programmes embody an element of 'selectivity' by virtue of the particular activity being chosen, e.g. regular R&D, generic–cooperative R&D, or technology transfer/adsorption. Thus Israel's 'Industrial R&D Fund', while formally 'neutral' in the allocation of its incentives, and given its dominance over other programmes for long periods of time, embodies strong selectivity of 'regular R&D' in relation to other possible technological activities. See, e.g., Lall and Teubal (1998).

12. Initial conditions in the ideal HTP model, which to our mind reflect the conditions prevailing in Israel in 1969, assume (a) that R&D was virtually non-existent

within the business sector, and (b) that its diffusion was a strategic priority of the country (a necessary condition for growth of the business sector and of the economy as a whole).

13. Learning, including experience-based learning, triggered by increased R&D in the business sector is *the* principal factor leading to enhanced R&D/innovation capabilities.

14. Both are based on studies of Israeli high tech during the 1970s (see Teubal et al., 1976 and Teubal, 1982, both reprinted in Teubal, 1986).

15. See also Avnimelech and Teubal (2002c).

16. An expanded discussion of Yozma's impact and a systematic comparison between the Yozma and Inbal programmes can be found in Avnimelech and Teubal (2002c).

17. Yozma's successful implementation owes a lot to 'policy learning and experimentation'. The high rate of SU failure during the late 1980s led to a quest for ways of solving the problem, including a visit of the Chief Scientist to Silicon Valley. The outcome was identification of what may be termed a 'systemic failure' in the country's national system of innovation: venture capital. For an expanded discussion of Yozma's impact, see Avnimelech and Teubal (2002c).

18. This section is based on interviews conducted in the summer of 1999 somewhat updated with information from NASSCOM (2002). The policy issues and suggestions that emerged are relevant if global IT high-tech product markets rebound in the next couple of years or so; and similarly with regard to global technology capital markets (e.g. NASDAQ).

19. Wipro is a Tier 1 player in the software and services industry. Following NASSCOM (2002), there are five such companies in India (defined as having an annual turnover of $200 million or more) and representing 33–35 per cent of the overall software export market during 2000–1. These global companies offer a comprehensive services portfolio, boast a line-up of Fortune 500 customers, and will continue to log in above industry growth rates during 2001–2. They include Tata Consultancy Services, Wipro Ltd, Infosys Technologies Ltd, HCL Technologies and Satyam Computer Services Ltd. Spinoffs and spillovers from this group (and from somewhat smaller Tier 2 players) will contribute to the new model of high tech discussed in this chapter.

20. For details of the interviews, see Teubal (2000b: 155–6).

21. NASSCOM (2002: 32) lists a set of 'factors of strength' of the Indian IT industry, some of which are important for generating a future 'capability' for the creation of high-tech SU companies and a 'product' software, R&D-based, IT segment. The current factors of strength include: cost–value proposition; a vast base of English-speaking, skilled manpower; high quality orientation (major expansion in the base of SEI CMM level 5 companies); experience and state of the art hardware and software platforms; flexibility and adaptation of Indian professionals for on-time, on-schedule delivery of projects; the high reliability factor of Indian software export companies; strong educational orientation (ideal for the production of high class engineering graduates skilled in computer sciences and engineering); a vast base of Fortune 500 customers who are increasingly outsourcing to India; and support from successful Indians in Silicon Valley. To this we could add government incentives, e.g. tax incentives to software exports.

22. Although there seemed to have been some investments by another company or some private placements. Israeli counterparts to SAS, e.g. Orkitt, have actually benefited from IPO and from investments by foreign and local financial institutions (including venture capitalists).

23. Participation in the Standards Committee mentioned would be one way of getting plugged into world knowledge networks. Also, venture capital could play a role in this respect. Finally, it must be mentioned that knowledge links build up gradually and cumulatively as a result of the expansion of the firm and of the industry as a whole.

24. A detailed discussion of the liberalization and deregulation steps taken during the 1990s can be seen in Dossani and Kenney (2002). Their analysis shows that notwithstanding the undoubted advances, important obstacles still remain (at least they did a couple of years ago).

25. It is a major issue whether or not India would like to implement an 'incentives' programme in support of R&D/innovation. While such programmes could make a significant contribution to the high-tech cluster, its effectiveness would depend on good design and non-bureaucratic, learning-enhancing implementation.

26. The importance of 'indigenous' global companies for a balanced accumulation of assets is also borne out by the study of very successful companies in Israel's data security industry. See Teubal and Avnimelech (2002).

27. The Hughes example might also contribute 'indirectly' to the next phase of development of the Indian software and IT industry by acting as a strategic/organizational/ business model that could be replicated by other MNEs.

28. This has been confirmed by the very rapid growth that took place after 1999.

29. An example is the VC company founded by Narayana Murthy, the founder of Infosys, among India's leading software companies. Also, the high quality links between large Indian software companies and large multinational corporations also facilitate the identification of the 'technology needs' of the latter. This could potentially be a very valuable asset, spurring the process of SU formation in India.

30. The analysis that follows presupposes that the global IT high-tech market will recover in the next two–five years or earlier.

31. The emergent characteristics of the reconfigured high-tech cluster were: a VC market/sector comprising large numbers of SU and VC; an increasing weight of SU 'output' in total high-tech output; and strong links with global capital markets.

32. In a previous work (Avnimelech and Teubal, 2002c) and following Dossani and Kenney (2002), we point out the significance of some of the positive developments in India's VC industry during the 1990s. This is reflected also in NASSCOM (2001: 119–20) which points to the comparatively large amounts of funds invested and the minimal reduction in VC investments during 2001–2 compared to 2000–1 ($1.1 billion against $1.2 billion); and to the fact that over seventy VC funds operating during 2001–2 with total capital management of $5.6 billion. The data, however, are not clear about the *structure and organizational forms of VC funds/companies*, nor about the share of investments which are '*early phase investments*', a critical aspect of the Silicon Valley model of high tech. That is why it is not clear to us whether *VC emergence*, in the sense of *a cumulative process of growth* that took place in Israel's VC industry during 1993–8 has really taken place (probably not). For further insights in India's VC industry, see Bowonder and Mani (2002).

References

Arora, A., V. S. Arunachalam, J. Asundi and R. Fernandez (2001) 'The Indian Software Services Industry', *Research Policy* 30 (8): 1267–87

Avnimelech, G. (2002) 'Exploring VC Added Value: a Study of the Israeli VC Industry', MA Degree Paper, Tel-Aviv University, Tel-Aviv.

Avnimelech, G. A. Gayego, M. Teubal and B. Toren (2000) 'Country Report: Israel, TSER (Targeted Socio-Economic Research) Project', 'SMEs in Europe and Asia', typescript.

Avnimelech, G. and M. Teubal (2002a) 'Israel's Venture Capital Industry: Emergence, Operation and Impact', in D. Citendamar (ed.), *The Growth of Venture Capital: a Cross Cultural Analysis* (Westport, CT: Praeger).

——(2002b) 'Venture Capital: Start Up Co-evolution and the Emergence and Development of Israel's New High Tech Cluster – Part 1: Macroeconomic and Industry Analysis', *Economics of Innovation and New Technology*, 12 (5), June 2003.

—— (2002c) 'Venture Capital Policy in Israel: a Comparative Analysis and Lessons for Other Countries', paper presented at EC-sponsored Workshop on 'Financial Systems, Corporate Investment in Innovation and Venture Capital', Brussels, 6–8 Nov.

—— (2002d) 'Venture Capital-Start-Up Co-evolution and the Emergence and Development of Israel's New High Tech Cluster – Part 2: Implications of a Microeconomic Analysis' (forthcoming).

Bartzokas, A. and M. Teubal (2002) 'A Framework for Policy-Oriented Innovation Studies in Industrializing Economies', *Economics of Innovation and New Technology* (special issue on Innovation Policy in Developing Countries) 11 (4–5), Aug.–Oct.: 477–96.

Blass, A. and Y. Yafeh (2001) 'Vagabond Shoes Longing to Stray: Why Foreign Companies List in the US', *Journal of Banking and Finance*, 25 (3): 555–72.

Bowonder, B. and S. Mani (2002) 'Venture Capital and Innovation: the Indian Experience', paper presented at the International Workshop on 'Financial Systems, Corporate Investment in Innovation and Venture Capital', Brussels, 6–8 Nov.

Bresnahan, T., A. Gambardella and A. Saxenian (2002) 'Old Economy Inputs for "New Economy Outcomes": Cluster Formation in the New Silicon Valleys', paper presented at the 2002 Druid Workshop, June.

Business Week (2002) 'Calling Bangalore: Multinationals are Making it a Hub for High Tech Research', Manjeet Kripalani, 11 Nov.: 24–5.

CBS (Central Bureau of Statistics, Israel) (2001) 'Development of Information and Communications Technologies in the Last Decade', March.

Cetindamar, D. (ed.) (forthcoming) *The Growth of Venture Capital: a Cross Cultural Comparison* (Westport, CT: Praeger).

Dossani, R. and M. Kenney (2002) 'Creating an Environment for Venture Capital in India', *World Development*, 30 (2): 227–53.

Gates, B. (2002) 'Slowing the Spread of Aids in India', *New York Times*, 9 Nov.

Gelvan, D. and M. Teubal (1997) 'Emergence and Development of a Venture Capital Industry in Israel: an Evolutionary and Policy Approach', paper presented in Symposium in Honour of Alexander Volta, Como, Italy.

Gompers P. and J. Lerner (2001) 'The Venture Capital Revolution', *Journal of Economic Perspectives*, 15 (2): 145–68.

—— (1999) *The Venture Capital Cycle* (Cambridge, MA/London: MIT Press).

IVA (Israel Venture Association) (1997) *1997 Yearbook: a Survey of Venture Capital and Private Equity in Israel*, ed. Giza Group.

——(1998) *1988 Yearbook: a Survey of Venture Capital and Private Equity in Israel*, ed. Giza Group.

——(1999) *1999 Yearbook: a Survey of Venture Capital and Private Equity in Israel*, ed. Giza Group.

——(2000) *2000 Yearbook: a Survey of Venture Capital and Private Equity in Israel*, ed. THGC Giza Group.

——(2001) *2001 Yearbook: a Survey of Venture Capital and Private Equity in Israel*, ed. IVC (IVC Research Center).

Justman, M. (2001) 'Structural Change and the Emergence of Israeli's High Tech Industry', in *The Israeli Economy 1985–98: From Government Intervention to Market Economy, Volume in Honor of Michael Bruno* (Falk Institute for Economic Research), Jerusalem, Israel.

Justman, Moshe and E. Zuscovitch (2000) 'The Economic Impact of Subsidized Industrial R&D in Israel', paper presented at the EUNIP Conference, Eindhoven Technological University, Tilburg.

Kenney, M. (2001) 'Regional Clusters, Venture Capital and Entrepreneurship: What Can the Social Science Tell Us About Silicon Valley?', forthcoming in an OECD proceedings workshop.

Lall, S. and M. Teubal (1998) ' "Market Stimulation" Technology Policies in Developing Countries: a Framework with Examples from East Asia', *World Development*, 26 (8): 1369–85.

Metcalfe, S. (1996) 'The Economic Foundations of Technology Policy: Equilibrium and Evolutionary Perspectives', ch. 11 in P. Stoneman (ed.), *Handbook of the Economics of Innovation and Technological Change* (Oxford, UK and Cambridge, MA, USA: Blackwell).

Murray, G. (1999) 'Seed Capital Funds and the Effects of Scale Economies', in *Venture Cap: International Journal of Entrepreneurial Finance*, 1: 167–82.

Myers, S. C. and N. S. Majluf (1984) 'Corporate Financing and Investment Decisions When Firms Have Information That Investors Do Not Have', *Journal of Financial Economics*, 13: 187–221.

NASSCOM (2002) *The IT Industry in India: Strategic Review 2002* (New Delhi: National Association of Software and Service Companies).

——(2003) *The IT Industry in India: Strategic Review 2003* (New Delhi, National Association of Software and Service Companies).

Nelson, R. (1993) *National Systems of Innovation* (New York: Oxford University Press).

——(1994) 'The Co-evolution of Technology, Industrial Structure and Supporting Institutions', *Industrial and Corporate Change*, 3 (1): 47–63.

Saxenian, A. (1998) *Regional Development: Silicon Valley and Route 128*, 8th edn (Cambridge, MA and London: Oxford University Press).

——(2002) 'The Silicon Valley Connection: Transnational Networks and Regional Development in Taiwan, China and India', *Science, Technology and Society*, 7 (1): 117–49.

Schertler, A. (2002) 'Path Dependencies in Venture Capital Markets', Working paper 1120, Kiel Institute for World Economics.

Stiglitz, J. E., and A. Weiss (1981) 'Credit Rationing in Markets with Incomplete Information', *American Economic Review*, 71: 393–409.

Teubal, M. (1982) 'The R&D Performance Through time of High-tech Firms: Methodology and an Illustration', *Research Policy*, 11: 271–87.

——(1986) *Innovation Performance, Learning and Government Policy* (Madison: University of Wisconsin Press).

Teubal, M. (1993) 'The Innovation System of Israel: Description, Performance and Outstanding Issues', in R. Nelson (ed.), *National Systems of Innovation* (New York: Oxford University Press).

——(1996) 'R&D and Technology Policy at NICs as a Learning Process', *World Development*, 24: 449–60.

——(1996) 'A Catalytic and Evolutionary Perspective to Horizontal Technology Policy', *Research Policy*, 25: 1161–88.

——(1999) 'Towards an R&D Strategy for Israel', *Economic Quarterly* (Hebrew), 46 (2): 359–83. English version in http://atar.mscc.huji.ac.il/-economics/facultye/teubal/rd.pdf.

—— (2002a): 'What is the Systems of Innovation (SI) Perspective to Innovation and Technology Policy (ITP) and How Can We Apply it to Developing and Industrialized Economies?', *Journal of Evolutionary Economics*, 12: 233–57.

—— (2002b) 'Observations on the Indian Software Industry from an Israeli Perspective: a Microeconomic and Policy Analysis', *Science, Technology and Society*, 7 (1): 151–86.

Teubal, M. and E. Andersen (2000) 'Enterprise Restructuring and Embeddedness: a Policy and Systems Perspective', *Industrial and Corporate Change*, 9 (1): 87–111.

Teubal, M., N. Arnon and M. Trajtenberg (1976) 'Performance in Innovation in Israel's Electronics Industry: a Case Study of Biomedical Electronics Instrumentation', in Teubal (1986), pp. 10–31. First published in *Research Policy*, 5 (1976) 354–79.

Teubal, M. and G. Avnimelech (2002): 'Foreign Acquisitions and R&D Leverage in High Tech Industries of Peripheral Economies: Lessons and Policy Issues from the Israeli Experience', forthcoming in *International Journal of Technology Management*, 24, Special Issue, 'Evaluating Innovation Policies New Objectives, New Strategies, New Results?'

Teubal, M., G. Avnimelech and A. Gayego (2002) 'Company Growth, Acquisitions and Access to Complementary Asseets in Israel's Data Security Sector', *European Planning Studies*, 10 (8): 933–53.

Toren, B. (1990) 'R&D in Industry', in D. Brodet, M. Justman and M. Teubal (eds), *Industrial Policy for Israel* (Hebrew), Jerusalem Institute for Israel Studies.

Trajtenberg, M. (2000) 'R&D Policy in Israel: an Overview and Reassessment', Working Paper 7930, National Bureau of Economic Research, Cambridge, MA.

6

Software Product Development in India: Lessons from Six Cases*

Rishikesha T. Krishnan and Ganesh N. Prabhu

.

1. Introduction

While the software industry is considered a highly successful economic growth engine in India (NASSCOM, 2002a), its rapid growth in recent years has been achieved by firms primarily providing manpower-intensive customized software development and maintenance services to foreign clients (Arora et al., 2001). While this business model has enabled Indian software companies to transit smoothly from software 'body-shopping' services to offshore software development in India, it has also made them vulnerable to the business cycles in client countries. The software services model is manpower intensive, and growth is achieved only by a proportionate increase in the number of software engineers employed. This results in large organizations that become increasingly difficult to coordinate and control. The competitive advantages of this business model are narrow (Arora, Gambardella and Torrisi, 2001) and may over time be eroded by lower cost countries like China.

One alternative to the software services model is a business model centred on software products. While the distance from India of the largest market for software products (the US) makes a continuing assessment of user needs in that market difficult, there are other options such as addressing the needs of the Indian market or creating 'core products' (Prahalad and Hamel, 1990) that could form the basis for software solutions in Indian and foreign markets. The availability of products suited to Indian user needs might induce Indian manufacturing companies to overcome their tendency to use 'custom development for standard functionality'[1] (Accenture, 2002: 31) and thereby enhance their ability to leverage information technology. From the perspective of national competitiveness, it could be beneficial to have more diversified software firms whose clients use 'packaged solutions' that incorporate best practices for standardized functions at lower costs, while primarily utilizing customized software services for unique applications (Accenture, 2002: 54).

Indian software companies may be able to create software solutions for clients more easily and quickly if they build these solutions around products they have developed. Packaged products could also enable firms to benefit from the multiplier effect: by selling multiple copies of the same software at low marginal costs. Notwithstanding these potential benefits, few Indian firms have made a serious attempt to create a portfolio of software products, nor has there been a growth of independent software product companies. The Indian software industry association NASSCOM has listed 'low presence in global packaged software market' and 'lack of original technology development orientation' as the two major weaknesses of their industry (NASSCOM, 2002a: 32).

This study attempts to understand the issues that impact the creation and management of software products in the developing country context of India. We draw lessons for policy and practice from the collective experience of software product development in six diverse software product development projects in India, and use the insights so gained to examine their implications for software firms in general, the software industry, policymakers in India and, by extension, other developing countries.

2. Research on product development

Before exploring some of the specific issues regarding software products and the influence of the geographical context, it will be useful to summarize the findings of the extant generic research on the management of product development.

The key objectives in product development are to minimize time-to-market, and to maximize the fit between customer requirements and product characteristics (Schilling and Hill, 1998). Achieving these objectives helps a company to rapidly recoup its development costs and garner reasonable economic returns in highly uncertain environments. Companies seek to get to market early, develop products with external and internal 'integrity' (Clark and Fujimoto, 1990), make optimum use of development and other resources, and develop not one but a stream of new products over time.

Companies are advised to pay adequate attention to the 'fuzzy' front end[2] of the product development process (Khurana and Rosenthal, 1997), listen to the voice of the customer (Griffin and Hauser, 1993), improve intra-organizational communication, develop a common language to communicate and share product development ideas, and to deploy cross-functional teams in a structured product development process (Ulrich and Eppinger, 1995).

A clearly articulated strategic intent (Hamel and Prahlad, 1989), a development strategy that chooses the right set of projects and helps integrate strategic planning with R&D strategy (Wheelwright and Clark, 1992), strong top management involvement at early stages of the project, empowerment of project leaders as 'heavyweight project managers' (Clark and Fujimoto, 1990), transferring and leveraging skills and competencies across the company (Prahlad and Hamel, 1990), and setting targets for revenues from new products are considered best practices. Top management is urged to create an organizational climate in which honest failures are tolerated, creativity rewarded, and inter-functional and inter-divisional barriers lowered (Kanter, Kao and Wiersema, 1997).

Some of the attributes of software products, and the context in which product development is undertaken, influence the complexity and challenges involved in software product development in India. These issues are discussed in the following sections.

Software products and software product development

Computer software is the stored, machine-readable code that instructs a computer to carry out specific tasks. The three types of software are: (a) *tools* used to generate applications to retrieve, organize, manage and manipulate data, (b) *applications* designed to solve specific problems inherent across all industries or in a particular industry or business function, and (c) *system-level software* that controls the internal operations of a computer (Mowery, 1999). All three types of software can be provided in either 'standard' or 'customized' form. The term 'software product' generally refers to a traded, standard software programme, though some of the more complex forms of software products also involve some degree of customization. In this chapter we focus exclusively on application software projects.

Software products differ from physical products in a few respects. While physical products need to have production issues explicitly addressed during the product development process, and late changes in product designs can have cost and time implications, software products do not have such constraints. Instead, other issues like compatibility with hardware platforms and operating systems, both of which change rapidly, become critical. Software products are easier to replicate, either through piracy or by copying key features, and providing adequate protection to intellectual property rights is difficult. Network economies play an important role in software products: having a community of users and an installed base of systems software is often essential, as it facilitates interaction and file exchange among users. While architecture and compatibility issues are important, specification of features can often be delayed to near launch date to incorporate the latest needs of the target customers.

Generic packaged software applications often need large volumes to break even. Software duplication costs are low in comparison to those of development, maintenance and marketing. There are high costs associated with maintaining and servicing a product over its lifetime. Users expect frequent upgrades and demand the option to shift to an upgrade at a small incremental price. Upgrades have to be compatible with earlier versions and need to retain features to which users have become accustomed. Once the user gets used to a particular software package, there may be a 'lock-in' effect, as switching to another software programme requires learning. Launch and promotion costs are often high as companies stage public relations events, advertise value propositions, and enforce product cannibalization to market newer versions. Marketing software products in international markets may need localization of the product itself as well as the marketing mix.

The US market is the largest in the world for packaged software, accounting for nearly 50 per cent of the $200 billion global market for packaged software (OECD, 2002: 320). As 'user-friendliness' and adaptation to local operating conditions are critical in the case of application software, proximity to users is essential in developing appropriate products and being effective in the product development process (Mowery, 1999: 163). Therefore, US-based software firms that develop application software products hold an advantage over other firms that have no presence in the US (Mowery, 1999: 160). The offshore structure of software production, which is well suited to customized software development, is not suited to the short development cycles, rapid prototyping, and high responsiveness to user needs that are essential for packaged software development.

Product development in the Indian software industry

Indian software companies have largely stayed away from product development. Even industry majors that set ambitious targets for product revenues have given up their targets over time. For example, the major firm Infosys Technologies had about 4 per cent revenues from software products in 2001–2 (SEC, 2002), though at one time they hoped to achieve a target of 40 per cent revenues from products by 2000 (Prahlad, 1996).[3]

There are some reasons for Indian software firms to desist from developing products. India is well established as a source of software services, and there are large firms that are successful role models for new firms and smaller firms to emulate. This has established services as the dominant logic among Indian firms. Software services enable Indian companies to be highly profitable with relatively low risks and ensure regular immediate cash flows, in contrast to product development that involves large initial investments and future, uncertain cash flows. The major software services firms have high valuations and generate high expectations from investors and analysts who expect these firms to 'de-risk' their ventures. The software industry is characterized by low physical and high human capital intensity (Mowery, 1999: 156). The steady supply of qualified software professionals, capable of generating revenue immediately through services, has probably added to the inertia of success among software service firms as their business model is not seriously threatened.

The software services business model is based on limited, client-specific relationship marketing to generate business, and efficient project management and quality management to execute it. Indian software firms have been content to leave the conceptualization and design of a software solution to a client-appointed information technology consultant and undertake only the coding and implementation of the software. Such software projects are usually well defined and have clear deliverables. In contrast, software product development is viable only if the firm can internally conceptualize unique applications and capture value largely through the marketing part of the value chain. The limited demand potential of the Indian domestic market and the large geographical distance from the largest market for packaged software, the US, makes the entry and marketing of software products a difficult proposition. Software product firms need to have appropriate reference clients to convince other clients that they should buy expensive software products, and Indian client installations are often not considered appropriate reference installations. Further, maintenance over the lifecycle of a product in foreign markets is expensive, as is the provision support in multiple locations worldwide, though limited support can be provided over the Internet. There are problems with software piracy and the lack of adequate venture capital that make software product development in India difficult.

Product development can enable software firms to be at the leading edge of technology by exploiting synergies between their service and product businesses. There are, however, evident difficulties in managing both types of projects. Nambisan (2001) found in a survey of 137 firms (with a predominantly Indian sample) that 87 per cent of product ventures initiated by software service firms were unsuccessful, primarily due to inappropriate transfer of organizational practices and development culture. Some Indian software firms may also face an additional barrier because they are locked in at a lower level of innovation through prolonged involvement with low end service projects (D'Costa, 2002).

However, software product development has the potential to yield high returns to Indian software companies (Krishnan and Prabhu, 1999). Among software professionals, there is often a higher level of prestige associated with working for software product firms as against mere software service providers. Software product development projects could therefore potentially attract high quality Indian software development talent that currently migrates to US software product firms. While the lack of proximity to the large US market may be a hindrance, many Indian firms have a strong US presence for provision as software services that can potentially be extended to the development of software products. There are product application areas in developing countries that are not served by products from developed countries. There is a potential for Indian firms to develop niche products at low costs specifically for the Indian market and then extend these products to other developing country markets to generate volumes. For example, Soft Systems, India developed a low-cost specialized enterprise resource planning software package for managing plantations in India, and now has 560 installations across twelve countries (Jishnu, 2002).

Product development and innovation in India

It is intriguing that there have not been more visible efforts at software product development, particularly when the software industry is not affected by the factors that constrain other Indian industries. There is a pattern of limited product innovation that characterizes the Indian industry across all sectors of the economy. Much of this is due to the legacy of a protected economy where innovation was unnecessary and often thwarted by government policy (Forbes, 1999; Bowonder and Richardson, 2000). The scarcity of investment capital made most entrepreneurs risk-averse. Many engineering products manufactured in India were governed by technology licensing agreements that placed restrictions on their slightest physical modification or even improvement. Import restrictions made it difficult for companies to source particular components or skills and capabilities they lacked. Scarcity of design skills and experience, lack of appropriate engineering resources, lack of a strong market orientation, and centralized control by business family heads have been some of the other constraints to product development in other sectors in India (Krishnan and Prabhu, 1999).

None of the above factors is germane to the Indian software industry. Further, in recent years, after the liberalization of the Indian economy was initiated in 1991, there has been an increased interest in product development manifested by Indian companies in diverse industries (Forbes, 1999; Krishnan and Prabhu, 1999). In an increasingly competitive and crowded marketplace, the ability to develop and launch new products has gained in importance, both to create product differentiation as well as increase primary demand. As the software industry requires low physical and high human capital, Indian software firms could be expected to be at the forefront of product innovation. This is not evident, however. India has an abundance of programming and software development skills, yet creates few packaged software products. Software industry insiders attribute this lack of a package orientation to factors in the larger innovation system outside the software companies. Desai (1998) believes that 'innovation can flourish only in an ecosystem that has the elements of market, money, university, cluster of companies, attitudes, culture and the appropriate regulatory and legal environment', while Mehta (1998) emphasizes that software product development requires 'an R&D culture, market intelligence, skills to develop user-friendly software and documentation, availability of funds and special marketing skills'.

3. Understanding recent product development in India

The Indian software industry provides a rich research context for an understanding of the factors and processes that influence software product development in a developing country context. Given the late evolution of product thinking in Indian industry, and the dominant service orientation of the software industry, it is likely that the major challenge in software product development in India is developing a product orientation. This consists of being able to conceptualize a product in terms of what need it meets, what the target market is, and being able to devise a distinctive product that adequately meets user needs and yet differentiates itself from competitive offerings in ways that customers value. This task is complicated, as research suggests that service and product businesses differ in terms of project management, culture and organizational practices (Sawyer, 2000; Nambisan, 2001).

It is also likely that firms that focus on niche markets in India and then extend the product to other developing country markets over time are more likely to succeed. Also, Indian firms that build products around customized software they have developed earlier may be more likely to succeed. In India, product development speed and efficiency considerations may be secondary to considerations of fit with customer requirements. In the light of these initial propositions, we study a diverse set of software product development efforts of Indian companies to understand the factors that affect the initiation and implementation of software product development projects. We also attempt to understand the motivations and commitment of pure product companies in India that operate in a context where service companies are dominant and successful. We seek to understand whether the developing country context, and the sequence of entry from services to products, creates unique opportunities and difficulties for software companies that undertake software product development projects in India.

Given the relative lack of literature on the variables and factors affecting software product development in India, we chose to use a qualitative exploratory research method, the case method of research, that is considered appropriate for such research contexts (Yin, 1994). We conducted in-depth case studies of six software product development projects developed by six software firms in India. We chose one software product in each firm and traced the process of initiation and implementation of the software product development effort within the firm. Through the study of company records, in-depth interviews, secondary material, and industry/press reports we constructed detailed case studies of the product development process for each of these projects.

Our approach has involved a multiple case study (Yin, 1994). Potential cases were identified from newspapers and magazines. The projects studied were only of applications software products, and were chosen to provide a variety of industrial contexts, types of firms, types of markets and levels of customization. We covered projects from both 'pure-product' companies and 'service-product' hybrid companies. We examined both commercial successes and failures, products selling in large volumes, niche products, and products that emerged from customized software development projects. By a process of analysis within cases and synthesis across them, we have gained key insights regarding software product development in the Indian context.

We analysed the cases across nine dimensions from four important themes that reflect the issues emphasized in previous sections. First, the product-market choice issues were looked at in terms of product definition and positioning, company size and choice of product, and whether the product choice emerged from technology push or market pull. Second, the product design and user interface issues were explored through the interplay of technology choice and product architecture, product architecture and customization. Third, customization and version management as well as marketing and product launch issues were investigated as a single dimension. Finally, the influence of internal organizational factors such as reward and incentive systems and quality systems on the product development process was examined across cases.

Six companies, six products

Summaries of the products studied and the companies in which they were developed are given in Table 6.1. We also provide a brief description of each firm and its product. The case studies are based on data collected up to June 2000. Subsequent events, to the extent known to us, have had no impact on our general findings and conclusions.

Infosys Technologies and BANCS 2000

Infosys Technologies is one of the largest software firms in India and the first Indian software firm to be listed on a US stock exchange, the NASDAQ. Its major business is in software services with its revenues from software products being about 2 per cent of their total revenues. It is known for excellence in management and corporate governance.

Table 6.1   Companies and products studied

The company	The product
1. Infosys Technologies Ltd, India's best known large software firm.	BANCS 2000, a banking product for the domestic and international market.
2. Ramco Systems, one of India's larger product-focused software firms.	Marshal (later re-named e-applications), an enterprise resource planning product.
3. Tata Consultancy Services, India's largest software company. Part of the Tata conglomerate and privately held.	EX, financial accounting product positioned as the world's friendliest accounting software.
4. Concept Software, a small software company focusing on multi-language desktop publishing products.	InPage, an Arabic script-based multi-language desktop publishing software product.
5. Eastern Software Systems, a small software company focusing on enterprise resource planning products.	MakESS, an enterprise resource planning product targeted at small companies.
6. RiteChoice Technologies, a small software company focusing on the stockbroking domain.	Spectrum, a product to manage the back office and middle office of a stockbroker.

The development of the BANCS 2000 product owes its inception to a pilot project for bank computerization initiated by the Indian Banks Association in 1989. Infosys was one of eight firms chosen for participation in this project. Infosys decided to create a 'foundation framework' and an integrated approach to this product, even though this delayed the first deliveries, in the hope of being able to create a more robust and easily expandable and scalable solution for marketing to other banks. The major challenge faced by Infosys has been to meet customer expectations for customization and for an offering that was differentiated from that delivered to other customers, while at the same time maintaining a single code base (believed by Infosys to be an important aspect of product development). The formal inauguration of the product took place in 1994, though some bank branches were already working with the product earlier.

Notwithstanding its small size in relation to the service business at Infosys, the banking project had, since its inception, commanded a high level of top management interest as it was seen as the basis for the future creation of a larger product business. A major revamp of the product was undertaken in 1997 to enable it to meet the requirements of foreign banks for such things as multi-currency operations and centralized banking operations. Subsequently, the product has been Internet enabled through a new utility called Bank Away. The product has been adopted by some Indian private sector banks and has found markets in South East Asia and the Middle East. It faces tough competition from at least ten major competing products worldwide. As the product requires a relatively high level of customization, a key factor in influencing prospective sales is the demonstration of installations with high profile customers in foreign countries. Banking products remain the only significant product offering of Infosys. Other products developed by Infosys for retailing and warehousing were spun-off to Yantra Corporation in the US, in which Infosys now has a minority stake.

Subsequent to our study, Infosys completely re-engineered the product and named it Finnacle. Finnacle is now reputed to be among the world's top three banking products.

Ramco Systems and Marshal

Ramco Systems is part of a large south Indian industrial group with major interests in cement and building materials. The vision of creating a world-class software product company revolving around enterprise applications goes back to the late 1980s when the vice chairman and founder of Ramco Systems was a graduate student in the US.

Product development on the Marshal product started in 1989, and the first release was in 1993, based on a robust technical architecture that had been conceived in 1992. A number of releases followed in the Indian market till 1995. A major effort to upgrade the product to international standards followed after 1995, with about 400 software professionals involved, leading to the release of Version 3.0 in 1997. Version 3.0 combined good functionality with strong product architecture and was launched in a number of international markets.

The product has been relatively successful in certain markets and geographies, e.g. human resources applications in British legacy markets (Malaysia, Singapore, India, UK); enterprise asset management in capital-intensive industries such as power, gas and aluminium, where maintenance is critical; in process industries like food, chemicals and textiles, as the structure of the software was well-suited to these businesses. The installed base as of May 2000 was 156 customers in 650 locations and 11 000 users in eleven countries. The largest implementation was in the Swatch group (seventeen locations). The product was Internet enabled and relaunched as 'e-applications' in 1999.

Tata Consultancy Services and EX

Tata Consultancy Services (TCS) is the largest software firm in India and part of the Tata business conglomerate. Though a majority of its revenue comes from software services, TCS has pioneered or developed several software products in India in the areas of banking, accounting, insurance and health care. They have developed several software development tools such as MasterCraft, Adex and Assent that offer them an advantage in software product development.

EX is TCS's major mass-marketed packaged software. Positioned as the world's friendliest accounting software, it is equally amenable for single-person, small-business and large-firm accounting. It was the first mass-marketed Indian software product. It was launched in 1991, with an innovative stage play that featured well-known Indian stage actors, full-page newspaper advertisements, launch events in major cities, and wide distribution of information brochures.

The present product, EX Next Generation 1.5, is a comprehensive business accounting software with document designer and extensive reporting capabilities for medium-sized businesses. For larger corporations with higher volume requirements, EX Next Generation 1.5 Multi-User is positioned as a robust, reliable and extendable accounting solution. The product has developed over several versions, both in terms of feature upgrading from small single-user to multi-user versions, and an increasing capacity for the development of international versions. TCS runs its own accounts on EX. The product was distributed through 'Keydealers' and direct 'Keymen' commission agents, and backed by online user support. TCS collected user feedback through a registration process that was linked to upgrades. Attractive package design, multiple computer media options, and bundled offers supported sales. A 'transparent' hardware lock (a hardware lock that did not block a port) protected the software from piracy. TCS considers this product conceptually strong, user-friendly, feature rich and affordably priced. EX offers off-the-shelf installation and training. Over the years, the product has been backed by continuing promotion focusing on user friendliness. The product is estimated to have 80 000 users. It won the Best Software Product Award from the Computer Society of India as well as the Most Popular Software Award, the Best Packaging Award, and the Best Communication Award of the society.

Since its launch, upgrades of the software for new features were essentially through software layering and add-on coding over the basic software. In 2000, a new and independent team initiated a major restructuring of the EX package. The restructuring was aimed at enhancing quality, features and performance by using an entirely new software code built using internally developed software tools while retaining a major part of the graphic user interface that was familiar to EX's current users.

Concept Software and In-Page

Concept Software is a small software firm based in Delhi promoted by two engineering graduate classmates from the Indian Institute of Technology at Kanpur. The partnership firm started with several small product development projects that had mixed success. The last of these software development projects was to develop Russian language word-processing software. While that project was not a commercial success, the partners gained valuable knowledge in the design and development of generic word- and character-processing software.

The partners realized that the best application area for their knowledge of character processing was in the development of Arabic script-based word-processing software. Unlike English, which requires only a simple placement of letters alongside each other, the Arabic-based scripts use compound lettering that require complex changes in the shapes of basic letters as extensions to a character are added. This means that, while the number of characters is limited (unlike the large number of characters in the Chinese script), a simple set of characters and extensions are insufficient for the Arabic scripts. Words need to be built by developing complex shapes within a single complex character as multiple characters are added on a keyboard. Arabic script software that was available before Concept Software's InPage made compromises with the authentic shapes of the script, to suit software limitations, that were aesthetically unacceptable in communities that view the Arabic script as an aesthetic form. These software packages also made the script difficult to read. Publishers of the best newspapers and books in the Arabic scripts did not use such compromised software and relied on handwritten calligraphy.

Concept Software was the first and only firm to build an Arabic script software, InPage, that used a compounded lettering scripting technology developed internally for a limited set of languages based on Arabic-based scripts. An employee trained in classical Arabic scripts, and trained by the partners in computer programming, helped the firm develop a very large library of compounded Arabic letters that appeared and changed on screen as individual letters of the alphabets were typed using a conventional keyboard. They also developed a set of ready-made and commonly used Arabic mastheads as graphic files within the package. These were popular Arabic verses and quotations that were scripted into very complex aesthetic shapes that could not be created through the keyboard. Both the compounded lettering and ready-made graphic files soon made InPage the undisputed best Arabic script software in the world.

Concept Software launched the first version of InPage with a software lock at a fairly high price. However, the software lock was soon 'broken' and the package was widely pirated at low prices in several countries. Concept Software subsequently built an improved version and marketed it at a far lower price than its first version, with a hardware lock that has not been broken so far. The product is currently a monopoly and no product of comparative quality and features exists. Almost all Arabic newspapers and publishers in the world use either of the two versions of InPage. Most of the high end users have purchased authentic copies of the new version of InPage. However, the pirated low priced copies of the earlier version of InPage represent the major competition for the new version, especially among individual buyers. The market for this product is largely in the Arab countries and marketing is primarily through the firm's agents based in the UK, as the company does not have the resources to sell directly to the many Arab countries.

Eastern Software Systems and MakESS

Eastern Software Systems (ESS) is a small software firm based in Delhi that has built an enterprise resource planning (ERP) software package, MakESS, targeted at small firms. Competing ERP products from international industry majors such as SAP and BAAN are priced at over US$50000 in India, far too expensive for small Indian firms who cannot afford such high investments and do not see commensurate benefits justifying such a price. On the other hand, low-featured, customized ERP products, that are developed by small firms for US$2000 or less in India, are quite unreliable.

Seeing the gap develop in the small firm market for ERP software, ESS developed MakESS in three interlinked versions. The entry-level package (human resource management only) retailed for about US$2000 (useful for almost any product or service organization), a second full version suitable for non-manufacturing firms at US$10000 (this included the human resource package), and a third full version for manufacturing firms at US$16000. With over 100 installations in India, some in fairly large multi-location firms, MakESS has occupied a niche as a relatively low cost, value-for-money, ERP package in India.

The firm promotes modification of client business practices to best practices that are incorporated in the software, but unlike larger ERP firms, is relatively more willing to customize the package for specific requirements by charging the client additionally on a person-month basis. By making the package highly user friendly and targeting firms in specific industries that can inherently adapt easily to it, the firm saves on installation, customization programming and support costs. For example, pursuing this marketing strategy, the firm has built an innovative add-on special module for milk procurement activities in milk cooperatives (a specialized application not available in other ERP software) and is targeting hundreds of milk cooperative plants throughout India through the National Dairy Development Board.

The firm recently released its Internet-based ERP version on a 'no initial fee–low monthly charge' basis. The firm sees Internet versions as an extension of the market to smaller firms rather than a shift in the core market of larger firms that are more likely to opt for Internet-based versions. Major software firms worldwide have reposed faith in ESS as they hold minority equity stakes in the firm.

RiteChoice and Spectrum

The Spectrum product is the outcome of a decade-long effort to provide a product that can manage all the essential operations of a stockbroker. Started as a partnership in 1988–9, its first product was launched in 1989 and reflected 'stockbroking as taught by brokers'. A LAN-based, scaled-up version was launched in 1991. RiteChoice was started in 1992. A new prototype concept was subsequently created in 1995, and upgraded and ported to Oracle as Spectrum 2000E.

The Spectrum product has client–server architecture, and can handle back-office (clearing, settlement, brokerage) and middle-office (risk management) functions for multiple exchanges, multiple locations and multiple instruments. It is designed for large brokerages with multiple branches and many sub-brokers. A major feature of product development at RiteChoice has been the intense academic study of the broking process to gain domain knowledge before initiating product development. A concept paper incorporating state-of-the-art best practices in the area formed the basic user knowledge used for product design and coding. Experts vetted the proposed product design before actual product engineering took place. Their knowledge-intensive approach has been acknowledged by the minority investment of IT major Intel in this company.

Explaining product development in the six companies

In this section, we summarize and discuss our analysis across the six products and companies that we studied. The analysis is across nine dimensions covering four themes: product market choice, product design-user interface issues, marketing and product launch, and interface with organizational systems.

Product definition and positioning

An important aspect of software product development is the clear definition of the target market, the need being met and the distinctiveness or competitive edge of the product being offered (most visible in MakESS, Spectrum, In-Page, and later versions of Marshal). Clarity on these issues enables clear definition of the product itself, which is essential for the development of a product that has integrity, and that can be developed in a reasonable time frame without 'creeping functionality'. While it may not be possible to do all this the first time around, especially in a complex product, a successful product developer learns to address these questions rapidly and adequately (Marshal to a large extent, and to a lesser extent BANCS 2000).

Early product definition is more likely to take place rapidly in a 'product company' (Marshal) than a 'services company' (BANCS 2000) that also makes products, as in the latter there is a conflicting culture of a propensity to institute incremental changes to meet emerging customer requirements. A product company is more likely to place greater stress on functionality for each version.

Developing products for highly regulated industries in emerging markets necessitates the ability to keep track of new notifications and other developments and to continually update and upgrade the product. RiteChoice has found that the new transaction types and instruments allowed by the Securities and Exchange Board of India over time have necessitated frequent changes in the product. On the research side, they have to be continually ready for introduction of these new features at short notice.

Company size and choice of product

For small companies, niche products are an effective way of entering the product market (In-Page in Arabic publishing and Spectrum in stock-broking). Typically, niche products that address specific, usually narrower or lower order needs of a small group of users, are less complex. They are more customized and can be developed in relatively shorter time frames and typically do not need huge development resources. However, absence of a strong network of independent software dealers makes it difficult for these niche products to reach the relevant and possibly already distributed market, as it is prohibitively expensive to set up a separate marketing network for a single product or a small group of products. This problem exists in international markets as well, though the challenge in that case would be to set up a partner network that would enable greater market access and penetration (Concept Software has a sales agent in UK for world sales).

Software product development requires major investments in development time and money. Larger firms can hire a large number of developers and invest for long periods in developing new products that are either supported by revenues from customized software development (BANCS 2000) or implicitly by other businesses of the business group (Marshal). Smaller firms too can invest time and resources to product development projects if supported by larger firms (ESS has venture capital investments from large software firms). Smaller software firms with little external support have often to depend on client firms that are willing to allow the software firm to develop and experiment with new products as long as they get a reasonably customized product for themselves.

The strongest, inimitable, knowledge-based competencies seem to be in the small companies: in the case of In-Page, character and image manipulation; in the case of Spectrum, knowledge of stockbroking and related issues. The presence of a strong core group facilitates this process. In the case of In-Page software development, the two partners have been working together on several related ventures to build up their knowledge base. They have also internally trained a person, with classical Arabic knowledge from a traditional Arabic school, to work on software design: a unique combination that is possibly an inimitable asset for the firm. In the case of Spectrum, about one-third of the total strength of about sixty people have been working on the product for at least five years. The founder, S. Rangarajan, has been focusing on the product and the stockbroking sector for over a decade. In comparison, the large companies seem to have complementary competencies in tool development and building powerful architectures for their products.

Technology push or market pull?

Software product development can occur either on the basis of technology push or market pull. Indian firms seem to have been driven more by the former than by the latter. BANCS 2000 started with a specific requirement of a bank (external market pull) but later became technology-driven (client-server); In-Page was competence-driven: the firm wanted to know how to leverage the competence they had already developed in image and character manipulation. Marshal was started with a project to develop an enterprise solution for a particular industry group. The firm also had a desire to become a product player and extended the product to other industries till it became more technology-driven in its conceptualization of the product and its versions.

Software development depends on developing an iterative focus on technology push and market pull, never allowing one or the other to become dominant. Competitive advantages can emerge from either of the two forces as they can lead to unique product features that are valued by customers. Products can become more powerful by identifying and focusing on latent needs. For example, RiteChoice found that brokers do not have adequate information and control over how much they are funding their sub-brokers. Setting limits for each sub-broker by itself is not enough, as there would be an opportunity loss associated with one or more sub-brokers not fully utilizing their allotment. They therefore integrated a dynamic mode of risk management of sub-broker accounts into their product. This contrasts with Marshal, which was more dependent on information from consultants and others about customer needs. In both cases, the product companies were able to identify and develop unique features for their products.

Choices of technology and product architecture

Technology and choice of architecture are important as they have a continuing impact on the evolution of the product. Choice of a robust technology or framework facilitates upgrades and addition of features while at the same time ensuring compatibility with other hardware and software products. These technological choices are particularly important for complex and high value products that are likely to be in use by a customer over an extended cycle of up to ten years (Marshal, BANCS 2000).

While technology is an area of strength for Indian software product developers, there is also a tendency to try and solve problems with a technology solution rather than a marketing solution. For example, if the range of customer requirements are not clearly identified and prioritized in advance, developers may consider all requirements as equally important and build a complex product that addresses all possible needs, rather than building a simpler product that more effectively meets the prioritized needs of the target set of customers. This makes the engineering activity more complex, delays development, and may divert attention from real market problems that have to be resolved through hard marketing choice decisions (BANCS 2000). On the other hand, firms sometimes try to avoid adding features that were initially not considered important enough to be addressed, but are in increasing demand from the market, as they involve major changes in the basic software architecture and therefore extensive rewriting of code (BANCS 2000, EX). Once the market demand is persistent, the need is met initially by overlaying the basic software with an add-on layer that addresses the need: a compromise solution that increases processing time but reduces feature development time. Eventually, such features that emerge as essential over time are built into the main product only when the product is entirely re-engineered (EX) by a fresh software development team that often has to ignore all the software code written earlier as it is too complex to reuse.

Product architecture and customization

Customization of software products is relatively easier if the software is architectured to be modular and layered. However, modular and layered architectures compromise on processing speed and other output performance parameters. Therefore, customized software developed for single clients is usually built with more integral architecture to provide superior performance. Nonetheless, once successful at a single client stage, if such software is expanded into a product with the same integral architecture, it poses serious problems both for new feature building and customization. Software layering over the basic integral architecture becomes the preferred route in such cases, thus decreasing performance but allowing customized software to be 'productized'. However, with each layering the product becomes more and more difficult to modify, thus leading to a situation where eventually major re-engineering becomes essential.

An important decision in the product design and architecture is which variables to hard-code and which ones to parameterize (BANCS 2000). Hard-coding allows for faster software development and higher processing speed and performance. However, it compromises on flexibility for both the customer and the developer. From the customer's point of view, hard-coding makes related policy changes in the application that require changes in the software product settings difficult to implement without reworking the code. A pre-parameterized code allows the customer to make such changes internally and rapidly. However, it also requires the customer to maintain security features so that unauthorized persons do not make parameter changes. More importantly, it also requires the customer to think carefully into the future and estimate the range of parameterization that may be required. Some firms that are also involved in customized software development found that their customers were often not willing to engage in such advanced thinking. They preferred hard-coding to meet present software performance requirements rather than parameterization that involved higher development time and was of uncertain utility in the future. However, from the software product developer's point of view, greater parameterization is essential to develop a generic product, so that product features can be enhanced as customer requirements and expectations increase. To do so, the developer needs domain expertise and needs to forecast possible changes that are likely to occur in that domain. In the relative absence of this understanding, developers have to depend on user need statements that may be inadequate and compromise on future flexibility through lack of parameterization. This creates difficulties in the conversion of initially customized software into potentially packaged software products (BANCS 2000).

Customization and version management

One of the major trade-offs in software product development is between adding new and customer demanded features as and when they are discovered, either incrementally in the existing product, thus creating a range of minor version releases; or retaining each version for longer periods while customizing those features for those who demand them, thus creating a range of customized version releases. Firms do not seem to have arrived at an effective way of making this trade-off.

In cases where some of the customization is requested by the client firm in order to trade off against making changes in the existing work flow, the software firms concerned have sought to persuade the client into making work-flow changes on the grounds that the software incorporates 'best practice' in work-flow design (Marshal; BANCS 2000). However, in cases where the client firm does not agree to making work-flow changes, the smaller firms are more likely to agree on greater customization (MakESS) while the larger ones are likely either to opt out of such projects or not to market their products to firms that are likely to make such demands (Marshal). Smaller firms can enjoy an edge over larger firms by agreeing to higher levels of mutually justifiable customization, in comparison to larger firms that apparently cannot manage the complexities of customization given their larger client base and their larger development and maintenance groups.

The degree of customization that the software allows its users is a key factor for its acceptance. In a high value, complex product, it may be advisable to allow a higher degree of customization as this could provide a competitive edge (BANCS 2000). Marshal seems to have used this effectively by charging well for customization. MakESS seems to allow a greater degree of customization to take place if demanded and relies on the higher user-friendliness of the software to reduce the incidence of customization as it takes away their limited number of good software engineers from development. However, version control is a major concern from the software maintenance point of view.

Marketing and product launch

In virtually all the cases, there seemed to be an under-utilization of partnerships with other firms, particularly for marketing. Forging such partnerships would overcome the problem of setting up expensive marketing channels all over the world for what is essentially a limited product pipeline. While large companies like Ramco and Infosys could conceivably hope to set up an international sales network in the medium term, for small companies like Concept Software, partnerships are perhaps the only way of effectively reaching the market, though new channels like sales over the Internet are an alternative.

The timing of a product release is important in external markets. By the time Ramco launched its Version 3.0 in international markets, the market for ERP software was beginning to mature. Their late entry was partly compensated by their simpler design and reduced cost of implementation, but other problems like lack of endorsement from the 'Big Six' consulting firms, lack of an implementation methodology, and inflexibility in hardware and software platform choice could not be comprehensively overcome (Sadagopan, 2000).[4] These led to complex and slower implementation processes at client sites.

Reward and incentive systems

Top management support is important but not sufficient to ensure the growth of a product culture within a services company. Given the longer gestation period for products and the greater uncertainty involved, reward and incentive systems have to be made more attractive to get the best developers involved in the product development activity (BANCS 2000). On the other hand, developers are interested in acquiring new skills and are therefore willing to work at comparatively low salaries so long as they are engaged in projects that use the latest software tools and technologies (EX) that have broader applications and can help them secure higher paying positions in foreign countries. Firms may encourage a high turnover of software professionals at junior levels to bring in new software professionals who are younger and probably more hardworking. Projects that offer limited scope for lateral or upward (or outward) movement, due to their narrow application scope or the relatively dated nature of tools and technologies used, have difficulty in attracting developers. This is especially true when the mainstream customized development activity of the firm offers developers better and more varied application scope and range of software tools and technologies (BANCS 2000).

Quality systems

An essential aspect of developing world class products is the establishment of effective quality systems within the product development project and across the organization. The quality systems and productivity measures used for services can be inappropriate for products. Large firms like TCS and Infosys have developed elaborate quality systems for their customized software development projects. They have also sought to extend these systems to software product development. However, this is difficult in most cases (Nambisan, 2001). Initial (first version) software development often takes a relatively ad hoc development route in comparison to service projects, due to the high levels of uncertainty regarding potential customers and their requirements, and the large range of software development paths to choose from. Often the firm's standard quality systems come in at the point when a first workable version is available, and the systems are then quickly adapted to meet the need of controlling the quality of commercial versions and releases. At that stage, the quality systems start resembling the firm's systems for customized software development. On the other hand, pure product companies like Ramco and ESS have an internally developed quality system in place from the initial stages of product development and have improved these systems with their product development experience.

4. Moving ahead with product development

Coping with challenges

All the companies that we have studied up to June 2000 have persevered with their products with reasonable success (though profitability information is not available). A number of other Indian software companies that started on the product route (e.g. Mastek and Wipro Systems) have since then changed track and become predominantly software service companies. Software services companies such as Infosys, that at one time set ambitious targets for revenues from software products, have changed their minds.

Some smaller companies have persisted with niche products with mixed results. Our study confirms that successful product development is not easy. Should Indian software companies fight against these odds and commit resources to product development?

Given the physical distance of India from the world's largest market for software products, the US, it is unlikely that Indian companies can be successful in the development of products with very short lifecycles and low prices. There does, however, seem to be an opportunity for Indian companies to use their high quality software developers to develop products of intermediate to high complexity with longer lifecycles. Smaller companies could focus on products of intermediate complexity targeted at niche markets. The emergence of the Internet and electronic commerce as a sales and delivery channel opens a new route to reach out to customers outside India. Product functionality can also be made available to customers all over the world through Application Service Providers (ASP). The ASP route opens up new possibilities for alliances and partnerships.

Indian companies can also use their software technology skills to drive technology-based products such as tools and specialized utilities. With the increasing penetration of computers in the Indian market both among businesses and homes, there will also be greater opportunities for products targeted at the Indian market.

However, the strongest argument in favour of developing products is the gradual erosion of the cost advantage of Indian software companies primarily due to increase in employee costs. If it were not for the tremendous demand–supply gap in the global software industry, perhaps Indian software companies would have been facing a different situation than they are today. New entrants into the software industry, like companies from China, are reported to be making rapid advances in developing their skills and may have cost advantages over Indian companies. Product development is one way for Indian software companies to strengthen their competitive position in the long run.

Indian software firms may eventually have to move towards becoming 'solution companies' rather than service or product companies. Solution companies build a portfolio of product components and combine them in unique ways to provide complete software solutions for their clients' specific requirements. This requires a strong service orientation in a product-oriented company and an ability to conceptualize the entire solution space in the software firm's chosen market and develop a stream of product components to address those requirements. Solution companies can potentially exploit synergies between service and product projects, and Indian firms that are currently active in both areas have an opportunity to transform themselves into solution companies that are both effective and efficient.

What Indian companies and the government can do to further the development of a product orientation is discussed in the following sections.

Company initiatives

Companies involved in software product development need to have a subtle understanding of the issues related to customization and version management. Customization is not necessarily contradictory to a product approach; very successful products like SAP R/3 require a high degree of customization. What is more important, though, is understanding which features need to be in the core product, which parameters need to be user definable, and how to manage customized add-ons and modifications through the version upgrade path. Managing these trade-offs again requires close inter-functional working between the design, engineering, marketing and support groups. These capabilities will improve as companies go through repeated product iterations. To ensure that this learning takes place, companies need to put in place comprehensive review mechanisms.

Companies need to be careful in converting customized solutions developed for particular users into products. While the learning gained from the customized solution will have value in developing a related product, the reuse of customized software for developing more generic products is likely to result in limited acceptance by a wider group of customers, as customer-specific compromises emerge as inappropriate for a larger customer group.

There is a need for better version management and strategic product planning, which are currently underdeveloped areas in most companies. This needs people who have an overall understanding of the structure and technology of the product, an in-depth understanding of the market and its trends, and an ability to forecast customer needs and tap on latent needs. These people can plan versions that are technically designed to allow for faster development and release, yet are robust to allow customer- or developer-based modifications, and flexible enough to allow enhanced versions to be developed without complete re-engineering. This is indeed a tall order for one person, but firms that have the benefit of one or more such people have a definite edge in software product development over the long run.

Product development requires discipline: in analysis, decision-making and implementation. It involves intuitive understanding of markets, users and their needs combined with creative problem-solving, elegant design and robust architecture. It needs to be led by developers and engineers who are sensitive to the market, and marketers who are appreciative of engineering constraints. More effective cross-functional working and integration across these groups and with customers would facilitate better and early product definition.

Companies interested in developing the product business need to create a broader product pipeline to help justify the investments in creating a product-marketing infrastructure. Products with medium to high level of complexity and with well-defined and easy-to-address markets are good candidates for development by Indian companies. Companies with non-competing products could look at forming a marketing consortium to lower international marketing and support costs.

Smaller companies seem to be good at building inimitable competencies and appropriate domain expertise in niche areas that are too narrow to be of interest to large firms. Large companies seem to be good at developing appropriate tools and building new (software) technological frameworks that are too large in scope for small firms to build internally and exploit effectively. Both small and large companies need to find ways of working together to utilize these complementary and mutually reinforcing advantages. Large companies interested in the product business may find it advantageous to identify as acquisition targets the small companies that have strong competencies and domain expertise in areas that are emerging as important.

Service companies interested in developing the product business need to create separate incentive and reward systems to help motivate employees working on product development. In addition to ensuring that the product development takes place on the latest platforms and with contemporary technology, given the longer time horizon of product development, product developers need to be compensated with stock options on terms different from those used for people in the service business. This would ensure that the immediate revenue-based incentive structures in the services businesses do not pull away promising product developers into services.

To make the product development activity more market-oriented, companies might like to hire more management graduates in the product development business as well as encourage senior developers who take product leadership roles to undergo some formal management education.

Government policy

There are both direct and indirect ways in which the government of India can support the development of a product orientation in Indian software companies.

In the early years of the software industry, the government provided export-marketing support through a finance scheme operated by the Export Import Bank of India. Other development financial institutions have also provided various forms of support for the Indian information technology industry (George and Prabhu, 2003). Given the difficulties in creating an infrastructure for product marketing in foreign markets, the government might like to consider formulating appropriate schemes for provision of one-time support to Indian companies for creating their marketing infrastructure in foreign countries.

Steps to deepen the internal market for software products would provide impetus to Indian software companies to develop more products. Result-oriented incentives for potential client organizations to effectively adopt information technology can spur software development. One of the key measures in this direction is the prevention of software piracy and the protection of intellectual property. The government should continue and intensify policies to check software piracy and identify new ways of protecting intellectual property in software. As a large customer, the government norms for purchase of software for internal use should protect intellectual property and select the best class of software available anywhere in the world rather than favour indigenously developed software, as this will force software vendors to develop world-class products.

It is evident from our study that while Indian software product companies ideally need both a high degree of domain expertise and technological competence, the latter is more common than the former. The relatively low sophistication of most Indian user industries makes genuine domain expertise hard to find. Government policies that continue to emphasize that Indian industry needs to be globally competitive, and those that open the Indian market to foreign competition, are likely to increase the sophistication of domestic industry. These can indirectly help software firms to acquire the essential domain expertise to be internationally competitive in software products.

Notes

* Originally published in *Science, Technology and Society*, 7 (1) (January–June 2002). Copyright © Society for the Promotion of S & T Studies, New Delhi, 2002. All rights reserved. Reproduced with the permission of the copyright holders and the publishers, Sage Publications India Pvt Ltd, New Delhi.

We thank the editors E. Sridharan and A. D'Costa for useful comments on earlier drafts of this chapter. We thank too the six companies studied for providing us access and the members of their product development team for spending a considerable amount of time patiently articulating their organizational and partnership experiences. However, all conclusions reached and inferences drawn are those of the authors and do not necessarily represent the views of the companies studied.

1. This consists in getting a programme written for a standard business function such as accounting or inventory management rather than using a readily available software product.
2. The early stages of the product development process involve ideation, understanding user needs, forecasting demand and usage trends, and coping with technological uncertainties. These stages are sometimes referred to as the fuzzy front end of the product development process in view of the uncertainties involved. Companies take steps to assess and manage risks as the product development process proceeds, and uncertainties also reduce as the launch date comes close, thereby reducing the fuzziness involved.
3. D. N. Prahlad was then senior vice president at Infosys: interviewed in June 1996.
4. S. Sadagopan is an expert on enterprise resource planning (ERP) systems.

References

Accenture (2002) 'Making Indian Manufacturing Companies Globally Competitive', (New Delhi and Mumbai: Accenture). http://www.accenture.com/xd/xd.asp?it= enweb&xd=locations\india\india_ideas_3.xml.

Arora, A., V. S. Arunachalam, J. Asundi and R. Fernandes (2001) 'The Indian Software Services Industry', *Research Policy*, 30: 1267–87.

Arora, A., A. Gambardella and S. Torrissi (2001) 'In the Footsteps of Silicon Valley? Indian and Irish Software in the International Division of Labour', SIEPR Discussion Paper No. 00–41, June, Stanford Institute for Economic Policy Research, Stanford CA.

Bowonder, B. and P. K. Richardson (2000) 'Liberalisation and the Growth of Business Lead R&D: the Case of India', *R&D Management*, 30 (4): 279–88.

Clark, K. and T. Fujimoto (1990) 'The Power of Product Integrity', *Harvard Business Review*, 68 (6): 107–18.

D'Costa, A. (2002) 'Export Growth and Path Dependence: the Locking in of Innovations in the Software Industry', *Science, Technology and Society*, 7 (1): 51–89.

Desai, A. (1998) 'Presentation at the Workshop on the Context of Innovation in India: the Case of the Information Technology Industry', 24 July 1998, New Delhi.

Forbes, N. (1999) 'Technology and the Indian Industry: What is Liberalisation Changing?' *Technovation*, 19: 403–12.

George, G. and G. N. Prabhu (2003) 'Developmental Financial Institutions as Technology Policy Instruments: Implications for Innovation and Entrepreneurship in Emerging Economies', *Research Policy*, 32 (1): 89–108.

Griffin, A. and J. R. Hauser (1993) 'The Voice of the Customer', *Marketing Science*, 12 (1): 1–27.

Hamel, G. and C. K. Prahalad (1989) 'Strategic Intent', *Harvard Business Review*, 67 (3): 63–76.

Jishnu, L. (2002) 'The Greening of Achamma', *Business World*, 2 Sept: 50–2.

Kanter, R. M., M. J. Kao and F. Wiersema (1997) *Innovation: Breakthrough Thinking at 3M, Du Pont, GE, Pfizer and Rubbermaid* (New York: Harper Business).

Khurana, A. and S. R. Rosenthal (1997) 'Integrating the Fuzzy End of New Product Development', *Sloan Management Review*, 38 (2): 103–20.

Krishnan, R. T. and G. N. Prabhu (1999) 'Creating Successful New Products: Challenges for Indian Industry', *Economic and Political Weekly*, 34 (31), 31 July–6 Aug: M114–M120.

Mehta, D. (1998) 'A Time for Consolidation', *Information Systems Computer World*, 3 (17): 44.

Mowery, David C. (1999) 'The Computer Software Industry', in D. C. Mowery and R. R. Nelson (eds), *Sources of Industrial Leadership: Studies of Seven Industries* (Cambridge: Cambridge University Press), pp. 133–68.

Nambisan, S. (2001) 'Why Service Businesses are Not Product Businesses?', *Sloan Management Review*, Summer: 72–80.

NASSCOM (2002a) *Software Industry in India: a Strategic Review* (New Delhi: NASSCOM).

NASSCOM (2002b) *National Association of Software and Service Companies* (New Delhi: NASSCOM), website: http://www.nasscom.org.

OECD (2000) *OECD Information Technology Outlook: ICTs, E-Commerce and the Information Economy* (Paris: OECD).

Prahalad, C. K., and G. Hamel (1990) 'The Core Competence of the Corporation', *Harvard Business Review*, 68 (3): 79–91.

Prahlad, D. N. (1996) Interview. http://web3.asia1.com.sg/timesnet/data/ab/docs/ab1008.html.

Sadagopan S. (2000) Website of Prof. S. Sadagopan, http://www.iiitb.ac.in/ss.

Sawyer S. (2000) 'Packaged Software: Implications of the Differences of Custom Approaches to Software Development', *European Journal of Information Systems*, 9: 47–58.

Schilling, M. A., and C. W. L. Hill (1998) 'Managing the New Product Development Process: Strategic Imperatives', *Academy of Management Executive*, 12 (3): 67–81.

SEC (2002) Infosys Technologies Form 20-F for year ending 31 March 2002. http://www.sec.gov/Archives/edgar/data/1067491/000089161802002223/0000891618-02-002223.txt.

Ulrich, K. T. and S. D. Eppinger (1995) *Product Design and Development* (New York: McGraw-Hill).

Wheelwright, S. C. and K. Clark (1992) 'Creating Project Plans to Focus Product Development', *Harvard Business Review*, 70 (2), 70–82.

Yin, R. K. (1994) *Case Study Research: Design and Methods* (Beverly Hills, California: Sage).

7
The Silicon Valley Connection: Transnational Networks and Regional Development in Taiwan, China and India

AnnaLee Saxenian

Transnational entrepreneurs – US-educated immigrant engineers whose activities span national borders – are creating new economic opportunities for formerly peripheral economies around the world. Talented immigrants who have studied and worked in the US are increasingly reversing the 'brain drain' by returning to their home countries to take advantage of promising opportunities there. In so doing they are building technical communities that link their home countries to the world centre of technology, Silicon Valley. As the 'brain drain' increasingly gives way to a process of 'brain circulation', networks of scientists and engineers are transferring technology, skill and know-how between distant regional economies faster and more flexibly than most corporations.

The development of technical communities that span national borders and boast as shared assets technical information, trust and contacts has been largely overlooked in most accounts of globalization (Portes, 1996). This chapter suggests that transnational communities may become as important as more commonly recognized actors – states and multinational corporations – in the growth of new centres of technology entrepreneurship. The first half of the chapter begins by briefly outlining the argument and illustrating the contribution of a transnational community to industrial upgradation with evidence from Taiwan. It then examines the software industry in India, focusing on the case of Bangalore, and argues that in spite of a record of successful entrepreneurship in the US, Indian engineers have been slow to build a cross-regional technical community. This case suggests that the receptiveness of the domestic political and economic context is a critical precondition for developing and taking advantage of such transnational networks.

The second half of the chapter further explores how the local context shapes such cross-national people and knowledge transfers through a comparison of the experience of India and China in the 1990s. While data are limited and the institutional and economic differences between the two countries are complex, the material presented here suggests that Chinese policy-makers have succeeded in attracting return entrepreneurs through strategies that are similar to those pursued in Taiwan. The chapter concludes by pursuing some of the implications of this contrast for Indian policy-makers: in particular, the importance of fostering the development of local professional and technical networks to take advantage of the growing global networks linking the US and India.

1. Technical communities and industrial decentralization

Transnational technical communities are only possible because of advances in communication and transportation technologies and changes in the structure of technology markets and competition. In the 1960s and 1970s, the dominant competitors in the computer industry were vertically integrated corporations that controlled all aspects of hardware and software production (the IBM or 'national champion' model.) The rise of an alternative, more flexible industrial model (the Silicon Valley model) spurred the introduction of the personal computer and a radical shift to a highly fragmented industrial structure organized around networks of increasingly specialized producers. This presaged the widespread shift in the 1980s and 1990s from mass production to more flexible manufacturing systems based on firm-level specialization and extensive outsourcing (Powell, 2001).

Today, independent enterprises produce all the components that were once internalized within a single large computer corporation: from application software, operating systems and computers to microprocessors and other components. The final systems are in turn marketed and distributed by yet other enterprises. Within each of these horizontal segments there is, in turn, increasing specialization of production and a deepening social division of labour. In the semiconductor industry, for example, independent producers specialize in chip design, fabrication, packaging, testing, as well as different segments of the manufacturing materials and equipment sector. A new generation of firms has in turn emerged in the late 1990s that specializes in providing intellectual property in the form of design modules rather than the entire chip design.

This change in industry structure appears as a shift to market relations. The number of actors in the industry has increased dramatically and competition within many (but not all) the horizontal layers has also increased. Yet this is far from the classic auction market mediated by price signals alone; the decentralized system depends heavily on the coordination provided by cross-cutting social structures and institutions (Powell, 1990). While Silicon Valley's entrepreneurs innovate in increasingly specialized niche markets, intense communications in turn ensure the speedy, often unanticipated, recombination of these specialized components into changing end products. This decentralized system provides significant advantages over a more integrated model in a volatile environment because of the speed and flexibility as well as the conceptual advances associated with the process of specialization and recombination.

The deepening social division of labour in the industry creates opportunities for innovation in formerly peripheral regions – opportunities that did not exist in an era of highly integrated producers. The vertical specialization associated with the new system continually generates entrepreneurial opportunities. By exploiting these opportunities in their home countries, transnational entrepreneurs can build independent centres of specialization and innovation, while simultaneously maintaining ties to Silicon Valley to monitor and respond to fast-changing and uncertain markets and technologies. They are also well positioned to establish cross-regional partnerships that facilitate the integration of their specialized components into end products.

The social structure of a technical community thus appears essential to the organization of production at the global as well as the local level. In the old industrial model, the technical community was primarily within the corporation (Kogut and Zander, 1993). The firm was seen as the privileged organizational form for the creation and internal transfer of knowledge, particularly technological know-how that is difficult to codify. In regions like Silicon Valley, however, where the technical community transcends firm boundaries, such tacit knowledge is often transferred through informal communications or the inter-firm movement of individuals. This suggests that the multinational corporation may no longer be the advantaged or preferred organizational vehicle for transferring knowledge or personnel across national borders. Transnational communities provide an alternative and potentially more flexible and responsive mechanism for long-distance transfers of skill and know-how, particularly between very different business cultures or environments. Moreover, as multinational corporations decentralize, moving away from the traditional hierarchical 'hub and spoke' forms of organization towards more differentiated, globally distributed networks, their subsidiaries integrate into the networks of local technical communities (Nohria and Ghoshal, 1997).

In consequence, the distinction between multinational and entrepreneurial firms is diminishing. As recently as the 1970s, only the world's largest corporations had the resources and capabilities to grow internationally. These multinational corporations expanded primarily by establishing marketing offices or branches overseas. Today, by contrast, new transportation and communications technologies allow even the smallest firms to build partnerships with foreign producers and tap overseas expertise, cost-savings and markets. Start-ups in Silicon Valley today are often global actors from the day they begin their operations. Many raise capital from Asia, others subcontract manufacturing to Taiwan and China or rely on software development in India, and virtually all seek to eventually sell their products in Asian as well as American markets.

The scarce resource in this new environment is the ability to locate foreign partners quickly and to manage complex business relationships across cultural and linguistic boundaries. This is particularly a challenge in high-technology industries in which products, markets and technologies are continually being redefined, and where product cycles are routinely as short as six months. Producers of all sizes must exchange and develop knowledge and other capabilities in order to increase innovation.

First-generation immigrants, like the Chinese and Indian engineers of Silicon Valley, who have the language and cultural as well as the technical skills to function well in both the US and foreign markets, are distinctly well-positioned to play a central role in this environment. By becoming transnational entrepreneurs, these immigrants can provide the critical contacts, information and cultural know-how that link dynamic, but distant, regions in the global economy. They can create social networks that enable even the smallest producers to locate and maintain mutually beneficial collaborations across great distances and facilitate access to foreign sources of capital, technical skills and markets. The proliferation of such relationships over time can result in the creation of a transnational technical community, one that can transfer the market and technological know-how needed to support a dynamic of industrial upgrading.

Clearly, Silicon Valley is no longer the sole source of IT-related innovation in the world economy. Other US regions, from Seattle to Boston's Route 128, are increasingly sources of transnational entrepreneurship. International technical communities are also building horizontal connections between centres of expertise in Taiwan, Ireland, Israel, China and India, bypassing the US altogether. In consequence, while Silicon Valley remains a pre-eminent source of new information technology, the capacity for technological innovation today is far more geographically decentralized than at any time since the invention of the semiconductor. Also, the stable postwar core–periphery or hub-and-spoke hierarchies are giving way to globally distributed networks with multiple centres with distinctive specializations.

2. Transnational entrepreneurs and industrial upgrading in Taiwan

While innovation occurs within local technical communities, each with their own specialization, the connection to transnational networks ensures compatibility with market and technical developments elsewhere. The experience of Taiwan illustrates how a transnational community can contribute to domestic industrial upgrading. It also suggests that the state can play a key role in developing global technology connections as well as local capabilities.

In the 1960s and 1970s the relationship between Taiwan and the US was a textbook First–Third World relationship. US businesses invested in Taiwan to take advantage of low-wage manufacturing labour. Meanwhile, the best and the brightest Taiwanese engineering students came to the US for graduate education and created a classic 'brain drain' when they chose to remain to pursue professional opportunities in the US.

This relationship changed dramatically in the late 1980s. US-educated engineers began to return home, drawn by active government recruitment and the opportunities created by rapid economic development. The upgrading of Taiwan's technological infrastructure and capacities in Taiwan, through growing OEM ties to foreign customers and through local learning-by-doing, spurred a reversal of the brain drain (see Figure 7.1). At the same time, a growing cohort of highly mobile engineers began to work in both the US and Taiwan, regularly commuting across the Pacific. Typically, Taiwan-born, US-educated engineers, these 'astronauts' have the professional contacts and language skills to function fluently both in Silicon Valley and Taiwanese business cultures and to draw on the complementary strengths of the two regional economies (Saxenian, 1999).

Miin Wu is a classic transnational entrepreneur whose experience illustrates the importance of return entrepreneurship to the development of innovative capabilities in Taiwan. Wu immigrated to the US in the early 1970s to pursue graduate training in electrical engineering. Like virtually all his classmates from the elite National Taiwan University, he took advantage of the ample fellowship aid available in the US at the time for poor but talented foreign students. After earning a doctorate from Stanford University in 1976, Wu recognized that there were no opportunities to use his newly

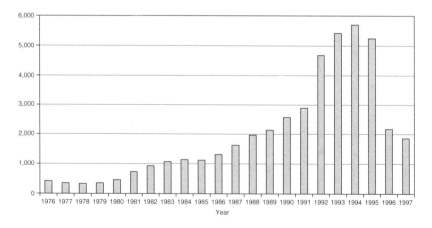

Figure 7.1   Returnees to Taiwan from the US, 1976–97

Source: National Youth Commission, Ministry of Education, Taiwan ROC, 1999.

acquired skills in economically backward Taiwan and chose to remain in the US. He worked for over a decade in senior positions at Silicon Valley-based semiconductor companies, including Siliconix and Intel. He also gained entrepreneurial experience as one of the founding members of VLSI Technology.

By the late 1980s, economic conditions in Taiwan had improved dramatically and Wu returned home to start one of Taiwan's first semiconductor companies. He located Macronix Co. in the Hsinchu Science-based Industrial Park and brought thirty senior Silicon Valley engineers, largely former classmates and friends, with him, along with over ten years of training, experience and professional relationships in Silicon Valley. He also transferred elements of the Silicon Valley management model to Macronix, including openness, informality and minimal hierarchy: all significant departures from traditional Taiwanese corporate models.

In 1995, Macronix went public on the Taiwan stock exchange and the following year became the first Taiwanese company to list on NASDAQ. The firm is now the sixth largest semiconductor maker in Taiwan, with over $500 million in sales and some 3000 employees. Macronix manufacturing facilities and a majority of its employees are based in Taiwan, but the firm maintains an advanced design and engineering centre in Silicon Valley and Wu continues to recruit senior managers from the Valley. He has also established a corporate venture capital fund that invests in promising start-ups in Taiwan and Silicon Valley with technologies related to their business. In short, Miin Wu's activities bridge and benefit both the Hsinchu (Taiwan) and Silicon Valley economies.

While the Hsinchu Science Park was not the cause of Taiwan's success in IT, its success reflects the fast expanding ties between the two regions. After its first eight years (1980–8) the Park was home to only ninety-four companies with under $2 billion in annual sales collectively, and attracted only a handful of US-educated engineers per year. By the early 1990s the Park had become a destination for hundreds of returnees annually, and they started new companies at an accelerating rate. By 1989, 2840 Taiwanese had returned from the US to work in the Hsinchu Science Park. Also, these returnees were disproportionately likely to start their own companies. Some 40 per cent of the companies located in the Science Park (110 companies out of a total of 284) in 1999 were started by US-educated engineers, many of whom had considerable managerial or entrepreneurial experience in Silicon Valley. These returnees, in turn, actively recruited former colleagues and friends from Silicon Valley.

The Park was attractive to engineers from the US in part because of its location close to the headquarters of Taiwan's leading public research institute, the Industrial Technology and Research Institute (ITRI) and its subsidiary, the Electronics Research and Service Organization (ERSO), which in the 1980s spearheaded a technological leapfrogging through the government-led transfer of semiconductor manufacturing technology from the US (Meany, 1994; Matthews, 1997). Hsinchu is also the home of two of Taiwan's leading engineering universities which had dramatically increased enrolments and research capacity in the 1970s and 1980s. Finally, the Hsinchu Science Park offered a range of fiscal incentives for qualified technology investments and provided returnees with preferential access to scarce, high quality housing and to the only Chinese–American school in Taiwan, both located on the Park grounds.[1]

In addition to permanent returnees like Wu, a growing population of 'astronauts' work in *both* places and spend much of their lives on aeroplanes. While their families may be based on either side of the Pacific (most often they stay in California because of the lifestyle advantages), these engineers travel between Silicon Valley and Hsinchu once or even twice a month, taking advantage of the opportunities to play middlemen bridging the two regional economies. This includes many Taiwanese angel investors and venture capitalists as well as executives and engineers from companies like Macronix with activities in the two regions. This lifestyle is, of course, only possible because of the improvements in transportation and communications technologies. However, it does not mean that these 'astronauts' are rootless. Their dense personal networks and intimate local knowledge of both Silicon Valley and Hsinchu play a central role in coordinating economic linkages between the two regions. Even engineers who remain in Silicon Valley are typically integrated into the transnational community. Many work for start-ups or large firms with activities in both regions. Some moonlight as consultants on product development for Taiwanese firms. Others return to Taiwan regularly for technical seminars sponsored by government agencies or professional associations.

As engineers travel between the two regions they carry technical knowledge as well as contacts, capital and information about new opportunities and new markets. Moreover, this information moves almost as quickly between these distant regions as it does within Hsinchu and Silicon Valley because of the density of the social networks and the shared identities and trust within the community. These transnational ties have dramatically accelerated the flows of skill, know-how and market information between the two regions. In the words of a Silicon Valley based Taiwanese engineer:

> If you live in the United States it's hard to learn what is happening in Taiwan, and if you live in Taiwan it's hard to learn what is going on in the US. Now that people are going back and forth between Silicon Valley and Hsinchu so much more frequently, you can learn about new companies and new opportunities in both places almost instantaneously.[2]

Others say Taiwan is like an extension of Silicon Valley. The former CEO of Acer America claims that the continuing interaction between Hsinchu and Silicon Valley has generated 'multiple positive feedbacks' that enhance business opportunities in both regions.[3]

A closely-knit community of Taiwanese returnees, 'astronauts' and US-based engineers and entrepreneurs like Miin Wu have become the bridge between Silicon Valley and the comparably sized region that extends from Taipei to Hsinchu Science Park. Shared educational experiences and alumni ties – most were graduates of National Taiwan University and other elite technical universities – in turn facilitated the returnees' integration into the local technical community. By transferring technical know-how, organizational models and contacts, they have accelerated the upgrading of Taiwan's technological infrastructure while also maintaining close ties with Silicon Valley. Taiwan is now the world's largest producer of notebook computers and a range of related PC components including motherboards, monitors, scanners, power supplies and keyboards. Taiwan's semiconductor and integrated circuit manufacturing capabilities are similarly state-of-the-art, on a par with the leading Japanese and US producers; and its flexible networks of specialized small and medium-sized enterprises coordinate the diverse components of this sophisticated infrastructure (Dedrick and Kraemer, 1998).

The growing integration of the technological communities of Silicon Valley and Hsinchu offers benefits to both economies. Silicon Valley remains the centre of new product definition and developer of leading edge technologies, while Taiwan offers world-class manufacturing, flexible development and integration, and access to key customers and markets in China and South East Asia. Taiwan has also become a significant and fast-growing source of capital for Silicon Valley-based start-ups. Unlike the arm's-length and top-down technology transfers between large firms that characterized the relations between Japan and the US in the 1980s, the Silicon Valley–Hsinchu relationship today consists of formal and informal collaborations between individual investors and entrepreneurs, small and medium-sized firms, as well as the divisions of larger companies located on both sides of the Pacific. In this complex mix, the social and professional ties among Taiwanese engineers at home and their counterparts in the US are as important as the more formal corporate alliances and partnerships.

Taiwan's policy-makers created an environment that attracted US-educated engineers home in growing numbers, but only after two decades of investment in the domestic environment. The elements of this environment included: a well-developed skill base and technical infrastructure, an attractive physical environment for entrepreneurs, a growing venture capital industry, and close professional ties to Silicon Valley (Saxenian and Li, 2003). Once in place, the transnational community accelerated the pace of innovation and industrial upgrading of Taiwan's PC and semiconductor industries beyond the expectations of the policy-makers. This experience suggests too that foreign-born engineers are only likely to return permanently to their home countries when they perceive that the professional opportunities outweigh, or at least match, those available to them in the US.[4]

3. Reversing the brain drain? The case of China

China, like India, has suffered greatly from the brain drain. In the 1990s these two countries each sent more students to the US for higher education than any other country. In 1998–9 alone, for example, 10.4 per cent of international students enrolled in US higher education, or 51 001 students, were from China, excluding Hong Kong, and 7.6 per cent, or 37 482 students, were from India (IIE, 2000). The dominance of Chinese and Indian students in US higher education is most pronounced at the doctoral level, and in particular the science and engineering fields. Between 1990 and 1996, 16 749 Chinese and 8211 Indian students received PhDs in the US, with 92 per cent (15 454) of the Chinese and 83 per cent of the Indian degrees (6786) in the science and engineering fields (NSF, 1999) (see Figure 7.2).

China and India are therefore particularly well positioned to benefit from 'brain circulation' and reversal of the brain drain. Data on the number of foreign students returning from the US to their home countries are limited, but it is clear that students from India and China have tended to remain in the US in greater numbers than their other foreign-born counterparts. An NSF study reports, for example, that in 1996, 87 per cent of Chinese and 84 per cent of Indian PhD students with temporary work visas planned to stay in the US after graduation, compared to only 48 per cent of Taiwanese students (NSF, 1999).

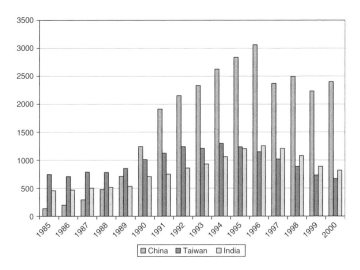

Figure 7.2   Doctorates awarded in the US to scholars from China, Taiwan and India, 1985–2000

Source: National Science Foundation, 1998 and 2002.

There is evidence, however, that US-educated Chinese students, like their Taiwanese counterparts a decade earlier, started returning home in growing numbers in the second half of the 1990s. A survey by the China Research Center and the US International Education Association found that 30 000 (18.8 per cent) of 160 000 students who studied in the US between 1978 and 1998 had returned to China (*World Journal*, 29 August 1999). A more recent study by the Beijing Science & Technology Committee claims that 140 000 students returned to China between 1996 and 2000, and that these returnees had started 3000 firms with a total output of $1 billion (*People's Daily*, January 2001). Another report claims that over 20 000 overseas students had returned to Beijing since 1988 to start companies.[5] (The findings of the latter studies should be treated with some caution because of their source and, in all likelihood, reflect trends rather than accurate numbers.)

In search of an explanation: the Chinese state and domestic context

Policy-makers in India and China have devoted substantial attention to promoting the development of the domestic information technology industries, and both countries boast rapid IT growth rates. However, their developmental trajectories differ markedly. China is a considerably larger producer than India with IT exports of $40.8 billion (not including $5.2 billion from Hong Kong) in 1998, compared to India's $1.2 billion. They are differently specialized as well (see Table 7.1). China is focused primarily on manufacturing computer and telecommunications systems and accessories for the domestic market, while India's IT specializes in providing software services for export. China's software sector, like India's hardware sector, remains very small (see Table 7.2). A full account of these divergent trajectories is beyond the scope of this chapter, but they provide background for explaining the nature of transnational linkages to Silicon Valley.

The development of transnational networks between Silicon Valley and China is best understood in the context of: (a) IT policies that support the commercialization of technology, (b) a well-developed physical and telecommunications infrastructure, and (c) the creation of two-way flows of

Table 7.1 High technology exports, China, Hong Kong, India: 2000

2000	High-technology exports		Royalty and licence fees	
	$ millions	*% of manufactured exports*	*Receipts $ millions*	*Payments $ millions*
China	40 837	19	80	1 281
Hong Kong	5 155	23	–	–
India	1 245	4	83	306

Source: World Bank (2002), 5.11; includes IT manufacturing only.

Table 7.2   Software output: China and other countries, US$ billion

	China	US	Japan	Ireland	India	S. Korea	Global
1999 sales	5.3	220	54	8.4	6.8	5.9	527
% of world market	1.0	42	10.2	1.6	1.3	1.1	100
2000 sales	7.2	240	57.2	8.9	8.9	8.3	596
% of world market	1.2	40.2	9.6	1.5	1.5	1.4	100

Source: China Software Industry Association (2001), p. 3.

ideas, information and contacts between Chinese engineers in the US and China. Since the 1980s, Chinese policy has aggressively targeted investments in IT-related manufacturing, promoted the commercialization of technology developed in universities and research institutes, and recruited overseas students to return to start IT companies. China has also devoted substantial resources to upgrading the nation's physical and technological infrastructure and capabilities. This contrasts with the more hands-off approach of Indian IT policy, which has focused on the promotion of exports and the development of software parks.

China's IT policy in the 1990s

In the postwar period China, like India, modelled its science and technology system after that of the former Soviet Union. Ministries of the central government owned and administered R&D institutes focusing on defence and other heavy industries such as machinery and mining. As civil use technologies accounted for a very small portion of China's research and production activities prior to 1980s, the state-owned research institutes, of which there were about fifty, were the driving engine for technological innovation and the development of heavy industry (Gu, 1999).

When China embarked on market-oriented economic reforms in the late 1970s, this system was challenged for its inefficiency and outdated focus on government demand, particularly military. The Chinese leadership sought to reorganize the national innovation system to increase productivity and to orient research towards civilian technologies such as electronics. Policymakers concluded that in spite of considerable research capabilities, the bottleneck for China's stagnating innovation system was the inability to commercialize basic and applied research, or in the words of Chinese scholars, the separation of research from production.

After a series of failed attempts to restructure its innovation system, the Chinese government identified the practice of encouraging spin-off enterprises by scientists and technologists from the state-owned research institutes as the most efficient way to accelerate industrial development. This involved three key reforms at the national level: (1) freeing researchers from the research institutes and laboratories to work in the private sector, (2) legal designation of a new category of non-governmental New Technology Enterprises, and (3) establishment of the Torch Programme and the Zones of New and High Technology Enterprises to encourage the commercialization of high-tech products.[6]

These reforms were influenced by the emergence in the 1980s of dozens of new technology enterprises on Zhongguancun Street in the Haidian district of Beijing. It quickly became known as the 'Street of Electronics' because most of the firms in this district were in the business of making and/or marketing electronics and computing-related products. By the end of the 1980s there were almost 100 firms in Zhongguancun, most of which had been started by personnel from local universities (including the elite Beijing and Qinghua Universities) and dozens of national research institutes.

Development Zones of New and High Technology Industry

Inspired by the success of such spin-off firms, the Chinese government initiated the Torch Programme, within the Ministry of Science and Technology, in 1988. One of the primary policy initiatives of the Torch Programme was to establish the 'Development Zones of New and High Technology Industry' in selected cities in the coastal and central parts of the country. The developmental zones were designed to promote on a wider scale the spin-off of high technology enterprises from state-owned R&D laboratories and institutions.[7]

While the Torch Programme identifies development zones, municipal governments govern them, granting the land and providing the basic infrastructure such as roads, water, power supply and other facilities. Municipal governments also organize the local administrative commission that accredits firms to locate in the zone as 'high and new technology' firms in line with the yardsticks stipulated by the central government. The municipal administrative commission also controls government investment funds to support start-ups or growing firms, and uses its authority to help arrange (state-owned) bank loans to firms in the zones. Firms that qualify to locate within these development zones benefit from state-of-the-art infrastructure and typically receive substantial financial advantages including tax holidays and low-cost (or free) land.

The Torch Programme launched twenty-five national level development zones in 1989, including the Beijing Development Zone of New and High Technology Industry. By the mid-1990s, they had established a total of fifty-two developmental zones located primarily in eastern and central China.[8] After a decade of development, these zones have attracted and helped to create China's most successful technology firms such as the Legend Group, which is located in the Beijing developmental zone. Legend was started by researchers from the Computing Institute of China's Academy of Science and is now China's leading PC-maker, with output of 13.6 billion RMB ($1.6 billion) and 30 per cent of the domestic PC market.

The Beijing Developmental Zone of New and High Technology Industry, centred in the well-known Zhongguancun area, is considered the most successful in the country. By 1999, the zone had 4837 enterprises with 196 139 employees, including 993 returnees from overseas, and total exports of US$5.48 billion. It included such well-known Chinese companies as Legend and Founder, as well as foreign companies such as HP-China. China's other leading technology zones include Shenzhen (located on the Hong Kong border) and Pudong district of Shanghai.

In 1999 the Beijing Municipal Government renamed the 20 000-acre zone as 'Zhonguancun Science Park' to consolidate and expand its function in technological innovation, with the hope that Beijing could become China's 'Silicon Valley'. This renaming of the development zone is part of China's plan to devote greater resources to the district in order to upgrade it to a higher level of technological innovation.[9] Senior administrators at Beijing University have recently started to actively assist and motivate start-ups from the Science Park to go public on the Hong Kong stock exchange. They report six IPOs in 2000, and anticipate more with the opening of the second market in Shenzhen in late 2001.

China's new system of innovation

China appears to have successfully linked its public Science and Technology efforts with the commercial activities of relatively autonomous industrial enterprises (Lu, 2000). The new innovation system institutionalizes the interaction of national science and technology programmes and public research institutes with industrial enterprises regardless of whether they are 'state-owned' or 'non-governmental'. China's most successful companies – Legend, Stone, Founder and Great Wall – are products of this interaction.[10] The Chinese government continues to target resources on IT-related research and development, investing approximately $3 billion to promote the computer industry alone between 1998 and 2000. Today, the focus of resources has shifted from computer manufacturing towards development of the software and semiconductor sectors.

The development of China's Science and Technology infrastructure reflects this commitment (see Table 7.3). From 1987–97, China had 454 R&D engineers and 200 R&D technicians per million compared to 149 and 108, respectively, in India. During the same period, China was training 43 per cent of its tertiary-level students in science and engineering, in comparison to 25 per cent in India. Also, while China's expenditures on R&D lagged at only 0.66 per cent of GNP between 1987 and 1997, compared to 0.73 per cent for India, the central government aggressively increased spending on science and technology in the late 1990s (World Bank, 2002). According to government statistics, total spending on science and technology in China grew 13 per cent in 1999, to US$15.5 billion. At the same time, R&D spending (a subset of overall S&T spending) grew nearly 18 per cent to US$8.2 billion,

Table 7.3   Science and technology indicators: China, Hong Kong and India, 1990–2000

	Scientists and engineers in R&D (per million people) 1990–2000	Technicians in R&D (per million people) 1990–2000	Science and engineering students % of total tertiary students 1987–1997	Scientific and technical journal articles 1997	Expenditures on R&D % of GNI 1989–2000
China	459	187	43	9 081	0.56
Hong Kong	93	100	36	2 080	0.06
India	158	115	25	8 439	0.62

Source: World Bank (2002).

or 0.8 per cent of GDP. This ratio of R&D spending to GDP was the highest ever recorded, but is still short of the stated goal of 1.5 per cent set in 1995 (US Embassy, 2000).

Government programmes are aimed also at expanding the domestic market for information technology. For example, a series of large-scale central government projects called the Golden Projects were launched during the 1990s, including the Golden Bridge (a national information network), the Golden Card (a nationwide system linking Chinese banks), the Golden Customs (a communication network connecting foreign trading companies with the Customs Bureau), and Golden Taxes (a computerized tax system). Not surprisingly, government purchases of PCs account for a substantial share of the Chinese market, with widespread use of computers as tools in large projects such as air traffic control, road transportation and construction management.

China's new technology enterprises are successfully commercializing technologies to meet industrial and consumer needs, both domestically and increasingly internationally. Chinese domestic producers have increased their share of the fast-growing domestic computer market from 30 per cent in 1990 to over 67 per cent in 1997.[11] As a result, China has changed from being a net importer to a net exporter of computer electronic products, with US$4 billion in exports in 1997 (Lu, 2000).

Infrastructure for IT development

China's physical and telecommunications infrastructure provides an important foundation for the development of its IT industry. The central government invested aggressively in upgrading roads, airports, ports and other physical infrastructure during the 1980s and 1990s, particularly in the heavily urbanized areas of the east coast. This has been critical to development of the computer and telecommunications equipment manufacturing sectors

Table 7.4   Adoption of IT in China, India and comparison countries, 2000/2001

	Personal computers (per 1000 people), 2000	Internet users (thousands), 2000	Internet secure servers, 2001	ICT expenditures % of GDP, 2000	Telephone mainlines (per 1000 people), 2000	Mobile phones (per 1000 people), 2000
China	15.9	22 500	184	5.4	112	66
India	4.5	5 000	122	3.8	32	4
Brazil	44.1	5 000	1 028	8.4	182	136
Israel	253.6	1 270	301	7.4	482	702
US	585.2	95 354	78 126	8.1	700	398

Source: World Bank (2002), 5.9 and 5.10.

and, along with the state-of-the-art facilities in the development zones, undoubtedly contributes to its attractiveness for returnees from overseas.

The development of the telecommunications infrastructure is equally important to the growth of China's IT industry. While India and China were relative equals in the early 1980s, China today outperforms India along every dimension of telecommunications performance (see Table 7.4). In 2000, China had 120 m main telephone fixed lines, compared to India's 27 m. While China's tele-density remains low by developed country standards, at 8.6 per cent (the world average is 12–14 per cent) it is well above India's 2.9 per cent.[12] Also, China now boasts over 19 million Internet connections and 65 million cellular subscriptions.

The quality and reach of the physical and telecom infrastructure makes China a more attractive location for foreign IT companies as well as for returning entrepreneurs. The annual flow of foreign direct investment into China in the late 1990s averaged over US$40 billion and accounted for over 13 per cent of gross fixed capital formation.[13] While breakdowns by sector are not available, anecdotal evidence suggests that a large share of the FDI in the late 1990s was in IT-related sectors. Most of the leading Silicon Valley IT companies have R&D labs as well as development and production facilities in China (either as wholly-owned subsidiaries or, more often, as joint ventures). These offer a low-risk way for overseas Chinese professionals to return home, and enhances the growing pool of technically and managerially sophisticated professionals available in the emerging centres of technology such as Shenzhen, Beijing and Shanghai.

There are, of course, many constraints on the development of the IT sector in China; constraints that will hinder the pace of innovation and entrepreneurship, and potentially limit the return of overseas students in years to come (Yu, 2000; Naughton, 1997). China today has a very limited rule of law, intellectual property rights are rarely protected, the capital market is not well developed, and the venture capital industry is dominated by government agencies. Indeed, the IT industry as a whole remains largely under the control of the government, either directly through partial ownership, or indirectly through its power over approval of stock market listings and bank lending. Corruption remains widespread at most levels of government in China, in spite of high-profile public efforts to discourage it (Chen, 2001). Finally, the continued attempts to control the contents of the media and the Internet have the potential to either slow the industry's development or provoke social and political conflict.

Building the bridge to Silicon Valley

Since the early 1990s, when China began allowing large numbers of students abroad for study, policy-makers have recognized the opportunity to tap the pool of foreign-educated Chinese for domestic development purposes. While the most desirable option would be to recruit all the 'overseas students' and get them back to China, this has proved difficult because of the large gap in living and working conditions between China and the developed West. Local and central governments have thus pursued two types of strategy.

Government support of technical and business exchange

Chinese policy-makers have devoted substantial resources to promoting technical and business exchanges that involve overseas Chinese students. Typically, this involves events such as conferences, investigation tours, joint research projects, and exhibits. Such activities are designed to involve scientists and researchers, business people and policy-makers in cross-regional exchanges of know-how and information. They also provide opportunities for overseas mainland professionals to build relationships with their domestic counterparts. In some cases a local and central government agency will develop a programme that directly funds such events; in others it will subsidize non-government agencies and the private sector to sponsor such activities.

In the late 1990s, Chinese policy-makers, academic institutions and technology companies increased their commitment to improving external communications, particularly with the overseas Chinese in Silicon Valley. They sponsored an increasing number of events and programmes in the US, while also inviting overseas Chinese academics and industry representatives to China to attend conferences and other events. In addition, the Ministry of Education established the 'Chunhui Programme' to finance short-term trips to China by overseas Chinese who were trained abroad to participate in technology-associated activities such as conferences, research projects or other authorized programmes. Many of Silicon Valley's Chinese professionals have participated in these programmes.

Programmes to encourage return entrepreneurship

Policy-makers in China, at both local and central levels, have also attempted to attract overseas students to return home to start their own technology enterprises. Representatives of cabinet-level ministries as well as municipal governments from large cities such as Shanghai and Beijing pay regular visits to Silicon Valley to recruit Chinese technology professionals to return home. The visiting Chinese officials usually hold dinners or meetings with mainlanders and use the occasion to publicize the favourable policy and business environment in China.

Many municipal governments have established 'Returning Students Venture Parks' within the Development Zones of High and New Technology Enterprise. These parks are exclusively for enterprises run by returnees, and while they offer infrastructure and financial benefits like other science parks, they also address the special needs of returnees such as accelerating bureaucratic processes involved with establishing residency or ensuring access to prestigious primary and secondary schools for their children (see Appendix).

By 2000, there were twenty-three 'Returning Students Science Parks' across China, and many other municipalities had policies to attract returning students but no park. The 'Returning Students Science Park' in Zhongguancun (Haidian) district of Beijing, for example, reports that it housed forty-eight companies and sixty-eight returning students in 1998. This is the oldest and largest of the three overseas student parks located in Beijing, which collectively houses 114 companies.

It is difficult to determine the extent to which such policies towards returning students have contributed to China's success in technology industries, or even to the rate of return of overseas students. However, it is worth noting that these policies are quite similar to those pursued by Taiwanese policy-makers in the 1970s and 1980s that played a central role in the creation of a transnational community linking Taiwan and Silicon Valley.

The evidence from Silicon Valley suggests that mainland Chinese professionals, like their Taiwanese predecessors, maintain professional as well as personal ties with China even while working in the US. There are half a dozen Chinese professional associations in the region that range in size from 200 to over 1000 members.[14] While originally formed to organize social activities and help new immigrants overcome the sense of isolation in a foreign culture, they have become important forums for exchanging news, contacts and business information about China. These associations sponsor business tours to China, receive delegations of Chinese government officials, and serve as conduits for Chinese firms recruiting in the Valley. In 1998, for example, the North American Chinese Semiconductor Association co-sponsored a two-week tour of China's semiconductor industry for a delegation of local engineers. The group produced a scientific report that was widely circulated among mainland Chinese in the Valley. The alumni associations of the elite Chinese secondary schools, such as Beijing University and Qinghua University, have active Bay Area chapters that provide an additional direct link back to China.

Mainland Chinese have primarily arrived in the US during the 1990s, and so have started far fewer companies than the Taiwanese and Indian engineers, who began coming to the US in the 1970s. However, those who have started companies have focused almost exclusively on developing products and services for the large domestic market. The dominant model among mainland start-ups is to incorporate in the US and locate headquarters in Silicon Valley while operating primarily on the mainland. While there may be an R&D office in Silicon Valley, all other functions are located in China. Consequently, these firms have more employees in China than in the US, and their top executives spend most of their time in China, or on aeroplanes between Silicon Valley and China!

UTStarCom, for example, provides telecommunications network infrastructure for the Chinese market. It was started by a US-educated engineer and is headquartered in Silicon Valley, where it has thirty employees, but it has 1000 employees in China, making it the third-largest producer in Beijing's Zhongguancun Science Park. Sina.com, which has followed a similar model, with its origins and base in Silicon Valley, is now the leading Internet portal in China. Both companies went public on the NASDAQ in 2000. Likewise, Jason Wu's NetFont, an Internet security software products company primarily targeting the mainland market, has ten people in Silicon Valley and sixty in Beijing. CEO Wu reports that he spends 90 per cent of his time in the China operations.

In sum, mainland Chinese engineers are returning home at an increasing rate and starting companies that serve the domestic Chinese market. Underlying this trend is the growing circulation of people and information between China and Silicon Valley, paralleling that established a decade earlier between Taiwan and Silicon Valley.

4. Reversing the brain drain? The Indian case

The technical and managerial capabilities of US-educated Indian professionals are clear from their continued entrepreneurial successes in Silicon Valley. By 2000, Indian engineers were at the helm of 972 Silicon Valley-based technology companies, which accounted for approximately $5 billion in sales and 25 811 jobs. Moreover, the pace of Indian entrepreneurship has been accelerating rapidly: while Indians were running only 3 per cent of the technology companies started between 1980 and 1984, they were running 10 per cent of those started between 1995 and 2000 (Saxenian, 1999).

The Indian community also institutionalized its social networks in the 1990s through the formation of two of Silicon Valley's most vibrant associations: the Indus Entrepreneurs (TiE) and the Silicon Valley Indian Professionals Association (SIPA).[15] While Indian immigrant engineers successfully mobilized their professional networks within Silicon Valley, they were initially slow to build ties with India. As they gained seniority in US companies in the 1990s, however, many NRIs were instrumental in convincing senior management that they should source software or establish operations in India to take advantage of the substantial wage differentials for software skills. In contrast with their Taiwanese and Chinese counterparts, the Indian community – in the absence of state promotion of global or local technical networks – has played a largely arm's-length middleman role linking US companies with software programming skill in India.

In 1999, Silicon Valley's most successful Indian entrepreneurs (and the founding members of TiE) began actively building bridges to India. Today, TiE has established chapters in Bangalore, Bombay, Delhi, Hyderabad, Calcutta and Chennai. The growing attention paid to these successful entrepreneurs, combined with the market successes of Indian IT firms like Infosys, Wipro and Satyam, have created role models for young Indian engineers and contributed to growing confidence and interest in IT entrepreneurship. The NRIs, have, in turn, been investing aggressively in promising start-ups and venture funds, and begun to serve as role models and advisers for local entrepreneurs.

While traffic between India and the US has increased substantially in recent years, US-educated engineers remain reluctant to return home permanently. There are no data on these trends, but long-time residents of Bangalore report that there has still been only 'a trickle' of permanent returnees to that city. Interviews in Silicon Valley suggest that Indian professionals in the US are likely to turn to India for software programming and development resources, and that many are interested in working in India for a limited period, running a US subsidiary or development office. However, few have followed the Taiwanese and Chinese pattern of returning home to start new technology companies.

One of the most significant roles the Silicon Valley community has played in India is in its attempts to influence government policy. In 1999, for example, Silicon Valley entrepreneur K. B. Chandrasekhar led a Committee on Venture Capital for the Securities and Exchange Board of India. The committee's report developed a comprehensive vision for the growth of India's VC industry, based on a survey of the global experience, and proposed a series of regulatory and institutional reforms to achieve this goal.[16] More recently, they have convened forums bringing together top policy-makers and NRIs to discuss deregulation of telecommunications. Efforts such as these could contribute to the creation of a more attractive context for return entrepreneurs, particularly if accompanied by other policy reforms directed at improving the local environment for innovation.

Indian engineers in Silicon Valley report that business conditions have improved dramatically in India during the past decade. The establishment of the Software Technology Parks (STPs) scheme has provided export-oriented software firms in designated zones with tax exemptions for five years and guaranteed access to high-speed satellite links and reliable electricity. The economic reforms that began in 1991 improved the domestic climate for IT production, particularly the removal of duties and licences on imports of software and industrial equipment (Schware, 1992; Sridharan, 1996; Heeks, 1996). Yet, even today, expatriates complain about bureaucratic restrictions, corrupt and unresponsive officials, and an infrastructure that causes daily frustrations: from unreliable power supplies, water shortages, and backward and costly telecommunications facilities to dangerous and congested high-ways (Krueger and Chinoy, 2000).[17]

The Indian software industry has boomed in recent years, but most of the growth is still driven by low value-added services (Arora et al., 2001; D'Costa, Chapter 1). The industry is dominated by a small number of large export-oriented domestic and foreign corporations that have minimal ties with each other, local entrepreneurs, or the science and technology research base in India. These companies have been so profitable that they are locked into successful routines: there are few incentives to address higher value-added segments of the market or to nurture entrepreneurs that might do so (Parthasarathy, 2000a and 2000b).

In consequence, there are few Taiwan-style 'astronauts' or US-educated engineers who have their feet sufficiently in both worlds to transfer the information and know-how about new markets and technologies or to build the long-term relationships that would contribute to upgrading India's technological infrastructure. This would include not simply transforming the software industry but also developing a viable hardware and manufacturing sector (Narasimhan, 1999; Parthasarathy and Joseph, Chapter 4).

Communication between the technology communities in India and the US is growing fast. Alumni associations from the Indian Institutes of Technology are starting to organize events in Silicon Valley. Some of the large software companies are establishing subsidiaries and alliances in the US. Also, venture capital firms are emerging to invest in firms that link Silicon Valley's technology and market access with India's software skills. Thus, while reversal of the 'brain drain' is not yet on the horizon, there is a small but fast-growing professional community linking Silicon Valley and regions like Bangalore, and one that could play an important role in upgrading the Indian IT sector in the future.

5. Conclusions and policy lessons

The current approach to IT policy in India addresses the immediate obstacles to growth identified by a small number of established, export-oriented software producers, and their high-profile association, NASSCOM.[18] This has proved to be successful: IT policy reforms, business confidence and investment have become mutually reinforcing. This was reflected in the escalating valuations of technology companies on the Indian stock exchanges in 1999–2000.[19] It is also reflected in the growing number of multinationals locating overseas development centres in the established IT regions, and this process of policy reform continues. The political influence of the software industry means that the government of India is undertaking important regulatory reforms, particularly in the telecommunications sector. Also, intensifying competition between state governments for IT investments should ensure improvements in transportation and communications infrastructure, at least in select urban areas.

The experience of Taiwan and, more recently, China, suggests that Indian policy-makers could play a more active role in improving the domestic environment for innovation. The Chinese government has, implicitly if not explicitly, recognized that entrepreneurship is a collective, not an individual process, and that innovation increasingly depends upon processes of collective learning, typically within localized communities (Saxenian, 1994). Such technical communities are built through collaborations of the sort that are rarely practised in India today: collaborations between firms of all sizes, ages and specializations, between firms and universities or research institutes, and between firms and financial institutions such as venture capital. Also, in a world of global communications and transportation, such collaborations increasingly bridge the technical communities in distant regional economies.

The Taiwan and China cases suggest several policy lessons for India, focused on enhancing the linkages between local skill, technology and markets. Over time, such an approach could attract growing numbers of US-educated engineers back to India and also:

- provide incentives, at either the central or local level, for collaboration between established firms, entrepreneurs, and science and technology research capabilities;
- ensure a level playing field between domestic and export-oriented firms to encourage Indian entrepreneurs to serve the domestic market;
- continue the pace of bureaucratic reform and infrastructure improvement, particularly accelerating the improvement of the telecommunications system;
- enhance communication and collaboration between Indian technical professionals in the US and India, including policies that encourage return entrepreneurship.

Most scenarios for the Indian IT sector envision Indian software companies developing innovative products and applications as well as continuing to provide low value-added services for export (NASSCOM, 1999, 2000, 2002). Yet they typically overlook the opportunities for a localized process of innovation both in manufacturing and services. IT producers typically must work closely with customers to develop expertise and to define and test new products. Yet, as long as Indian software houses continue to rely primarily on export markets, they forgo the opportunity to test and perfect new products through interaction with end-users (D'Costa, Chapter 3 of this volume).

India, like China, has the technology, know-how and skill base to experiment with developing new products and services for its large domestic market. Such an approach depends upon continued deregulation in telecommunications and provisions that products and services sold domestically enjoy tax benefits or subsidies that would lessen the current bias towards software export units. This would encourage entrepreneurs to develop economically viable ways to develop products to solve local problems.

IT offers potential efficiencies in a wide range of activities, from distribution and marketing to banking and agriculture. Farmers, for example, can use IT for managing their timetables, crop scheduling, soil testing, insect and rodent control, as well as for marketing and water management. Similarly innovative applications of IT can accelerate development of local language software and local content that will expand access to the benefits of the Internet to more Indians. There is also room for innovation in the provision of the fast growing IT-enabled services such as medical transcription or call centres. Such remote services could eventually provide more employment in India than the software services sector as they depend not on engineers but on large numbers of people with English language skills and who are willing to work for low wages.[20]

This approach could involve experimentation with applying technologies and capabilities developed in the West to the development of products that are appropriate to the Indian environment (Jhunjhunwala, n.d.). Products developed in the West are typically too costly and provide more features than are needed by the vast majority of the Indian population. If products and services were developed that were affordable and reliable, they could transform what is now a potential market into a very sizeable customer base. Take a product like an electronic pager. The pagers available in India today are produced in the West and sell for prices that are well beyond the means of most of the Indian population. However, the technology is so simple that a pager could be developed and manufactured locally for one-fifth of the Western cost. At this price it would be affordable to 20 per cent of the Indian population (which is a very large market). Such products would in turn be likely to have substantial export potential elsewhere in Asia, in Latin America, and in the rest of the developing world.[21]

India already has the design capabilities needed for new product development. These capabilities are evident in the growth of VLSI design in the overseas development centres of foreign companies, as well as in the activities of Bangalore-based firms like Sasken (formerly Silicon Automation Systems), and Encore Software that develop the sophisticated intellectual property components for semiconductor design. There is also evidence that returning entrepreneurs like those in Taiwan could become a source of innovative capabilities. Strand Genomics, a bio-informatics company that uses computing algorithm to accelerate drug discovery, was founded by two returnees from the US. The other five members of the senior management team also have technical degrees from US universities as well as substantial combined experience working in the US.

The challenge, of course, is for the US-educated and trained technologists to return to India and adapt their skills to an indigenous market that is unlikely to require the state-of-the-art features and applications developed in Silicon Valley. Collaboration between local start-ups and established producers with knowledge of particular domains could be especially important in the Indian context. A Bangalore company, Innomedia Technologies, for example, developed a low-cost technology for interactive television that uses existing cable-TV infrastructure to provide video on demand, interactive media, and online shopping. Once the technology was defined, the firm built an alliance with the large, established manufacturer, Reliance Industries, to undertake volume production and distribution. Such collaborations can, of course, involve partners from other regions in India, and even elsewhere in the world. The NRI community in Silicon Valley could become a resource in identifying and coordinating such long-distance partnerships.

However, the precondition is the creation in India of the local technical networks that support the recombination of capital, skill and technology into new ventures. Such an environment is emerging from an R&D group led by the Telecommunications & Computer Networks Group (TeNeT) at IIT Madras. This group includes university faculty, several small R&D companies formed by alumni, as well as distant collaborators. The group's mission is to make possible 25 million Internet connections in India in less than ten years. TeNeT has strategic alliances with IC manufacturers abroad to develop wireless access, fibre access, and Internet access systems specific to the needs of developing countries (Jhunjhunwala et al., 1998).

Comparable networks can be created in other regions. Policy-makers (state governments, ideally, as they are typically closer and more responsive to local needs) might provide incentives for collaborations between companies, or between companies and local universities or other research institutions. Alternatively, they might facilitate associational activities that bring together local producers, researchers and service providers to seek solutions to shared problems such as the shortage of skilled labour or the need for better infrastructure. This process should facilitate the creation of cross-cutting social and technical networks that, over time, support information sharing and collective learning.

The companies and institutions that currently characterize the Indian scene have the potential to create localized technical communities with differing specializations related to their institutional and resource endowments. India's public sector units, such as the aerospace and defence research outfits in Bangalore, could provide a source of technological opportunities if their boundaries were opened up and skill and know-how were allowed to flow more freely within the region. Similarly, venture capitalists and other service providers could, with time, become more knowledgeable about local capabilities, opportunities and resources in order to play a growing role in coordinating and facilitating local experiments across India.

Finally, while the Indian Institutes of Technology produce among the best engineers in the world, their graduates still leave the country in large numbers. This group, or even a small subset of them, could play a technological leadership role in India in the coming decades if more were to return or stay in the country. As it stands now, however, too few remain or return to make an impact. By accelerating the deregulation of telecommunications and other key sectors, upgrading the physical infrastructure, and enhancing conditions for entrepreneurship, the government could create conditions under which more NRIs would be willing to invest in the Indian economy. It is even possible that young Indian engineers would return in far greater numbers than in earlier generations if they saw viable economic opportunities at home. This could make a substantial difference to India's future.

Appendix

A briefing on China Suzhou Pioneering Park for Overseas Chinese Scholars

(Distributed electronically to Bay Area China Network (8/11/98) with subject heading: A Great Business Opportunity for You)

Sponsors:
Chinese Scholarly Exchange Service Centre, Ministry of Education
Torch Program Office, Ministry of Science and Technology
Jiangsu Service Centre for the Shift of Qualified Personnel
Jiancsu Science and Technology Commission
The Administrative Committee of the Suzhou New Technology District
Suzhou Science and Technology Commission

Location:
The Park is located in the Suzhou New District (Suzhou National New and High Technology Industrial Development Zone) to the west of the old city proper of Suzhou. The district is only 80 km away from Shanghai and 1.5 hour drive from Shanghai Hongqiao Airport.

Mission:
To create a favourable environment for exploitation of research results and development of small and medium-sized technology based enterprises by providing all-round service and quality facilities.

Target clients:
Technology-based companies and research institutes run by students and scholars studying or working or returned from abroad.

Incentives for tenants:
- Three-year refund of business tax starting the first day of operation
- Three-year refund of the local part of VAT

- Exemption from income tax in the first two profit-making years, six-year reduction of the rate by 50 per cent and then levied at a special rate of 15 per cent for the next three years
- Minimum registered capital of US$10 000 provided for technology consultancy or service provider, US$60 000 for manufacturing enterprises
- Application priority for different-level grants and funds
- Application priority for certificate of new and high technology product/ enterprise
- Building management and business services
- Free provision of registration formalities
- Provision of advice on policy and technical issues
- Business promotion
- Assistance in obtaining financing and refunds of duties
- Provision of training programmes

Progress to date:
A news conference was held in Beijing this February to declare the establishment of the Park. The six sponsors have jointly set up the Torch New & High Technology Investment and Guarantee Company and registration is now underway. The company is not-for-profit and will specialize in venture capital and credit guarantees for tenants of the park.

Building:
The Park owns one four-storey building with floor space of 10 000 square metres. It hosts eighty-eight units ranging from 20 to 100 sq metres. Services and facilities include the following:

- Conference room with conferencing facilities
- Seminar room
- Product display chamber
- Internet access, central air conditioning
- Reception
- Fax, typing, wordprocessing and photocopying services
- Air ticket booking, hotel room reservations
- 24-hour security services

Applicants and companies:
Till now, the Park has received more than fifty applications and thirty of them are in operation. Business of these companies mainly covers electronics, biotech, mechanics [sic], computer software and environmental protection. Presidents or managing directors of these companies have studied in the USA, Japan, France and UK.

China Suzhou Pioneering Park for Overseas Chinese Scholars invites you to apply today.

Notes

Originally published in *Science, Technology and Society*, 7 (1) (January–June 2002). Copyright © Society for the Promotion of S & T Studies, New Delhi, 2002. All rights reserved. Reproduced with the permission of the copyright holders and the publishers, Sage Publications India Pvt Ltd, New Delhi.

1. The incentives include low interest loans, a five-year income tax break for the first nine years of operation, the right to retain earnings of up to 200 per cent of paid-in capital, accelerated depreciation of R&D equipment, and low cost land. This information and the data on the Park in the following paragraph come from the Science Park Administration, Hsinchu Science-based Industrial Park.

2. C. B. Liaw interview, 28 August 1996.
3. Ron Chwang interview, 25 March 1997.
4. For more on the Taiwanese case, see Romer (1993); Ernst (1999); Saxenian (2000); Hsu (1999).
5. *People's Daily*, http://www.zgc.gov.cn/news/dailynews/000911-4.htm.
6. Other national science and technology programmes include the Climbing Programme (for basic research), the 863 Programme (for high technology research and development) and the Spark Programme (technologies that serve agriculture and small rural enterprises).
7. Another reason for launching the zones was to attract foreign investment into China.
8. Shenzhen Science Park was the first research park in China while the Beijing Park was first established in 1988 as the development zone, which strictly speaking is not the same as a Science Park. The development zone is more like an industrial park that emphasizes manufacturing rather than research. However, as is often the case with China, the distinction loses meaning in pactice.
9. This is a tricky political issue because many cities are competing for government support, including Shanghai, Shenzhen and Guangzhou. The government has not explicitly stated that it has chosen to target Beijing, but evidence is mounting.
10. For a detailed and insightful account of this interaction between state technology resources and new industrial enterprises in China's IT sector, see Lu (2000) and Lu and Lazonick (2001).
11. Not only do these firms have the advantage of market knowledge and proximity, but they have also been strategic in targeting the local market to increase market share. Legend, for example, has lowered prices considerably. Ninety per cent of its total PC shipments in 1997 were units that cost less than US$1500 and one-third of those cost less than US$1000.
12. In 1997 the wait for a new phone connection was 12.17 months in India, compared to 0.68 months in China.
13. This compares to an annual average FDI flow of US$2.7 billion to India between 1996 and 1999, which accounted for approximately 3 per cent of gross fixed capital formation in the same period (UNCTAD, 2000).
14. These are separate from an equal number of Taiwanese professional associations in the Valley. The Taiwanese and mainland Chinese have established separate organizations for many reasons having to do with history and culture, as well as the timing of their arrival in the US, but this may change in the future.
15. For more information on the development and organization of the Indian community in Silicon Valley, see Saxenian (1999).
16. See the 'Report of K. B. Chandrasekhar Committee on Venture Capital' to the Securities and Exchange Board of India at http://www.sebi.gov.in/.
17. A 1999 study by McKinsey & Co estimates that as much as $23 billion in IT export revenues and 650 000 jobs failed to materialize in India over an eight-year period because of the limitations of the telecom infrastructure.
18. The National Association of Software and Service Companies, NASSCOM, was founded in 1988 with thirty-eight members. By 1999 it had 464 members, and in December 2001 it had 854 members and accounted for almost 95 per cent of software industry revenues. NASSCOM's annual *Strategic Review* provides the only detailed and up-to-date figures on employment, revenues, exports and market share for the Indian software and other IT industries. This gives the Association leverage but is not an optimal situation for policy-makers, as there are many

potential sources of bias. Policy reform would ideally include the creation of a reliable, independent source of detailed industry data.

19. Software and related IT services companies now comprise 20–25 per cent of India's total stock market capitalization.

20. See 'Indian Business – Spice Up Your Services', *The Economist*, 16 January 1999.

21. Remarks by Ashok Jhunjhunwala, Conference on Equity, Diversity, and Information Technology, National Institute of Advanced Study, Bangalore, December 1999.

References

Arora, A., V. S. Arunachalam, J. Asundi and R. Fernandes (2001) 'The Indian Software Services Industry', *Research Policy 2001*, 30 (8): 1267–87.

Chang, S. L. (1992) 'Causes of Brain Drain and Solutions: the Taiwan Experience', *Studies in Comparative International Development*, 27 (1): 27–43.

Chen, M. J. (2001) *Inside Chinese Business: a Guide for Managers Worldwide* (Cambridge, MA: Harvard Business School Press).

China Software Industry Association (2001) *2000 Annual Report of China Software Industry*, Beijing.

Dedrick, J. and K. Kraemer (1998) *Asia's Computer Challenge: Threat or Opportunity for the United States and the World?* (New York: Oxford University Press).

Ernst, D. (2000) 'What Permits David to Grow in the Shadow of Goliath? The Taiwanese Model in the Computer Industry', in M. Borrus, D. Ernst and S. Haggard (eds), *International Production Networks in Asia* (New York: Routledge), pp. 110–97.

Grieco, J. M. (1984) *Between Dependency and Autonomy: India's Experience with the International Computer Industry* (Berkeley: University of California Press).

Gu, S. (1999) *China's Industrial Technology: Market Reform and Organizational Change* (London: Routledge).

Heeks, R. (1996) *India's Software Industry: State Policy, Liberalisation and Industrial Development* (New Delhi: Sage Publications).

Hsu, J. (1997) 'A Late Industrial District? Learning Networks in the Hsinchu Science-Based Industrial Park', doctoral dissertation, Geography, University of California at Berkeley.

Institute of International Education (IIE) (2000) *Open Doors 2000* (Washington, DC: IIE).

Jhunjhunwala, A. (n.d.) 'Can Information Technology Help Transform India?', Department of Electrical Engineering, Indian Institute of Technology, Madras, http://www.tenet.res.in/Papers/IT-Trans/ittrans.html.

Jhunjhunwala, A., B. Ramamurthi and T. Gonsalves (1998) 'The Role of Technology in Telecom Expansion in India', *IEEE Communications Magazine*, 36 (11): 88–94.

Kogut, B. and U. Zander (1993) 'Knowledge of the Firm and the Evolutionary Theory of the Multinational Corporation', *Journal of International Business Studies*, 24 (4): 625–45.

Krueger, A. O. and S. Chinoy (2000) 'The Indian Economy in a Global Context', background paper, Conference on Indian Economic Prospects: Advancing Policy Reform, 31 May–1 June, Center for Research on Economic Policy Reform, Stanford University.

Lu, Q. (2000) *China's Leap into the Information Age: Innovation and Organization in the Computer Industry* (Oxford: Oxford University Press).

Lu, Q. and W. Lazonick (2001) 'The Organization of Innovation in a Transitional Economy: Business and Government in Chinese Electronic Publishing', *Research Policy* (Amsterdam), 30 (1): 35–54.

Mathews, J. A. (1997) 'A Silicon Valley of the East: Creating Taiwan's Semiconductor Industry', *California Management Review*, 39 (4): 26–54.

Meany, C. S. (1994) 'State Policy and the Development of Taiwan's Semiconductor Industry', in J. Aberbach et al., *The Role of the State in Taiwan's Development* (London: M. E. Sharpe).

Naughton, B. (1997) *The China Circle: Economics and Technology in the PRC, Taiwan and Hong Kong* (Washington, DC: Brookings Institution Press).

Narasimhan, R. (1999) 'Deploying IT in India: the Need for a Larger Vision', lecture at the Indian Institute of Information, Technology, 22 Oct, Bangalore.

National Association of Software and Service Companies (1999, 2000) *The IT Software and Services Industry in India: a Strategic Review* (New Delhi: NASSCOM), http://www.nasscom.org.

——(1999) *Indian IT Strategies*, Report prepared by McKinsey & Co (New Delhi: NASSCOM).

——(2002) *The IT Industry in India: Strategic Review 2002* (New Delhi: NASSCOM).

National Youth Commission (1999) Report on Students Returning from Abroad, Ministry of Education, Taipei, Taiwan ROC.

National Science Foundation, Division of Science Resource Studies (1998) 'Statistical Profiles of Foreign Doctoral Recipients in Science and Engineering: Plans to Stay in the United States', by Jean M. Johnson, Arlington, VA: NSF 99-304, Nov.

Nohria, N. and S. Ghoshal (1997) *The Differentiated Network: Organizing Multinational Corporations for Value Creation* (San Francisco: Jossey-Bass Publishers).

Organization for Economic Cooperation and Development (1997) *Information Technology Outlook* (Paris: OECD).

Parthasarathy, B. (2000a) 'Globalization and Agglomeration in Newly Industrializing Countries: the State and the Information Technology Industry in Bangalore, India', doctoral dissertation, Spring, University of California at Berkeley.

——(2000b) 'An Asian Silicon Valley in Bangalore? Evidence for the Changing Organization of Production in the Indian Computer Software Industry', unpublished paper, Indian Institute of Information Technology, Bangalore.

Portes, A. (1996) 'Global Villagers: the Rise of Transnational Communities', *The American Prospect*, March–April: 74–7.

Powell, W. W. (1990) 'Neither Market nor Hierarchy: Network Forms of Organization', in Barry Staw and Lawrence L. Cummings (eds), *Research in Organizational Behavior* Greenwich (CT: JAI Press), pp. 295–336.

——(2001) 'The Capitalist Firm in the Twenty-First Century: Emerging Patterns in Western Enterprise', in Paul DiMaggio (ed.), *The Twenty-First-Century Firm* (Princeton and Oxford: Princeton University Press), pp. 33–68.

Romer, P. (1993) 'Two Strategies for Economic Development: Using Ideas and Producing Ideas', *Proceedings of the World Bank Annual Conference on Development Economics 1992* (Washington, DC: International Bank for Reconstruction and Development).

Saxenian, A. (1994) *Regional Advantage: Culture and Competition in Silicon Valley and Route 128* (Cambridge, MA: Harvard University Press).

——(1999) *Silicon Valley's New Immigrant Entrepreneurs* (San Francisco: Public Policy Institute of California), http://www.ppic.org/publications/PPIC120/ppic120.abstract.html.

——(2000) 'The Silicon Valley–Hsinchu Connection: Technical Communities and Industrial Upgrading', discussion paper, Stanford Institute of Economic Policy Research, Stanford University.

——(forthcoming) 'The Bangalore Boom: From Brain Drain to Brain Circulation?', in Kenneth Keniston and Deepak Kumar (eds), *Bridging the Digital Divide: Lessons From India* (Bangalore: National Institute of Advanced Study).

Saxenian, A. and Chuen-Yueh Li (2003) 'Bay-to-Bay Strategic Alliances: the Network Linkages between Taiwan and the US Venture Capital Industries', *International Journal of Technology Management*, 25 (1 and 2).

Schware, R. (1992) 'Software Industry Entry Strategies for Developing Countries: a "Walking on Two Legs" Proposition', *World Development*, 20 (2): 143–64.

Securities and Exchange Board of India (2000) 'Report of K. B. Chandrasekhar Committee on Venture Capital', SEBI, New Delhi, http://www.sebi.gov.in.

Sridharan, E. (1996) *The Political Economy of Industrial Promotion: Indian, Brazilian, and Korean Electronics in Comparative Perspective 1969–1994* (Westport, CT: Praeger).

UNCTAD (2000) *World Investment Report 2000: Cross-border Mergers and Acquisitions* (Geneva: UNCTAD).

US Embassy of China (2000) 'Tenth Five Year Plan for Science and Technology', Newsletter of the Environment, Science, and Technology Section, US Embassy of China, July.

World Bank (2002) *2002 World Development Indicators* (Washington, DC: International Bank for Reconstruction and Development).

Yu, G. (2000) 'Chinese Immigrants in Silicon Valley and Innovation in China: a Case Study of Beijing Science Park', Master's Thesis, School of Public Policy, University of California at Berkeley, Spring.

8
Capability Building and Inter-Organization Linkages in the Indian IT Industry: the Role of Multinationals, Domestic Firms and Academic Institutions[1]

Rakesh Basant and Pankaj Chandra

1. Introduction

Organizations develop linkages to access markets, capabilities and complementary assets, reduce risk and uncertainty or improve appropriability. Linkages also help reap synergies across economic entities and become competitive. Inter-organization linkages are characterized by a variety of features. These include types of entity involved (e.g. foreign/domestic, private/public), markets served (e.g. foreign/domestic), types of alliance (e.g. involving technology development and licensing, production, marketing and distribution, financial participation and the like). It is the interplay of these features that tends to decide the extent and nature of capabilities developed in the network.

While the role of inter-firm linkages in developing technological capabilities is recognized (Bell and Pavitt, 1997), the process and the circumstances under which such learning takes place are not well understood. If capability building through linkages is viewed as a function of the types of entities, linkages and markets involved, various strands of literature can provide some insights on the processes at work. The literature on multinationals and foreign direct investment (FDI), for example, suggests that under certain policy regimes, foreign linkages can facilitate the form of learning that arises out of knowledge spillovers and competitive pressures provided by foreign firms (see Kokko, 1992; Mytelka, 1998). Similarly, there is ample evidence to show that the interaction between academia and industry can result in significant knowledge flows and learning, especially in industrial-bound clusters (Basant, 2002). Studies have also shown that a movement in the hierarchy of linkages (i.e. marketing to manufacturing to technology development) or a move from one-way to two-way linkages (see discussion below) can have a positive impact on the technological capabilities of participating entities. This is particularly so when participants make technological investments and countries adopt pro-competition policies (Kokko, 1992; Mytelka, 1998). Moreover, studies on learning and exposure to markets would suggest that linkages focusing on more competitive and demanding markets (e.g. exports) would provide greater opportunities for capability building (Ernst, Gaaniatsos and Mytelka, 1998). Finally, it also needs to be recognized that capability-building processes emanating from linkages are also influenced by the strategic intent of the partnering entities.

As global and local linkages are increasingly becoming relevant for developing country firms' capability building, an understanding of how inter-organization networks evolve and function, and how developing country entities can benefit from these alliances, becomes crucial. This is particularly so for large emerging markets like China and India where both domestic and export markets can provide opportunities to learn from networks. These economies, especially the former, have become part of global networks with large inflows of FDI in recent years. In both these economies the IT sector has seen significant growth. MNCs have set up subsidiaries or formed linkages with local entities to serve domestic and export markets. Similarly, domestic organizations have also formed alliances to service these markets.

Information and communication technologies (ICT) are undergoing significant changes: software is rapidly becoming the core of most information and communication applications. This has created a new set of opportunities for software firms. For instance, it has been suggested that development of telecom-related software could prove to be a useful market opportunity for Indian software firms. However, in order to exploit such opportunities, access to hardware knowledge will be crucial. Technology cooperation between telecom hardware and software firms can provide such an opportunity (Basant and Chandra, 1997). It may be useful to explore how different types of organizations exploit these opportunities.

In the context of global patterns of alliances and the emerging opportunities in the telecom sector, this chapter explores the role of inter-organizational linkages in capability building. We follow a broad concept of organizations, which includes a variety of entities that are engaged in capability building and value addition. These include firms, academic institutions and research organizations. These organizations could be public or private and could be owned by domestic or foreign entities. More specifically, we explore how the features of alliances, types of participating entities, their strategic intent, and the nature of markets served have contributed to capability building. Given the strategic intent of using linkages to build capabilities for developing new products and services for commercialization, do organizations of different types follow different paths? Does the implementation of these strategies by different organizations result in different outcomes in terms of capabilities and spillover benefits? To explore these and related questions, we examine the nature and extent of inter-firm linkages in the telecommunication sector of the Indian IT industry, study two technology development networks created in the telecom sector by a foreign multinational in India and China, and contrast the nature of these foreign firm networks with that initiated by a domestic Indian organization. The foreign firm networks are of two types, one established by the multinational with firms in the host country and the other with a public sector academic institution. The network established by the domestic Indian organization comprises linkages between a public sector academic institution and domestic/foreign firms.

These comparisons provide useful insights into capability building through network linkages, as the nature of linkages, types of alliance partners, their strategic requirements, and the nature of markets served vary across the networks under study. Insofar as the partnering entities represent software and hardware capabilities, these cases exemplify strong interdependence between such competencies to exploit emerging opportunities in the ICT sector. The methodology used in this chapter involved analysis of primary survey data and case studies on Nortel's linkages with Indian and Chinese organizations, and the network developed by the Indian Institute of Technology, Chennai's TeNet Group. Details are provided in the respective sections.

The chapter is divided into five sections. In the next section we present the findings of a survey of linkages within IT firms that deal with telecommunication technologies. The cases of R&D networks of Nortel in both India and China are discussed in section three. We assess Nortel's role in developing technological capabilities among the Indian participants of the network. The section also compares the Nortel network in China with its network in India to examine the relative advantages of the two *vis-à-vis* the learning potential for the domestic economies. In section four we present a case study on technology development and commercialization in the telecom sector at the Indian Institute of Technology, Chennai through the formation of a network of alliances. The final section summarizes the key findings to highlight aspects of inter-organization linkages, that may result in higher learning for organizations in developing countries.

2. Inter-firm linkages in the Indian telecom sector

Firms are engaged in various forms of collaborative activity. Two types of inter-firm linkages can be distinguished: those that involve a one-way relationship leading to a flow of technology from the licensor to the licensee or from the mother unit to the subcontractors; and a two-way relationship involving joint R&D or research to create common standards. While the unidirectional linkages have existed for a long time, the two-way relationships are more recent; the newer forms of partnering in R&D, production and marketing have also become more prominent over the years (Mytelka, 1999; WIR, 1998). Recent data (1980–96) show a marked shift away from the quasi-exclusive reliance on one-way linkages to the development of two-way collaborative relationships in the 1990s, particularly in IT (WIR, 1998). Even traditional linkages are being transformed into two-way partnerships. For example, in customer–supplier relationships, suppliers are being drawn into joint research and design activities. The share of two-way relationships among the agreements involving developing countries is also on the rise, which suggests that firms in developing countries are gradually becoming viable partners in joint technology generation activities (WIR, 1998). In the following paragraphs we study the Indian telecom sector to understand the nature of such relationships and their role in building capabilities.

A recent analysis of secondary data has shown that firms in the Indian telecom sector are engaged in a wide variety of inter-firm linkages (Basant and Chandra, 2001). An interesting aspect of these linkages was found to be the relationships between software, hardware and service firms. It is therefore important to include these categories of firms in any analysis of the telecom-related IT sector. Consequently, we conducted a survey of 100 telecom-related firms to collect detailed information about their linkages with other firms. The names of the firms that were surveyed were generated from IT magazines. The survey focused on four locations, namely, Delhi, Mumbai, Bangalore and Chennai.[2] Each of these firms was visited by an investigator who filled out a questionnaire during personal interviews with senior managers. Our survey covered a large variety of firms.[3] Preliminary investigation showed that often enterprises have more than one alliance and within each alliance they work on multiple projects with their partners. Therefore, data on linkages were compiled at two levels: alliances and projects. In what follows, we discuss our findings from the survey.

Nature of alliances

Telecom IT firms were engaged in a variety of alliances (Table 8.1). The share of hardware firms in the total number of alliances was much lower than their share in the sample firms. While alliances with other software firms were dominant among sample software firms, these firms also had linkages with hardware and IT services firms. Often the same alliance involved a variety of activities or dimensions, e.g. technology transfer, licensing of brand and a subcontracting arrangement. To facilitate analysis, the alliance activities were divided into five broad categories relating to technology, production, finance, marketing and distribution, and those involving a management agreement. Table 8.2 reports the distribution of alliances across these categories and sub-activities within them.[4] The alliances covered a variety of activities: while technology, production and marketing, and distribution-related alliances were equally important, finance and management agreement-related linkages were found to be less popular.[5]

Table 8.1 Distribution of alliances by type of alliance partners

Firms	No. of firms	%	No. of alliances	%	Partner firm					
					Hardware	%	Software	%	IT service	%
Hardware	20	20.8	39	8.6	24	61.5	12	30.8	3	7.7
Software	38	39.6	101	22.1	19	18.8	80	79.2	2	2.0
IT service	38	39.6	116	25.4	42	36.2	33	28.4	41	35.3
Total	96		256							

Note: Four firms could not be classified in the three categories defined in the table. In the case of two alliances, the relevant details were not available.

Table 8.2 Percentage distribution of alliances by nature of alliance

Nature of alliance	Frequency	Percentage
Technology-related		
Joint research and development arrangement	68	26.4
Technology collaboration to establish standards	116	45.0
Cross-licensing	3	1.2
Licensing	12	4.7
All technology-related	143	55.4
Production-related		
Joint production contract	44	17.1
Subcontracting	60	23.3
Supply arrangement	66	25.6
All production-related	134	51.9
Finance-related		
Subsidiary	8	3.1
Financial collaboration	18	7.0
Joint ventures	32	12.4
Minority holding	5	1.9
Cross-holding	2	0.8
Bidding consortium	27	10.5
All finance-related	65	25.2
Marketing- and distribution-related		
Distribution and sales arrangement	121	46.9
Marketing arrangement	95	36.8
Licensing of brand	9	3.5
All marketing- and distribution-related	145	56.2
Management agreement	50	19.4
Total no. of valid alliances	258	

Within technology-related linkages, collaborations for establishing standards were dominant. Significantly, over a quarter of the alliances involved joint research and development agreements. Besides, many of the technology-related alliances involved joint R&D as well as collaborations for establishment of standards. Subcontracting and supply arrangements are dominant among the production-related alliances, and joint production activities are also quite important. Distribution and sales arrangements are the most common marketing- and distribution-related alliances. While marketing links are important, licensing of brands is not widespread. The IT Telecom sector seems to be different from many other sectors (see Basant, 2000) where Indian firms are actively seeking alliances for licensing brand names, especially foreign ones. Also, unlike many alliances in recent years, linkages among IT firms do not appear to focus principally on raising financial resources. Besides, there appear to be more 'two-way' alliances amongst sample firms.

Participation of foreign firms

Inter-firm alliances in the Indian IT sector have significant involvement of foreign firms (Table 8.3). In fact, for all categories of alliances, the incidence of alliances between domestic and foreign firms is significantly greater than that among domestic firms. Interestingly, the distribution of 'domestic' alliances by categories is not significantly different from that of 'foreign' alliances. Technology-, production-, marketing- and distribution-related alliances dominate for both domestic and foreign alliances, with finance-related linkages not being as important.

Objectives of alliances

Technology-based objectives were dominant for forming alliances (Table 8.4). These included exploitation of technological complementarities among partners, monitoring technological opportunities, accessing partners' technology, acquisition of world class practices, reduction in innovation time span, conducting basic research, and the like. Market expansion and

Table 8.3 Extent of participation of foreign and domestic firms in different categories of alliances (percentages)

Category	Distribution of alliances by categories		Share of alliances among domestic and foreign firms		Total valid responses
	Domestic	Foreign	Domestic	Foreign	
Technology-related	28.7	25.9	20.1	79.9	134 (100)
Production-related	21.3	25.2	16.1	83.9	124 (100)
Finance-related	14.9	11.6	22.6	77.4	62 (100)
Marketing- and distribution-related	25.5	27.6	17.4	82.6	138 (100)
Management agreement	9.6	9.7	18.4	81.6	49 (100)
Total number of alliances	94 (100)	413 (100)			507 (100)

Table 8.4 Distribution of alliances by objectives

Objective	Intentions frequency	Percentage	Realized frequency	Percentage realization
To reduce cost and risks	104	40.3	71	68.3
To seek financial support	44	17.1	27	61.4
Exploit technological complementarity among partners	184	71.3	142	77.2
To reduce innovation time span	73	28.3	41	56.2
To acquire larger market share	144	55.8	117	81.3
To conduct basic research	10	3.9	4	40.0
To monitor technological opportunities	139	53.9	104	74.8
Expansion of market	170	65.9	128	75.3
To access partner's technology	130	50.4	109	83.8
To monitor possible entry of potential competitors	57	22.1	30	52.6
To seek control over partner	9	3.5	2	22.2
Outsourcing of peripheral activities	17	6.6	7	41.2
To acquire world class practices	107	41.5	78	72.9
To activate subsidiary partnership	11	4.3	2	18.2
To strengthen customer–supplier partnership	95	36.8	59	62.1
To increase profitability	204	79.1	170	83.3
Others (new products, cost-effective outsourcing)	10	3.9	5	50.0
(Total no. of valid alliances)	258			

monitoring was the other important objective of reported alliances, and a large majority of firms (79 per cent) entered into alliances to increase profitability. A significant proportion of firms (40 per cent) also established inter-firm linkages to reduce costs and risks. In a large proportion of cases, the intended objectives were realized (Table 8.5). Overall, the realization of technological, market expansion and profitability objectives was greater than for other objectives. The alliances therefore seem to have a positive impact on sample firms' technological capabilities, market share and profitability.

Some other features of alliances and capability building

Several other benefits of alliances were also evident (Table 8.5). In almost all the alliances, the size of the projects and the number of employees devoted to the alliance increased over time. The proportion of alliances in which the partner helped set up factory or other facilities was rather low (22 per cent). This is possibly because not many alliances have involved manufacturing linkages. However, in only about 44 per cent of the cases did the partners help in improving managerial practices. Besides, in only about 53 per cent of the cases did the alliances facilitate improvements in shopfloor or

Table 8.5   Some features of alliances and their evolution

	Percentage
Size of the projects increased over time	91.6
No. of employees devoted to alliance increased over time	87.9
Partner helped set up factory/facilities	21.5
Partner helped improve shopfloor/programming practices	53.4
Managerial practices changed	43.9
Alliance helped to develop new products	44.8
Investment in hardware/software usable in other projects	66.8
Alliance helped in training people other than those involved in projects	69.6
Projects are mainly for the export market	34.3
IPRs are held by (or plan to hold):	
Partner	25.5
Firm	19.1
Both	21.7
None	33.8

Note: The number of responses varied for each question, and therefore the percentages were computed for valid responses only.

programming practices. While these low percentages may be partly reflective of the nature of alliances, one would have preferred a more positive impact of alliances on firm level practices. Perhaps firms are not consciously trying to exploit this benefit.

On the positive side, a large proportion of alliances (about 45 per cent) facilitated development of new products. This would certainly have enhanced the sample firms' product development capabilities. In about 41 per cent of the cases, the sample firms also had (either jointly with the partner or alone) the intellectual property rights (IPRs) over the technology generated through the alliance.[6] Interestingly, only about 65 per cent firms considered IPRs to be important in an alliance. Apart from the direct benefits in the form of product and/or process (e.g. factory, facilities) capabilities, the sample firms seem to be benefiting too from spillover effects. About 67 per cent of the sample firms reported that the investments in hardware/software made through the alliance are usable in other projects. In almost 70 per cent of the cases, the alliance helped in training employees other than those involved in the alliance projects.

Another interesting feature of the alliances needs to be noted: most of the alliances are for the domestic market with only 34 per cent of them focusing on the export market. It is difficult to ascertain the extent to which the domestic orientation of alliances is a reflection of sampling biases in the survey. However, to the extent that these estimates are indicative, they suggest a maturing of the domestic IT Telecom market, especially when one juxtaposes this with the fact that a majority of the survey alliances are between domestic and foreign firms.

Some dimensions of projects undertaken within alliances

On average, the sample firm made 73 per cent of the total financial investment in the project (Table 8.6). This is consistent with our earlier finding that the alliances captured in the survey were not primarily geared towards raising financial resources. Provision of design, software and hardware can be seen as important aspects of inter-firm alliances. The cases where both the firm and the partner provided these inputs can certainly be seen as 'two-way' linkages, and in most cases where the sample firm is providing the design, software and hardware, linkages are likely to be of the 'two-way' variety. This impression is strengthened by the fact that in over 81 per cent of the projects the sample firm played an important role in planning. Another important feature of the projects has been that in a large proportion of cases (58 per cent) employees with skills not hitherto available with the firm were hired for the projects. The projects therefore created opportunities for firms to enhance their knowledge base through recruitment of better-trained people. This advantage is over and above the benefit of training existing employees through such projects.

Table 8.6 Profile of the projects and the associated learning potential

Average share of the firm in investment		73%
Average share of the partner in investment		21%
Percentage of cases in which design was provided by:	Partner	43.2
	Firm	48.9
	Both	7.9
Percentage of cases in which software was provided by:	Partner	40.3
	Firm	32.3
	Both	27.4
Percentage of cases in which hardware was provided by:	Partner	41.9
	Firm	33.3
	Both	24.8
Percentage of cases where planning done jointly was significant		50.4
Percentage of cases where planning done jointly was moderate		30.7
Percentage of cases where planning done jointly was low		19.0
Percentage cases where firm has access to the final product		82.9
Percentage cases where a number of people were hired with new skills		58.2
Alliance involving hardware manufacturing:		
Percentage of cases in which manufacturing equipment was provided by partner		17.3
Percentage of cases where design improvement made to the product		47.1
Percentage of cases where new equipment was bought		58.9
Percentage of cases where equipment was modified		27.7
Percentage of cases where new products developed		37.1
Total number of projects		156

Capability building through alliances: summarizing the survey findings

The survey findings seem to suggest that inter-organization alliances in the IT Telecom sector have been used to access technology and complementary assets (e.g. marketing and distribution, manufacturing) and expanding markets. Accessing financial resources does not appear to be a key objective. Of course, firms try to reduce risks and costs, and improve profitability through such alliances, and in a significant proportion of cases these objectives are met. Moreover, apart from other benefits, these alliances have facilitated the building of technological capabilities among sample firms. As is the case in most situations, some firms have gained more than others. The survey data are inadequate to identify the characteristics of firms that benefit from alliances. Some of these characteristics will be explored through the case studies in the next two sections.

Further, while the alliances seem to have been largely 'successful', that does not mean that firms are completely comfortable with them. Many firms reported that they are not able to completely eradicate technological and market uncertainties through alliances. Difficulties in predicting product lifecycles, short technology lifecycles, and slow absorption of technologies make the operation of alliances difficult. Often, new agreements have to be entered into with changes in technology. Besides, firms have to live with ambiguously defined scope of participation in their alliances. Commitment to alliances varies a great deal across partners; often the alliances are very fragile. Add to that the differences in the work cultures, objectives and financial strengths of the alliance partners and one has a recipe for unstable relationships. This is particularly the case in alliances between foreign and domestic firms. Despite these and many other difficulties and challenges, a large proportion of the sample firms seem to have benefited from alliances. They are probably learning to learn from alliances. This is a positive sign, as technologically capable domestic firms can be competitive and remain valuable partners in any alliance.

3. Nortel's network: technology development processes in India and China

The nature and objectives of alliances in the IT Telecom sector discussed in the last section suggest that firms enter into these linkages for a variety of strategic reasons. While capability building has been an important outcome of these linkages, it is still not clear if certain elements of the linkages or characteristics/strategic intentions of the partner entities can influence the learning potential of the partnership. This and the following section explore these dimensions through two case studies.

This section focuses on an international technology development network of a telecom multinational (Nortel Networks, Canada) in India. It also discusses, albeit very briefly, Nortel's network in China. The nature of linkages, types of participating entities, and the nature of markets served are different in the two networks. Besides, Nortel has used different strategies in the two countries. Interestingly, the objectives and strategies of partner entities in these countries have also been different. Both of these are two-way partnerships which have significant learning potential for participating entities in developing countries. The conditions under which such capability building is facilitated needs to be explored. In order to achieve this we first discuss the characteristics of the two networks separately and then provide a comparison of their strategies and learning.

Nortel's network in India[7]

Nortel is a leading telecommunications firm from Canada which specializes in developing technology for digital networks. Its revenue in 2001 was US$17.5 billion. In 1989, the International R&D Group of Nortel entered into arrangements with two Indian software development companies: Sasken (earlier known as Silicon Automation Systems (SAS)) located in Bangalore, and Tata Consultancy Services (TCS) which has its headquarters in Mumbai. Two other companies were added to this arrangement in 1992. These were Infosys Technologies (Infosys) and Wipro Technologies (Wipro), both of which are located in Bangalore. These firms compete with each other in the domestic and international markets. Infosys was founded in 1981. It is a premier software development company with an annual turnover of about US$391.9 million[8] in 2000–1 and employs about 10 000 workers, 8725 of whom have software-related skills. Infosys focuses on software services in the areas of distribution, finance, retail, telecom, insurance, Internet and engineering services. In addition, they have products in the area of bank automation. Established in 1989, Sasken develops tools and services that enable the design of semiconductors, telecommunications, computing and networking equipment. The company's stated core competence is signal processing which has resulted in solutions for digital communications, with specific emphasis in multimedia technologies. In 2001, it employed about 947 people of whom 837 were software engineers. Its annual IT software and service revenue in 2000–1 was US$29.1 million. Set up in 1968, TCS is Asia's largest consulting group with activities that range from management consulting to IT solutions, offshore development and branded software products. About 16 880 people work for TCS whose sales turnover in 2000–1 was US$647.8 million. Wipro Technologies was started in 1980. Wipro has about 9250 employees with an annual turnover of US$544.9 million in 2000–1.

The Nortel alliance is unique in a number of ways. It was envisaged as a long-term stable relationship among 'peers'. The Indian partners were asked to contribute to the mainstream of Nortel's work and the implicit division of labour that keeps 'architects' in the north and 'coders' in India was sought to be broken. Nortel therefore did not view its Indian partners merely as a cheap source of software production; financial gain by squeezing the partners is not the long-term goal. Instead, they are willing to help them evolve into genuine two-way partners.

Genesis and formation of the network

The International R&D group at Nortel started to think about forming linkages with firms in India in the late 1980s. Two senior employees of this group, both of Indian origin, spearheaded this effort. While the major impetus for forming this alliance came from Nortel, some of the Indian partners were also actively looking for such linkages. As a part of their preparation, Nortel checked with Texas Instruments and Hewlett Packard about their experiences of working in India. With the help of individuals in these and in other companies known to the Nortel initiators, a long list of potential partners was developed. Nortel selected the four Indian firms on the basis of very specific skills and capabilities they had developed over the years. Three broad reasons led to the emergence of this partnership: interest of the two Indians at Nortel to develop long-term links with India; emergence of India as a strong, low cost software development centre; and Nortel's desire to externalize its R&D work to reduce its costs. The Indian firms were looking to earn foreign exchange, keep their best people within the country, enter into domains like telecom, and for opportunities to learn the latest technology and management practices and climb up the product complexity ladder.

Organization of the network

The partnership is not an equity-based joint venture. It is an ongoing contractual relationship between Nortel and its partners; each relationship is individually defined. Nortel made the bulk of the physical investment. At each partner's location, Nortel has created an infrastructure which is comparable to that in Canada. Apart from the state-of-the-art telecom hardware, Nortel has installed large capacity dedicated lines for communication with its partners.

Linkages between the Indian firms and Nortel are not organized in a way that requires interaction among the Indian partners. Such collaboration is limited, informal, and typically focuses on sharing some standards and practices but largely on communication infrastructure-related issues. Training of partner firms' employees is common. Each Indian partner has an independent project relationship with Nortel. Allocation of projects to each partner by Nortel is governed by its overall strategy to map disciplines across partners and avoid overlap. Each partner in India has specializations and 'collectively' the four Indian partners are growing in the image of Nortel's mother lab in Ottawa, which works on a broad spectrum of telecom products. As the firms do not work together, Nortel remains the 'director' of the network.

The Nortel projects, which started with low skill assignments such as pro-gramme testing, have gradually evolved into fully-fledged offshore development centres for Nortel to develop, modify and support software products or software components of Nortel products. The initial projects were arm's-length technical contracts with very limited interaction between the development teams of Nortel and the Indian firms. This relationship evolved with the successful completion of many of these projects. Gradually, Nortel commissioned larger and more complex development projects requiring more sophisticated hardware and communication infrastructure along with enhanced interaction between Nortel and the Indian teams. At the offshore development centres, Nortel has installed advanced telecom hardware for testing this software. It is hoped that with the synergistic interaction between increased access to telecom hardware and software, communication infrastructure, and the improving project skills, these alliances will graduate to product design and development centres. Most of the current work focuses on the further development of existing Nortel products; only a small proportion can be categorized as research.

It must be re-emphasized, however, that at this point in time, each Indian partner works on independent projects; Nortel integrates these projects. There are reasonably well-defined rules for protecting Nortel's intellectual property. Trust plays a key role in avoiding leakages of proprietary knowledge. While the relationship does not prohibit collaboration of Indian companies with Nortel's competitors, movement of persons working on Nortel projects to substantially similar projects of competitors is not permitted. An agreement on non-disclosure at the corporate level is signed and each person working on Nortel projects individually signs such an agreement. Anything the partners develop with Nortel belongs to latter unless they agree to negotiate and to share. Interestingly, within the Indian firms' premises, Nortel projects are located in physically separate areas with restricted access. Each of the Indian partners has different types of relationships with many international firms. For instance, one of these Indian firms also has a Nortel-like offshore software development centre for NCR. The Indian firms have a large number of Fortune 500 firms as customers around the world, such as Microsoft, IBM, Oracle, Fujitsu, Philips, Hitachi, Sharp, Toshiba, National Semiconductors and Texas Instruments. The Indian companies compete fairly aggressively in the international market for projects. Theoretically, therefore, potential for learning across alliances is high and has been exploited by the participating firms.

Nortel's strategic intent

Software is increasingly substituting for a variety of tasks which were earlier performed by telecom hardware. Software development in North America has become extremely expensive due to the shortage of skilled manpower. It seems that Nortel's strategic intent was to outsource software development for telecom devices from relatively inexpensive offshore locations. Indian firms provided a rich pool of software development capabilities as well as the ability to gear up fast to develop new application software. However, their telecom-related knowledge base was limited. This provided excellent opportunities for collaboration between firms with complementary capabilities. Nortel made specific efforts to develop/update the telecom hardware/ software-related knowledge of its Indian partners. While the expectation of cost savings was important and it came to fruition with Nortel saving about $50 million per year due to the network, the long-term perspective was probably more important.

However, cost saving alone does not justify the investments Nortel made in the partnership. Nortel has been seeking opportunities to adapt its telecom technology for the Asia-Pacific market. It has so far been unsuccessful in entering the Indian telecom market; its international competitors like Siemens, Alcatel, AT&T and Ericsson are already present in India. This alliance therefore not only provides Nortel access to the inexpensive software development resources in India, but also allows them to enter the Indian market with products specially designed for India.[9] Moreover, an R&D arrangement of this kind brings product development activity closer to the markets in the Asia-Pacific region. The concept of a more open 'two-way' partnership (although somewhat asymmetrical) was partly necessary to attract good Indian firms and provide stability to the relationship.

Benefits to the Indian firms

The benefits of this alliance to the Indian companies have been numerous. The firms together earn about US$50 million per year for India. The major gain has been in developing telecommunications-related knowledge and acquiring expertise to produce to world standards and satisfy global markets in this sector. As Nortel was not averse to sharing and connecting Indian firms to the world market, the partners learned the whole package, got exposed to how Nortel functions, how it deals with the customers, and the like. The Indian partners also received training on telecom technology and Nortel's products. Such learning opportunities arose during visits by Nortel experts to Indian sites as well as visits of Indian engineers to Nortel's facilities overseas. Specific learning occurred through the use of new telecom-related software (especially in switching), entry into new market segments relating to various telecom product lines, development of new products (largely in the form of new features on existing products), acquisition of knowledge relating to international programming standards as well as protocols/standards in telecom process (process and quality standards for developing highly complex products), and the like.

Strategically, the entry of Indian firms into the telecommunications software market has been a significant outcome of this alliance. The alliance not only facilitated entry into this market segment but also created learning opportunities that may eventually help the Indian partners to become important players in this emerging segment.[10] The Indian firms feel that their association with Nortel has accelerated the development of their technological capabilities in this business. There have been two other spillover benefits. The alliance has enhanced the credibility of and has provided better visibility to the Indian partners. This has in turn helped them attract other customers. The Nortel development centres have had strong demonstration effects within each company.

Looking ahead

The long-term sustainability of this alliance will depend on the nature of learning by the Indian partners and the extent of locked-in investment by the participating firms. Though Nortel has invested significantly in this partnership, it is not clear what role this alliance plays in its global network of alliances. Likewise, the Indian firms have developed similar linkages with other MNCs, although probably not as intensive. There is no doubt that Nortel has shared proprietary technology with the partners. As the technological capabilities of the Indian partners improve, Nortel will have to share more such technologies to sustain the alliance. A significant part of the knowledge embodied in this technology is tacit and its misappropriation difficult to monitor and detect. However, the credibility of the Indian partners and, therefore, their ability to attract partners in the future is highly dependent on their protecting Nortel's intellectual property. It is this 'shared vulnerability' that is most likely to keep the alliance alive and help it grow. Some of the Indian partners may be asked to do the sunset phase of some telecom products, including dealing with Nortel's customers using older technologies. Working with Nortel on its new products also cannot be ruled out, although this might prove to be riskier for Nortel. In any event, it is important to note that if this relationship continues to grow as vigorously as it has in the past, at some stage the issue of the ownership of intellectual property will also have to be addressed.[11]

The organizational arrangement was probably optimal for Nortel. It is clear that intensive interaction among the Indian partners would have helped them learn more from the alliance.[12] However, the Indian partners may not have preferred such an arrangement given the fact that they vigorously compete with one another. In fact, Nortel claims that collaboration among the Indian firms was part of their vision and they did make some rudimentary efforts at inducing greater collaboration among them. However, the Indian partners did not seem very enthusiastic. Being competitors and collaborators at the same time is probably not very easy. Nortel also appreciates many of the concerns raised above, including those relating to IPRs and is open to sharing proprietary benefits, as they have done in the case of one of the partners (see note above). Their expectation is, however, that such sharing of IPRs would require the Indian partners to bring more to the table, be more entrepreneurial and take risks to develop new products and markets. Two of the Indian partners prefer the 'command-execute' mode and are reluctant to take risks, while the other two are more entrepreneurial. As a result, the relationship between Nortel and the two entrepreneurial partners has matured more than its linkages with the other two firms.[13]

Nortel's network in China

In this section we briefly describe Nortel's technology developments in China. In contrast to India, Nortel has established eight joint venture facilities and one R&D centre in China. The R&D lab was set up in 1994 as a cooperative arrangement between Nortel and Beijing University of Post and Telecom (BUPT) in order to transfer telecom technology to the Chinese government. As part of the set up, a few key personnel were deputed both by the University and Nortel. Nortel provided the initial capital (e.g. switches, office set-up, computers, software, and the like) while the University provided space and researchers. Initially the mandate of the project was to make Chinese adaptations to Nortel's software. Now it has moved to undertaking a number of projects within China for a variety of agencies, including MPT, in addition to specialized subcontracting work for Nortel. There are two distinct areas at this research centre: one devoted solely to Nortel's product development and the other for both Nortel and MPT projects.

The BUPT–Nortel R&D Centre is situated on the BUPT campus. Two directors-general head the lab: one each from Nortel and BUPT. It employs eighty-five employees of whom sixty are software designers. Most employees were from BUPT, though a few have been hired from Qinghua, Beijing and other universities. The lab hires those graduates and employees of the university who are telecom/wireless/radio engineers and have a computer background. Several professors of the university are also involved with the activities of the lab. The lab faces a high turnover of engineers: as their work at the lab is research-oriented, many go abroad (chiefly to the US and Canada) for graduate studies. Nortel sends over some people from other facilities worldwide to this lab.

The lab is developing software for mobile networks, wireless in local loop (WLL), MTX switches, broadband networks, FWA products, and is also helping MPT to develop telecom standards. Nortel has four WLL sites in China. Some are GSM while others follow the CDMA standard. However, most of the GSM research at the lab is being done for China Telecom while the CDMA work is being done for Nortel. Some other projects that the lab has done over the years are: software for handset interface (this was bought over by Nokia), messaging for wireline, wireless and Internet, enhancements to existing software for MPT, and field installation at the national and provincial levels, customization of some features for various municipalities on their telecom equipment, base station work for Nortel Maitra (contract work for GSM development in France, and the like). This lab has created a niche for its products in China. There are very few firms that are developing telecom software, especially in the area of switching (MTX switches) or base station software, which is the focus of the lab, as they require special capabilities. Its principal competitor is Lucent China, which is working in the area of wireless telephony. There are a few Chinese software firms that are developing software for some low to medium quality technology for switching that is still being used by China Telecom.

The first project of the lab was to develop a GSM provision centre (i.e. storage of customer profiles) which was a local Chinese requirement from its wireless equipment vendors. Now the lab is developing messaging models for various platforms: fixed to wireless, intra-mobile and Internet. This project is an example of how the complexity of tasks that are performed at the lab has risen. Also, with this product the lab is starting to compete globally. The BUPT–Nortel facility is becoming more integrated with Nortel, following Nortel standards and practices. While the Nortel hardware has not changed much, their software has changed rapidly, and they have also increased the spectrum of languages that are being used at the lab.

Nortel's linkages: comparing China and India

In comparison to Nortel's network in India, its alliance with BUPT has the following differentiating characteristics:

- BUPT and Nortel are involved in joint development of software with Nortel personnel present as opposed to subcontracting in India. This was operationalized by setting up a research centre at a telecom university in China with joint management; while in India separate linkages were formed with four Indian companies working independently of each other.
- The alliance with the telecom university has the potential of upgrading the technology, teaching material, and skills of both faculty and students. Besides, the location also provides an academic and research focus. In essence, Nortel was participating in developing manpower for the industry as well as future researchers. In the Indian case, only the four firms benefited.
- The alliance in China had a strong domestic market focus, assisting in the development of the local telecom sector. The Indian firms were developing products for Nortel's markets abroad. It appears that Nortel's objective in India was to tap the superior software capabilities while the focus in China was to support the large local market.
- The Chinese professionals participating in the alliance combined software skills with strong telecom knowledge. In the Indian case, Nortel provided the telecom knowledge while the domestic firms brought in their software skills.
- In both the alliances, projects have moved up the complexity ladder. It is believed that the Indian projects were more complex than those in China though this needs to be confirmed.

- The number of professionals involved in the Chinese alliance was much smaller than that in India (around 800 in 2001).
- While the Chinese alliance may be developing less complex projects, they were more focused in terms of developing *complete* products. The Indian teams were developing parts of a product, which was being integrated by Nortel.

Some of these differences can be explained by the fact that China has a large telecom market (about US$1 billion in 1999). In addition, Nortel has a large presence in the Chinese telecom market and forms a part of a large segment of the telecom supply chain in China (e.g. from manufacturing semiconductors to transmission devices and telecom services). Their eight joint venture facilities are spread out in eastern China, and therefore there is a strong need to service the domestic developments. Nortel is barely present in India. Nortel's strategies are obviously affected by these considerations.

An interesting question arises out of the above comparison: do public–private partnerships yield better spillovers to the society in terms of long-term capability building? While more empirical work is needed to evaluate this hypothesis, the case study in the next section provides us with more insights on this issue.

4. Wireless technology at the Indian Institute of Technology, Chennai

An access network connects homes and offices to the local exchange. While the fibres in the trunk exchange network were dramatically increasing the bandwidth over the backbone and reducing its cost, the 'last mile' problem of wired access remained, which restricted penetration (especially in India where population density in urban centres is very high). Technology developed by the TeNeT group at the Indian Institute of Technology (IIT), Chennai, created a new standard in the usage of wireless for the access portion of the network or WLL at considerably low costs. More interestingly, it is a story of how R&D developers at an academic institution (that is publicly funded) formed inter-organization linkages to commercialize and successfully deploy technology globally.[14] This case study highlights the structure and processes that the group utilized to develop and commercialize hi-tech solutions on a large scale.

The TeNeT group was formed by nine faculty members, in the mid-1980s, from the Electrical Engineering and Computer Science departments of IIT, Chennai, with the objective of creating indigenous technological solutions for a reduction of the access network costs in India (which contributes to over 65 per cent of the total network costs). The group started by developing TDM–TDMA–PMP systems for C-DoT. The positive spillover was that a large number of students got trained in this process. In 1995–6, the group started to work on wireless-based solutions for the access problem. The group developed its low cost wireless technology using the DECT standard (other standards like GSM, IS95 or PHS could not provide high capacity WLL at low cost, required more base stations to serve more consumers, consumed more power because of the need to operate switches in an AC environment, and were highly proprietary, etc.) with the help of a number of student projects at IIT, Chennai. This technology was simple, robust and used standard connections: a proof of concept was established in the IIT labs. At about this stage of development, the group faced a dilemma. To deploy this technology for the betterment of telephony in developing countries, the technology had to be commercialized. The issue, however, was how to make that happen in an academic setting.

MIDAS Communications Technologies

IIT addressed this dilemma through a bold leadership initiative: permitting the group to help set up an enterprise. IIT and the new company would jointly own the initial product based on this DECT technology, while the company was to be fully owned by the promoters. The group wanted to develop the firm without financial support from government and to compete with the best in the world, both in terms of technology and cost. The group persuaded nine of their former students to start a company called MIDAS Communications Technologies that would commercialize the innovation.

MIDAS was started with equity provided by these former students. The TeNeT group provided technical support. IIT and MIDAS jointly owned the product, CorDECT. In the initial days, the firm 'operated' out of IIT laboratories where all worked together on the CorDECT project. Early on in the project, the group realized the critical role of high-quality, specially designed ICs in the development of their product and also appreciated that such ICs (especially in small volumes) could not be developed in India. Analog Devices, USA, evaluated their technology and agreed to develop the ICs designed by IIT and market these outside India. They also agreed to help the group license these ICs within India. Most importantly, however, Analog Devices agreed to advance funds to the group against future royalty payments. The group raised funds also by licensing their technology to other companies in India. This funding helped raise several research projects that got MIDAS off the ground.

By 2000, MIDAS had 128 people working across all departments. Seventy per cent of their employees were working in the design and development area, both in wireless (e.g. CorDECT) and fibre applications. MIDAS has developed fifteen vendors that manufacture various components and assemble their finished products (on a technology licensing and transfer basis). They have conducted trials in Brazil while they found licensees in Nigeria, Kenya, Fiji, Madagascar and Argentina who purchased CorDECT technology and performed tests locally.

Banyan networks

While MIDAS was trying to address the last-mile problem of telephone access by WLL, there was the Internet revolution. IIT recognized at an early stage that this would require local wired access for handling data through the net. It once again helped start a company with its former students that would work on the data–voice convergence. This time the company was formed with the help of former IIT students and external promoters. Ray Stator of Analog Devices provided angel funding. Banyan also invited another well-wisher, Arun Jain (chairman of Polaris Software Lab, Chennai) to become the chairman of Banyan and provide leadership to the group. Informally, Polaris had been involved in helping the team with business planning.

Banyan innovated a number of related products. Banyan, IIT, and Analog Devices developed one of its earlier products, 'Nova Ethernet Switch', jointly. Analog Devices started a new company to market this product in the US. The product was a finalist in the Las Vegas IT show. Another product, DSP (Digital Switch Processing), was licensed to Fujistar. Then came DIAS (Digital Internet Access System), a product that enables simultaneous data and voice transfer. DIAS combines the wireless technology of WLL with wired ethernet connections for voice and data transfer over the Internet. Banyan licensed technology to firms manufacturing MIDAS' products in India.

Banyan hired a professional manager from a consulting firm to head the organization. Arun Jain played a useful role as the chairman of the firm to restructure the organization and create well-defined roles for the IIT and Banyan teams: a clear improvement over the organizational structure and practices at MIDAS. Equity from external agents was brought in, another step in professionalizing the commercialization process of IIT's technology. Intel Corporation, USA, joined as the lead investor in Banyan with ILFS (which receives funds from the Tamil Nadu Venture Fund) coming in as the second investor.

Nilgiri Networks and nlogue.com

One of the original members of the TeNeT group, Timothy Gonzalves, took leave from IIT, Chennai, and started a firm in Ooty called Nilgiri Networks. This firm is developing 'network management systems' for products developed by the group as well as other products. Polaris Software Lab is a co-promoter of this company. They have recently developed a product called 'Cygnet'. The most recent venture of the IIT, Chennai, group is a new company called nlogue.com[15] whose objective is to run telecom and Internet business on a franchise basis in rural areas and small towns of India using the access network developed by MIDAS and Banyan. The plan is to provide the subscriber with a CorDECT box that will provide telephone and Internet services at no Internet charge. The only variable cost is the cost of the local telephone connection. The group is conducting a pilot project in

Nellikuppam, Tamil Nadu, using EID Parry's sugar factory as the base Access Centre.

This case is a unique example of academic entrepreneurship based on technological innovation: a strong testament of academic leadership, societal concerns and technological learning through inter-organization linkages. It is this last issue that we would like to explore further, though all three are closely linked in this case. Some key questions explored are:

- What did IIT, Chennai, have as a core strength that enabled it to incubate firms successfully?
- What was the basis of forming the various inter-organizational linkages?
- What was the learning of the various entities through this formation?

The core of this entire effort revolves around the vision, leadership and concerns of Ashok Jhunjhunwala. He brought in the technological base, linkages with well-trained students, a strong concern for societal change in developing countries, and an ability to bring together a team of well-trained people with international exposure in addition to the reputation of being part of an excellent institution. The group was able to draw upon the large IIT faculty, alumni and friends network to move forward its technological and business plans. Then came the technological expertise of the TeNeT group. They possessed world-class technological capabilities to transform innovations into commercial applications. IIT provided a conducive environment for application research, with a large pool of enthusiastic and bright students. The student researchers were involved in developing the 'proof of concept' with prototype and allied companies undertaking manufacture. The TeNeT group managed to create a well-defined focus in their research for a significantly long duration of time and could enthuse the academic community at IIT to participate with them. Another feature of their efforts was the ability of the group to quickly recognize the implications of emerging trends in technology and then ride the waves of technological development. This allowed them to look for novel technological solutions to the persisting last-mile problem through WLL and then recognize the role of Internet and build research products around this development. This ability kept them at the forefront of the technological revolution in IT and telecommunication. The IIT, Chennai administration also exhibited some leadership in recognizing the potential of the efforts of the group and allowed them to play the role of academic entrepreneurs.

The core strengths of the IIT team, when coupled with the low cost of performing R&D in India, provided a formidable combination for forming partnerships with firms that possessed other complementary assets. Some Indian firms were looking for new products for the Indian market. Several of the fifteen vendors of MIDAS also benefited from this approach. The IIT–MIDAS team also played the coordinator's role when they held the hands of manufacturers and established the production requirements. Interestingly, initially, IIT, Chennai, performed all the R&D as well as commercialization activity: now the IIT team concentrates more on academic R&D while MIDAS and Banyan perform the commercialization activity. This also reflects the changing roles of different players as the technology supply chain becomes more sophisticated and the inter-organizational partnerships mature. Perhaps, as this evolves further, MIDAS and Banyan may start performing more applied research themselves while the IIT team may shift upstream on the technology supply chain: performing more fundamental and theoretical research in this area. Earlier, MIDAS provided about 25 per cent of the research budget while IIT brought in the remaining 75 per cent. Now, MIDAS contributes 85 per cent of research expenditure while IIT provides the balance.

The formation of partnerships was based on derivation of mutual benefits, though elements of risk-taking were involved: a common feature of most technology linkages. The academic linkages of Ashok Jhunjhunwala helped to forge technological and commercial links both for the TeNeT group as well as for MIDAS and Banyan. One of the most enduring linkages of the entire IIT–MIDAS–Banyan network has been that with Analog Devices. Analog Devices were interested in the activities of the group, as they were chip-makers who were looking for chip designers. As they were not equipment producers, they did not foresee any competition from MIDAS. Moreover, each time MIDAS used their DPS chip (a general-purpose chip) for building its designs, it increased the sales of Analog Devices. MIDAS also helped this company find several good chip designers in India (including some in the IIT team). In return, the IIT team benefited by securing the help of the company in producing small volumes of specialized ICs for them, finding in the company a marketer of their IC designs, and a venture capitalist for their projects. In the initial stages of Banyan, a number of engineers from Analog Devices helped Banyan in the resolution of technical problems, and also helped them in procuring components from the US.

Similarly, Intel's participation as the lead investor in Banyan Networks was motivated by its interest in selling its chips for new applications, especially in emerging technologies. It was also a pre-emptive strategy in the event of the group at IIT developing a competitive technology. Banyan benefits, other than through direct funding, by networking opportunities with a variety of Intel's other partners and the opportunity to attend various product portfolio conferences globally (and especially in the Asia-Pacific) and thereby track developments in chip designing and new applications.

The most interesting linkages have been formed between the 'member companies' of the group. The different companies, i.e. MIDAS, Banyan, Nilgiri and nlogue.com represent different stages of the wireless based technology chain for delivering low cost telecommunication options in India and other developing countries. MIDAS have used Banyan's wired capabilities in their wireless products while Banyan are using MIDAS' CorDECT boxes in designing its wired solutions. Similarly, Nilgiri is developing network management systems for MIDAS and Banyan products in addition to other platforms. nlogue.com is simply a management of franchise effort using technologies developed by the other three companies. This may be the beginning of an integrated solution management endeavour jointly by all the firms. Network linkages have also helped generate minimum order sizes/large orders (and hence obtain volume discounts) for various components (Basant and Chandra, 2001 for details).

The above case study is a good example of network-based enterprise development with technology R&D as the core. It also reflects new vistas of public–private (and academia–industry) partnership and shows rudiments of organic evolution of a focused technology cluster. This 'Centre–Satellite' model with a strong central R&D infrastructure and dynamic satellite application firms covering different stages of the technology supply chain provides a viable model for technology development and implementation in India. More details on these cases and analysis can be found in Basant and Chandra (2001).

5. Conclusions

Indian firms in the IT Telecom sector have entered into a variety of inter-organization alliances in recent years. Our analysis suggests that these linkages have helped Indian organizations build technological capabilities. This chapter analysed inter-organization alliances and their role in capability building at different levels. Insights from the results of a primary survey and case studies were used to identify the key processes at work. In what follows we try to highlight some of the key conclusions.

While the survey results identify a variety of mechanisms that lead to learning, the case studies provide scope for comparing three very different types of technology-based alliances:

1. those established by an MNC with host country firms;
2. those established by an MNC with a host country public sector academic institution; and
3. those established by a host country academic institution with domestic and foreign firms.

Thus, the types of entities involved in the alliances were MNCs, host country firms, and academia. Each of them followed different strategies. The nature of alliances and markets served were also different. In what follows, we highlight the role of each of these factors in capability building.

On firm strategies and nature of alliances, the Nortel case studies suggest that MNCs may follow different strategies *vis-à-vis* inter-firm technology linkages in different host countries. MNCs might follow a *domestic market supported* R&D model in countries where the *market is large and growing* and where the MNCs have a *significant presence*, while following *domestic market independent* R&D strategies where the *market is relatively small* and the MNC presence is insignificant but where *specialized skills are available*. The latter strategy permits the use of the specialized and often low cost skills of the host country by the MNC. These two strategies will have obvious implications for learning among the host country entities in the alliance. MNCs may wish to share more technology, especially of the tacit variety, where they have greater control over the use of that technology. The links of Nortel manufacturing facilities with Nortel–BUPT provided such control in the case of China, while Nortel retained the role of managing the network and integrating the technologies developed by different partners in India to try and retain this control. While in both situations, the domestic country entities learned, in India they learned through more *complex individual* projects; in China, learning came from integration, i.e. undertaking simple but complete projects. While market focus and degree of control do affect the nature of projects undertaken in an alliance, better software skills in India may also have played a role.

Unlike the Nortel network in India, which was developed through the initiative of the MNC, the IIT network was the result of an indigenous initiative, and while the former was *domestic market independent* the latter was *domestic market supported*. Significantly, the IIT network also used MNCs to its advantage whenever there was a need for such a link, the link with Analog Devices being the most important. Nonetheless, the network and the focus of its research activities were largely controlled by the domestic entities. The IIT link fitted in with the MNC strategy to pre-empt competition and get access to good quality and inexpensive chip designers.

Rapid changes and convergence in telecom technologies and continuing unbundling of telecom service provision provide scope for strategic alliances between developing country firms and MNCs to exploit complementary capabilities. Firms with good skills and capabilities along with risk-taking ability are likely to gain more from such alliances. However, learning from alliances will need to be a strategic intent of the host country firms and they will need to make conscious efforts to learn from different projects and consolidate the learning across projects. Mechanisms will need to be devised to disseminate the learning within the organization. Movement of key personnel from one project to another may facilitate diffusion of knowledge within the organization. Our findings suggest that firms are already exploiting such spillovers but need to be somewhat more proactive about such learning.

Learning about standards and getting observed in the international market are important advantages of inter-firm alliances. The developing country firms may, however, need to worry about a trade-off. While long-term association with a single partner develops trust and facilitates technology transfer and learning, it may result in a 'lock-out' in a rapidly changing technological environment.

The cases of the Nortel–BUPT and IIT networks provide important insights into the role of academia in alliances. Participation of academia in technology networks creates significant technology spillovers; the IIT network was able to generate the same kind of externalities as were achieved by BUPT, China, through its links with Nortel. Academic institutions like the IIT or BUPT can attract a variety of MNCs as partners due to their research capabilities. The presence of segment-specific skills (like telecom in our cases) might facilitate rapid learning and provide an impetus for incremental and eventually significant innovations. Active participation of academia in such networks can go a long way in generating such a skill-pool, as spillovers through training and research are very high. A reduction in the technology gap through these processes can further enhance capability building.

The IIT network emerged from the vision of the group as they consciously sought to combine social objectives with scientific and technological objectives without losing sight of the commercial viability of such an effort. In one sense, the researchers at IIT were as close to the technology frontier as the Nortel researchers. Consequently, they were able to identify technological opportunities in just the same way as would a sophisticated lab of a large MNC. Without such perspectives on technological trends and opportunities, the IIT-type network is unlikely to emerge and contribute to capability building.

The cases of the Nortel and IIT networks highlight the potential of developing, nurturing and sustaining such hi-technology networks in developing countries. Given India's reasonable capabilities in telecom technology and high knowledge base in software, and given the tremendous potential of synergies between these two knowledge systems, one would have expected arrangements akin to the Nortel and IIT partnerships to emerge within the country among Indian software and telecom hardware firms. That this has not happened could partly be because the telecom activity was largely in the domain of the public sector, which did not face any competition either in domestic markets or through export activity in demanding markets. Consequently, the state did not recognize the value of innovation-related interactions between manufacturers of telecom equipment (e.g. ITI) and technology developers (e.g. C-DoT, IIT and software firms). Only now does one see the emergence of competition in the telecom sector. Besides, convergence of technologies is creating newer opportunities for inter-firm alliances. One would therefore hope for more such alliances emerging in the coming years.

Notes

1. The authors are grateful to Ashok Jhunjhunwala for his time and insights and for facilitating interaction with various IIT, Chennai faculty and related firms. The authors are extremely grateful to the firms who participated in our survey and in-depth case studies. The research assistance provided by Neeraj Jain is also gratefully acknowledged.

2. The available published information did not permit detailed stratification of firms to enable an appropriate sampling strategy to be used. We hope, however, that the insights derived from this survey will be indicative of the processes at work.

3. Basant and Chandra (2001) provide details on the distribution of firms.

4. If an alliance had multiple dimensions (e.g. involved technology transfer and joint production), it was counted in both categories, i.e. technology- and production-related. The distribution of alliances by detailed categories shows that a large number of them cut across the broad categories defined above (Basant and Chandra, 2001, Appendix I provides details). However, while technology, marketing and distribution (and to some extent production-related) alliances are often found in 'pure' forms, this is rarely the case with financial collaborations. In virtually all alliances where financial links exist, technology, production or marketing linkages are also part of the inter-firm relationship. Thus, financial participation is always bundled with other linkages.

5. Joint ventures constitute the most important form of finance-related alliances. While the bidding consortium is an emerging form of inter-firm alliance in this sector, minority and cross-holdings are not very common.

6. In about a third of the cases, nobody owned the IPRs, presumably because the partnership did not lead to any tangible intellectual property that can be protected. Nonetheless, product focus and the creation of IPRs in these alliances seem to be higher than suggested by discussions with people involved with industry. Even if such tendencies have been overestimated due to a sample bias, the broad trends seem to suggest participation of Indian firms in more complex alliances with a product and IP focus.

7. The description is based on a short questionnaire and in-depth interviews of firms participating in the network undertaken in 2000.

8. For 2000–1 we have used an exchange rate of Indian Rs 48.5 = 1 US$.

9. Nortel subsequently established a subsidiary in India but the existing alliances continue.

10. It has already started to happen. See discussion below.

11. Recent developments have made IPR-related issues more relevant. One of the partners in India has developed three innovations, patent applications for which have been filed by Nortel in North America. The Indian firm and Nortel are co-patentees and will share the royalties based on a geographical division. The Indian firm certainly has rights over the Indian market but it is not clear if it has any other rights.

12. Though knowledge spillovers through employee turnover continue to occur.

13. One of the partner firms in India has developed a new technology (that delivers high bandwidth over copper wire) on their own. This technology was offered to Nortel but they had their own one-megabyte modem, which is a competitor technology, and therefore they declined the offer. However, the Indian company now has two potential clients in the US and thus has been recognized as a world source of technology. While Nortel claims that its alliance with this growing Indian partner was instrumental in instilling confidence in them, the MNC will have to deal with the issue that this Indian firm and other partners may also initiate competing technologies in the future.

14. The group has developed the following systems over the years and has commercialized them: CorDECT, a WLL solution for access networks (including integrated access centre technologies to be located at street corners), DIAS, a direct (wired) Internet access system, OPTIMA, fibre in the loop solutions (where the

fibre connects the access centres while the backbone has a radio link), and CYGNET, a network management system.

15. Two professors of the TeNeT group, Ashok Jhunjhunwala and Bhaskar Ramamurthy, have now established a section 25 (not for profit) company which will hold equity in nlogue.com.

References

Basant, R. (2000) 'Corporate Response to Economic Reforms', *Economic and Political Weekly*, 35 (10), 4 March: 813–22.

——(2002) 'Knowledge Flows and Industrial Clusters: an Analytical Review of Literature', *Working Paper No. 40 (Economics Series)*, East West Center.

Basant, R. and P. Chandra (1997) 'Linking Telecom Technologies: Complementarities, Capabilities, and Policies', *Vikalpa*, 22 (3): 39–54.

——(2001) 'Inter-firm Linakges in the IT Industry in India: a Case Study of Telecom Technologies', mimeo, Indian Institute of Management, Ahmedabad.

Bell, M. and K. Pavitt (1997) 'Technological Accumulation and Industrial Growth: Contrasts Between Developed and Developing Countries', in D. Archibugi and J. Michie (eds), *Technology Globalisation and Economic Performance* (Cambridge: Cambridge University Press), pp. 83–137.

Ernst, D., T. Gaaniatsos and L. Mytelka (eds) (1998) *Technological Capabilities and Export Success in Asia* (London: Routledge).

Hegedoorn, J. and C. Freeman (1994) 'Catching Up or Falling Behind: Patterns in International Technology Partnering', *World Development*, 22 (5): 771–80.

Kokko, A. (1992) 'Direct Investment, Host Country Characteristics and Spillovers', mimeo, Economic Research Institute, Stockholm School of Economics.

Mytelka, L. K. (1998) 'Locational Tournaments for FDI: Inward Investment into Europe in a Global World', Division of Investment, Technology and Enterprise Development, mimeo, UNCTAD, Geneva.

——(1999) 'Mergers, Acquisitions and Inter-firm Technology Agreements in the Global Learning Economy', paper presented at the European Socio-Economic Research Conference, Brussels, 28–30 April.

World Investment Report (WIR) (1998) 'Trends and Determinants' (New York: United Nations).

9

Originative Innovation and Entrepreneurship in the Software Industry in India

Abhoy K. Ojha and S. Krishna

1. Introduction

The software industry in India is an undisputed source of reliable, high quality reliable software services. India has been rated as the first choice for software outsourcing. Much of the success of the software industry in India can be attributed to the availability of a low-cost, well-qualified workforce that can speak and work in English (Correa, 1996), and the compatibility of the Indian social and historical context with the needs of the global software services industry (Krishna, Ojha and Barrett, 2000).

However, after the recent slowdown in the global economy, there is a concern about the sustainability of Indian software growth. A substantial part of exports is based on low end programming (Abraham, Ahlawat and Ahlawat, 1998), and even this activity is highly concentrated in a few firms that dominate the export market (Correa, 1996). A recent Forrester Report (2001) indicated that over 50 per cent of companies relying on outsourcing software do so to reduce costs, and 90 per cent of them use offshore providers only for routine application maintenance and development. Further, rising costs in the Indian industry, rapid technological changes, and new entrants from other countries are likely to endanger the gains made by the Indian software industry.

The recommendation to the software industry to address these concerns is to have more firms move up the 'value chain' (Abraham, Ahlawat and Ahlawat, 1998; Kumar, 2001; McKinsey, 1999). This essentially means that Indian firms need to have a greater involvement in activities that add value to the end product or service, and provide a greater return on investment. For this to happen, firms need to move from business models based on mere programming skills to those based on higher levels of domain knowledge and consulting skills to provide total solutions to business problems. Also, a larger number of firms should develop products and components in their area of expertise.

For any national industry to develop through different stages of maturity, there is a need for a balance of entrepreneurial human capital and professional human capital (Iyigun and Owen, 1998). Entrepreneurial human capital is the collective capacity of an industry, contributed by entrepreneurs, to perform unconventional and innovative things that meet market needs. It is the entrepreneurs who provide an industry with new ideas, products and ways of doing things. Entrepreneurial skills are acquired by being involved in the entrepreneurial process, and schooling can rarely contribute to the development of these skills.

Professional human capital refers to the technical capacity of an industry to be involved in a chosen technology domain. While entrepreneurs provide the unusual ideas, it is the professionals who provide the accumulated technical skills and knowledge to facilitate their implementation. Professional human capital develops when people in a society acquire the necessary technical skills and knowledge by investing in schooling. To some extent these skills can also be acquired at work.

Both types of human capital are essential for any industry to succeed as they complement each other. However, in developing countries, entrepreneurial human capital plays a more important role than professional human capital. In any economy, individuals may choose to become entrepreneurs or professionals. Entrepreneurship is risky. There is a substantial possibility of an entrepreneur's venture failing. On the other hand, professional activities provide safe returns but are dependent on opportunities provided by the entrepreneurs. Hence, in an economy in which economic activity is low, entrepreneurial human capital is critical to initiate economic activity to enable professionals to find gainful employment. The lack of entrepreneurial human capital in the early stages of development is one of the explanations provided for the failure of former East bloc economies to develop globally competitive industries despite a highly educated labour force. As economic activity grows, although there will be a growth in the number of entrepreneurs, the ratio of entrepreneurs to professionals normally declines (Iyigun and Owen, 1988), and the role of entrepreneurial human capital is less critical.

There is significant professional human capital available in India to allow the software industry to move up the value chain. However, there is a dearth of entrepreneurial human capital in India that has prevented it from playing a dominant role in the global marketplace in almost any industry, including software. While software entrepreneurs from India have been successful in Silicon Valley in the US, very few have returned to India to start firms (Saxenian, 1999). In order for it to sustain its growth, the Indian software industry needs to encourage and nurture fresh entrepreneurial human capital that will be relevant for the next higher phase of the industry's development.

Manimala et al. (2001) in the *Global Entrepreneurship Monitor India Report 2001*, which will be cited extensively in this chapter, have highlighted the fact that entrepreneurship is not well developed in India, even outside the software industry. Their study, based on a comparative analysis of data from twenty-nine countries that cover a broad spectrum of economies, provides a good overview of how entrepreneurship in India stands in relation to other countries.

We classified the activities in the software industry in India into two categories that we have labelled (i) derivative, and (ii) originative. Derivative activities refer to work directed at modifying hardware and software that is already in use. Such activities may include (i) maintenance, (ii) enhancement through addition of new features, (iii) porting on to new hardware/software environments, and (iv) systems implementation involving minor software or hardware development. Derivative activities typically involve catering to the needs of a single client. There is little scope for innovation as tasks, environment and even schedules are predefined. These carry less risk. However, they also mean fewer rewards. Originative activities refer to activities that are oriented towards producing a product/service that is original. This could mean the development of a product or new algorithms, user interfaces, data organization, applications, ways of integration, or tools. Originative activities invariably involve products or services targeted at several clients and have long gestation periods before revenues trickle in. These activities carry high risk but provide great opportunities for innovation and very high returns.

We believe that the Indian software industry's emphasis should shift from derivative activities to originative activities in order to move up the value chain. In recent times, there have been several new ventures in the software industry in India that have been established to develop high value products and solutions (Viswanathan, 2000). The purpose of this study was to examine the background and attributes of the entrepreneurs who have chosen to operate in the software industry in India with originative activity in order to understand what it takes to be successful at it. Also, entrepreneurship and innovation do not occur in a vacuum (Manimala et al., 2001; Montealegre, 1999; Sanchez and Perez, 1998; Saxenian, 1999). They require a context that is supportive of such activities. Hence, an additional aim was to look at the context of the software industry from the perspective of these entrepreneurs in order to comprehend the features of the environment in India, in general, and the software industry, in particular, that hinder originative activity.

2. Innovation and entrepreneurship

Background of entrepreneurs

Past research and popular wisdom argue that persons from certain backgrounds are more likely to become entrepreneurs and be successful. Bhide (2000) found that individuals from middle-class backgrounds are more likely to start promising businesses than individuals from either extremely wealthy or extremely deprived backgrounds. According to him, people from extremely wealthy backgrounds do not want to enter the highly uncertain, high technology markets, preferring to remain in their established businesses. On the other hand, persons from deprived backgrounds normally lack the educational backing and confidence to enter such uncharted territory. Other research found that technology entrepreneurs came from families where the father was a self-employed professional or an independent business owner (Sanchez and Perez, 1998), suggesting that entrepreneurs were influenced by their fathers' ability to be on their own, which gave them confidence to be on their own in turn. Manimala et al. (2001) found that in India people from higher income families were more entrepreneurial than others when it came to higher value activities.

Technical knowledge in the area of activity seems to be essential in the high technology area. However, too much prior training and education raises the opportunity costs and risks of starting a small, uncertain enterprise (Bhide, 2000). Consistent with this argument, Sanchez and Perez (1998) found a significant number of high technology entrepreneurs had bachelor degrees, most had masters degrees, and very few had doctoral degrees. In India, Manimala et al. (2001) found that the rate of entrepreneurship increases with education but declines after graduation. Although this study was undertaken outside the software industry, it suggests that, as in other countries, there is an inverted 'U' relationship between education and entrepreneurship.

Past research has also found that entrepreneurs in the high-tech industries are relatively young, ranging in age from twenty-three to forty-four, and work experience from three to sixteen years (Sanchez and Perez, 1998). Bhide (2000) also argues that the entrepreneur's previous experience, even if it is relatively brief, mitigates the risks of inadequate research and improves the prospects of success. He found, however, that individuals who have the initiative and the incentive to start their own business, but lack sound business experience, seldom succeed. Manimala et al. (2001), on the basis of their study of entrepreneurship in India, suggest that 'the kind of energies and innovative and flexible ideas required for entrepreneurship is available primarily with young people'.

Sanchez and Perez (1998) found that most high technology entrepreneurs who have only technical knowledge but no managerial expertise had significant problems addressing management-related issues. Most entrepreneurs who are engineers spend most of their time doing technical work, and face considerable problems with financial resources and suppliers, and recruiting and retaining staff. They also found that ventures started by a team with a mix of technical and managerial knowledge had greater levels of success. Bhide's (2000) findings in the context of the US were similar.

Entrepreneurial attributes

The literature is rich in studies that have sought to identify the attributes of successful entrepreneurs that separate them from others. Popular conceptions of an entrepreneur suggest a highly energetic, achievement-oriented personality as a prerequisite for entrepreneurial success. For example, Hunger and Wheelen (1996: 371) argue that

> Successful entrepreneurs have a sense of urgency that makes them action-oriented. They have a high need for achievement, which motivates them to put their ideas into action. They tend to have an internal locus of control that leads them to belief that they can determine their own fate through their own behaviour. They have a significantly greater capacity to tolerate ambiguity than do many in established organization. They also have a high need for control and may be viewed as 'misfits who need to create their own environment'. They tend to distrust others and often have a need 'to show others that they amount to something, that they cannot be ignored'.

Stewart, Watson, Carland and Carland (1998) found that entrepreneurs were higher in achievement motivation, risk-taking propensity, and preference for innovation than both corporate managers and small business owners. Similarly, Sanchez and Perez (1998) found that entrepreneurs have a moderate to high need for achievement and power, and a low need for affiliation. However, other studies argue that contrary to what informal observation or early studies suggest, entrepreneurs do not appear to differ greatly from non-entrepreneurs with respect to various aspects of personality (Baron, 1998). Similarly, Drucker (1998) asserts that, 'What all the successful entrepreneurs I have met have in common is not a certain kind of personality but a commitment to the systemic practice of innovation.'

A second issue that has concerned students of entrepreneurship is the motivation of entrepreneurs to pursue uncharted careers even when they could have led comfortable lives pursuing more stable and well-paying careers. Sanchez and Perez (1998) found that the primary reason for highly educated and skilled persons to choose to become entrepreneurs rather than continue in large organizations is a need to be independent. The role of the monetary gains that normally accrue with a successful venture were incidental.

Manimala et al. (2001) found that entrepreneurship is not seen as a good career choice in Indian society. While successful entrepreneurs are respected, it is still largely seen as an option exercised by persons who are unemployed. In other words, individuals in India need to overcome societal discouragement to become entrepreneurs. The same study also reported that in relation to other countries the education system in India does not encourage self-reliance or entrepreneurship. Hence, entrepreneurs in India require an even stronger motivation than in other societies to choose entrepreneurship as a career, although the study does suggest that such discouragement does not exist in certain segments of society that have traditionally been associated with business.

The third attribute of entrepreneurs that has been written about is their risk-taking ability. Manimala et al. (2001) suggest that Indian society is low on risk-taking. Indians have a preference for careers that provide long-term jobs with a steady income, rather than careers that may have unpredictable returns. In that sense, India fits Iyigun and Owen's (1998) description of an economy that might get caught in a development trap because of a lack of entrepreneurial human capital even as it has sufficient professional human capital.

However, Bhide (2000) suggests that most entrepreneurs in the high technology arena do not take high risks. They nonetheless do seem to have an ability to tolerate ambiguity, which is a state in which they have to make decisions without clear problem definition or adequate information. Entrepreneurs often work under conditions that are characterized by high levels of uncertainty, novelty, emotion, and time pressure that tend to overload their information processing capacity. Together, these factors increase the entrepreneurs' susceptibility to cognitive biases, including (i) counterfactual thinking, (ii) affect infusion, (iii) planning fallacy, and (iv) self-justification. These biases lead to greater self-confidence than is rationally justifiable (Baron, 1998), allowing them to deal with ambiguous situations that others find very risky (Bhide, 2000).

The ability to build and maintain networks is an important attribute of entrepreneurs. Hunger and Wheelen (1996) contend that entrepreneurs build a network of people with key skills and knowledge that can be called upon for support. On the other hand, Bhide (2000) found that entrepreneurs do not rely on prior relationships to make their early sales. Most get orders from customers who were more or less strangers. Saxenian (2000), however, found that a significant factor for entrepreneurship among Indian and Chinese immigrants in the Silicon Valley was the ability to build and maintain networks. Khanna and Palepu (1997) claim that networks may be more important in the Indian context. As the institutions in India are quite weak, reliance on a network of personal relationships to negotiate through difficult situations is essential.

Another attribute of significant interest is the ability of entrepreneurs to have very creative ideas. A perception, based on stories in the popular press, suggests that successful entrepreneurs start with very creative ideas, which is the source of their success. However, research indicates that typically an entrepreneur starts with products or services that are quite similar, at least in their tangible attributes, to the products or services offered by other companies. They do not start with a unique or proprietary product, and their success is largely due to the 'exceptional execution of an ordinary idea' (Bhide, 2000). The innovations are generally incremental or easily replicable and normally do not qualify for a patent and are too visible to protect as a trade secret. Most start by serving local markets or a small number of customers with specialized needs, which they use to establish a springboard or base for a more ambitious subsequent initiative. They often encounter surprises and setbacks that require them to modify or completely revamp the original business idea. This implies that entrepreneurship may have little to do with the 'grand idea' than with small ideas that address real problems in the market. These findings are consistent with Drucker's (1998: 156) assertion that:

> To be effective, an innovation has to be simple, and it has to be focused ... effective innovations start small. They are not grandiose ... Innovation is work rather than genius. It requires knowledge. It often requires ingenuity. If diligence, persistence, and commitment are lacking, latent ingenuity and knowledge are of no avail.

3. Context of innovation and entrepreneurship

Entrepreneurship and originative innovation do not happen in a vacuum. Although entrepreneurship may eventually be a result of individual effort, personal efficacy is more likely to be developed and sustained in a supportive environment than in an adverse one. A supportive environment is also more likely to breed entrepreneurial success, which in turn further enhances entrepreneurial efficacy. Entrepreneurs require a fertile environment to flourish (Manimala et al., 2001; Martinsons, 1998; Montealegre, 1999; Sanchez and Perez, 1998; Porter, 1990).

Firstly, entrepreneurs need to have markets that will encourage and accept what they have to offer. Typically, successful entrepreneurs have their start-ups in very uncertain markets. The uncertainty does not assure attractive returns, but it does allow them to use their meagre initial resources for a better prospect of making a profit than the typical popular business which faces stiff competition. In highly uncertain markets, customers and suppliers lack reliable information about their alternatives, giving new start-ups an odd chance to make a profit (Bhide, 2000). What differentiates an entrepreneur from the rest is the ability to utilize this foothold to establish a business that determines the parameters of comparison.

In markets, as in India, where information technology penetration is low, the markets are not dynamic enough to accommodate untested products, and hence are unlikely to provide a fertile ground for development of entrepreneurship. Using Porter's (1990) framework, which emphasizes local market demand as a key determinant of industry success, this can be seen as one major reason why originative work in India has not taken root. As reported by Lal (1999), information technology adoption in the electrical and electronic industry in India is poor because of low educational qualification of management, low existing technological capabilities, low skills in the workforce, and lack of vision for growth. Manimala et al. (2001) found that although market openness and ease of entry in India had improved in recent times, the conditions were still much worse than high entrepreneurial countries like the US and also below the average of the twenty-nine countries surveyed.

The second significant support they need from their environment is financial, particularly in the early days. Most start-ups do not have the assets that a traditional investor would consider valuable. The founders, therefore, have to rely on their own resources or raise funds from relatives or friends who are willing to overlook the founder's limitations. They have little to offer investors besides their hopes and dreams (Bhide, 2000).

Today, there is an abundance of venture capital for the software industry, but it has not found many suitable candidates. This has a little to do with the lack of experience of the staff in the venture capital industry, most coming from traditional commercial banking, but a lot to do with a lack of management and financial knowledge among most entrepreneurs in the Indian software market (*Business World*, 2000). This is similar to Manimala et al.'s (2001) finding that, in India, despite significant improvements in availability of venture capital, personal resources remained a key source of funding for entrepreneurs.

The third kind of support that entrepreneurs require is infrastructure (Cabral, 1998; Martinsons, 1998; Montealegre, 1999; and Sanchez and Perez, 1998). This may range from universities and research and development organizations that act as sources of technological expertise and potential technology entrepreneurs, to physical infrastructure such as technology parks to adequate roads, communication facilities, and the like that are essential for conducting business. Manimala et al. (2001) reported that India had, on average, the lowest scores on adequacy of physical infrastructure among the twenty-nine countries surveyed.

While providing the infrastructure mentioned above is also largely the responsibility of the government, it may be argued that its involvement in supporting business through infrastructure provision is indirect. However, the government also has a more direct role in supporting entrepreneurship. A significant number of people have strongly argued against the role of government in the economy. More recent evidence and literature suggests, however, that there is definitely a role for the government in guiding the development of an industry (Martinsons, 1998; Montealegre, 1999). Governments can work towards creating an efficacy-enhancing environment by making resources both available and visible, publicizing entrepreneurial successes, increasing the diversity of opportunities, and most importantly, avoiding policies that create real or perceived obstacles (Chen, Greene and Crick, 1998).

Manimala et al. (2001) reported that, while India did not have the lowest scores on various elements of government policy and programmes for new firms evaluated in their study, it ranked below the average of the twenty-nine countries on every element. Their study clearly suggests that the government has a lot to do to encourage entrepreneurship in India.

4. Research methodology

The research was based on the case study method. There were no explicit hypotheses at the beginning of the study. The prime focus was to understand the elements of the background and attributes that make for a successful entrepreneur. Inherent in this line of enquiry was the desire to identify elements that discourage entrepreneurship in the IT industry in India. The second focus of the study was to identify some key features of the context in India in general, and of the IT industry in particular, that discourage entrepreneurs from establishing firms with a focus on originative work. It is understood that there are some enabling features in the context, but they were outside the agenda for this study.

A few entrepreneurial firms operating in India that had a primary focus on originative activity were identified. The sample captured a cross-section of entrepreneurs: some very successful, some not so successful, some who have been entrepreneurs for a long time, some that were just starting, some that relocated from the US, some that were homegrown. Sixteen entrepreneurs and/or their close associates from eleven different firms involved in high value activity were interviewed. Table 9.1 shows the list of firms selected and the people interviewed along with brief background information. The interviews were conducted on an open-ended basis after the interviewees were informed of the purpose. The duration of the interviews ranged from about an hour to over four hours each. They were all recorded, transcribed and converted to computer text files. Documentation and news clippings on the entrepreneurial ventures were also obtained. While the interviews formed the primary source of data, publicly available material on the selected companies, documents provided by them, and information available on their websites were used to support the interview data, and also enhance an understanding of software entrepreneurship in India.

The first part of the data analysis was oriented towards seeking similarities and differences in the background and attributes of the entrepreneurs involved with originative activity in the software industry in India with that of entrepreneurs in other contexts, as discussed in the literature above. The second part of the analysis focused on understanding the context within which these entrepreneurs operate, with particular reference to features that hinder entrepreneurship.

5. Findings of the field study of the software industry in India

Background of software entrepreneurs engaged in originative activity

Family background

Our sample showed that entrepreneurs involved with originative activity in the software industry in India are primarily from middle-class backgrounds,

Table 9.1   Companies in the study and people interviewed

Company	Person interviewed
Aditi Technologies Pvt Ltd was founded in 1994 to provide services, but later developed the product Talisma (now a separate entity called Talisma Corporation).	**Pradeep Singh** Founder and Chief Executive Officer, BTech (Elec.) from IIT Delhi, MBA from Harvard Business School. Worked with Microsoft, Texas Instruments and McKinsey Consulting. **Rekha M. Menon** Country Manager, India, and Vice-President, Human Resources. MBA from XLRI Jamshedpur. Worked with Akzo Nobel and Levis and consulted for the US Environmental Protection Agency.
Aztec Software and Technology Services (P) Ltd was founded in 1996 to create technology and products. 'JPact' (Java Powered Access Technology) is the first product.	**V. R. Govindarajan** President and Chief Technology Officer. MS in Computer Science from University of Massachusetts at Amherst. Worked for Digital Equipment Corporation (USA) and Tata–IBM.
Datanet Corporation Ltd was founded in 1995 with the objective of providing software solutions. Datanet has specialized in two technologies: Business Process Automation (BPRO) and Computer Telephony Integration (CTI).	**A. Prabhakar** Chairman and Managing Director BE, ME and PhD from Indian Institute of Science, Bangalore. He has worked in IIT, Delhi, as Asst. Professor and subsequently with ITI Ltd. He left ITI Ltd as Director (R&D) at the age of 56 to start Datanet Systems Ltd. **G. H. Visweswara** Executive Director. BE (Electronics). Worked for 20 years with ITI.
Dharma Systems, Inc is a leading supplier of e-business integration technologies. In early 2000, it introduced eUnify, a software solution designed to help web-integrators with rapid solutions that involve legacy systems.	**Dinesh Kavoor** Director. BE from IISc., Bangalore. He has worked for CMC and Wipro.
eCapital Solutions was started in 1999 with a mission to deliver solutions to global customers and is funded by the Chase Manhattan and CIBC–Oppenheimer groups.	**V. Sriram** Director (Operations). BE (Elec. & Com.) from Delhi College of Engineering. He worked for CMC and Hewlett-Packard India.

Table 9.1   (continued)

Company	Person interviewed
Encore Software Ltd was founded about 20 years ago and is a dynamic product development company in information technology that combines core technical expertise with a global business perspective. Its latest high-profile offering is the 'Simputer'.	**Vinay. L. Deshpande** Chairman and CEO. BE, MS (Electronics) from Stanford University. **Samyeer Metrani** (formerly founder of Xpert Systems). Manager, Software Development. BA, PGSM from IIM, Bangalore. He had founded Xpert Systems and also worked for Proline Software. **Prithuraj Puttaraju** (formerly founder of Xpert Systems). Business Development Manager. BE (Mechanical). He founded Xpert Systems with Samyeer Metrani.
iCODE Software Pvt Ltd was founded in 1994 and with headquarters in Fairfax, Virginia. Its products are accounting software packages called Accware and Accware Online, and Everest.	**Sanjay Shah** Vice President, R&D. BTech. IIT Bombay and MS (Computer Science) from Virginia Polytechnic Institute and State University. He worked for Tectonics and Mentor Graphics.
JL Informatrix Ltd was started in 1989 to provide software solutions primarily in the area of accounting and finance. It acquired a company founded in 1993, Nucleus Informatrix (NI), which was developing a product to enter the product domain.	**D. Kalyanaraman** Chairman and Managing Director. BTech from IIT, Chennai and PGP from IIM, Calcutta. He worked with companies like Godrej, MICO, L&T, and Digital in various managerial positions and has around 25 years of experience in industry.
Network Solutions was started in 1993 as an enterprise-wide network integration company. It has developed a product to facilitate this.	**Sudhir D. Sarma** Managing Director. BE (Electrical) from MS University, Baroda. He worked with ORG Systems, Hewlett Packard, and Motorola.
Macmet India Ltd was founded in 1974, as a trading house representing reputable multinationals in core sector industries. Its simulation division is developing simulation software for the power and defence sectors.	**H. J. Kamath** President. BE, PGP from IIM, Calcutta. **K. Kalyanaraman** General Manager (Projects). BTech (Aero) from IIT, Madras. He worked with the Indian Air Force
System Antics focuses on robotics software. It has built industrial robots and plans to build an underwater robotics arm and space robots.	**Jagannath Raju** Chief Executive Officer. BTech (Electronics) from the IIT, Madras, MS from University of California, Berkeley, and MS and PhD from MIT.

with little or no family history of business or entrepreneurship. Except for Shah of iCODE, all the entrepreneurs in our sample were from middle-class families that had no exposure to running a business. One of the disadvantages such entrepreneurs face is the lack of support from existing family structures. Also, there is a lack of appreciation in the larger family system of why a person should give up a promising career in the US, or a multinational in India, to establish a firm of his own, and that too in originative activity. While most entrepreneurs indicated that they did not experience any problems from their immediate family, they said that it was quite difficult to satisfy the concern of members of their extended family and social network of their decision to become entrepreneurs.

However, there are instances of persons from business families who have also undertaken originative work in the software industry. For example, Shah of iCODE Software explained how he was under constant pressure from his immediate family, both explicitly and implicitly, to become an entrepreneur. He gave up a lucrative job to start a business in the US, and more recently moved the development business to India. A family background in business not only facilitated the decision but also pressured him to give up his job to become an entrepreneur. There was also the case of a traditional family-owned business entering the originative arena. Macmet, which is wholly owned by the family that also owns Ambuja Cements, has ventured into developing simulation software for the power and defence sectors in India, with the intention of tapping global markets at a later stage. The family have essentially acted as financiers, and have left the management of the firm to professionals, Kamath and Kalyanaraman, whom they know and trust.

Technical knowledge

The entrepreneurs in our sample had varied educational backgrounds. Some did not have a very strong academic background but had a passion for technology and innovation, particularly in the software industry, that fuelled their drive to become entrepreneurs. For example, Metrani, currently at Encore, does not have formal engineering education (he holds an arts degree) but he had a fascination for computer technology from his school days, and took the plunge into entrepreneurship when he saw an opportunity. A somewhat different case is that of Sarma of Network Solutions, who has a formal degree in electrical engineering because that is what he got admitted to on the basis of the entrance criteria in his college, but he always wanted to study electronics. He neglected his formal education and continued his pursuit of electronics on his own. Eventually, he took the decision to launch himself as an entrepreneur.

There were many entrepreneurs who had strong academic backgrounds. For example, Singh, the founder of Aditi, is an IIT, Delhi, graduate. Similarly, Shah at iCODE is an IIT, Bombay, graduate with a MS from the US. Raju, the man behind System Antics, is an IIT, Madras, graduate with MS and PhD degrees from the US. Other people with similar profiles include Deshpande of Encore, Govindarajan of Aztec, and Shashidhar (whom we could not interview). A more homegrown case is that of Prabhakar of Datanet. He has a doctoral degree from the Indian Institute of Science and was an assistant professor at IIT, Delhi, before he joined ITI. He continued his affiliation with academics through involvement with the Indian Institute of Science, including guidance of doctoral students, before becoming an entrepreneur.

Work experience

Our data show that prior work experience is an asset for entrepreneurs. Metrani and Puttaraju, now with Encore, jumped into entrepreneurship without prior work experience. In addition to producing customized software for high technology applications, they also produced a shrink-wrapped product and tried to market it in the Indian and US markets. Unfortunately, they had problems raising financial support to sustain the product, and had to give up their dream.

All the other entrepreneurs had a little to a great deal of experience before becoming entrepreneurs. Shah worked for a couple of years for Techtronics, then ran a start-up selling hardware for another few years before he ventured into originative work, producing accounting software. Sarma worked for several years at an Indian software firm before he joined a multinational company and then quit to start out on his own. Singh worked in a senior position at Microsoft before he started his venture. Most of the others we studied, including Govindarajan, Sriram of eCapital, and Kavoor of Dharma, had several years of work experience before they became entrepreneurs. It is also interesting that some very senior people, close to what may be termed retirement age, have decided to venture out on their own. Prabhakar and his team at Datanet are examples in this category.

However, a more convincing reason to suggest that past work experience is an asset for entrepreneurs is an examination of the decision processes of venture capitalists who have entered the software industry in India. Suresh Rajpal (whom we could not interview), who was heading Hewlett-Packard operations in India, was sought out by a group of venture capitalists to head the organization they wanted to fund. He was able to put together a team of people whom he could rely on based on past experience to establish eCapital Solutions. Similarly, Mindtree, a recent high profile start-up company, has also been started by three people who have had tremendous experience in the industry, and have also received substantial venture capital support based on the expertise of their founders.

Management knowledge

Deshpande, who had attempted to develop some very good product ideas that did not initially succeed in the market, attributed the initial setbacks to lack of managerial thinking. He explained that, as engineers, 'We were more excited by the engineering challenges than the commercial reality.' Metrani and Puttaraju also attributed their inability to sustain their venture to a large extent to the lack of adequate management knowledge. However, most of the entrepreneurs in the sample had strong managerial experience, and many had formal management education. Those who did not have management expertise or a desire to be involved in managerial activity, had partners or senior associates with strong managerial experience.

However, two of the entrepreneurs thought that management knowledge hurts entrepreneurship. Kalyanaraman of JL Informatrix, who had received management education from a premier school, argued that management education makes individuals risk-averse. Also, the options available to them in large organizations increase their opportunity costs, making entrepreneurship a difficult choice. On the other hand, Sarma, who had no formal management degree, suggested that his lack of traditional managerial knowledge helped him to become a successful entrepreneur because he was not tied down by conventional managerial thought. It allowed him to implement certain practices that he felt might not have been possible had he had a management degree.

Attributes of software entrepreneurs engaged in originative activity

Personality

Not all the entrepreneurs in our sample fitted the popular notion of highly dynamic persons, bursting with energy in pursuing their dreams. However, Singh, for example, did come across as a highly energetic person, speaking passionately and trying to do other things even as he spoke to us. On the other hand, Sarma came across as a person in control, showing no signs of agitation, spending a lot of time with us despite his heavy schedule. Similarly, Govindarajan was a relaxed man during the time he spent with us. In that sense, external appearances are not good indicators of the energy people bring to their organization. In their own ways, all entrepreneurs bring energy to their team, inspiring them to work for long-term objectives.

However, they all shared some common qualities. They all had very high levels of self-confidence. They displayed confidence in the course they had chosen as a career, confidence in the product area they had selected, and confidence in their own ability and in the ability of their core team to deliver on the promise. Both Raju and Singh exuded confidence in the ability of their team to bring an Indian product to the global market, and do for their employees what Microsoft had done for its employees in terms of wealth creation and sharing. Similarly, Shah showed tremendous confidence in the ability of his team to deliver from his Bangalore operation all their needs, including promotional material such as CDs, the graphic interface, and the like. On a different scale, Prabhakar was confident that his software product was going to revolutionize banking in India. In addition to having a high level of confidence, they also seemed to have the capacity to enthuse like-minded persons to join them in their endeavour.

Motivation

This study indicates that the entrepreneurs have very strong motivations to become entrepreneurs, but their source of motivation varies from person to person. For Singh, it was some concept of giving back to a society that he had grown up in. For Prabhakar and his team at Datanet it was their desire to produce a product they had worked on for the Indian market, even as the management at ITI was losing confidence and decreasing expenditure on R&D. Prabhakar described his establishing a start-up as an attempt to prove to sceptics that such products can be developed in India. Deshpande has experienced several ups and downs in his long stint as an entrepreneur, but he still has the fire in him to continue. On the other hand, Puttaraju indicated that he decided to become an entrepreneur because his visa application to the US for higher studies had been rejected and he wanted to do something. While other reasons would have definitely played a role, we believe the fact that the venture was not a considered and motivated decision would have affected his decision to abandon it.

Another dominant reason for most entrepreneurs to choose their career path is a desire to be independent. For Shah, it was because he did not want to be lost in a large organization. For Kalyanaraman of JL Informatrix the desire to be on his own stemmed from the need to be one's own boss. Most of the persons we met shared these sentiments in one way or another. They felt constrained by the processes and systems of large organizations, and this drove them to establish an organization that allowed them to be at the top.

While most entrepreneurs did not give making money as the prime reason for why they became entrepreneurs, most did indicate that it was definitely a desire. However, Sarma provided an interesting twist to the idea of making money through an entrepreneurial venture. He suggested that being on one's own, rather than with a large company, might lead individuals to acquire wealth that they could truly call their own. He wanted to avoid getting accustomed to perks in large companies that would disappear when he changed jobs or quit.

Another overwhelming motivation was a conscious or unconscious expression of pride in the country. Over and above the 'normal' motivations, these entrepreneurs were motivated by an urge to seize the opportunity to create space for India in the high-tech markets of the world. This was expressed in variety of ways in almost all the interviews we conducted. For Deshpande, the thrill of only partially meeting his goal of putting India on the software map after a long tenure as a software entrepreneur was noticeable. For Singh, his motivation was rooted in his desire to overcome the sense of humiliation he felt at seeing the India stall at international computer fairs. His deep-seated urge is to prove to the world (and himself) that

Indians can provide international quality products that will be accepted for their performance and not for their source of origin. Govindarajan, who had returned to India with a multinational, became an entrepreneur when he realized that the multinational firms wanted to use India as a source of cheap labour and not for products. He admitted that he was not a 'natural' entrepreneur, but pride in his identity and also his pride in being Indian prompted him to join others to start a firm. Shah explained that he had named the latest version of his product developed in India, 'Everest', because it provided a touch of India (although it is in Nepal).

Ability to deal with risk and ambiguity

According to Deshpande, Indians are inherently risk-averse largely because of family pressures. He explained how he himself did not experience any pressure from his immediate family, but had to deal with the concern of the larger family. This view was shared by a few of the others too. However, there was little evidence among the people we interviewed that they were unaware of the risks associated with entrepreneurship. Most of these people had quit comfortable high-paying jobs, some in the US, to start their firms, fully aware that their venture might not succeed. They did not see it as a risk because most had comfortable personal savings to rely on, as well as a secure confidence that they had the skills, market-oriented and/or technical, that would allow them to return to the status quo if their venture failed. For example, Metrani and Puttaraju had launched a firm early in their career and experienced difficulties, and have taken up jobs that repositioned them exactly where they would have been had they continued in jobs.

Most of the entrepreneurs we spoke to had a strong reputation in the industry, particularly in the firm they last worked with. While none of them explicitly articulated it, they were aware that finding employment would not be a concern if they abandoned the venture. Indeed, they argued that many more people should become entrepreneurs, as it is not as risky as people who have not been entrepreneurs in the software industry make it out to be. All the people we spoke to were aware of the risks of becoming an entrepreneur, but were also conscious that the stakes were not as high as in other industries.

Networks

Our study shows that networks play a significant role in the success of a new venture. The networks are based on past professional interactions as well as college and/or family circles. The entrepreneurs were very clear that the ability to rely on past networks to provide basic or emergency help is an asset. Networks can be of help in a variety of situations. They may ensure a sale or a contract to initiate revenue flows. For example, the first project that eCapital undertook was on the basis of the contacts that Suresh Rajpal had as head of the India operations of Hewlett-Packard before starting on his own. Similarly, Singh started his services venture on the basis of a contract with Microsoft, his former employer. When, as a company policy, such contracts were being terminated, it was his access to Bill Gates that allowed him to persuade Microsoft to make an exception. Networks can also help in terms of obtaining financial assistance. As we will discuss later, it is very difficult to obtain financial assistance for start-ups in originative work. However, Deshpande admitted that while he and his partner got their first funding from family and personal savings, they were able to obtain funding from a bank on the basis of personal influence. Similarly, Shashidhar of Dharma also benefited from personal networks when he obtained funding from another bank. On the other hand, Raju of System Antics was able to obtain funding from Singh of Aditi for his own venture when others had refused. While it may be that Singh had more confidence in Raju's entrepreneurial skills on the strength of close contact, we believe the trust was further enhanced by friendship. Similarly, Prabhakar was able to raise capital from friends who were then settled abroad.

Focus on simple ideas

The product domains that most of the firms were involved in were not in any way revolutionary. All the successful firms were established around an idea that had developed in the mind of the entrepreneurs in their last job or prior experience as a user of a service. For example, Dharma Systems Inc was established to provide high end consulting services in database management. Neither domain nor their product, called eUnify, is revolutionary, but there is enough uncertainty in the global market for a new opportunity to emerge. This opportunity was also used to develop other products for the market. Similarly, Aztec emphasized the need to focus on a narrow range of activity, and gradually built a product, called Jpact, based on accumulated experience. The other organizations in our sample also had a narrow focus and each had a product that was an extension of something they were already doing as employees of another company or in the early stages of their own venture. For example, Datanet Corporation is developing products for transaction automation in the banking sector. This is an extension of the work that the core group of the organization was doing when they were employees in the R&D Division of ITI. Aditi Technologies' (now Talisma Corporation) product emerged out of the need for customer tracking required for the Microsoft services they offered. The internal software that they developed was further enhanced to make it suitable for other organizations with similar needs. Similarly, iCODE's first product was accounting software, similar to many products that were already available in the market: it was only customized for particular kinds of organizations. Once established, they developed a Windows version of their software for wider applications. Similarly, Macmet India Ltd is also an attempt to leverage on previous experience in a very narrow domain, that is not attractive for many organizations.

On the other hand, there was an example of a product, similar to a palmtop computer, from Encore Software Limited (formerly nCore), that was revolutionary. It was ahead of the market, but had to be discontinued even after a small batch of production and successful application of the product by a few customers because of cash flow problems. Now the same firm is involved with another revolutionary product called 'Simputer'. In many ways this product is also experiencing the problems faced by any radical product, but the firm, which is well established now, has a greater ability to sustain the efforts to have the product accepted in the market.

Context of originative innovation in the software industry in India

Market support

Most of the entrepreneurs in our sample were developing products for the international, particularly US, markets. For example, Aditi's product was developed for the US market although now they are also marketing it in India. Dharma Systems, which is actually a subsidiary of an American company, is entirely focused on the US market. iCODE has products that are targeted at American and European markets. Most of the entrepreneurs indicated that the Indian market was not ready for the kind of products that they were building or the volume needs were not large enough for them to pay attention to it.

The few that have tried to develop products for the Indian market have faced tremendous problems. Puttaraju described his frustration with attempts to build products for the Indian market primarily because of its small size. Raju had a similar opinion about the Indian market. Deshpande also described his difficulty in getting Indian firms to accept his products, although he did admit that there were small pockets in organizations that do give Indian products a fair chance. In addition to not being accepting of products from Indian companies, the payment schedules of large companies, particularly government organizations, are so slow that it is difficult for small start-ups to maintain cash flow.

However, there are some people who want to explicitly target the Indian market first and then take the product to the international market. For example, Datanet Corp is trying to build products for the banking sector notwithstanding the fact that lead-time is long and the banking sector is very conservative in adopting new technologies. Similarly, Macmet has a desire to use the Indian market to test its product before going global.

Financial support

Almost all the people we spoke to had tremendous problems getting finance from banks or venture capitalists. Visweswara described the multiplicity of problems, particularly having to face archaic and bureaucratic banking procedures to obtain finance from banks in India for their venture. The same message was reinforced by Prabhakar, who argued that lack of finance may be a major reason why many entrepreneurs have to choose to provide software services to foreign clients (derivative work) rather than build products (originative work). Metrani and Puttaraju, who have abandoned their venture and taken up jobs with Encore, identified cash flow problems and their inability to get funding as the principal reasons for their failure. Deshpande identified lack of financing as a key reason why his firm had not grown at the rate it could have. He reasoned that even in cases where finance was available it was not commensurate with the requirements. He described the problem of entrepreneurs trying to get funding for products as a chicken and egg problem. Banks were prepared to provide funds only after a product was developed or sold, when there was no longer a need for funding.

It is because of lack of funding that almost all the entrepreneurs, who are driven by the need to do originative work, also dabble with derivative work to maintain the cash flow. This compulsion to straddle both types of work leads to tremendous internal pressure in the organization. Aditi Computers undertook derivative work to finance product development. Govindarajan explained how the lack of funds had forced them to undertake services, which ultimately let to a delay in their product. Similarly, Sarma explained his reasons for getting into consultancy first rather than product development, although his original aim was to develop products. He has now developed a product. Prabhakar talked about the pressures from the investment community (and others) to abandon product development and enter the service industry, which he has so far resisted.

In the absence of publicly available funds, most entrepreneurs have relied on private funds. For example, Macmet has been funded entirely by its parent company. Since the parent company is in a traditional industry it can be evaluated by all the traditional methods, and loans can be obtained on the basis of the strength of that. Others have relied on friends. Some companies that have access to outside funds (e.g. iCODE) or are actually subsidiaries of American companies (e.g. Dharma Systems) have relied on friends from outside India to raise money. Dharma Systems has been able to raise capital in the US so the Indian unit has not had to deal with the problem of finding financial resources.

Infrastructure

There was clear unanimity that the telecommunications facilities that are available to the industry have improved considerably but are still inadequate to meet its needs. The need for a telecommunication infrastructure is absolutely critical to the software industry, but the entrepreneurs are not happy with the level of support they have received. They would definitely want the government to help directly by improving the facilities, or indirectly by opening up to enable private investors to provide such facilities.

Since the time the interviews were conducted there has been considerable progress in the telecommunications infrastructure.

In addition to telecommunication facilities, there is a need for good office space for software firms to start up without any waste of time. Most entrepreneurs suggested that the availability of physical infrastructure was so poor that they had to spend considerable time in the initial stages arranging things not related to the business. For example, Shah indicated that there were severe problems with the physical infrastructure in comparison to his experience in the US. According to Singh, the infrastructure problems are so severe that it is very discouraging for an entrepreneur to want to start a business in India. The only reason he, or other entrepreneurs of Indian origin, have been able to deal with the situation is that they could relate some of their experiences to their growing up in India. Anybody not familiar with the Indian context would find it difficult to take things in their stride. The government has tried to address these issues by establishing software technology parks, as in Bangalore. However, these do not seem to be meeting the needs of homegrown entrepreneurs. Some of them indicated that the costs were too high for young cash-strapped entrepreneurs.

In addition to very specific infrastructural requirements like telecommunications and physical infrastructure, there is a need to address issues related to general city conditions. As most of the software firms are dealing with international markets, international travel by the employees and clients is quite frequent. This requires the city to have a good airport with convenient flight connections. Also, city infrastructure, such as well-maintained roads, adequate street lighting, good garbage clearance facilities and the like indirectly make entrepreneurship easier by helping to attract and retain qualified employees.

Role of government

One of the needs most consistently emphasized by the entrepreneurs was a single window that would advise them on all government-related requirements to enable the entrepreneurs to devote their full time to the new venture and also remain within the law. Sarma described a situation in which he was hauled up because he was unaware of some government norm which was extremely easy to comply with. Menon related how the need to run to different offices to obtain clearances for various things had delayed her projects. Shah said that the absence of a single window facility had resulted in his being unaware of facilities that are actually provided for entrepreneurs. He believed that if the government was really serious about the incentives, a single window should provide all the relevant information.

A complaint high on the list of all the entrepreneurs was the level of corruption in all the government departments. There was a strong opinion that the government needs to simplify its procedures so that entrepreneurs are easily able to comply with them without being harassed by government agencies for violations that they were unaware of. They expressed a strong desire to be left to pay attention to the technological and market needs of their innovative ideas, rather than spend time negotiating their way through cumbersome government procedures.

However, one area in which government involvement was thought to be desirable was providing visibility to the industry, and also seeking to establish an image of quality for the entire industry. It would be easier for smaller firms to participate in the global market as a collective entity rather than having to prove themselves individually. For example, Deshpande explained how his firm might have been more successful if the Indian industry had already had an image of quality. At the present time his firm has to establish its image with each customer individually, and the latter are surprised by the excellent quality they receive. The government of India needs to actively help small entrepreneurs get a foothold in the market by building an international image of good quality for the Indian software industry. The larger players in the software services segment have taken a long time to establish their individual images. The newer firms could benefit from that success if government actively promoted the industry.

6. Promoting entrepreneurship in the Indian software industry

We can draw some broad conclusions from the findings of this study. Each of these also has implications for the development and nurturing of originative innovation and entrepreneurship in the software industry in India.

The first set of conclusions relates to the background of the entrepreneurs. Unlike other industries in India, most of the entrepreneurs in the software industry come from a middle-class non-business background, and a few from business families. This finding is consistent with Bhide's (2000) and Manimala et al.'s (2001) arguments that high value entrepreneurship attracts persons from families that are neither very rich nor very poor. However, it is much easier for persons from business backgrounds to make the move to become entrepreneurs, which is in line with the Sanchez and Perez (1998) findings, and also Manimala et al.'s (2001) argument that entrepreneurship is encouraged in families traditionally associated with business. This implies that software entrepreneurs in India can come from all family backgrounds and be successful, although persons from families with prior business experience may find it easier to obtain family support. The above conclusion also has implications for society. Several potential entrepreneurs, mostly from non-business families, are probably unable to pursue their dreams because of lack of support from their immediate family. Society needs to be more accepting of entrepreneurship and encourage close relatives to become entrepreneurs and not see it as an option only for people failing to find employment.

While lack of formal educational qualifications or not very high levels of qualification have a deterrent effect on entrepreneurship, it is also true that more often than not entrepreneurs in the software industry have strong academic backgrounds, with many having a masters or doctoral qualifications. This finding is also consistent with Bhide (2000) and the Sanchez and the Perez (1998) finding in their study of high technology firms, but a little different from Manimala et al.'s (2001) because their focus was not on high technology industries. What unites the entrepreneurs in the software industry in India are not their formal qualifications but their in-depth knowledge of the technology/domain on which they have focused. This implies that entrepreneurs who want to engage in originative activity in the software industry need to be highly conversant with the technology in their domain. Formal qualifications in the technology are desirable but not necessary. However, unlike traditional industry where entrepreneurs functioned principally as financiers and managers, there is no substitute to knowledge of the technology. If entrepreneurs intend to act as financiers, they have to be able to leave most of the business decisions to technically competent people, which is a departure from the more capital-intensive industries of the past.

Prior work experience is a critical asset for entrepreneurial success in the software industry to be successful. The experience is best if it is in the same technology as the new venture. However, experience is an asset even if it is not in the technology domain of the new venture, because it at least brings with it an understanding of all that is required to run a business. This implies that work experience, particularly in the domain of the product, is desirable, although experience in other industries is also an asset. Lack of experience is a limitation, as indicated by Bhide (2000) and Sanchez and Perez (1998), but by and large the entrepreneurs were young, as Manimala et al. (2001) found. Hence, young entrepreneurs who may be enamoured by the idea of creating a revolutionary product might be better advised to acquire a few years of experience before taking the plunge. It can greatly enhance the prospect of success.

Successful entrepreneurs or their senior associates have the requisite management expertise. However, some of the entrepreneurs felt that conventional management theories based on studies of large organizations need to be adapted before being applied to entrepreneurial ventures. This suggests that while technical knowledge is critical, managerial knowledge is also essential for the success of a firm, as suggested by Bhide (2000) and Sanchez and Perez (1998). An entrepreneur who is very technically oriented, and has no desire to address managerial issues, should co-opt team members or senior employees with managerial expertise to undertake the managerial responsibilities.

The second set of conclusions related to the attributes of entrepreneurs. From external observation it would appear that entrepreneurs in the software industry in India are not necessarily highly dynamic persons.

However, as found by Stewart et al. (1998), Sanchez and Perez (1998) and Bhide (2000) in their studies, and as suggested by Drucker (1998), they all exude tremendous confidence in themselves and their venture, and have the ability to enthuse others to work for their dream. This implies that a person who wants to become a high technology entrepreneur has to have a very high level of self-confidence and self-belief. If entrepreneurs are not confident of their own abilities they will not be capable of handling the pressures of a start-up nor will they be able to attract good talent to their team. However, there is no need to have the external trappings of a dynamic person. We believe that many more people can become successful originative entrepreneurs if they do not associate external dynamism as essential for starting a business.

Successful originative entrepreneurs share all the motivations of entrepreneurs in any other field or country, as reported by Bhide (2000) and Sanchez and Perez (1998), making money being only one of the goals. The findings also suggest that the stigma against entrepreneurship in India (Manimala et al., 2001) does not exist in the software industry. Most of the entrepreneurs had quit comfortable high paying jobs to launch firms focused on originative activity. An additional motivation, not reported in other studies, is the deep sense of pride in being Indian that motivates software entrepreneurs to seize the opportunity that the software industry offers to put India on the global map in a high technology industry. This suggests that entrepreneurs need to have motivation beyond just making money for otherwise they might not find it fruitful. It is the larger inspiration that sustains them against the odds they experience. The desire to put India on the global technology map is definitely an asset, allowing entrepreneurs to sustain their passion and overcome many difficulties. This implies that the government and society should endeavour to heighten this emotion to encourage originative entrepreneurship in the software industry in India.

As is true in other contexts, as reported by Bhide (2000), the originative entrepreneurs in the software industry have an ability to deal with ambiguity without necessarily being risk-takers. The risk is not as high as people who have not been entrepreneurs think it is, but the ambiguity is high. Hence, entrepreneurs in the software industry need to have a high ability to deal with ambiguity, but should not be overly concerned about the risks, as the downsides of entrepreneurship are not very high. In a society that is risk-averse (Manimala et al., 2001) and is vulnerable to the development trap (Iyigun and Owen, 1998), this is a significant finding. We believe that many more people could become originative entrepreneurs if only they were able to overcome the imagined risks of becoming entrepreneurs. Successful entrepreneurs should play a greater role in mentoring potential entrepreneurs.

Originative entrepreneurs, as most other entrepreneurs, have a natural ability to keep connected with all kinds of persons in their domain and even outside it (Bhide, 2000; Saxenian, 2000). However, some of these networks may actually be cultivated as there are mutual benefits to all those within a network, and this is particularly true in India (Khanna and Palepu, 1999). Hence, potential entrepreneurs should have an ability to develop and maintain a large network of professionals, family and friends. This often requires an entrepreneur to devote time and energy to sustaining the network. This is a worthwhile effort as the members of the network are of tremendous help in assisting a fledgling venture to negotiate potential dead ends.

As suggested by Bhide (2000) and Drucker (1998), successful entrepreneurs focus on a simple idea in a niche area in a dynamic market rather than a grand idea that is going to change the world. The innovation is typically not revolutionary but addresses a problem of the targeted market. This finding has a message for potential entrepreneurs. The probability of success is greatly improved if the entrepreneur has a focus on a niche area and initially targets simple products. More complicated products should be kept for the next stage when the entrepreneur has come to grips with the teething problems of the start-up. We believe that many more start-ups would survive if they abandoned grand ideas and pursued more simple products in the initial days.

The third set of conclusions relates to the context of the software industry in India. Most of the entrepreneurs find the Indian market discouraging, which is consistent with Lal's (1999) and Manimala et al.'s (2001) findings, and very negative for the growth of the industry (Porter, 1990). It is because of this that they target the international market. The few who would want to target the Indian market are people who have strong roots in India and prior experience providing products/services to its market. This suggests that key decision-makers need to make a conscious decision to give Indian software products a fair chance, and avoid overlooking them in favour of imported products. The government can play a central role in changing the situation. Firstly, it can increase information technology implementation in the government-controlled sector of the economy and encourage the implementation of information technology in the private sector through tax incentives and/or requirements of computer-based reporting, liberalization of the telecommunications industry, and the like. A spurt in demand will make the Indian market more attractive for many more entrepreneurs and motivate them to enter the originative domain with India in mind.

Despite all the public attention focused on the issue and increase in the availability of venture capital (*Business World*, 2000; Manimala et al., 2001), finance is not easily available to people who really need it and is targeted towards people with many other options to raise capital. There is a need to have venture capital that focuses on entrepreneurs who cannot get easy access to capital: young people without a track record in the industry but with a dream. Financing small start-ups, particularly in the originative domain, remains a problem, despite the entry into India of several venture capital firms. The government can encourage the banks to develop better ways of evaluating software ventures, so that capital is more easily available. However, the government should not enter the domain with its own finance company.

There has been an enormous improvement in the telecommunications infrastructure since the interviews for this study were conducted. However, other infrastructure for the software industry needs to be improved, as it is critical (Cabral, 1998; Martinsons, 1998; Montealegre, 1999; and Sanchez and Perez, 1998). Given Manimala et al.'s (2001) finding that India ranked lowest on physical infrastructure among twenty-nine countries, it is clear that entrepreneurs in India face a huge disadvantage in relation to other countries. Service-oriented firms themselves have been successful despite the infrastructure, and not because of it. As of now, infrastructure at the technology parks is more affordable to service-oriented firms, and not to entrepreneurs on a very tight budget in the initial phase. The standards need to be improved so that they are attractive to entrepreneurs in the originative domain.

The government needs to simplify its procedures. There was a strong consensus that the government should create a 'single window' system for entrepreneurs for such matters as registration and customs and excise duties to conformity with labour and city zoning laws. Entrepreneurs would like to comply with all the requirements without being hassled so that they and their teams can concentrate on the real work of creating globally competitive products. The government will need to do a great deal if it wants to avoid the opprobrium of India being ranked below average on all elements of government policies and programmes among the twenty-nine countries, as reported in Manimala et al. (2001).

Finally, the government can play a role in creating a brand image for the Indian software industry. Smaller entrepreneurs need to be able to benefit from the collective goodwill of the software industry. The government can supplement the efforts of industry associations to build an image for the software industry, both internationally and in India. While the image of the software service industry is quite strong, some coordinated assistance from the government will help translate this to goodwill for the product-oriented firms.

References

Abraham, T., S. Ahlawat and S. Ahlawat (1998) 'The India Option: Perception of Indian Software Solutions', *International Journal of Technology Management*, 15 (6/7): 605–21.

Baron, R. A. (1998) 'Cognitive Mechanisms in Entrepreneurship: Why and When Entrepreneurs Think Differently Than Other People', *Journal of Business Venturing*, 13: 275–94.

Bhide, A. V. (2000) *The Origin and Evolution of New Businesses* (New York: Oxford University Press).

Business World (2000) 'Venture Capital and Indian Startups', *Business World*, 14 Feb, 45–50.

Cabral, R. (1998) From University–Industry Interfaces to the Making of a Science Park: Florianopolis, Southern Brazil', *International Journal of Technology Management*, 16 (8): 778–99.

Chen, C. C., P. G. Greene and A. Crick (1998) 'Does Entrepreneurial Self-Efficacy Distinguish Entrepreneurs from Managers?', *Journal of Business Venturing*, 13: 295–316.

Correa, C. M. (1996) 'Strategies for Software Exports from Developing Countries', *World Development*, 24 (1): 171–82.

Drucker, P. F. (1998) 'The Discipline of Innovation', *Harvard Business Review*, Nov–Dec: 149–57.

Hunger, J. D. and T. L. Wheelen (1996) *Strategic Management* (Don Mills, Canada: Addison-Wesley Publishing Co).

Iyigun, M. F. and A. L. Owen (1998) 'Risk, Entrepreneurship, and Human Capital Accumulation', *AEA Papers and Proceedings*, 88 (2): 454–7.

Khanna, T. and K. Palepu, (1997) 'Why Focused Strategies May be Wrong for Emerging Markets', *Harvard Business Review*, July–Aug: 125–34.

Krishna, S., A. K. Ojha and M. Barrett (2000) 'Competitive Advantage in the Software Industry: an Analysis of the Indian Experience', in C. Avegrou and G. Walsham (eds), *Information Technology in Context: Studies From the Perspective of Developing Countries* (Aldershot, UK: Ashgate Publications), pp. 182–98.

Kumar, N. (2001) 'Indian Software Industry Development: International and National Perspective', *Economic and Political Weekly*, 10 Nov: 4278–90.

Lal, K. (1999) 'Determinants of the Adoption of Information Technology: a Case Study of Electrical and Electronic Goods Manufacturing Firms in India', *Research Policy*, 28: 667–80.

Manimala, M. J., S. Prakhya, M. Y. Gopal and J. Shields (2001) *Global Entrepreneurship Monitor: India Report 2001* (Bangalore: Raghavan Centre for Entrepreneurial Learning, Indian Institute of Management).

Martinsons, M. G. (1998) 'Hong Kong Government Policy and Information Technology Innovation: the Invisible Hand, the Helping Hand, and the Hand-Over to China', *IEEE Transactions on Engineering Management*, 45 (4): 366–80.

Montealegre, R. (1999) 'A Temporal Model of Institutional Interventions for Information Technology Adoption in Less-Developed Countries', *Journal of Management Information Systems*, 16 (1): 207–32.

Overby, C. S., B. Doyle, J. Sweeny and T. Watson (2001) *The Coming Offshore Services Crunch* (Cambridge, MA: Forester Research Inc).

Porter, M. (1990) 'The Competitive Advantage of Nations', *Harvard Business Review*, March–April: 73–93.

Sanchez, A.M. and O. U. Perez (1998) 'Entrepreneurship Networks and High Technology Firms: the Case of Aragon', *Technovation*, 18 (5): 335–45.

Saxenian, A. (1999) *Silicon Valley's New Immigrant Entrepreneurs* (California: Public Policy Institute of California).

Stewart, W. H., W. E. Watson, J. C. Carland and J. W. Carland (1998) 'A Proclivity for Entrepreneurship: a Comparison of Entrepreneurs, Small Business Owners, and Corporate Managers', *Journal of Business Venturing*, 14: 189–214.

Viswanathan, V. (2000) 'High Tech Start-ups', *Business World*, 4 Sept: 22–30.

10
Stages in Multiple Innovations in Software Firms: a Model Derived from Infosys and NIIT Case Studies

Deepti Bhatnagar and Mukund Dixit

This chapter presents a model of stages in multiple innovations in software firms derived from in-depth studies of innovations in two Indian software firms, Infosys and NIIT. The firms stand out in the Indian software sector in terms of the rapidity of their growth, the recognition received and the impact made by them in influencing the practices of firms following similar lines of business. They provide a contrast in terms of the scope of their activities and market foci. Infosys has focused dominantly on the international market while NIIT has harnessed the opportunities provided by both the domestic and international markets. The case studies are based on data gathered from each company's annual reports, websites, published articles, the company's own publications and interviews with key executives. We began by tracing the early stages of the companies, the conditions in the external environment and their early innovations. By external environment we refer to the set of forces that influence a firm's choices and their implementation but are outside its control. We followed the response of the environment to the innovations of the companies and the companies' own response to it in terms of further innovations. The chapter is organized as follows. We present a brief review of the relevant literature and follow it with case studies of Infosys and NIIT. This is then followed by a distillation of a model to explain multiple innovations in software firms.

1. A definition of innovations

We have adopted a broader view of innovation to include outcomes that are *totally new* and are being *adapted by the organization for the first time in the industry* in which it is operating. We consider innovation as the end, also distinguishing between innovation and the innovating process. For example, the idea of a 'dedicated offshore centre' is an innovation. Answers to questions like Who developed the innovation? What were the alternatives considered? Why? How was the decision made? would constitute the process of innovation. The focus of our study is more on innovation, its triggers and enablers, and less on the process innovation. We are seeking to identify innovations in *business concepts* and their *management* developed by the firm's employees, including its promoters. This means that the focus is not on innovations by outsiders like public policy-makers, customers and suppliers.

2. A review of the relevant literature

The relevant literature on innovations is vast. This covers areas such as innovations in strategy (Day, 1990), marketing (Johne and Snelson, 1988), new technology (Rothwell and Whiston, 1990) and organization theory (Damanpour, 1991). However, as Dougherty (1996) remarked, all this research does not seem to contribute to noticeably enhanced organizational capability to manage innovations. In reviewing the literature we find that activities intended to usher in innovation, such as a paradigm shift in strategy (Johnson, 1988), adopting new marketing tools (Mahajan and Wind, 1992), and using the organization's past experience to derive lessons about the future (Van de Ven and Polley, 1992), do not necessarily and automatically result in absorption of innovation. Cozijnsen (1989) concluded that many innovation efforts seem to fail because employees cannot handle an innovation correctly or simply reject it. It was suggested (Cozijnsen, 1993) that instead of viewing innovations from a single dimension, it is important to explore multiple organizational dimensions such as innovation policy, including the R&D policies from a strategic perspective (Buys, 1983), the innovation rate reflecting the diffusion and adoption perspective (Rogers, 1979), innovation willingness, including personality variables, and the compatibility of innovation with existing values (Cozijnsen, 1993), the capacity to change in relation to major functions of the organization (Vrakking, 1988), and the organization's potential to steer and control complex innovation processes (Carnall, 1990). Innovations occur because of a set of enabling factors and processes. Favourable public policy, enlightened management, or slack provided by the management are examples of enablers.

Continuing the exploration of the basic question as to why complex organizations obstruct activities that can lead to product innovation, and following Jelinek and Schoonhoven (1990), Dougherty (1996: 425) used the metaphor of 'tension' to convey the challenges faced by organizations in 'iterating between diverse activities, working around barriers, combining insights, and resolving the conflicts of seemingly opposing forces, all of which can be found in the innovation process'.

According to Dougherty (1996), four sets of activities contribute to the development of new, commercially successful products. These include working with potential customers to link needs with technological possibilities (tension of outside versus inside); organizing for new workflow so as to promote cross-functional collaboration (tension between the new versus the old); evaluating and monitoring the innovation (tension of determined versus emergent); and developing commitment to innovation (tension of freedom versus responsibility). The first tension involves a pull between the market, including customer needs, and market structure (outside), on the one hand, and the firm's organizational and technological capacity (inside), on the other. Organizing for creative problem-solving, according to Dougherty (1996), consists of a second tension between the old and the new, as existing practices designed for old products obstruct the development of new approaches, relationships and procedures required for selling the new product. The third tension in product innovation embodies a pull between top-down plans for innovation (determined) versus bottom-up emergence of innovation (emergent). It is argued that in order to bridge this gap, eliminate the tension and promote ongoing innovation, organizations need to develop fundamentally new capacities for organizational action. Lastly, product innovation is facilitated when people sense freedom to generate new ideas and create novel solutions to problems. However, this clashes with the organizational expectation that the employee should feel a sense of responsibility to work within organizational constraints and towards organizational goals. Thus, developing a commitment to innovations, according to Dougherty (1996), entails a tension between freedom and responsibility. Managing innovations involves managing the above four tensions. While many organizations, because they are oriented towards maintaining the status quo, emphasize one side of the balance, namely the inside, the old, the determined and the responsible, many organization theories seem to advocate the other side of the balance so as to facilitate innovation, namely the outside, the new, the emergent and the free. It is argued that, in order to bridge this gap and eliminate the tension so as to promote ongoing innovation, organizations need to develop fundamentally new capacities for organizational action.

In our research, we have carried forward the idea of organizational tension, imbalance and the need to further restore balance. We view innovations as outcomes of dynamic interaction between the organization and the environment. As mentioned earlier, our focus is on organizational innovation, i.e. how organizations adapt themselves to meet the challenges of a changing environment. We have analysed two organizations in the Indian software industry and distilled a model of stages in multiple innovations in software firms. A brief account of the two organizations, and the external and internal circumstances in which innovations occurred in these organizations, are presented below. We use the term 'context' to capture both the external as well as internal circumstances.

3. The organizations

Infosys and NIIT were started around the same time (in 1981 and 1982 respectively) by groups of professionals with comparable academic backgrounds and larger-than-life visions for their organization. Each organization has created an opportunity space of its own and has become a trendsetter. Their achievements and innovations have triggered several similar initiatives by other enterprises. Both place a high premium on developing their people resource. Both the enterprises have promoted a culture of being socially sensitive, and have operated within a self-imposed code of ethics. As corporations, they are looked upon as role models and have inspired many IT entrepreneurs in the country to have a bold vision and work towards achieving it within a value-based framework. These organizations and their promoters have acquired a high degree of respect, and their impact is demonstrated by the fact that they have been influencing the thinking of policy-makers.

4. Infosys Technologies Limited

Infosys Technologies Limited (Infosys) started small, but with a vision of 'building a leading organization on values'. The demand conditions in developed countries like the US and supply conditions in India provided it with an opportunity to visualize a business concept, innovate and grow. Infosys was set up in July 1981 in Pune as Infosys Consultants Pvt Ltd by a team of seven professionals under the overall leadership of Narayana Murthy, a postgraduate in computer science from IIT, Kanpur. Narayana Murthy held a key position in PCS, a computer company, and was involved in projects that designed and executed software projects for clients in the US. In the following paragraphs we provide a description of the early days of Infosys, key changes in the profile of the company, salient features of its business model, and the management practices, with special reference to people management issues.

The first decade: difficulties and facilitators

Initially Infosys worked as a subcontractor for DBC, a US company that got software projects and subcontracted them to Infosys. Their first assignment was the development of an online production control package for a client in the apparel industry in the US. In the course of this assignment Infosys noted that there were opportunities to undertake a significant part of the development work in India itself and save on costs without sacrificing quality. Based on this, Infosys decided to import a computer on its own and set up a software development centre in India. Articulating this opportunity and pursuing it logically was Infosys' first innovation. Difficulties in harnessing the opportunity included time loss in getting the licence to import the computer, refusal of financial assistance by leading banks, and delays in receiving clearances from the Department of State in the US to export the computer. At one time Narayana Murthy had to present his case to the State Department and argue that clearances be speeded up. Against the blockers there were facilitators, such as Karnataka State Industrial Development

Corporation, Saraswat Co-operative Bank, Karnataka State Financial Corporation, and MICO Industries. Narayana Murthy's technical background and abilities to persuade and persist enabled him to get the required support.[1]

In 1982 the company shifted its location from Pune to Bangalore to take advantage of the space provided by MICO industries, an auto-components company producing spark plugs, to instal the Infosys computer. MICO was planning to instal a computer on its own to meet its in-house IT service requirements. Infosys negotiated with them to allow it to instal the computer at their premises and offer the services. As the arrangement was economical to both, the deal went through. Infosys continued its work with DBC till 1987. That year it decided to pursue business opportunities on its own and discontinued its contract with DBC. The company had faced difficulties in getting the right kind of assignments and receiving payments on time. In one case it had to threaten to walk out of the assignment. Early independent projects included an assignment from Reebok, France, a bank computerization project with Canara Bank in India,[2] and a joint venture with Kurt Salmon & Associates. Infosys set up an office in Atlanta, Georgia, in 1989. That very year the company faced a crisis. One of the founders left to settle in the US. Narayana Murthy convened a meeting of the founders and offered to buy out their stakes if they were also contemplating a shift. Rather than selling out they rallied behind him and offered full support:

> In 1989, we almost closed down business. The turning point was when one of the founders left the firm and migrated to the United States. Infosys had customers but was still fledgling. Because the factor conditions hadn't changed dramatically, we were forced to send people outside of India at the client site. This wasn't the vision we had for the company, we wanted to add maximum value inside of India.[3]

The growth decade

The company reaffirmed its faith in the vision and set out to strengthen its implementation. This effort was supported by the policy changes that favoured liberalization and globalization in India. Between 1990 and 2000, the company grew to cater to the needs of several large international customers in the list of the top 1000 global companies. Besides expanding the Bangalore unit, it set up units in Chennai, Hyderabad, Mangalore, Bhubaneswar, Pune and Mohali, and offices in the US, Germany, the UK and Japan. It set up a Global Development Centre in Toronto, Canada, an office in Hong Kong, and had plans to set up a development centre in London.

In keeping with its growth, the number of employees increased from 73 in 1988 to 7500 in the first quarter of 2000. In 1993, the number of employees was 450. It increased to 2605 in 1998. Revenue from business operations was Rs 1.2 million in 1982. By the end of fiscal year 2000 the revenue had soared to Rs 9214.6 million.

To finance the setting up of a 160 000 square feet software development centre in Bangalore, the company made an initial public offer (IPO) on the Bangalore Stock Exchange in 1993. Later, to finance further expansion and set up new facilities in other cities, it raised foreign currency resources by floating American Depository Receipts and listed itself on NASDAQ in March 1999. It became the first Indian company to publish its annual report in accordance with international accounting standards.

The founders consistently emphasized their vision and concretized it in terms of approach to identifying and harnessing business opportunities, building an open, innovation-seeking and learning-supportive organizational culture, a stringent recruitment system, an employee development scheme, use of IT in innovative ways, knowledge management initiatives, support from demanding clients, favourable public policies, and taking the fullest advantage of an educational and population environment offering a virtually unlimited supply of aspiring candidates through a process of rigorous selection and advanced training. The company's expertise was in legacy platform and its ability to rapidly assimilate new technologies enabled it to offer a highly compelling value proposition to the top companies.

Infosys' success in creating a successfully replicable business model attracted the attention of policy-makers, making them aware of the potential and constraints of the software sector. Software exports got identified as a key focus area and tax incentives were given to set up software development centres in specially developed information technology parks.

Defining the concept of business and sustaining it

One of Infosys' early innovations has been the conceptualization and implementation of the *offshore development concept*. The Infosys model sought to maximize the development efforts in India and minimize the stay of Indian professionals in the US, and thereby to gain cost advantage. Successful implementation of the model required that Infosys assure the quality of development and monitoring of the project. It also meant that Infosys recruited professionals with skills in programming, customer requirement analysis, forecasting, customer interface, and project management. Such skills were not readily available. However, there were fresh graduates with qualifications in engineering and science for recruitment and training. This imbalance between what is desired and what is available, prompted the organization to innovate the concepts of 'learnability' as an attribute of the individual and 'learning value add' as the responsibility of the organization.

The company has deliberately focused on getting business from international clients. The contribution to revenue from domestic clients is less than 3 per cent. Its five largest clients accounted for 29.2 per cent of turnover in 1999. The clientele has evolved over the years through the company's marketing efforts and references by satisfied customers. The company has built a consistent record of delivering what it promised to its customers.

Based on its experience in implementing the offshore development model, the company has created an innovation in the concept of a dedicated offshore development services centre (OSDC) in which a software development team is dedicated to single-client use. The team uses the technology tools, processes and methodologies unique to the client. It has focused on new services like packaged application implementation of e-com/Internet/Intranet services. Over 80 per cent of the revenue in 1997–8 and the 90 per cent of that in 1999 came from repeat clients.

Infosys has used its project experience to conceptualize and develop branded products and services (see Krishnan and Prabhu, Chapter 6, for product development possibilities from services). Branding of services is new to the industry. Infosys has also created proprietary tools, techniques and methodologies, and trained its employees to execute projects using these. The contribution of these services to overall revenue is less than 10 per cent, but they provide a basis for building future growth.

These developments have been induced by the drive of the management to add value to the activities of the company and maximize the revenue earned per professional in order to stave off competitive pressures from other firms offering similar third-party services at lower cost in an increasingly cut-throat information technology environment.

Aspects of human resource management

Recruitment

As of 31 December 1998, the company had approximately 3500 employees including approximately 3000 IT professionals. Recruitment is done around the year. The company attracts talents by emphasizing company attributes such as strong and focused core values, ambitions of entering the global big league, a fun work environment with a high levels of professional freedom and responsibility, the opportunity for exciting careers as software engineers and project managers in an international context, knowledge management initiatives, and incentive systems like stock options that recognize and reward individual contributions.

Recruitment is on the basis of academic record and learnability. Learnability emphasizes not merely academic qualifications but an ability to learn new things quickly. Infosys designed a unique test to check on learnability. In addition, the company looks for abilities to work in teams and avoids individuals with dishonest tendencies.

Over the years, the number of applications received has soared. In 1998 the company received 74 400 resumés. It tested 22 483 people and offered jobs to 2004. In fiscal year 2000 the number of resumes received increased to 184 000 and Infosys hired 2050 candidates. Such a spurt in the number of applications received, and individuals tested and recruited, has created a context for innovating in the area of application processing, test administration, organizing interviews, communication with the candidates, and training the candidates once they join. The HR department has automated these processes with the help of IT. The IT software tracks the progress of the candidates at various stages of selection. The education and research division of the company has developed self-learning and testing modules using IT. This has minimized the requirement of face-to-face classroom learning and maximized the opportunities for recruiting and training more people.

Infosys promises its employees three types of value additions, namely, learning value addition, emotional value addition (implying emotional assimilation of employees with the organization), and revenue value addition (a competitive salary, performance-linked incentives and stock options).

The culture of transparency and openness

The company has an open door policy. Anyone can meet the members of the top management, and can also access a central database and get responses to frequently asked questions. Information about service rules and the values of the company is maintained on the Intranet.

Efforts are made to understand the employees' aspirations and expectations through employee surveys and 360° feedback. The company's Intranet provides opportunities for carrying out surveys and feedback on management initiatives. The Infosys home page has a feature called 'anvil' which provides opportunities to employees to test new ideas and share their experiences with experiments. For example, the Nortel team in Infosys shared its learning from the Nortel HR systems. Similarly, the tax calculations systems were put on an Excel sheet. This facilitated easy tax filing by the employees.

The company treats failures on the basis of issues and not on the basis of the persons involved. A root cause analysis of the failure is carried out and areas for improvement are identified. This is shared with all the people who can benefit from this analysis.

Initiating a culture of giving back

In 1998 Infosys set up the Infosys Foundation to give something back to society. The work of the foundation in areas such as health care, social rehabilitation, rural development, learning, education, and promotion of traditional arts was initiated in Karnataka state, and was later extended to other states like Maharashtra, Tamil Nadu and Orissa.

In 1997, the company independently initiated three social programmes. *Catch them young* attempted to spot bright young talent and provide intensive education in IT. *Train the trainer* imparted advance IT education to college lecturers. The *rural reach* programme attempted to impart computer skills to village children. In collaboration with Microsoft, it has donated PCs to schools under the *computer@classroom* programme. Infosys employees have tended to imbibe this value of giving back. Members of the top

Box 10.1 Innovations in Infosys

- Articulating a vision that explicitly incorporates innovation, values and integrity.
- The conceptualization of the business module where the customer is an international customer and the service providers are domestic skilled software engineers.
- Building on the concept of the offshore model and creating the concept of a dedicated offshore development centre.
- Careful attention to long-term sustainability of the organization by diversifying the client base, geographical markets, service offerings and technology platforms.
- Creating the concept of knowledge bank and providing opportunities for storing knowledge and making it reusable.
- Synthesizing learning across projects and developing proprietary tools, methodologies, framework, services and products.
- Emphasizing learnability in selection of people and providing opportunities for learning and acquisiton of the necessary skills and knowledge.
- Development of a unique campus-like organizational culture that supports sharing, learning, experimentation and flexibility.
- Instant recognition of the contribution of employees.
- Organizing a value workshop to reinforce the values of the organization and integrating the youngsters with them.
- Being transparent in all respects and developing an open door policy.
- Constantly searching for new standards of achievement and getting the achievement evaluated by independent international agencies.
- Use of information technology in managing human resources tasks, especially large-scale processing of applications short-listing candidates and organizing selection.
- Use of information technology for facilitating learning through self-taught modules and tests.
- Raising resources and the image of the organization by registering on the NASDAQ.
- Retaining employees not only through a culture of belonging but also through an Employees Stock Option Plan (ESOP), and also backing the ESOP through NASDAQ shares.
- Introduction of a clearly stated corporate governance system focusing on the role of inside and outside director, age limit for the directors, and the nature of performance audit.
- Building a culture of giving back to society.

management have led the mission by donating generously to their alma mater. The innovations in Infosys are listed in Box 10.1.

5. NIIT

NIIT was founded in Delhi in 1981 by three young and enthusiastic engineers, Rajendra Pawar, Vijay Thadani and P. Rajendran. As the world was entering the information era, NIIT visualized extensive requirement for 'computer-skilled' people, and set about the task of creating an abundant supply of such skills through extensive training and education programmes.

Early years and the evolving vision

The company started its business of training and education with its early vision of 'Bringing People and Computers Together... Successfully'. The mandate the organization gave itself was to make people in India not simply computer-literate but also computer savvy. The emphasis was on creating a distinct quality image. Thus, its mission has been to provide computer training to a wide range of people, from students seeking a career in computers and, of late, children, housewives, senior citizens and the physically-challenged seeking familiarity with computers in order to enhance their day-to-day effectiveness, to professionals and managers requiring advanced computing skills.

With the passage of time, NIIT broadened its competence and activity base. In addition to providing computer training, it entered the field of software solutions and the two activities provided synergy for growth. As mentioned earlier, the late 1980s saw a dramatic change in the country's business environment. In the year 2000, in terms of revenues for NIIT, learning solutions and software solutions were almost equally balanced.

As opportunities multiplied in the significantly changed IT industry, NIIT rewrote its vision statement to reflect the company's priorities for the future. Particularly relevant to us is the first part of the vision statement which emphasizes growth through people, and NIIT commits itself to 'foster career building *by creating opportunities that demand learning, thinking and innovation from each one of us*'. It goes on to state, 'We recognize *the necessity of making mistakes and risk-taking when it contributes to learning, innovation and growth of each one of us*' (our emphasis). By highlighting the importance of individual innovation, and conveying a readiness to accept well-meaning mistakes and reasonable risk-taking in the mission statement, NIIT seems to be indicating that learning and innovation are expected to be a mainstream activity.

Strategic choices

From the early years, computers came to be extensively used for accounting and wordprocessing purposes, and were also seen as a much more versatile and efficient substitute for the typewriter. The NIIT model of spread of computer education has almost been like the spread of typewriting schools in the 1970s: you are sure to find one in any middle-class neighbourhood. Such a pervasive presence across the country was made possible by the franchising strategy pioneered by NIIT. The strategy combines high geographic penetration with consistency in delivering high quality training. Under the franchise arrangement, NIIT provides technical training, hardware and software support, and training inputs to local units which carry out computer training for a variety of courses designed by NIIT under the NIIT brand. This entails standardization of the design, inputs and delivery for training programmes, and also a consistent concern for and monitoring of quality. NIIT's innovation lies in being the first Indian organization to visualize the suitability of the franchisee arrangement to its business needs and to harness it to propel its own growth. Subsequently, of course, many other IT organizations have followed the franchise route, and it continues to be a popular choice for offering computer training on an extensive scale.

Today, NIIT has a base of over 1000 corporate clients, wholly-owned subsidiaries in the Asia Pacific region, Europe, Japan and the US, and operations in thirty-eight countries. NIIT was adjudged the 'Company of Choice' by 500 Indian information systems managers, an indication of its popularity among IT professionals (*Computer World*, 31 August 1999). NIIT has made some striking innovations with regards to business, socially relevant issues, and 'people-friendly' policies and practices.

Over the years, through continuing effort, NIIT has built synergy between its two activities of training and software. Training has moved from classroom training to technology-based training to Internet-based learning with the help of live education, automated learning centres, multimedia software products, and integrated learning solutions. Likewise, in software the company has moved from contract programming services, offshore software projects, and on-site services to being a solution provider and systems integrator. Live learning in the world of business garnered from its software activity is used as a source of knowledge to strengthen the training and educational activity. NIIT has emerged as one of the top producers of educational multimedia material. Its 'learning capsules' have become branded products that are used extensively in the field of IT training both for IT professionals and top corporates, as well as for ordinary people who want to learn to use computers.

The courses are branded and promoted as if they were consumer goods. The entire NIIT education portfolio can be grouped under three brand names, namely Futurz, CATS (Curriculum for Advanced Technology Studies) and SWIFT. Futurz consists of a variety of e-commerce programmes, including NIIT's comprehensive flagship programme iGNIIT. The unique feature of iGNIIT is the inclusion of one year's industry exposure through Professional Practice (PP) as part of the programme curriculum. This gives the students a valuable opportunity to apply their programme learning to live challenges at the workplace. Based on the feedback received from captains of the industry, the scope of the programme is regularly broadened to include fresh inputs like e-commerce computing, technology edge, quality management and personal effectiveness. The NIIT curriculum design around Microsoft technologies offers students the advantage of acquiring proficiency for Microsoft certification. Evolved on the basis of the Indian ground realities of economic disparity, and aimed to give a fair opportunity to all deserving candidates, iGNIIT includes a seven-year bank loan which covers the cost of the programme and also a multimedia PC with Internet access and printer. The Curriculum for Advanced Technology Studies (CATS) provides exposure to the latest state-of-the-art technologies and developments in the IT field to IT and management professionals. Microsoft online training programmes are aimed at enhancing the skills of technical and software developers in the Microsoft back office/networking products and development tools. Such courses prepare students for certificate examinations in order to acquire MCSE/MCSD/MCP certification and the like.

SWIFT programmes include short-term courses designed to spread computer literacy and proficiency among the masses. The objective is to demystify computers for those who feel intimidated by technology, with courses designed for housewives, professionals such as lawyers, doctors and government employees, and the elderly.

NIIT launched 'NIIT NetVarsity' in mid-1996 as an online learning facility that offers web-accessible modules to learners across the globe and has emerged as one of the top producers of educational multimedia material. As of June 2000, it had developed 334 educational multimedia titles under brand names such as Vista, Vista Multimedia and HyperLEARN.

Socially relevant initiatives

NIIT has undertaken some socially relevant initiatives, such as a programme known as LEDA (Learning through Exploration, Discovery and Adventure) in which schoolchildren are taught on the basis of a multimedia series. It has also begun a programme called DigNIITy to offer computer literacy to senior citizens. The programme is intended to serve a dual purpose. It acknowledges the need and desire of people over sixty years of age to learn computer skills which can integrate them better with an increasingly computer savvy world. It also helps prepare the more ambitious and enterprising among the elderly for a second career. NIIT has launched the Total Freedom Scholarships to enable economically less privileged students to go through the NIIT GNIIT programme. In collaboration with the Rajiv Gandhi Foundation and the Spastics Society of Tamil Nadu, NIIT launched 'Computer Aided Teaching Technology and Rehabilitation for the Disabled' (CATERED) which is an attempt to enable spastics and the visually challenged to familiarize themselves with the power of computing. For the disabled, NIIT has developed an educational system called I-Learn.

Research and development

Emphasis on R&D to constantly innovate new methods of training as well as to develop systems and software is an important value in NIIT. The R&D centre carries out basic research, technology forecasting, initiatives in technology support and the like. Its contributions are flowing in back to the industry to improve software practices across the world.

NIIT's quest for knowledge creation led to its pioneering efforts in the field of cognitive engineering. The NIIT R&D group showcases a novel experiment in collaborative breakthrough research with the Indian Institute of Technology, Delhi, in the field of cognitive systems. The group organizes annually an international conference on cognitive systems to throw light on the latest advances in research on and understanding of human cognition.

Some of the technological breakthroughs for which NIIT filed for patents include Cognitive Kiosk for Rural, Outdoor and Tropical Environment, Handy Audio Replay Kit (HARK), Web Appliance for Remote Presence (WARP), and Sensor-enabled Computer-based Training System. The Technology Support Group (TSG) filed a patent for Software Engineering Tools (SETS), described by NIIT as 'the world's first evolutionary, full life-cycle software application delivery over the net'. TSG has also created a 'unique process automation suite of tools to track process data and reviews, and provide visibility to end customers on delivery process', all over the Net.

Thus, NIIT's commitment to knowledge generation and innovation has led it to groundbreaking basic and applied research in the IT field and has presented India with an interesting model of collaborative research between industry and academia.

Developing human capital

Another innovative element of NIIT strategy has been its commitment to developing its people resources. The organization does not necessarily scout for the ready-to-start-work resources in the IT market and hire it at the best salary in the IT industry. Young candidates with a sound potential to learn, and with a basic value congruence, are recruited and given rigorous technical training to turn them into competent IT professionals. In addition to a professional flair, the people selected are expected to have commitment to values such as a positive regard for one another, integrity, business ethics, speed, innovation, quality and MERIT (Meeting Every Requirement In Time). Before starting on the job, employees discuss their roles and responsibilities for the coming year and clarify expectations. They are expected to monitor their progress by filling in a monthly focus report. Thus, exposure to demanding projects and other developmental experiences at NIIT, their rapid assimilation into performance-driven project teams, and the force of the NIIT work culture builds opportunities for growth and stretch for new entrants. These developmental efforts help newcomers discover their untapped potential and provide a boost to their professional growth. Through this involvement, NIIT develops moderately high achievers into first-rate professionals.

In an industry with an unusually high rate of technological obsolescence, NIIT offers a variety of in-house and external training programmes to its members, to keep them field-attuned with the latest developments in IT. NIIT has its own School for Employee Education and Development (SEED) at Chennai and Delhi. To emphasize that self-learning is an individual responsibility which the company would be happy to support, NIIT launched a scheme called the SPIRIT fund (the Self-Propelled Initiative for Renewal and Individual Transformation). A certain amount of money is allocated to every NIITian for self-growth. People are free to use this fund for any self-development programme they are interested in. The scheme also covers the spouse and children of NIITians. The corpus remains the same for all employees irrespective of their position in the organization, and the money cannot be carried forward to the next year. Thus emphasis is on continuing self-development which cannot be postponed to the following year.

The company runs a Managing Director's Quality Club that not only ensures defect-free products and services but also makes an attempt to initiate and instil quality initiatives among its members. The club endeavours to sustain and advance the quality movement through the Personal Quality Initiative (PQI), with the assumption that unless people are committed to quality at an individual level, quality at the organizational level cannot be sustained. Every individual maintains a scorecard to record improvements on a self-selected personal parameter such as a commitment to quit smoking, coming to the office on time, and similar things.

In order to promote leadership throughout the organization, NIIT has developed the concept of leadership circles. The company believes that the best way to learn is to teach, and additional training has the capacity to stretch itself. Thus, NIITians who have ten to fifteen people reporting to them become home team leaders and are expected to develop leadership attributes in their teams. The home team leaders impart training along the instructional modules and material developed for such purposes. In this way, ordinary leaders are converted into trainers and the circle is repeated.

The HR policies of NIIT follow a lifecycle-based compensation design. The company gives an annual dating allowance to NIITians who are single. On the wedding anniversary of any member, the company gives a gift cheque to the spouse of the member along with a best wishes card. Acknowledging the fact that around 35 per cent of NIITians are women, maternity leave along with flexible working hours are available to women employees. Mothers of young children can exercise the option of coming for half a day or alternate days, or alternate months. The company also offers to make a PC and a modem connection available at home to enable mothers to work from home.

Given the fact that the average age of an NIITian is in the mid-twenties, and that the young are open to risk-taking, experimentation, and work better in a dynamic environment, the culture is non-hierarchical and democratic. People are encouraged to ask questions, clarify doubts and take risks. Job rotation is a common phenomenon, with movements of executives from training to HRD, to consulting, to research and development, and so on. The rotation is intended to help NIITians to personally grow and develop a holistic understanding of the overall business. The innovations in NIIT are listed in Box 10.2.

Box 10.2   Innovations in NIIT

- Visualizing the requirement of 'computer skilled' people in the information era. Initiating computer business and training on the basis of its vision *'Bringing people and computers together ... successfully'*
- The strategy of spreading computer education for high geographic penetration through franchise agreements.
- Value of giving importance to individual innovation, and conveying a readiness to accept well-meaning mistakes and reasonable risk-taking,
- Moving from classroom training to technology-based training to Internet-based learning with the help of live education, automated learning centres, multimedia software products and integrated learning solutions.
- The concept of branding courses like consumer goods to target distinct target segments, such as young undergraduate students, working executives, computer professionals and eager learners in all age groups.
- Recognizing Indian ground realities of economic disparity, and evolving a financing scheme that gives a fair opportunity to all deserving candidates.
- Commitment to develop people resources through rigorous technical training. Training also imparted through its own school for Employee Education and Development (SEED) at Chennai and Delhi. Also, development of leadership circles in order to facilitate the development of team leaders.
- Collaboration with the Indian Institute of Technology, Delhi, in the field of cognitive systems. Other technological breakthroughs include Cognitive Kiosk for Rural, Outdoor and Tropical Environment, Handy Audio Replay Kit (HARK), Web Appliance for Remote Presence (WARP), and Sensor-enabled Computer-based Training System.
- Conferred the National HRD Award in 1998 for its 'People Vision'. Setting of new standards and creation of several best practices in HRD. For instance, it launched a scheme called SPIRIT fund (the Self-Propelled Initiative for Renewal and Individual Transformation) which allocates a certain amount of money to every NIITian for self-growth.
- Initiation of a leadership club that endeavours to sustain and advance the quality movement through the Personal Quality Initiative (PQI) with the assumption that unless people are committed to quality at an individual level, quality at the organizational level cannot be sustained.
- Constant innovations in training in terms of content and material so as to offer new courses that are commensurate with the latest developments in the IT field.
- Use of innovative measures to integrate families with NIIT.
- A non-hierarchical, democratic and supportive work culture that encourages openness, risk-taking, experimentation and easy interactions among employees.
- Undertaking socially relevant initiatives such as LEDA (Learning through Exploration, Discovery and Adventure) and DigNIITy that are computer literacy programmes for children and senior citizens respectively.

6. Infosys and NIIT as innovating organizations: key questions

It is evident from the above account that Infosys and NIIT have built their organizations by

- articulating their vision and communicating it clearly;
- investing in HR and building new competencies;
- introducing new services and seeking new clients;
- strengthening relations with existing clients;
- subjecting themselves to stringent external evaluations; and
- developing a culture of giving; of returning something back to society.

We found Infosys and NIIT crafting their own responses where no existing precedents existed. As they grew from small to big, so did the nature of their challenges. What, however, remained unchanged was their belief in their vision, a willingness to be different, and daring to take risks and create their own standards, and forge their own responses in seeking to meet the challenge of innovation and growth. The organizations moved on to become what we call a 'learnable organization'. To us 'learnability' means a willingness to undertake new and unfamiliar tasks, to struggle and study and grope, and to endeavour to reach a deeper understanding and produce a superior solution for the client. Both the organizations invested and nurtured this internal attribute of organizational learnability in taking on new projects, venturing into new technologies, and building partnerships and alliances. R&D centres were created explicitly to put into effect this need for ongoing innovations. Thus, a culture of learning, innovations and risk-taking in business was created and fostered. In phase two of their growth, we found the environment too making demands on these organizations in terms of new tasks and solutions. Thus, added to the self-generated urge for innovations now there were external demands to take on the unfamiliar and the unknown.

With growth came the challenge of retaining people and providing them with opportunities for professional development in an environment marked by high employee turnover. This led to innovations in building a sense of belongingness among people. Both Infosys and NIIT have been innovative in their own ways in meeting this challenge. The case studies reveal that the organizations had a range of innovations to their credit, and all these did not occur simultaneously. The response of the external environment, customers, suppliers and regulators to the first innovation paved the way for subsequent ones. Forces leading to the first innovation were different from those in the subsequent ones. The key questions in this regard are:

- How does the first innovation of the organization take place? What are the triggers and facilitators?
- How do subsequent innovations take place?

- What is the role of external responses to the first innovation in triggering or constraining subsequent innovations?
- How does one link the various forces leading to multiple innovations?

An examination of the triggers for innovation and the innovations themselves in the two organizations suggests a stage model for multiple innovations. The literature on innovation has focused on processes in single innovations such as Post It notes (Nayak and Ketteringham, 1994) or Sony Walkman (Morita, 1994) for generating innovations. In this study we have examined multiple innovations as the outcomes of ongoing interaction between the organization and its external environment. To enable us to present the model we introduce certain key terms.

Key terms for the model

To enable us to present the model we introduce certain key terms.

Triggers for innovation

The triggers for innovations are those aspects within or outside the organization that prompt the innovations.

Enablers of innovation

The existence of triggers by themselves does not lead to innovation. It is the enablers, either within or outside the organization, that enable the innovation to take place. These enablers help the organization to seize the innovating opportunities, generate options, and make a choice. They also help in implementing the choice. The internal enablers we have been able to identify are the leadership style of the top management, the culture of experimentation and tolerance of failure, the ambience of learning and sharing, recognition of innovation as a part of the mission of the enterprise, the appraisal and recognition systems of the management. The external enablers are developmental financial institutions, the network of educational institutions, R&D laboratories, the community of investors and their confidence, customers and their feedback, and public policy-makers.

Strategic imbalances as triggers for innovation

We define strategic imbalance as the gap between what is desired and what is available in the context of the linkage between the organization itself and the organization and its external environment. This imbalance is a major trigger for inducing innovation. It prompts the organization to rethink the opportunities and threats in the external environment, and its own strengths and weaknesses, and develop options to bridge the gap. We have been able to identify the following types of imbalances.

Internal imbalance

This is the imbalance between the way the organization conceptualizes and articulates its vision – what it wants to accomplish, the kind of customers it want to serve and the products and services it wants to offer, the competencies it desires to build – and its current realities. It may have humble beginnings; its size may be small; monetary, technical and people resources may be scanty or non-existent. The environment may be indifferent, unsupportive or hostile. In other words, the 'present' is fraught with questions, problems and uncertainties. As the founders passionately believe in their vision, the gap between what the organization is and what they want it to be spurs both product and process innovations.

Confronted with an uneasy imbalance between aspiration and reality, key decision-makers may look more at the potential of their meagre resources and stretch and enhance them rather than get mired by the constraints they are facing. They may look for helpful support in the external environment and leverage on it. For example, with his conceptualization of the offshore software development model, Narayana Murthy stretched his capabilities to communicate and negotiate, and got MICO industries to rethink its decision to import a computer and the Department of State, US, to allow Data General Corporation to export the machine to India. The arrangement Infosys worked out with MICO was very innovative. It provided Infosys with a base without jeopardizing the freedom and flexibility of MICO industries. A firm base with a computer enabled Infosys to bid for projects in the US and bring them to India.

In its early vision of 'Bringing people and computers together, successfully', NIIT realized that its internal resources were inadequate to manage the logistics of the extensive network of training centres it wanted to start across the country in order to work towards its vision. This imbalance led to an innovative arrangement. Rather than tone down its ambition or recruit a large number of people as software trainers, NIIT chose to establish a franchise arrangement with local people for which NIIT provided the overall design, curriculum, material, training and initial hand-holding. It specified stringent guidelines in relation to quality parameters and the required infrastructure, and evolved its quality monitoring mechanisms. NIIT lent to these centres its brand name in return for a fee charged from the franchisee. This arrangement was an innovative response to the internal imbalance experienced by the company.

External imbalance: type I

We define external imbalance type I as a gap between what is required by the vision or dream of the founders and what is readily available in the environment to realize it. What may be needed may be a particular type of resource, say, skilled labour, or a particular type of customer. This gap prompts the organization to take an alternative perspective of whatever the environment can offer and innovate around it. For example, both NIIT and Infosys did not get ready-to-use talent. They took a developmental view of whatever was available: graduates who could learn, imparted to them rigorous training in the knowledge and skills required for high quality performance, and realized their vision. The concepts of 'learnability' and 'learning value add' got innovated in the process.

External imbalance: type II

This is the imbalance between what the external environment expects the organization to do and what the organization is *immediately* capable of doing. The expectations from the stakeholders in the environment challenge the organization to do something to meet them. The response to this challenge could lead to process or product innovations. For example, as Infosys succeeded in meeting the quality expectations and deadlines of the customers and satisfied them, the customers' expectations increased. They started giving Infosys larger and more complex projects with tougher time and cost deadlines. Infosys responded with a round of innovations centred around new tools and methodologies for project monitoring. In this context, one can also discuss innovations that can be generated in response to restrictions from the environment on what the company can or cannot do.

The model of stages

In the two cases developed by us we have been able to identify a dynamic interaction among the imbalances and enablers leading to innovations in stages.

Multiple innovations: stage I

In the first stage, stage I, the founders clarified and articulated their expectations from the organization they had created. The reason for creating an organization of their own was, besides the joy and satisfaction of such a creation, that the founders held certain values dear to them and wished to build an organization around these. They expressed their dissatisfaction with the status quo and committed themselves to doing something different, and thus developed a shared resolve to build an organization that would embody their vision. As they began their search for this common ground, sometimes through sheer intuition and a lucky break, but more often through arduous discussions and brainstorming, challenging and building upon each other's ideas, adding and pruning, and repeated iteration, they evolved a conceptualization of their vision. This conceptualization included the products or services the promoters wanted to offer the customer which he would want to seize and the impact they wanted their organization to have. The vision was far removed from their current reality in terms of size and endowment of resources. An internal imbalance occurred.

At this stage, there was also realization that the environment was not ready to respond readily to all the demands they wanted to make. An external imbalance of type I also occurred. In order to 'emerge as a world class software solutions provider', which was the vision that Infosys gave itself, it required from the environment world class infrastructure (equipment, power, connectivity to the market, access to centres of knowledge, exposure, etc.); world class people (in terms of their skills, understanding, work attitudes and a global mindset that cares for quality and timely cost-effective delivery, and not excuses for shoddiness and delays); and world class support from the regulatory framework. The domestic environment in India in the early 1980s posed enormous handicaps on each of these parameters. The infrastructure in terms of the facilities for installing the latest generation of computers was extremely unsatisfactory. Power supply was uneven. The regulatory regime did not permit easy import of equipment, even manuals and floppies. Encouraging and supporting IT organizations aspiring to be global players was not on the agenda of any government or political party. Infosys needed, but was not at all certain about the supply from the environment, high-quality, trained manpower with a global mindset which was a sine qua non for a knowledge-based industry like IT. Thus, there existed a vast strategic imbalance between what the organization needed from the environment to fulfil its vision of the future and what the environment could supply.

Such a 'strategic imbalance' offers a unique opportunity to any organization to innovate. Not all organizations are willing or able to seize it, but organizations with a visionary leadership are able to convert this very imbalance into powerful triggers for innovation. An imbalance between demand and supply can be remedied in three ways. Organizations can lower their expectations and demands from the environment by diluting their own vision, which many companies do. Faced with harsh realities, they tone down their vision, de-scale the aspirations, and continue to be reasonably successful in the light of watered-down self-expectations. The second option is to alter the environment itself. This entails demanding and ensuring from the environment a supply of upgraded, high quality inputs so that organizational needs are met. As the stakeholders are many, and changing each one, and that within a desired time-frame, is extremely difficult, this is just a theoretical option. The third possibility, and this is, in the short run, what innovating organizations do, is to creatively build internal resources and capabilities so as to neutralize or surmount the industry environment's many handicaps.

As the educational environment in the country was not geared to supplying world quality manpower for world class performance, Infosys and NIIT developed their own strong training establishments to meet this need. In a situation where power supply is unpredictable, but Infosys needed to have uninterrupted power to ensure timely completion of projects, it acquired a power-generating capability. When NIIT wished to popularize computer training in the country, but the environment did not offer easy availability of infrastructure, the company devised the franchisee arrangement in which NIIT's core strength of high quality computer training was leveraged but other issues of managing the local infrastructure were left to the local partners to handle.

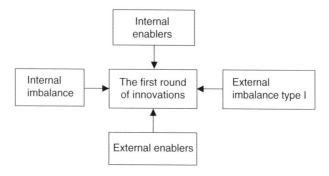

Figure 10.1 Multiple innovations: stage I

Infosys stayed with its vision and innovated; it created a culture that could support learning. It looked at learnability in the candidates. Similarly, NIIT looked for people with potential. In its search, the organization was facilitated by the existence of a network of technical institutions that graduated a large number of students. The internal enablers that helped both the organizations to bridge the gap were a shared vision of the founders, their technical capabilities, and family support for this adventure. An organizational culture of teamwork, transparency and autonomy encouraged experimentation and innovative responses. Similarly, external factors played an enabling role. There were customers who were willing to give the company a chance. There were also developmental financial institutions with a flexible approach to project review that provided the resources.

This stage can be represented as in Figure 10.1.

Multiple innovations: stage II

What happens to the innovations of the organization in the first stage decides the shape of the next phase. The organization gets a fillip to innovate further if the environment receives the innovation favourably and demands more. A successful innovation generates new expectations from the environment and also new external enablers. As innovating organizations continue their effort to devise new, homegrown solutions to reduce the strategic imbalance, their innovativeness begins to get noticed. Customers become aware that some organizations have shown the grit to meet their exacting quality standards and punishing deadlines. There is therefore a demand for more of the same from the same customers, 'repeat orders' for the innovative initiative. Thus, feedback from the environment reinforces the innovative streak. The word spreads with time, and more and more customers express a willingness to do business with such a dependable organization. It also builds new internal enablers: a culture of experimentation receives support, the founders articulate their vision more clearly, and

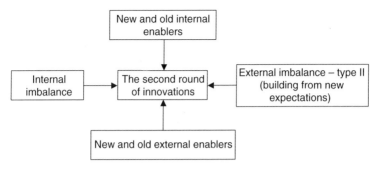

Figure 10.2 Multiple innovations: stage II

the organization's overall image is enhanced. When the expectations are beyond what the organization can readily deliver, an external imbalance of type II occurs. The organizations are challenged to innovate again. Both new and old external enablers and the new and old internal enablers spur the second round of innovation. Such innovations can be continuing or discrete. This stage is captured in Figure 10.2.

Thus feedback from stakeholders and their new expectations provide triggers for the second wave of innovations. This time the compulsion for innovation comes from outside, and innovating organizations have to keep on generating internal energy to meet those expectations. In comparison to the first round, the challenge in the second round is to whip up sufficient internal excitement about the external triggers so that people feel enthused to live up to those challenges. Once again, the role of leadership becomes critical. Leaders now have to establish a strong link between the demands of the external stakeholders and their organization's vision so that likely innovations to help meet external expectations can be seen as enhancing the organization's capabilities and strengths.

For Infosys, this stage meant expectations from customers that they undertake more projects and work on more complex ones. The new expectations led to innovations in tools, methodologies, products and services. For NIIT, this meant developing new training programmes and also diversification into software development and forging a synergy between learning solutions and software solutions.

Multiple innovations: stage III

The response to the above round would decide the next phase. If these innovations were well received, there would be another round of expectations and development of new enablers. This would lead to new imbalances and another round of innovations. The multiple stages can be visualized as in Figure 10.3.

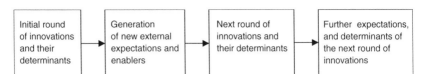

Figure 10.3 Multiple innovations: stage III

En route the organizations revisit their vision and articulate a new one. In the NIIT's case the innovations and positive feedback from the stakeholders prompted the organization to revisit the vision and articulate a larger one. In that of Infosys, the founders added a global context to the vision. This set the stage for another round of innovations. In the process, a culture builds up in which innovations are actively encouraged. In an industry experiencing a stiff 'talent war', competitors are tempted to copy these innovations, As such emulation and imitation, though flattering, can blunt the innovating organization's competitive edge, organizations are under pressure to constantly innovate to retain their lead.

Linear representation, as above, should not be construed as one development strictly following the other. The organization could return to the earlier developments and get stuck or move forward. This zigzag is possible if the power of one development is not sufficient to push the organization to the next. Elaborating this further, however, is beyond the purview of this chapter.

7. Conclusion and implications

Multiple innovations occur in organizations in stages. They occur when there is a strategic imbalance between the organization's vision of what it wants to achieve and the internal resources (such as technical capabilities) available. The organization stretches itself and innovates in a variety of ways, including strong capability development programmes, innovative team structures, and people management practices in order to bridge the gap. The next stage of strategic imbalance indicates a gap between organizational expectations from the environment (such as world class infrastructural support, a pool of world quality manpower, accessibility to centres of knowledge and the like) and the current environmental reality which may be far removed from the expectations. Innovative organizations like Infosys and NIIT take recourse to a variety of creative measures in order to expand and utilize their resources innovatively to overcome environmental handicaps and bridge the strategic gap. A third category of strategic imbalance exists when there is a gap between the environment's expectations and an organization's ability to meet them. The successful past track record of organizations prompts clients to make challenging demands on them in terms of complex software solutions and exacting time and quality specifications while the organization's existing set of capabilities and commitments preclude delivery of such expectations. The mismatch between exacting environmental demands and an organization's ability to meet them prompts another round of innovations. Thus our model suggests that at each stage of organizational growth, an imbalance between aspirations and reality provides powerful triggers for innovation. However, such innovations do not follow routinely. As is evident from our analysis, internal and external enablers play a crucial role. Internal enablers that are critically important are a leadership that encourages risk-taking and innovations, a culture that rewards experimentation, tolerates failures, and provides enough space and encouragement to people to dare to think differently, and an atmosphere in which learning, learnability, teamwork and knowledge-sharing are highly valued. Organizations desirous of instilling innovation orientation need to pay attention to these internal enablers and evolve ways of cultivating and retaining them.

Equally important is the role of external factors as enablers. Specifically, with regard to regulators, providing a level-playing field to Indian IT organizations in terms of infrastructural support, availability of world class facilities, supportive legislation, and explicit political will can act as powerful boosters. The implication for policy-makers is that sufficient freedom to devise their own compensation and reward mechanisms, including ESOPs, can significantly help innovative organizations in attracting, developing and retaining talented people who are the mainstays for ongoing innovations in any organization.

Notes

1. Bhatnagar, S.C. (1993): *Infosys Limited: Profile of a Software Company*, IIMA case no. CISG 15, Indian Institute of Management, Ahmedabad.
2. Ibid.
3. Infosys, HBS case no. N9-800 – 103 prepared by William J. Coughlin, July 2000.

References

Bhatnagar, S. C. (1993) 'Infosys Limited: Profile of a Software Company', IIMA case no. CISG 15, Indian Institute of Management, Ahmedabad.

Buys, J. A. (1983) 'Innoveren is mensenwerk. Tijdschrift voor Organisactiekunde en Sociaal Beleid', 37 (Sept./Oct.), cited in A. Cozijnsen and W. Vrakking (eds), *Handbook of Innovation Management* (Cornwall: T. J. Press Ltd).

Carnall, C. A. (1990) *Managing Change in Organizations* (New York: Prentice-Hall).

Coughlin, W. J. (2000) 'Infosys, Financing an Indian Software Startup', HBS case no. N9-800–103, July.

Cozijnsen, A. J. (1989) 'Het innovatievermogen van politie-organisaties. Onderzoek naar de mogelikheden van een non-profit organisatie om complexe vernieuwingen succesvol doore te voeren (Deventer:Kluwer Bedrijfswetenschappen)', cited in

A. Cozijnsen and W. Vrakking (eds), *Handbook of Innovation Management* (Cornwall: T. J. Press Ltd).

Cozijnsen, A. J. (1993) *Prediction Innovation Success with the DIPO-instrument* (Cornwall: T. J. Press Ltd).

Damanpour, F. (1991) 'Organizational Innovation: a Meta-analysis of Effects of Determinants and Moderator's', *Academy of Management Journal*, 34: 555–90.

Day, G. (1990) *Market Driven Strategy: Processes for Creating Value* (New York: Free Press).

Dougherty, D. (1996) 'Organizing for Innovation', in S. R. Clegg, C. Hardy and W. N. Nord (eds), *Handbook of Organization Studies* (London: Sage Publications), pp. 424–39.

Jelinek, M. and C. Schoonhoven (1990) *The Innovation Marathon: Lessons from High Technology Firms* (Oxford: Basil Blackwell).

Johne, F. A. and P. Snelson (1988) 'Success Factors in Product Innovation: a Selective Review of the Literature', *Journal of Product Innovation Management*: 114–28.

Johnson, G. (1988) 'Rethinking Incrementalism', *Strategic Management Journal*, 9: 75–91.

Majahan, V. and J. Wind, (1992) 'New Product Models: Practice, Shortcomings and Desired Improvements', *Journal of Product Innovation Management*: 128–39.

Morita, A. (1994) 'Selling to the World: the Sony Walkman Story', in J. Henry and D. Walker (eds), *Managing Innovation* (London: Sage Publications), pp. 185–91.

Nayak, P. R. and J. M. Ketteringham (1994) '3M's Little Yellow Note Pads: Never mind. I'll do it myself', in J. Henry and D. Walker (eds), *Managing Innovation* (London: Sage Publications), pp. 215–23.

Rogers, E. M. (1979) *Diffusion of Innovations* (New York: Macmillan).

Rothwell, R. and T. Whiston (1990) 'Design, Innovation and Corporate Integration', *R&D Management*, 20: 193–201.

Van de Ven, A. and D. Polley (1992) 'Learning While Innovating', *Organization Science*, 3: 92–116.

Vrakking, W. J. (1988) 'Innovative Management vermogen opvoeren; observaties over de koppeling tussen de innovatiewetenschap en de innovatiepraktijk (Alpen a/d Rijn: Samsom)', cited in A. Cozijnsn and W. Vrakking (eds), *Handbook of Innovation Management* (Cornwall: T. J. Press Ltd).

11
Conclusion: Global Links, Domestic Market and Policy for Development

Anthony P. D'Costa and E. Sridharan

1. Introduction

The Indian software industry has come a long way from its humble beginnings in the 1980s. The industry has grown at an impressive rate over the past decade and has in aggregate, and for its major companies, attained brand name recognition in selected software service niches. Its export-driven model now commands the world's attention for skilled professionals and offers hope to many developing countries which are struggling to cope with a hyper-competitive post-WTO global economy. Yet, there is a broad consensus among the contributors to this volume that the Indian software industry is overwhelmingly concentrated in software services and, more recently, in low-tech IT-enabled services. In this concluding chapter we reiterate some of the principal challenges facing the industry and suggest broad policies that will enable the Indian industry to take the high road to innovation. There are two complementary strategies that reinforce each other: tapping the advantages offered by the global economy to develop national technological capability and serving the domestic market to diversify the foundations of the software industry. Both are likely to contribute to a stronger innovative capability. Based on this understanding, we also lay out some likely scenarios for the Indian industry in the next few years.

2. Overcoming challenges in the software industry

India's strong presence in software services has been concentrated dispro-portionately in certain activities such as custom applications development and legacy application management, maintenance and migrations, and in certain domains like finance, communications and media. Overwhelmingly, these services are dependent on the dominant US market. Product innovation has been marginal in India. All agree that service exports constitute an impressive achievement. Most suggest, however, that the industry needs to shift its focus to higher value-added activities. There are many reasons for this. First, innovating will assist the Indian industry to diversify domains and markets, and preserve and enhance its competitiveness. Second, it will have a larger multiplier effect on India's overall development. Third, there are recent developments that illustrate India's undue exposure to export market vulnerabilities. For example, some states in the US as well as trade unions in the UK are attempting to restrict outsourcing work to India. If the pressure to move away from low value service exports is already building up how can the transition be made? Will purely market-driven development, as it is currently practised, lift the Indian software industry to an innovation-driven higher value-added trajectory, or will policy intervention be needed to complement the shifts in corporate strategy?

In identifying some of the challenges confronted by the Indian industry, D'Costa (Chapters 1 and 3) argues that user-feedback linkages are critical to software innovation. Such feedback is difficult to capture fully given the immense geographic, cultural and, hence, psychological distances. These gaps are inevitable in an intercontinental type of outsourcing arrangement, whether onshore or offshore. The advances in telecommunications and the Internet do not fully compensate for the importance of face-to-face interaction between Indian software developers and foreign users. There are additional challenges, as exhibited by the three forms of decoupling of the industry: between software and hardware, between the export and domestic markets and between software services and software products (D'Costa, Chapter 1). Without a sustained effort in overcoming them, especially fostering the second area of each of these pairings, a rounded and innovation-oriented development trajectory is unlikely to take off. There is a fourth form of decoupling (Sridharan, Chapter 2), starkly observable when compared to the IT industries of the US and Israel. In India, the link between the civilian sector and national security sector, akin to a closed black box, is quite weak. This is unfortunate as the defence, space and missile programmes encompass complex information and communication technologies which could upgrade the civilian industry to a higher technological trajectory.

To overcome some of these shortcomings, D'Costa (Chapter 3) argues that two macrostrategies are necessary, namely reduction of export dependence, especially on the US market, by promoting domestic market development; and a diversification of external markets, especially to East Asia. These strategies are likely to push the Indian industry away from low value services to the huge embedded software demand in East Asia, marrying India's engineering domain expertise with IT expertise. There is no doubt that domestic diffusion of IT to create domestic demand and promote niche innovation, including software products catering to domestic needs in parallel with exports, will be critical.

These interpretations are generally consistent with the other studies in the volume. For example, Parthasarathi and Joseph's (Chapter 4) econometric analysis of a large dataset of Indian software firms finds no statistically significant evidence of export-orientation positively affecting innovative performance, even though formal R&D tends to understate actual incremental innovative activity in an industry like software. They emphasize, like D'Costa, the complementary role of the domestic market in promoting innovation entailing enterprise solutions. They advocate consciously targeting IT demand from large public sector core infrastructural and heavy industrial projects in the tenth five-year plan (2002–7) to promote IT innovation for the home market. This is expected to lead to spillovers by way of exports of more complex products and services aimed at large enterprises. The authors recommend targeting the energy (oil, gas, coal, electricity generation), transport and telecom sectors' needs for process control and enterprise resource planning (ERP).

From a different angle, Saxenian (Chapter 7) also advocates leveraging the domestic market for technological innovations. China is a good example of such leveraging. China's domestic-oriented public sector computer manufacturing firm Legend has only now begun testing export markets (Bradsher, 2003). Similarly, a collaborative effort in India leading to the design of 'Simputer', a low-cost computer aimed at the domestic market, is an encouraging sign. Saxenian and several other authors (Basant and Chandra, Chapter 8; Avnimelech and Teubal, Chapter 5; Krishnan and Prabhu, Chapter 6) explore the ways in which technology links with multinational corporations can be strengthened. More pertinently, tapping Indian technical talent residing in the US would be a strategic choice that both industry and government can pursue. Saxenian advocates the promotion of policies *à la* Taiwan and China to encourage Indian techno-entrepreneurs from Silicon Valley to initiate business in India. The creation of local and cross-national technical networks such as the TeNeT group centred around IIT, Chennai, is illustrative of return entrepreneurs and technical networks. Such networks bring about technology transfer that is far more valuable than mere foreign direct investment. To attract such talent from abroad and promote local innovation it would be prudent to promote domestic IT diffusion and infrastructure development.

Similar to the Israeli experience, Avnimelech and Teubal (Chapter 5) argue that favourable background conditions have emerged in India for local growth. Over the 1990s, Israel itself began to display characteristics of the Silicon Valley 'model'. According to the authors, what needs to be done in India is roughly similar to what was effected in Israel, that is, based on policy-oriented research, introduce key enabling policies at the macro-, meso- (or cluster) and micro- (or firm) levels. These would be a combination of horizontal and targeted policies to promote innovation and the globalization of asset markets, which is expected to promote the co-evolution of large numbers of venture capitalists and start-ups. However, Avnimelech and Teubal do not stress domestic market-oriented solutions in their approach for promoting innovation (unlike D'Costa, Chapter 2; Parthasarathi and Joseph, Chapter 4; Krishnan and Prabhu, Chapter 6; Saxenian, Chapter 7). Based on the Israeli experience, the authors anticipate that heightened financing of new firms is likely to generate competitive products. In addition, Israel's tapping of the Israeli/Jewish technical community in the US and elsewhere, and promoting civilian spinoffs from military R&D, particularly defence electronics and communications, offer significant strategic lessons for building Indian innovative capability.

Consistent with leveraging foreign firms for domestic innovative capability, Basant and Chandra (Chapter 8) demonstrate how technological spillovers from collaborations with foreign firms are maximized. They focus on inter-firm and industry–academia collaboration in the telecom sector to demonstrate the importance of foreign and collaborative arrangements in penetrating the world market. This is a significant issue as R&D outsourcing and chip design, both aimed at world markets and led by multinationals but increasingly in collaboration with Indian firms, are taking off. These collaborations emphasize the creation of broad and deep pools of specialized skills to attract collaborative ventures and absorb foreign technology. It is evident that a pool of technical skills and domestic collaborative technological networks with academia, as in the TeNeT group case, are vital for effective technology absorption, diffusion and spillovers. Consequently, the development of such local technological capability in IT and telecom generate export activity. India, they argue, is characterized by multinational strategies that are independent of the domestic market as the domestic market is small. However, domestic skills are of high quality. This corroborates Sridharan's (Chapter 2) observation of recent high-tech developments in the Indian IT industry, including R&D outsourcing and chip design investments. Given increasing technological convergence trends within the various IT sub-sectors, it is realistic to expect the creations of local technical, commercial and entrepreneurial networks in India.

Echoing D'Costa and Saxenian, Krishnan and Prabhu (Chapter 6) emphasize the importance of a vibrant domestic market for IT solutions to software product innovation. Given geographic and cultural distances, Indian firms venturing into software products for world markets should target longer lifecycle, intermediate to high complexity products commanding high prices. Under these constraints, tools and specialized utilities for niche markets and not short lifecycle, low-price products ought to be targeted. They argue that a shift to products is desirable for the industry as its cost advantage in software services will in time be eroded. This is in line with the argument (Desai, 2002) that the global software manpower supply shortage is over. They argue that Indian firms should become 'solutions' firms, building on product components, thus marrying services skills to products for client-specific solutions. This lays out a path to exploiting services–product activity synergies, thereby effectively recoupling the service–product divide. Firms need to have a deep understanding of customization and version management, something that can be derived, we can add, from their concentration in the areas of custom applications development, legacy applications management, maintenance and migration to new platforms. Krishnan and Prabhu point out that most Indian product firms target overseas markets due to the unremunerative character of the domestic market, further suggesting the importance of deepening the domestic ICT market to sustain product development.

In their case study of originative innovations by techno-entrepreneurs in Bangalore, Ojha and Krishna (Chapter 9) agree that most such entrepreneurs target world markets with niche products, not domestic markets, for the reasons mentioned above. They too argue, like Krishnan and Prabhu, Saxenian and D'Costa, that the creation of a vibrant domestic market for solutions, by the diffusion of IT and telecom connectivity, is the key to promoting domestic techno-entrepreneurship and product innovation as well as the creation of local technological networks and return entrepreneurship.

Bhatnagar and Dixit (Chapter 10), in their study of the continuing organizational innovation in Infosys and NIIT, make the case that firms need to pay special attention to organizational innovation to meet the challenges of external and internal imbalances. However, their chapter can be read as an argument that current software service activity auto-generates incentives to continually innovate, at least organizationally, to remain competitive. This need not be at the expense of creating a domestic IT market to promote innovation. They address the question Sridharan raises in Chapter 2: whether the service-driven export model auto-generates incentives to continually innovate to move up the value chain to more complex services, software products and hardware–software integrated products. Sridharan (Chapter 2) has drawn an analogy with the initial state-orchestrated growth of the Korean and Taiwanese semiconductor industry. This industry, which was overwhelmingly world market-oriented, managed to vertically integrate backwards: from chip assembly to wafer fabrication, design and R&D. It would appear that the software services export model does auto-generate some incentives and pressures for innovation, but it is an open question whether this would be adequate for firms to move beyond streamlining existing software services capabilities to products and 'solutions', or to migrate laterally to high-tech R&D, hardware production and chip design services.

The studies in this volume, notwithstanding their diversity of methodology and issue area, do point to the need for broadly facilitative public policies for the creation of a vibrant domestic market. This can be realized by the rapid diffusion of IT and telecom connectivity, greater investment in higher technical education and research, and targeted policies for the promotion of venture capital, high-tech investment, and outsourcing of R&D and chip design to India. All this would appear necessary for the creation of originative entrepreneurship, both local and 'return', and local and cross-national technical networks, which in turn would facilitate the

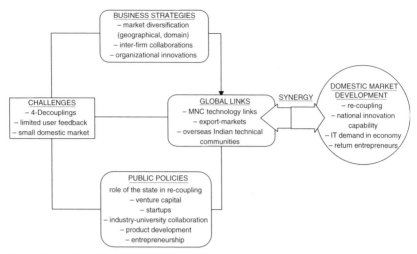

Figure 11.1   Global links and strategies for domestic market development

diversification of the industry's activities, domains and markets. We present a stylized interpretation of the Indian software industry, mapping out the global challenges and opportunities, the significance of the domestic economy and the various strategic and policy options for the creation of a synergy between the external environment and local efforts (Figure 11.1).

3. Three possible scenarios

Based on the findings of the individual contributors, we sketch three possible scenarios, low, medium and high, for the Indian software industry over the next few years. In the low scenario, India continues the transition from on-site to offshore software services, driven basically by the logic of market developments and remains confined to a limited range of activities. In the medium scenario, India diversifies its activities, domains and markets somewhat, helped to a degree by facilitative policies such as greater telecom and Internet connectivity and investment in human resources.

In the high scenario, we foresee a long-term move up the value chain. This trajectory is expected to transcend the four decouplings alluded to earlier by the following three, increasingly interlocking, developments. First, continued software services growth led by the existing major firms is likely to continue, steadily diversifying activities, domains and markets. Second, low-tech IT-enabled services led by multinationals will be a major growth area, notwithstanding protectionist sentiments in particular locations and sectors in the US and UK. The rapid growth in ITES has the potential to reinforce software services as well as cumulatively reinforce other multinational investments in India. Third, multinational relocation of R&D and chip design, and some outsourcing of these activities to India to new and existing Indian firms and multinational joint ventures are expected to grow. What is interesting is that the relocation of R&D and outsourcing arrangements are also taking place in a range of non-IT industries, with seventy MNCs relocating R&D facilities to India since 1997, and the total number of MNC-owned R&D facilities in India, including those set up before 1997, exceeding 100 by early 2003 (Dubey, 2003). Should chip design pick up, the Indian industry can expect numerous start-ups over the next few years.

Taken together, these developments will lead to the growth of new local and cross-national technical networks and support technological spillovers from world market-oriented activities. If public policy and market developments rapidly diffuse IT and telecom connectivity in India, and if higher technical education and R&D get adequate policy support, these trends will be enhanced. India's new IT trajectory could be further advanced with out-contracting of defence projects and the commercial spinoffs from the hitherto hermetically sealed national security sector.

Within the next decade, these innovation-related developments have the potential to overcome the four decouplings. With technological convergences and multiple overlapping, local and cross-border networks of technical personnel spanning industry and academia, and engaging existing local firms, new players and multinationals, we can anticipate, qualitatively, a very different Indian industry. Thus, chip design and R&D outsourcing in telecom and emergent bioinformatics product segments, combined with 'solutions' provided by older, large software services firms, could form complex linkages among themselves in new domains and niche markets.

In an optimistic scenario, these linkages may even cross traditional boundaries to link up with traditional engineering industries and other R&D-oriented industries such as pharmaceuticals and biotechnology. Consequently, globalized high-tech complexes could emerge in India for the first time. If they were to materialize, these complexes could approximate those in Israel, Taiwan and Korea. The individual studies in this volume as well as the current developments in the industry suggest that environmental conditions are favourable for the realization of the high scenario. However, it has been amply demonstrated that pressures emanating from the world market will not be sufficient to push the industry to a higher technological trajectory. In order to get the industry out of existing lines and domains of activity the state, through market-complementing public policies, must assist the industry in this endeavour, especially by enhancing the country's infrastructure, venture capital formation, and higher education and research systems. Building a dynamic industry also requires corporate strategies, anticipating the industry's comparative advantage. Proactively tapping the vast global opportunities will be an integral part of such strategies. There is no doubt that a synergy between the domestic and foreign markets seems to be the most promising path for India's high road to innovative capability.

References

Bradsher, K. (2003) 'Chinese Computer Maker Plans a Push Overseas', *New York Times*, 22 February, B1, B4.
Desai, Ashok V. (2002) 'The Dynamics of the Indian Information Technology Industry', Centre for New and Emerging Markets, London Business School, London.
Dubey, Rajeev (2003) 'India as a Global R&D Hub', *Business World*, 17 February.

Index

Rural Automation Exchanges (RAX)
    108n
Russia 8
    H1B visas for   15

Sadagopan, S.   161n
sales revenue, of ICT and software firms
    4
Sampson, G.   84

Sanchez, A. M.   222, 223, 224, 226,
    227, 240, 241, 242, 244
Santa Cruz Export Processing Zone,
    Mumbai   56, 88
Santangelo, G. D.   53, 54
SAP, Germany   42, 43, 65, 150
Saraswat Cooperative Bank   250
Sarma, Sudhir D.   230, 231, 232, 233,
    238, 239